Kenneth O. Morgan is one of Britain's leading modern historians. He is a Fellow of the British Academy, Honorary Fellow of The Queen's College and Oriel College, Oxford University, and entered the House of Lords in 2000. He is the author of over 30 books, including *The People's Peace: Britain since 1945; Modern Wales: Politics, Places and People* and *The Twentieth Century*.

AGES OF REFORM

Dawns and Downfalls of the British Left

Kenneth O. Morgan

I.B. TAURIS
LONDON · NEW YORK

Published in 2011 by I.B.Tauris & Co Ltd
6 Salem Road, London W2 4BU
175 Fifth Avenue, New York NY 10010
www.ibtauris.com

Distributed in the United States and Canada
Exclusively by Palgrave Macmillan
175 Fifth Avenue, New York NY 10010

ISBN: 978 1 84885 576 2

1006348097

A full CIP record for this book is available from the British Library
A full CIP record is available from the Library of Congress

Library of Congress Catalog Card Number: available

Printed and bound in Great Britain by CPI Antony Rowe, Chippenham

MIX
Paper from
responsible sources
FSC
www.fsc.org   FSC® C013604

Elizabeth, avec toute ma tendresse

Contents

Preface

Fifty years ago, I was taking my first tentative steps as a professional historian: I had just been appointed to a temporary (word emphasised in my contract) research post at the then University College of Swansea. My research topic was politics and society in late-Victorian and Edwardian Wales, and I could not have been more fortunately based than in Glanmor Williams's History department. But the book that made the greatest impression upon me then was on American history, written by a professor named Richard Hofstadter at Columbia University. It was entitled *The Age of Reform*, and had been published in 1955, subsequently winning the Pulitzer Prize. I hoped to teach and research on American as well as British history at Swansea, if possible, and Hofstadter's book I found endlessly exciting. In fact, it was a disenchanted, highly controversial critique of the Populist and Progressive movements in whose shadow American intellectuals of the New Deal generation had grown up. And yet, as Hofstadter wrote, his criticisms came from within, out of the traditions with which he felt most comfortable. They were the more telling for that.

As luck had it, Hofstadter's book was in my hand luggage when I first stepped off the boat in the United States, in New York Harbour in July 1962, to spend a year on a fellowship at Columbia. At that time, customs and immigration officials were mainly anxious to keep out Communistic (rather than obscene) literature. The aggressive (and no doubt overworked) man on the quayside seemed disinclined at first to let through either me or Hofstadter's book to pollute the minds of the American young. *The Age of Reform* seemed to him a dangerous left-wing tract (though actually its main thrust was to highlight the illusions and ambiguities of the Progressive left). Time passed. Then I mentioned, almost in desperation, that Hofstadter might be all right because he was based at Columbia in the very heart of the island of Manhattan. The customs man suddenly unfroze, smiled, announced that Columbia was where some family relative was at school, and wished me well. So I avoided Ellis Island and spent the next 14 months on the upper West Side most happily. In fact, I notionally had Hofstadter as a kind of supervisor during my time at Columbia. It did not work out ideally, partly because Hofstadter was personally distant and only seldom came into college, partly, I am sure, because of my own nervousness in putting historical points to the great man, as a mere beginner in American history. *The Age of Reform* was in any case by then being severely criticised in its methodology and judgements by other distinguished historians, including that famous historian of the South, C. Vann Woodward. Hofstadter's work had a rough ride in the very first *New York Review of Books* published during a long New York newspaper strike early in 1963, and its authority was now somewhat tarnished.

Nevertheless, Hofstadter and his book (indeed, all his equally controversial books) remain memorable for me. This was neither because of his research methods nor because of his conclusions. He ignored those manuscript and other primary sources which are the staff of life to the rest of us: he wrote privately that 'the archive rats' simply drained the excitement out of their subject. He turned to more speculative social sciences rather than the objective evidence when he wrote of 'paranoid styles' and 'psychic crises'. His treatment of Populism and Progressivism, much influenced by his own experience as an ex-Communist liberal intellectual during the McCarthy era, was so severe as to be destructive. And yet the literary sparkle and sheer intellectual brilliance of his analysis of US reform movements have inspired my own historical efforts ever since, in evaluating Britain's own Ages of Reform. So this collection of shorter pieces, focussing on the British progressive left over the past 200 years, written mostly since 1990 but with a far longer ancestry, is a delayed, but I hope not too inadequate, tribute to the abiding influence of this complex scholar who died of leukaemia at just 54, one of the very few truly great men I have met.

The first section of this book covers aspects of Liberalism, mainly within the Liberal Party. I look at the 1832 Reform Act which still seems to me to deserve a place in the Liberals' Valhalla, and at Gladstone, an Oxford/Anglican traditionalist who became ever more radical with age and gave moral leadership to a democratic mass movement, as much because of the Irish Home Rule split as in spite of it. I also look at the popular impact and media presentation of the Boer War (re-christened the Anglo–South African War during a centenary conference at which I spoke in Pretoria), a moment of modernity both in domestic politics and in repelling a rampant racist imperialism. Those brave Liberals and early socialists who crusaded against 'methods of barbarism' on the Veldt were much in my mind when I spoke in parliament in 2003 against the invasion of Iraq, undertaken amazingly by a Labour government: I venture to include this speech in the book. I have much to say on David Lloyd George, our most radical prime minister and almost single-handedly responsible for the progressive social thrust of the New Liberalism, and on the 1906 Liberal government which for its boldness outdid every other centre-left government we have known other than that of Attlee. Lloyd George, when I began working on him in the early 1960s, had become a public whipping-boy, condemned across the political spectrum for causing a collapse in public and private virtue. Fortunately, a combination of the opening up of his papers in the Beaverbrook library in 1967, under the memorable custody of Alan Taylor, and a liberating 'permissiveness' which blasted away much of the hypocrisy of bourgeois Puritanism, saw Lloyd George's reputation as a radical reformer amply restored. There were very dark phases in his career – the Black and Tans in Ireland, the flirtation with Hitler – but then Gladstone, too, is besmirched by Egypt, and Churchill by India. At any rate, Lloyd George now has his statue put up in Parliament Square, a 'dynamic force' in bronze set up alongside five static Tories, a general and a right-wing King.

I am much gratified that I had something to do with this rehabilitation myself, starting with my first (very short) book on L.G. as a Welsh radical back in 1963, going on to writing his entry in the *Dictionary of National Biography* (2004). It seemed sadly ironic that the Liberal Democrats, at a debate in Brighton in September 2007 in which I participated, voted heavily for the 'greatest ever Liberal' being John Stuart Mill, a great philosopher but a cautious, apprehensive democrat, who never ran anything, was a hopeless MP, lost his seat in 1868 in a Liberal near-landslide, and led numerous admirable crusades most of which failed. Clearly Lloyd George who actually ran the country in peace and war and served in government for 17 years had no chance against him (Gladstone and Keynes ran equally badly, incidentally). For much of its history, the Liberal and (often) Labour left, has been undermined by high-minded, elitist distaste for power, and the Brighton vote rather illustrated it. I also look at some wider contexts of British Liberalism, the links with France and with Germany, and Lloyd George's attempts to harmonise relations with the two. A final essay in this section discusses the much ignored role of British Liberalism as a beacon for Hofstadter's Progressives across the Atlantic. Toynbee Hall and the London County Council were Edwardian Britain's version of thirties Communism as an inspiration for radicals. Progressivism was a unique ideological strand in the so-called special relationship, perhaps as important as diplomacy or war.

The second section covers a later long phase of reform, dominated in one way or another by the Labour Party from the end of the First World War onwards. Here I try in places to explore Labour's ideas. This is an elusive enterprise, despite the ideological force of the Webbs, the Coles, Tawney, Laski and Crosland, and the left-wing intelligentsia more generally, memorably depicted by John Vincent as treading the rolling road from Bush House to Golders Green like Chaucer's pilgrims, en route for a new Jerusalem in NW 3. Certainly British socialism has been singularly protean. It has been much more than what Herbert Morrison called 'what a Labour government does', yet adopting the various guises (or disguises) of ethical fellowship, workers' power, planning, equality, modernisation, nationalism and much else. Each had its place in the sun, before darkness descended. By the new millennium, the Labour Party, of which I have been a member since 1955 throughout a surfeit of black defeats and pinkish dawns, could scarcely be called a Socialist Party at all. I particularly examine nationalisation, the epitome of the socialist idea in 1945, but now almost the left's last, worst choice even at a time of capitalist collapse, and the refusal of the centre-left to reject a hereditary monarchy suffused in the symbolism of class. Some external perspectives also come in – great successes such as the ending of Empire and more positive relationships with Europe from Gaitskell to Blair; less happily, the 'special relationship' with the US, largely the work of Labour governments, with creative outcomes under Bevin and, to a degree Wilson and Callaghan, but with a catastrophic denouement in Iraq.

There are also Labour's heroes, an inescapable feature of the cultural landscape of a 'people's party' that denies having a cult of great men. On one of the greatest, Keir Hardie, I wrote a full biography. Of the others, Nye Bevan still seems to me a prophetic figure, simplistic in his economics, yet still audaciously relevant in his social and cultural insights, the paradigm of what it meant to be a socialist. Michael Foot, who, like Jim Callaghan earlier, asked me to write his life, is always identified with internal division and a catastrophic election campaign in 1983. The 'donkey jacket' at the Cenotaph was his Turin shroud. Foot was not really a theorist, certainly not an economist of any kind, he had no affinity for power, and much of his career was taken up by negative crusades against his party's leadership. And yet, in his seriousness about words and ideas, his concern for culture, high and low, and above all an abiding passion for history, inherited from his Liberal father, he represents to me many of the nobler values which the left has cherished. As an octogenarian, his campaign on behalf of bombarded Croatians was as moving as the 86-year-old Gladstone's on the massacred Armenians a century before. Writing about Foot and Callaghan, naval patriots of Plymouth and Portsmouth, born to Drake's Drum and the Pompey Chimes, gave new excitement to my career after academic exile as a vice-chancellor, and rekindled my idealism as well. Both Callaghan and Foot, in their different ways, had a strong sense of history. It was a message which New Labour fatally neglected.

Much of our recent past has seen times of destructive disillusion for the British left. At the time of writing the government of Gordon Brown, an introverted though highly gifted man, seems to be driven by misfortune and the media into electoral and ideological collapse. The British left in 2009 has seriously lost momentum, even vision or purpose, after 12 years in office. Socialist priorities like the redistribution of wealth or social equality and libertarian ones like individual freedom under the law are flouted. Our political culture, once predictably bi-polar, now seems far more miscellaneous than at any time since 1945, with liberals, nationalists, Greens, UKIP and even the dangerous BNP striving for support. The political and constitutional system (very much including the voting system) commands less respect than for generations, for reasons that go far beyond the recent scandals of MPs (and some peers') expenses. Nevertheless, single-issue pressure-groups of miscellaneous idealists, even a huge mass protest like the Iraq march in which I took part in March 2003, are no substitute for a strategy for power, even though this strategy may now demand a confluence of parties and movements (probably aided by electoral reform) as its basis. This is too critical a moment to be tribally dogmatic about the varying shades of meaning attached to such protean terms as liberal and progressive. I am not by instinct or inclination a propagandist, and cherish the critical disciplines of the objective professional historian which I have been throughout my career. But I always naturally belong in left field – social democratic with a strong leavening of Liberal democratic republicanism on civil liberties, and respect for Plaid Cymru as it expands the cautious aspirations of 'unhistoric' Wales, and also strongly Green and pro-European, along with an instinctive global fraternalism. If the 2010 general election were to throw up some form of Progressive co-partnership or even a rainbow coalition of the liberal left, I would be perfectly content. The British left has been my torment and my joy, ever since Richard Hofstadter and my Swansea comrades inspired me to write about it. History should be, among other things, about the politics of hope, and I hope it justifies this book.

Kenneth O. Morgan
Long Hanborough, Oxfordshire
October 2009

Liberals

Chapter 1

The Great Reform Act of 1832

When I became a member of the Reform Club, I knew that it was a requirement to subscribe to the principles of the Great Reform Act. I did not, however, know that you also had to lecture on it! My historical research has invariably been far removed from the events of 1832. Indeed, my most substantial recent work has been a biography of a living former prime minister, Lord Callaghan. It is perhaps tempting to reflect fancifully on Lord Grey's 'winter of discontent' or to imagine the Duke of Wellington asking 'crisis, what crisis?' It is true that Lord Callaghan and the Duke of Wellington do have two things in common – Irish ancestry and the fact that their administrations were both defeated on a vote of confidence in the House of Commons. But there any point of contact comes to an abrupt end.

Even so, all historians of modern Britain, whatever their area of specialism, are aware of how the Great Reform Act casts its mighty shadow over the political history of this country. It was a major point of transition. It showed the emerging force of public opinion. It illustrates the beginnings of mass democracy. It was the greatest triumph in modern times of the people over what William Cobbett famously christened 'the Thing'. The Reform Club is right to celebrate it in the millennium year, and the Act is well worth re-examining all over again.

(i)

For many decades, it seems, the Great Reform Act has had bad reviews. In the hundred years following its passage, it was the object of almost uncritical veneration from authors writing in the old Whig-Liberal tradition. It was indissolubly linked with the immortal memory of Charles James Fox, with the passionate philippics of Lord Macaulay, and the literary glories of the Macaulay/Trevelyan dynasty. George Macaulay Trevelyan's biography of 1920 hailed Lord Grey, the hero of 1832, as a patrician popular tribune, a kind of Tony Benn *avant la lettre*, a man whose career went far to 'ennoble the annals of statecraft'.[1] This was the Whiggish tradition with which I grew up as a schoolboy in the late 1940s. But in the years since then historians seem to have settled on a far more critical judgement.

There have been two main, albeit very different, schools of criticism of the Reform Act, conservative and radical. With regard to the first, many historians have emphasised that the effect of the Great Reform Act was not change, but continuity. They have stressed that not much changed; the climactic events of 1832 were almost much ado about very little. This notion of continuity is a natural one for the craft and outlook of the professional historian. Indeed it is a theme that thrusts itself before us in the contemporary political world. For myself, as I look across the House of Lords, I cast my gaze on a distinguished and active figure on the Liberal Democrats benches. He is Earl Russell, the great-grandson of Lord John Russell, the politician who actually introduced the Reform Bill in the Commons in March 1831. But an awareness of continuity can also merge into an ethic of conservatism and this needs to be critically addressed.

The argument advanced two major themes, political and social. It emphasised that after 1832 the political system changed only modestly. With reason did Charles Wood, one of Grey's closest ministerial associates, observe in 1831 that the Bill was 'anti-democratic and pro-property'.[2] Alternatively, Lord Brougham declared that 'By the people, I mean the middle classes, the wealth and intelligence of the country, the glory of the British name.' No democrat he. It has been noted that there were more electoral abuses after 1832 than there were before. After all, there were many more different ways of being qualified for the franchise. Greater complexity meant greater abuse, and greater demands on the ingenuity or cunning of the political solicitors and others involved in determining the legal qualifications for the franchise in the new age of voter registration. There were just as many small boroughs, and just as much, if not more corruption. Dickens's Eatanswill, after all, describes the electoral system from a post-1832 perspective. Seventy 'proprietary' boroughs, owned by a single magnate, remained intact, and indirect control was more rampant still. In some boroughs, the electorate went down rather than up after 1832. Overall, it is agreed by historians that there was no immense change in the electorate. Frank O'Gorman has calculated that the percentage of adult males with the franchise went up merely from 14 per cent to 18 per cent, hardly a revolutionary transformation. Leslie Mitchell has rightly pointed out that the Act looked backwards: it was more concerned with 'exorcising the ghosts of the 1780s and 1790s than with laying the foundations of the Victorian order'.[3] Lord Macaulay in his *History of England*, as is well known, linked the Reform Act of 1832 with the Glorious Revolution of 1688 as a 'preserving revolution', a strategic controlled change that was intended to conserve.[4] No further change would be needed in any future that anyone could conceive. As everybody knows, Lord John Russell became known as 'Finality Jack' for advancing the view that 1832 was 'a final settlement'.

The social system after 1832, so historians rightly tell us, changed even less. In the counties, the historic 40-shilling freehold dating from medieval times remained the basis, though in somewhat extended form. Many of the enfranchisement provisions of the Great Reform Act in the counties, the 'Chandos Clause', carried in committee to enfranchise £50 tenant farmers (important in rural Wales), the enfranchisement of particular categories of leaseholders and the £10 copyholders, were intended to reinforce the hold of the aristocracy and the broad acres of the countryside over parliamentary representation in the House of Commons. Similarly, the new system had the indirect effect of preserving the ascendancy of the landed interest over the system of local government. This, indeed, continued to be the case down to the Act of 1884 and in England (though not in Wales) beyond that in many rural areas. The role of the Whig aristocracy, the mighty names of Bedford, Devonshire, Spencer, Argyll, heirs of the victors who brought William of Orange to the throne in 1688, remained powerful in politics down to the 1880s as all readers of Trollope and the saga of the Duke of Omnium will immediately recognise. Gladstone's first two Cabinets, those of 1868–74 and of 1880–5, were overwhelmingly Whiggish, with urban radicals such as John Bright and Joseph Chamberlain strictly marginalised. Gladstone confessed himself to be, socially, 'an out and out inequalitarian'.[5] The Great Reform Act was a supreme exercise in social exclusion. There was symbolic argument over voters with an uncertain qualification, notably non-resident owners of a 40-shilling freehold in the boroughs. The Tories argued that they should vote in the boroughs, lest deferential rural seats be swamped by more radical, perhaps dissenting, urban voters. They urged the need to demarcate distinctly the agricultural and the manufacturing interest. The Whigs, by contrast, urged that the two should not be rigidly kept apart. After losing out on the Chandos Clause, the Whigs won their point on this. Even so, the Reform Act might well take its place in the roll of honour of today's Countryside Alliance, foxhunting and all.

It was not only cautious historians but also radical politicians who came to take this negative view of the Reform Act. The Welsh and the Scots looked to the Acts of 1867 and 1884 as the *fons et origo* of democratic politics, not 1832. David Lloyd George, when campaigning against the House of Lords on behalf of his People's Budget in 1910, spoke of a reform that 'awoke the spirit of the mountains, the genius of freedom that fought the might of the Normans. ... The political power of landlordism in Wales was shattered as effectively as the power of the Druids.'[6] But he was talking of the general election that followed the 1867 Reform Act, not the dormant era of landlord control after 1832. An earlier Welsh radical, Henry Richard, elected member for Merthyr Tydfil in 1868, described the state of Welsh politics between 1832 and 1867 as one of 'feudalism', of 'clansmen struggling for their chieftains'.[7]

Alongside all these interpretations, there has also been a fierce onslaught from radical or left-wing historians or commentators. There is abundant evidence to support their view. Indeed, passionate disappointment with the outcome of the Great Reform Act was voiced at the time by 'Orator' Hunt in the House of Commons in 1832 and by the National Union of the Working Classes. The Chartist Movement from 1839 onwards was galvanised by the class bias and the cynical limitations of the Act of 1832. For the urban population of the newer industrial areas, especially in the North of England, the political effect of the Act was minimal. Socially, its most visible and notorious legacy was the erection of the workhouse, the 'poor Law Bastilles' created by the 1834 Poor Law Amendment Act, a physical symbol of class rule based on the cruel philosophy of 'less eligibility', that ultimately the root cause of poverty lay in the poor themselves. Marxists have seen the entire Reform debate in 1830–2 as irrelevant, a bourgeois fig leaf covering up the primitive nakedness of the capitalist order. The act was simply the triumphant statement of the conquerors, the rising bourgeois class. Real change in society would not come from tinkering with the superstructure as in the Reform Act but from fundamental transformations in the economic and social substructure as the evil contradictions of the capitalist system worked themselves out. Real change would come from below, from the mature class consciousness of the exploited proletariat in the mines, the mill and the backstreets. As the Yorkshire miners' leader Herbert Smith observed in the 1920s, in an admittedly opaque phase capable of a variety of interpretations, 'on t'field, that's t'place.'

(ii)

But, for all the force behind these various negative interpretations, they are not in my view at all good enough. To deal with the second, radical critique first, the mainstream of the working-class movement in Britain eventually drew from the 1832 Reform Act the moral that emancipation – freedom for the workers – would best come from political methods. Indeed, as one who has spent much of his time as a Labour historian, this conclusion seems to me to stand out in British history over the past 150 years. All six points of the Charter were concerned with the reform of parliament. Champions of anti-parliamentary forms of change, the Owenites, millennial radicals of various kinds, were marginalised. Later on, the pivotal moment in the political history of the working class came in 1899–1900 when Keir Hardie persuaded the trade unions that they should enter the political arena and form a great 'Labour Alliance' with the socialist societies, notably his own Independent Labour Party (ILP). The workers should capture and use power, not destroy it. He argued passionately, and successfully, against syndicalists, industrial unionists and other who took a contrary view.[8]

The same conclusion was eventually reached by another great working-class tribune, Aneurin Bevan, himself much attracted by notions of workers' control at the time of *The Miners' Next Step*, the famous quasi-syndicalist pamphlet published by the Unofficial Reform Committee at Tonypandy in 1912. In his political testament *In Place of Fear* (1952), Bevan commits himself to the parliamentary view of socialism. He argues that the most revolutionary force in the world, one which the more doctrinaire Marxists never really understood, was democracy.[9] Even Nye himself was an advocate of the incremental, peaceful route to socialism, a revolution made by consent. It was in 1832 that this notion first began.

And what about the arguments in favour of 'continuity'? Too often, it seems to me, historians, however imaginative, can lack a sense of occasion. Their own careful, scholarly constructs, put together patiently in the quiet of libraries or the hothouse atmosphere of the university seminar, fail to take account of the world outside and emotions and passions of the time. For, by any test, 1832 was a huge departure. It is visible even at the time if you look in the right place. Linda Colley has written that the course the Whigs adopted in 1830–2 was 'politically perilous'. Norman Gash's work focussed heavily on the surviving anomalies, the remaining smaller boroughs, on remaining pockets of royal influence like Windsor or Brighton.[10] There were indeed some of them. But you might also reach different conclusions about the impact of 1832 if you looked at Manchester or Merthyr Tydfil.

Beyond that, 1832 changed the influence and Crown and the House of Lords forever. Henceforth it was with the elected representatives of a reformed system that the initiative would reside. It led to the nationalising of politics, and the growth of nationwide parties – indeed, the foundation of this Reform Club in 1836 is testimony to that. With its 656,000 voters, the electoral roll in Britain after 1832 was the most democratic in Europe. The £10 householder, a property owner of course but an identifiably representative one, had a symbolic and psychological power. The Reform Act also embodied wider changes, notably in connection with the established Church. Indeed, if one takes the cycle of change from the Repeal of the Test and Corporation Act in 1828, through Catholic Emancipation in 1829 to the passage of the Reform Act, it is the old Protestant establishment that is the ultimate victim, as the church and chapel politics of subsequent decades were to demonstrate. Gladstone in

1838, still in his High Tory period, saw in the Reform Act of 1832 'a certain element of Anti-Christ'. His famous tract on the relations of Church and State in 1838 is seen by Jonathan Clark, in a powerful work of sustained scholarship, as 'the swansong of the old society', a society fatally undermined in its philosophical foundations in 1832.[11]

So it is reassuring to conclude this part of the discussion with the thought that in May 1836 the creators of the new Reform Club got it right. It shows how some of the Whigs even then saw the wider implications of the change that had taken place, the need to have a *point de réunion* with the radicals and the Irish. Sir William Molesworth, a young radical MP, went over the top in extolling its significance. 'Our success is certain. It will be the best club in town, and the effect will be to break the Whig party by joining the best of them to the Radicals, and the club will be the political centre of the Empire'. Brooks, the traditional Whig Club, was, he added 'not liberal enough, too expensive and not a dining club'.[12] It would embrace the widest possible constituency; hence the presence of Daniel O'Connell and other Irish members amongst the founders, as fine portraits in this club abundantly commemorate. There could have been an even more notable recruit. The young Benjamin Disraeli was for six months in 1834–5 a member of the Westminster Club, the precursor of our own club, but had to resign in the face of political criticism.[13]

The founding fathers of our club, excited by the mood of reformist euphoria after 1832, set their sights high. The Reform Club would not only rival the Carlton Club across Pall Mall in organising the Whig-Liberal cause and providing a central meeting point. It would be superior to the Tories of the Carlton in every way – in the intelligence of its members and in the beauty of its architecture. The relatively young Charles Barry, architect of the Italianate Travellers Club at 102 Pall Mall and later of the Houses of Parliament, was chosen to design it, in preference to Charles Cockerell or Decimus Burton, who had built the nearby Athenaeum. Barry was to create for the Reformers a superbly distinctive Italianiate Palazzo at 104 Pall Mall. It was possibly modelled on Sangallo's Palazzo Famese in Rome, certainly based on the concept of the 'double cube' of Inigo Jones and, beyond that, the Renaissance gospel of Palladio and Alberti, and the classical principles laid down by Vitruvius in times of antiquity. There was also the matter of food. The eminent *chef de cuisine*, Alexis Soyer, was taken on by the Reform Club, to create a legendary reputation for gastronomic distinction.[14] A whole edifice of liberal ideology would be built on the succulent foundations of Lamb cutlets Reform. It would go on to promote, energise and organise the reformist dynamic of the mid-Victorian age.

(iii)

How and why did the Great Reform Act happen? On one level, it was the outcome of a triumph of political manoeuvring. Reform, after all, had to be passed by an unreformed House of Commons. The Act became possible because the Tories, dominant in politics since the heyday of the Younger Pitt, were fundamentally split. Some of the far-right Ultras were determined to vote down Wellington and Peel after the alleged 'betrayal' of Catholic Emancipation in 1829, even if that meant letting in the old Whig enemy. Several Ultras voted against Wellington's government in the vote of confidence in November 1830. Meanwhile, the Whigs were vitally reinforced by Liberal Tories after the sudden death of their leader, George Canning, in August 1827 after only four months as premier, and the row over the disfranchisement of the rotten boroughs of East Retford and Penryn in 1828. This brought in ex-Canningites such as Melbourne, Palmerston, Stanley, and Goderich (and, of course, William Huskisson, shortly to be killed in a bizarre accident that saw him run over by one of the new steam-driven railway engines at the opening of the Manchester to Liverpool line). Their influence on the Grey government was in some ways disadvantageous. Melbourne in particular proved to be a Conservative and even malign influence who rejoiced in the savage suppression of the agricultural labourers caught up in the Captain Swing movement. But their presence encouraged a view that this was above all a moderate change in 1832. The representation of property and of traditional forms of influence was enshrined in the Act. They sought to get rid equally of the Old Corruption of George III and his placemen and the New Corruption of the Younger Pitt, and to create a healthier, viable system on the basis of the existing distribution of property, agricultural and industrial, rural and urban, in a way that would last.

In the end, the Whigs in 1832 conducted an exercise in limitations. They focussed on the fact that their redistribution was essentially limited and moderate. If 56 rotten boroughs had been abolished under Schedule A of the Act, only 22 new borough seats were created, 14 of them in the north. The secret ballot, originally a part of Russell's proposals to the great alarm of landowners everywhere, was dropped in committee. The enfranchisement of women, which some believed, with scant evidence, had resulted in some women exercising the vote at least in local elections in the distant past, was specifically excluded. The Reform Act made a point of asserting that it applied only to adult males, confirmed in the case of *Chorlton v. Lings* in 1868.[15] There was no further change on this point until the end of the First World War.

The Whigs focussed on events in parliament. They were only indirectly influenced by popular tumult outside. But everyone knew that it was a time of massive political and social tension at home and abroad. In Britain there were the Captain Swing riots of farm labourers in Kent and south-east England, which were brutally put down, there were strikes by Doherty's followers in Lancashire textile areas, there were revolutionary ideas of co-operation, communitarianism, monetary reform and free thought amongst the Owenites. A free-thinking artisan like the shipwright, Thomas Gast, veered between a miscellany of radical options.[16] There was a background of still greater turbulence abroad. There was the shock effect of the revolution in France that saw the establishment of the July Monarchy of Louis Philippe in July 1830, the revolution in Belgium (which aroused fears of French encroachment in that politically sensitive land), and insurrectionary movements in Spain, Italy and Poland. Across the ocean, British radicals were impressed by the new egalitarian pressures shown in the United States in the movement of Jacksonian Democracy. Here were poorer farmers, craftsmen and working men who invaded the White House in their joy at the election of Andrew Jackson, 'Old Hickory', and who challenged fundamentally the patrician world maintained for three decades by the federalist politicians who took their cue from George Washington.

Against this varied and tumultuous background, the Reform Bill first went through the Commons in the spring of 1831 in an atmosphere of near hysteria. Its second reading was carried by just one vote, 302 to 301. Macaulay's famous letter to Ellis describes the psychological and indeed physiological effect of these events on the Tory leadership as seen by this normally restrained and self-contained observer.

> The shouts broke out and many of us shed tears. I could scarcely refrain. And the jaw of Peel fell, and the face of Twiss was as the face of a damned soul, and Herries looked like Judas taking his necktie off for the last operation. We shook hands and clapped each other on the back, and went out laughing, crying and huzzaing into the lobby.
> On his way home, Macaulay conveyed the great news to his cab driver, who declared 'Thank God for it, sir'.[17]

Sir Robert Peel, even more notorious for his iron self-control, his smile in Daniel O'Connell's famous phrase 'like a silver plate on a coffin', greeted the news of a dissolution on 22 April with 'a harangue of sound and fury'. His oration, reported J.C. Hobhouse, was cut short by Black Rod 'just as he seemed to fall into a fit' while Hardinge, another Tory, forecast that there would be gunfire in the streets.[18] The consequence, however, was a huge Whig-Liberal victory in the general election, an overall majority of perhaps 140, a disaster for the Tories comparable with 1906, 1945 or 1997. Little wonder that the Iron Duke was heard to observe, 'Damn democracy'.

The Lords, the ultimate bastion of reaction, a Torres Vedras line against change, were even more intemperate. Lord Londonderry had to be held back by fellow Tories to prevent him from rushing across and assaulting Grey and other Whig peers. When the Lords later debated the second reading in October 1831, the Lord Chancellor Brougham spoke for over three hours with powerful effect, addressing the reporters present as much as the assembled lords, remarkably enough. Melodramatically, he pleaded on his knees with his fellow peers to pass the bill. As a result, a combination of arthritis and the effect of many tumblers of mulled port apparently made it difficult for him subsequently to rise and put the question. The Lords were impervious to his eloquence, and the bill was thrown out by 41, leading to an inevitable serious constitutional crisis.

There now followed an explosion of popular protest – mass uprising in Bristol and Merthyr Tydfil (which I discuss below), along with troubles in Derby and Newcastle and Nottingham and Preston, and menacing movements in Birmingham and Manchester, and potentially London. Things then seemed to calm down, and an amended version of the Reform Bill scraped through the Lords on 14 April 1832 by nine votes. But on 7 May Lyndhurst, a high Tory, got his critical amendment to delay the disfranchisement of the rotten boroughs passed by 35 votes. There followed the tumultuous 'days of May' with the famous attempt inspired by Francis Place to defeat the Duke of Wellington by 'going for gold', that is a mass withdrawal of specie from the banks. There were rumours of class violence, national bankruptcy, the triumph of republicans and anarchists and of anti-Christ. Gun shops did a brisk trade. Followers of Attwood and Place engaged in vague drilling. In a tragi-comic meeting at Windsor on 8 May, William IV had appeared to reject the view of Grey and Brougham, the prime minister and lord chancellor, that he should pledge himself to create enough new peers to ensure the passage of the Reform Act. King William declined to become a Lloyd George, or perhaps Tony Blair, before his time. Indeed, he sent Grey and Brougham empty away without even offering them any sustenance. The result, according to popular legend, was that the two statesmen had to repair for a meal to a post-house in Hounslow, where a vigorous debate over the table ensued as to whether their mutton chops should or should not be accompanied by kidneys.[19] The next morning, the Grey government submitted its resignation.

In the end, not only the culinary needs of Grey and Brougham but the constitutional needs of the country were met. Wellington was unable to take office, the King agreed à *outrance* to create a batch of 50 new peers to pass the bill if necessary, the Lords gave way and passed the third reading by 106 to 22. On 7 June 1832, with the King showing his dissent by refusing to give royal assent in person as was usual, the bill became law.

Throughout the focus of attention was on parliament in London. Sydney Smith genially suggested that one direct consequence of the crisis was the diminutive stature of Lord John Russell, the chief combatant of the hour for the government. Russell, said Smith, had originally been over six feet tall. 'But, engaged in looking after your interests, fighting the peers, the landlords and the rest of your natural enemies, he has been so consistently kept in hot water that he is boiled down to the proportion in which you now behold him!'[20] But Smith's levity concealed the tensions of the time, a parliamentary crisis and a crisis of civil society without precedent since the clash between King and Commons in the early 1640s. That former crisis was finally resolved by force of arms. Many politicians and owners of property, who checked their pikes and muskets before they went to bed, believed that the confrontation of 1832 might well result in a similar outcome.

(iv)

But the act is ultimately important not for its political and constitutional aspects. Its passage illuminates the social impact of industrialism, the massive change that had taken place in Britain, the first industrial nation, since the outbreak of the Revolutionary and Napoleonic Wars. There had been scattered groups of reformers from the early 1790s, the Corresponding Society, the Friends of the People associated with the radical young Charles Grey. Later, especially after 1815, there arose a rash of local Hampden Clubs, and isolated events like the marches of the so-called Blanketeers from Manchester. But they soon welled up into a broader, increasingly co-ordinated movement of nationwide social protest, triggered off amidst the economic distress and hardship of the time. The dynamics of a raw industrial, capitalist society were thereby laid bare.

It is customary to distinguish between middle-class and working-class radicalism in this broad movement. Actually, I am not quite sure how clear the distinction was in the new emerging towns of the industrial age, frontier communities as raw and unformed as the cowboy or mining settlements of the American Wild West. Asa Brigg's superb social dissection of the parliamentary reform movement, still the best analysis a full half-century after it was written with its author still in fine historical fettle, shows vividly the complexities of social categorisation of this kind. In Birmingham, for instance, Thomas Attwood's Political Union straddled classes and social groups in a way that reflects the structure of the small industrial businesses of the emergent black country.[21] Broad-based pressure emerged from manufacturing and commercial interests in the new industrial towns, their grievances voiced in powerful new provincial newspapers like the *Manchester Guardian* or the *Leeds Mercury*, or in the newly formed Chambers of Commerce whose interests turned out to be far more than purely commercial. In 1831–2 the Whigs appealed four-square to them. One of the consequences of the massacre at Peterloo in 1819 was a belief by the Manchester of Commerce that the very basis of the structure of local authority, including the maintenance of law and order could no longer be rationally defended by men of property and demanded a fundamental reform.

Focussing more specifically on the nascent urban and industrial working class, there is no doubt that 'the dangerous classes' kindled real terror. Fear of these new Jacobins, Robespierre with a Rochdale accent, was omnipresent. The 'mob' turned into a crowd, and the crowd turned into a class. Manchester radicals in 1819 hailed 'the artisan, the mechanic and the labourer, from whom all riches sprang',[22] a statement of the labour theory of value long before Marx. A subterranean culture was exposed of the friendly societies and obscure libertarian sects and the unstamped press and the popular clubs, with their membership, as Edward Thompson delighted to emphasise, said to be 'unlimited'.[23] They evolved modernised forms of popular protest; they embodied the revolutionary power of the printed word, as illustrated in Cobbett's terrifying 'democratical and Jacobinical talk'. New strategies of popular mobilisation were outlined in mass reform meetings. A particularly terrifying case was the riotous meeting held in Spa Fields in Clerkenwell, in December 1816, when the revolutionary (and inebriated) Watsons, father and son, called for the large crowd to invade and force open London's prisons, and themselves advanced menacingly as far as the outer wall of the Tower of London. One John Castle called for 'the last of Kings to be strangled with the guts of the last priest'. Unfortunately, he turned out to be a government spy. The angry passion of Spa Fields slowly petered out.

The reform movement, like any other popular upsurge, needed its martyrs. And, of course, it found them at Peterloo in 1819. This was truly a terrible event. A peaceful meeting of 60,000, gathered in St. Peter's Field in Manchester to hear pro-reform speeches by Orator Hunt and others, was charged by a maddened and undisciplined yeomanry. Eleven were killed and over 400 were injured, including many women and children.

A tiny child was trampled to death. And, as is customary in British disasters from that time to this, mining accidents, train crashes or whatever, no one was ever prosecuted or publicly held to account. Peterloo was a great moral turning point, industrial Britain's Amritsar or Sharpeville. Its ideological impact was overwhelming. It was a moral triumph for the dispossessed and the disinherited. It inspired Shelley's immense polemic *The Mask of Anarchy*, a devastating if complex poem written in Italy in 1819 and deemed by Leigh Hunt to be too dangerous to be published until 1832. Shelley's climax is still overwhelming:

> *Rise like lions after slumber*
> *In unvanquishable number*
> *Shake your chains to earth like dew*
> *Which in sleep had fallen on you*
> *Ye are many – they are few*[24]

After Peterloo, things were never the same. There appeared to be a more tranquil period in the mid-1820s. Trade picked up, unemployment fell, the workers busied themselves with nascent trade unions and co-operatives. But there was a mounting feeling of impending change being inevitable thereafter. Truly this was a landmark in the formation and the consciousness of the industrial working class.

Social upheaval did not in itself force through the passage of the 1832 Reform Act. But it was an omnipresent threat in the near background. Orator Hunt jeered at Whig fears after disturbances and the billeting of troops in his own constituency at Preston. 'I challenge you to get up a *Whig* riot throughout the country!'[25] Troops were billeted in many parts of the country. The social context was particularly clear in two very different places, both of them violently confrontational – Bristol, with the ancient quayside of its docks from which John Cabot had once sailed to America, and Merthyr Tydfil, on the rim of the Welsh industrial region with its gaunt new ironworks. In both places, there was a considerable loss of life. At first glance, many contemporaries assumed that this was just a replay of traditional rioting and vandalism. In Bristol there was a special destruction – the Mansion House and Customs House were destroyed, prisoners released from Bristol gaol, the celebrated Bishop's Palace burnt down, and the contents of the Bishop of Bristol's ample wine cellar flogged off on College Green at a penny a bottle! Between 120 and 250 Bristolians were killed or wounded by the dragoons. There were five public executions; others were transported to Van Diemen's Land and stayed there.[26] In Merthyr, with its background of trade depression, unemployment and resentment at truck shops and wage cuts in the Crawshay ironworks, there was a ferocious clash between demonstrators and the local militia and troops from the Argyll and Sutherland Highlanders. Eleven unarmed men were shot down by troops within the Castle Hotel and killed and many others injured by bayonets. There was one memorable public execution, that of a young local miner, Richard Lewis. Accused, on virtually no evidence, of stabbing a Highland infantryman, Donald Black, Lewis was hanged and thereafter immortalised as Dic Penderyn.[27]

But these were uprisings, not simple riots. The context was intensely political. What triggered off the Bristol riots was the visitation of the assizes by the local recorder, Charles Wetherell, MP for Boroughbridge (with its 48 electors), a most reactionary and vituperative Tory opponent of the Reform Bill. His very presence in the city at such a time was highly inflammatory. So too was the blinkered response of the two local bishops, of Bath and Wells and of Bristol, both of whom voted against the Reform Bill in the Lords. The destruction of property in Bristol was very specific and so, too, was its periodicity. The rioting ended abruptly when its objectives were achieved. Throughout, the Bristol Political Union was an important guiding force, training its fire on the oligarchy who ran the local closed corporation; its vice-president, William Herapath, a professor of toxicology, was later, incidentally, to find fame as expert witness in the trial of 'Palmer the Poisoner'.

In Merthyr, as Gwyn A. Williams has shown, there was a distinctive, popular tradition of 'Jacobinism' amongst the local craftsmen and 'shopocracy' dating from the 1790s. In 1830 there were in consequence huge reform meetings in Merthyr and Dowlais, and massive pressure on local industrialists and would-be politicians like John Guest. The Merthyr uprising was intensively ideological: it is an early instance of the red flag being flown in a popular protest. Class hatred of Crawshay and the ironmasters was fused with rage against the political order, including the 'shopocracy' itself. The riots in Merthyr followed a massive reform rally at Waun Mawr, with mass banners proclaiming 'Reform'. There were popular heroes to hand like 'Lewsyn yr Heliwr' and a famous martyr in Dic Penderyn. Dic is Wales's, perhaps Britain's, first working-class hero. His memory was used politically to put popular pressure on Guest to support the cause of reform years later in 1837. But, long since, Dic Penderyn's last dramatic words on the scaffold – '*O Arglwydd, dyma gamwedd!*' – 'Injustice', have rung down the years.[28] I see that the Queen, already under pressure to apologise to the Maoris for the Treaty of Waitangi, the Australian aborigines for the theft of their land, the Afrikaaners for the deaths of children in the concentration camps during the Boer War, and the Irish people for the Great Famine, has in some quarters been urged to apologise to the people of Wales as well for the undoubtedly unjust execution of Dic Penderyn 169 years ago. In my view, there are rational arguments against selective retrospective state apologies. But it might nevertheless be a shrewd move for the Prince of Wales, whose contact with his supposed people is at best episodic, if he, too, were some time to remember publicly the martyrdom of Dic Penderyn.

(v)

After 1832, the rhetoric and reality of Reform were never the same. There were the most profound social and political implications. Politics exploded, breaking out from small, localised undercover societies, and went out into the country at large. The advance of literacy was a major factor in this process. From Cartwright to Cobbett to Cobden and Bright, the tide rolled on. The history of the Reform Club itself is an important and distinguished part of that process. Very soon, the reform of parliament led to assaults on other established institutions in the 1830s – on the slave system, local government, the poor law and especially the privileges of the established church. The Protestant establishment was on the defensive henceforth – indeed, the Church Defence campaign came into being, a movement that was to lose the overall campaign in Wales. The outcome came in moves to disestablish the Church (successful in Ireland and in Wales) but also a wider disestablishment of the traditional secular order. The defeat of the landed gentry during the repeal of the Com Laws in 1846 was one early consequence.

The change in the reform movement was very noticeable in Chartism. The emphasis now changed from the need to cleanse parliament from old corruption and to create a quite different relationship with the Crown and the executive, to working out new ideas of representation. What was under discussion now was not simply the independence of parliament but its legitimacy, its relationship no longer with the Crown but with the people. Change was inherent even in the terms of the Reform Act of 1832. There was a steady increase in the electorate by the 1860s through the inflationary impact on property values, which led to the rise in rentals and thereby to the numbers of £10 householders who could exercise the vote in borough constituencies. The £10 qualification had been attacked by radicals in 1832 who pointed out that, in most parts of England, a £5–7 valuation was the norm. But by the 1860s, the £10 valuation contained revolutionary potential. By now, Lord John Russell was 'Finality Jack' no longer. He admitted his huge mistake and became a champion of reform once again. The American Civil War of 1861–5 was an important event in British history too, as the close friendship of Cobden and Bright with the American radical abolitionist, Charles Sumner, indicated. The encouragement it gave to a revived parliamentary reform movement in Britain marked the death-knell of the post-1832 compromise. Reform, far more sweeping this time, came again in 1867 and 1884, and of course in 1918 and 1928 with the emancipation of women and nearly universal suffrage. But these later developments, momentous though they all were, proved less traumatic than the first breakthrough in 1832.

The process of change since 1832 has been an erratic one. Reform of our unwritten, unstructured constitution has not been a dominant theme in modern British history. Labour governments have tended to have other priorities and Labour prime ministers have been constitutional conservatives for the most part. The Lords was partially reformed over 88 years between the Parliament Act of 1911 and the abolition of most hereditary elements in 1999. Even today we have the extraordinary spectacle of 90 hereditary peers and a handful of bishops lingering on in a half-amended second chamber. Women did not receive the vote at all until 1918 and only in 1949 was the final process of Lords reform as then conceived carried out. Advocates of proportional representation, of course, assert that something far more fundamental is needed, and, with the fading out of a politics dominated by two major parties, their time may yet come.

Even so, we can now look at the 1832 Reform Act with fresh eyes. It was the first, vital step. Then and later, it was assumed that parliament was the epicentre of the political world and the glory of the nation. While the French or the Italians might deride their own legislative assemblies as corrupt talking-shops, the British revered theirs. Every schoolboy knew of the symbolism of Big Ben. During the Second World War, as Mrs. Thatcher proclaimed in her 1988 Bruges speech, it chimed out for freedom. The Army Bureau of Current Affairs classes, started up amongst the troops in the war, extolled the historic virtues of 'the mother of parliaments' and spoke proudly of the Levellers and the Putney debates. That, in 1945, was what we were fighting for, the historic embodiment of our sovereignty. Today, by contrast, parliament seems marginalised, diminished, not just in the face of an overmighty executive, but in terms of wider pressures of globalised economic forces, involvement in Europe, a revolution in information technology and in the power of the media. Today, Lord John Russell would first explain his proposals for parliamentary reform not on the floor of the House of Commons but to John Humphreys on the *Today* programme. I guess he would do so very effectively, if the interruptions allowed him to.

But now the reform mantle of 1832 is being taken up again. We have the extension of reform to the localities – to Scotland, Wales, Northern Ireland, to London and perhaps in time to the regions of England as well.

Accountability has acquired a new sheen. A raft of reform ideas is being proposed by many groups of which Charter 88 and Democratic Audit are only two, taking the logic of 1832 to a more natural conclusion, in pursuit of a revitalised civic, republican ideal, based on a philosophy of human rights, enshrined in the European Convention. This creates a quite different institutional and intellectual climate. Professor Norman Gash, in a celebrated phrase, wrote of the Reform Act of 1832, that 'what the Whigs did was necessary but that what the Tories said was true'.[29] In fact, most of what the Tories said was rubbish. The Great Reform Act did not mean an end to monarchy, the established Church, religion, property rights, the full panoply of the capitalist system – regrettably so, some might perhaps feel. But the Tories were right in one key respect in 1832. In Peel's famous phrase, the door opened then can never be closed. The forces of change flow on once again, and perhaps in time irresistibly. The process of political reform is still on our agenda. Indeed it is perhaps more vigorous in this Millennium year than at any time since Lord Grey lived in Downing Street. That this should still be so is an immemorial tribute to the achievement and the unfinished business of the Great Reform Act of 1832.

Chapter 2

Gladstone and the New Radicalism

Gladstonianism was a powerful factor among the Liberals in rallying and reuinifying them down to the 1906 general election, with its great imperatives of freedom of trade, religious equality and international peace founded on national self-determination. It remained of importance in building up the tradition of Liberal 'guiding principles' after 1918 (notwithstanding Lloyd George's memorable onslaught on Herbert, Viscount Gladstone in 1922 as 'the finest living embodiment of the Liberal principle that talent is not hereditary'). In the Liberal schisms of the 1920s the Gladstone tradition was still important in the reconstruction of 'the immortal principles of the great Liberal Party' and its various regional bases.

Even in the 1980s the tortuous attempt to construct a viable relationship between the Liberals and the Social Democrats within the Alliance was marked in the case of Roy Jenkins, himself an eminent biographer of the Grand Old Man, by frequent Gladstonian references to a 'union of hearts' and to there being no limit to the onward march of a nation (the European Community notwithstanding).

To an extent that is often forgotten, Gladstone was also a potent force in the birth and early growth of the Labour Party. He had a profound influence on Labour pioneers such as Arthur Henderson, Philip Snowden and George Lansbury. Keir Hardie, in effect the founder of the Labour Alliance in 1900, had an intense devotion for Gladstone as a great liberator of the masses, 'God bless him! May he be spared to accomplish the great work to which he has put his hand,' he wrote in 1887.[1] He wrote a passionate tribute to Gladstone in the *Labour Leader* when the great man died in 1898, including in his eulogy the liberation of Ireland, and the challenge to the House of Lords and vested interests generally. 'Gladstone's work has made Socialism possible', Hardie wrote.[2] The Liberal heritage was a vital factor in the history and ideas of the Labour and socialist movement at least down to 1945, as the writings of men such as Tawney and Laski indicate. In some respects, as in the attempt to redefine socialism as personal freedom, it had its relevance even in the 1980s, almost a century after Gladstone's death.[3]

Nor was Gladstone's legacy, real or assumed, confined to the political left. Where radicals saw the great emancipator, New Conservatives (sometimes christened neo-Liberals) extolled the great economist, even while they made Disraelian genuflections to 'one nation'. The prolonged attempt by Mrs. Thatcher and her followers in the 1980s to restore faith in strict economy, private enterprise and market forces was a concentrated attempt to elevate once again the principles of Gladstonian economics after years of harassment and heresy by the aberrant followers of Keynes. So there is every justification in looking anew at Gladstone's style and principles.

A most important light is shed on Gladstone's abiding influence by his attitude towards the politics, culture and nationality of Wales. There is no doubt that in his later years Gladstone became a great national hero to the Welsh, amongst whom he made his home in Hawarden in Flintshire – witness the immense acclaim given to his mass address at Singleton Abbey in Swansea in 1887, or his dramatic speech at Cwmllan, at the foot of Snowdon in 1892.[4]

Yet it has been widely assumed, both by Conservative churchmen and by several Welsh nonconformist radicals of the quasi-nationalist *Cymru Fydd* (Young Wales) school, that Gladstone was basically hostile to the Welsh Nonconformist presence that emerged in the Liberal Party between the 1860s and the 1890s. There is often assumed to have been a fundamental tension between the high church squire of Hawarden and the great mass of Welsh nonconformists. William George, Lloyd George's brother, called Gladstone 'a drag on the wheel'; the Unionist squire of Trevalyn Hall (not far from Hawarden), Arthur Griffith-Boscawen, said much the same.[5]

Furthermore, it has been claimed that this is a symptom of a wider weakness endemic in the Liberal Party in the later nineteenth century – the pressure upon Gladstone by 'faddists' or purveyors of 'crochets' in the party, especially after the split over Irish Home Rule in 1886.[6] The supreme symbol of this is taken to be the 1891 Newcastle Programme (which had Welsh disestablishment as the second in its lengthy list of items), which Arthur Balfour derided as 'a programme of varieties'. The Welsh radical element in the Liberal Party is taken as a symbol of the sectionalism that created turmoil within the late Victorian Liberal coalition. The influence of the so-called Celtic Fringe is considered to be a damaging factor down to 1914, and thus a major cause in the ultimate death, 'strange' or otherwise, of Liberal England (and Wales).[7] I wish here to examine this view, which seems to me basically mistaken.

Wales, in fact, played only a marginal and episodic part in British political life from the Tudor age down to the 1860s. There were only occasional noises off in the valleys, as in the Merthyr uprising of 1831, the Rebecca riots or Chartism. Welsh politics, wrote the radical Henry Richard in 1866, were essentially 'feudal'.[8] Even so, Gladstone, as he emerged to full political stature, encountered an important range of influences that kept him in close touch with Welsh affairs. He married a Welsh woman, Catherine Glynne. He lived in Hawarden. In 1866, he was much impressed by the letters published by Henry Richard that drew attention to the public neglect of Welsh interests.[9] Gladstone was also increasingly drawn into the Welsh political and cultural scene, as in his memorable attendance at the Mold *eisteddfod* of 1873 when he praised 'the ancient history, the ancient deeds and the ancient language of your country, the Principality of Wales'.[10] Through Henry Austen Bruce, his home secretary from 1868–74 and member for Merthyr Tydfil, he became involved in Welsh education and the campaign for a national university.

Above all, there was Stuart Rendel, the member for Montgomeryshire from 1880 to 94.[11] He became a particularly close friend of Gladstone. He was his host several times at his villa in Valescure on the French Riviera; his second daughter, Maud, married Gladstone's third son, Henry; he was a pall-bearer at Gladstone's funeral. Rendel was neither a great intellectual nor a powerful orator. But he was a very shrewd political strategist. Although an Englishman, an Anglican and (remarkably) a wealthy arms manufacturer, he had a clear conception of the need to recognise the Welsh political identity, focussing on the supreme issue of the disestablishment of the church in Wales, and of how to merge Welsh national causes of various kinds with a wider organic Liberalism.

After 1890, Rendel became somewhat out of touch with some aspects of Welsh politics, as his concern with the tithe riots of the late 1880s indicated. He had scant sympathy with the aggressive, almost separatist, nationalism of younger men like David Lloyd George. But Rendel retained a powerful influence on Gladstone right down to 1894, when he went to the House of Lords on the premier's retirement. Stuart Rendel was in many ways a genuine radical – witness his later strong support for Lloyd George during the Boer War and the campaign for the 1909 'People's Budget'. He remained a benevolent influence in Wales, notably as a generous benefactor of the University College of Wales, Aberystwyth, where several chairs and a hall of residence bear his name to this day. By educating Gladstone in the national and political needs of Wales, he played a notable and creative part in transforming the social and political outlook of the Liberal Party.

Gladstone's direct contact with Welsh politics down to the Irish Home Rule schism of 1886 was intermittent, though important. In particular, as a deeply committed Anglican, he viewed with great anxiety the rise of a popular nonconformist movement in Wales to disestablish and disendow the Anglican Church there. Gladstone maintained that there was no parallel with the Irish Church that he himself had disestablished in 1869. He spoke strongly against Welsh disestablishment on Watkin William's motion in the Commons in May 1870. The prime minister emphasised that the Welsh Church enjoyed 'a complete constitutional, legal and historical identity with the Church of England'.[12] A separate measure to disestablish the church in Wales was, therefore, unthinkable.

On the other hand, Gladstone did also appreciate the perceived inadequacies of the church in Wales at the time. After all, fully three-quarters (perhaps four-fifths) of the worshipping population of Wales attended nonconformist chapels, not the mother church. As Colin Matthew has shown, he accepted and endorsed the growing religious pluralism within the United Kingdom, developing since the 1840s. He made the significant admission that there was indeed a Welsh Church problem – and a Welsh political problem extending far beyond it. He devoted, therefore, much time and trouble to selecting a Welsh speaking bishop for the see of St. Asaph in 1870, and again for the see of Llandaff in 1882. He took it very seriously. He had also evidently totally changed his view on the Welsh language which had created 'unfavourable impressions' in his mind back in 1856.[13]

Thus in January 1870, he wrote, 'I have not since taking my present office felt more strongly the gravity of any matter of duty requiring to be done than this of the Welsh bishopric'.[14] In December 1882, he added complainingly, 'A vacancy in a Welsh see costs me more trouble than six English vacancies.'[15] The effects could be comic. He wrote to Henry Bruce in January 1870, 'If you read in the papers some morning that I have been carried to Bedlam and that a straight waistcoat is considered necessary, please to remember it will be entirely owing to the vacancy in the see of St. Asaph.'[16]

The personal results were not altogether happy. Joshua Hughes, eventually appointed to St. Asaph in 1870, was not a distinguished bishop. He had, it emerged, acquired only a B.D. (Lampeter) not a B.A. (Cambridge) as recorded in Crockford's.[17] Richard Lewis, appointed to Llandaff in 1882, was termed a 'pis aller', and 'an inferior Basil Jones' (a reference to the Bishop of St. David's, himself by no means an intellectual giant).[18]

Even so, Gladstone's concern with Welsh church appointments had indirectly a most powerful effect on the movement for Welsh disestablishment and church reform, even if this was largely accidental. In paying such intimate attention to the need for a Welsh-speaking bishop, sympathetic to nonconformists, Gladstone was making a notable public concession. He was acknowledging implicitly that the disestablishment of the Welsh Church was justifiable, not on the Liberationist argument of freeing all churches everywhere from the trammels of the state connection, but on the specific grounds of Welsh nationality. Wales, it emerged, could be recognised as a nation, as Ireland had been in 1869. By 1885, when 30 of the 34 Welsh constituencies returned Liberals and greatly helped Gladstone back to Downing Street for the third time, the great majority of the Liberal Party, especially of course in the principality, was in sympathy with Welsh disestablishment. Gladstone was coming to accept the great tide of popular feeling, which he himself had indirectly stimulated. By 1885, indeed, he was making private admissions that he might well have to reverse his view on Welsh disestablishment,[19] as his son Herbert's 'Hawarden Kite' was dramatically to show he had also done on Irish Home Rule.

Gladstone also stoked the fires of Welsh national sentiment elsewhere. He made, as we have seen, a powerful emotive declaration of support for Welsh cultural nationalism at the Mold *eisteddfod* in 1873. He also intervened strongly in the Commons on behalf of the Welsh Sunday Closing Bill in 1881, which he justified on national grounds as a sanction for separate Welsh legislation on a matter on which Welsh nonconformists had particularly strong feelings.[20]

Above all, he was pushed by Bruce, Rendel and others into endorsing the Welsh crusade for higher education. He publicly endorsed Hussey Vivian's motion on behalf of Welsh intermediate schools in the Commons in 1879.[21] He appointed the epoch-making departmental committee on Welsh higher education in 1880–1 which, led by its chairman Lord Aberdare (formerly Henry Bruce), called powerfully for a Welsh intermediate school system and for two Welsh university colleges.[22] Gladstone also reluctantly provided some state funds for the new colleges at Cardiff and Bangor in 1883. Even more reluctantly, he endorsed support for a third college, the University College on the seafront in Aberystwyth, which had existed since 1872 and had already produced such distinguished students as O.M. Edwards and Tom Ellis.[23] Unforeseen at the time, the social and cultural base for a Welsh national movement had thereby been provided. The schools and colleges created by the Welsh educational crusade – involving such emotional symbols as *Sul y Brifysgol*, when poor chapel-goers gave their pence to a national university on 'University Sunday' – were to provide the new middle-class elite that dominated Welsh political, commercial and cultural life down to 1914. The University of Wales, *Prifysgol y Werin* (The People's University) by its very existence challenged the hierarchical, static world that Wales had known over the centuries.

By the mid-1880s, the change in the tone of Welsh politics was very pronounced. The older type of Welsh Liberal, men like Henry Richard,

Lewis Dillwyn, George Osborne Morgan and Hussey Vivian, was being supplanted by younger, more radical, more intensely nationalist figures such as Torn Ellis and the very youthful Lloyd George. By 1885 Wales had become the most Liberal part of the British Isles. It was, of course, particularly affected by the Reform and Redistribution Acts of 1884–5. With 30 Liberal members it had become an unconquerable bastion of the British left.

Most significantly, in the Irish Home Rule schism of 1886, it responded overwhelmingly to endorse Gladstone's position on Ireland. Despite the impact of Joseph Chamberlain and the radicalism of his Unauthorised Programme, which had an especial appeal for nonconformists and disestablishers, the Protestant Welsh in thousands turned decisively towards Gladstone.

Only a small minority flirted with Liberal Unionism – and several of those few, including Sir Hussey Vivian, the editor-publisher Thomas Gee of Denbigh, and (almost) the youthful David Lloyd George, swung back to Gladstonianism soon after the polls.[24] In Montgomeryshire, Rendel, who clung on to his marginal seat with much difficulty, urged Liberal activists to 'say as little as they can' about Ireland, and to concentrate on disestablishment, land reform, and the towering personality and moral leadership of Gladstone.[25] The relative unanimity of Wales in 1886 (and again in 1900 during the Boer War) was in marked contrast with the divisions of Liberalism in Scotland and its large-scale retreat in much of southern England. It was Welsh national consciousness that largely contributed to this result.

After the Irish Home Rule split in 1886, there was a major transformation of the Liberal Party. There was the new prominence of Labour and the unions, of agrarian radicalism, of urban progressives in London – and of Welsh and Scottish nationalists. It was, contrary to what many historians have alleged in Dangerfield-like terms, an optimistic, forward-looking period, the years which gave birth to the New Liberalism of Hobhouse and Hobson, of Rowntree, Masterman and Chiozza Money, of Churchill and Lloyd George. Political developments in Wales were an important part of this optimism.

There was the creation of a distinct Welsh parliamentary party, with its own whips, chaired by Stuart Rendel from 1888 onwards. There were the emergence of distinct Welsh political priorities: church disestablishment, education, temperance, land reform and a qualified form of governmental devolution. There was a new political structure in Wales, with the North Wales and South Wales Liberal Federations coming into being – both of them affiliated with the National Liberal Federation in London, unlike their comrades in Scotland. There was also a new elite of political leadership – Tom Ellis, Herbert Lewis, Sam Evans, D.A. Thomas in the mining valleys and, above all, Lloyd George, returned to parliament for Caernarfon Boroughs in a by-election in 1890. Others, like Ellis Griffith and Llewelyn Williams, were following on. Even Rendel himself was gradually being phased out. Gladstone was being forced to respond, and respond positively, to their pressure.

Certainly the Liberal leader was far from happy about some aspects of this. He was worried about the growth of agitation over the land tenure system in Wales, with its alarming parallels to the Land League of Michael Davitt in Ireland. He kept silent over the tithe disturbances and the government's various Tithe Bills of 1889–91 – an almost unique act of self-denial on an ecclesiastical topic. He was, however, forced to acknowledge that there was, if only on cultural grounds, a separate Welsh agrarian question, with largely nonconformist, Welsh-speaking tenant farmers deeply alienated from their Anglican, Tory, anglicised landlords. Great dynasts like Sir Watkin Williams Wynn, Lord Penrhyn or Lord Cawdor were finding that the sands of time were running out. Gladstone, somewhat characteristically, appeared to give public support to Tom Ellis's Welsh Land Bill of 1892 – even though in the end he voted against it. He also strongly endorsed Rendel's Welsh Intermediate Education Bill of 1889, which many of the clergy, and St. David's College, Lampeter, viewed with intense suspicion.[26] The eventual Act of 1889 was a powerful one, creating a nationwide network of secondary 'county' schools, and making Wales a bastion of state secondary education which it remains to this day. Gladstone also caused a sensation by a particularly emphatic endorsement of the Welsh language and its value, at the Wrexham national eisteddfod in 1888.[27]

He also made a decisive shift on Welsh disestablishment. After 1886 one prominent Liberal after another came out in support of it in principle: Morley, Harcourt, Rosebery, even Spencer, the famous 'Red Earl' (a reference to the colour of his beard and certainly not to his politics). Francis Schnadhorst, the party organiser, encouraged the growth of the North Wales and South Wales Liberal Federations, both of which had disestablishment as their first objective. Gradually, indeed delphically, Gladstone also responded. As an Anglican, he was repelled by the anticlericalism of men like Sam Evans and Lloyd George, notably when the latter attacked the 1891 church congress at Rhyl for 'floating on barrels of beer'. But, almost imperceptibly, in a sea change as it were, Gladstone moved to a complete reversal of his views on Welsh disestablishment. It might be noted here that his son, the Reverend Stephen Gladstone, the Rector of Hawarden, became a committed disestablisher.

Thus we have Gladstone in June 1887, in terms of remarkable obscurity even for him, stating that he was 'endeavouring to give to the demand for information that is not unnaturally entertained whatever satisfaction the question may permit'.[28] In 1890 Gladstone actually voted on behalf of Scottish disestablishment and declared that the question in Wales was 'ripe for decision'. In February 1891 he both spoke and voted for it in the Commons. He placed his argument on the firm ground of Welsh nationality. He declared that the Welsh Church had become the church of the few, and the church of the rich.[29] Wales was a nation of nonconformists. A great intellectual crisis had thus been overcome. At Newcastle in October 1891, as noted, Welsh disestablishment was the second item on the Liberal programme, with Gladstone's benevolent assistance.

(i)

When he formed his fourth and final government in August 1892, Gladstone was very aware of the problems of Wales. After all, he had a majority of only 40; the Welsh Liberal members numbered 31 and theoretically held the balance of power. He actually formed his government in Rendel's elegant home at 1 Carlton Gardens, just behind Pall Mall. He accepted all the three main points that Rendel put to him. He went ahead with a charter for a national university of Wales, ignoring the clerical protests that emanated from St. David's, Lampeter. With some reluctance, he appointed a Royal Commission rather than a mere committee, to inquire into the Welsh land question. Finally, he drafted a Suspensory Bill to suspend the vested interests created within the Welsh Church, an earnest of goodwill regarding future disestablishment and disendowment. In addition, a talented young Welsh MP, Tom Ellis of Merioneth, was made a junior whip.

Despite much sceptical criticism from the Welsh newspapers, Gladstone was now clearly moving towards the framing of a Welsh Disestablishment Bill. 'Vote! Vote! Vote! for Irish Home Rule and Welsh Disestablishment,' he shouted in the House when provoked by Randolph Churchill.[30] In the late autumn of 1893, a Welsh disestablishment measure was being drawn up by government draftsmen, and indeed was to be introduced by Asquith, the home secretary, the following May, after Gladstone had retired as premier.[31] It is worth noting, incidentally, that despite much political and historical controversy on the point, Monmouthshire was firmly included as being part of Wales in this bill.

Gladstone retired as premier in early March 1894. He was followed by Lord Rosebery, a change greeted with some rebelliousness by Welsh Liberals who had little regard for an imperialist peer as prime minister. It seemed as if an important chapter in Welsh politics was at an end. However, it was not quite over. In June 1895, *The Times* announced, quite unexpectedly, that Gladstone had cancelled his 'pair' with Villiers over the Welsh Disestablishment Bill now going through its committee stage in the House. It emerged that Gladstone objected to two disendowment provisions, notably the secularisation of cathedrals. (Gladstone's grandson, W.G.C. Gladstone, MP for Kilmarnock, also objected on this point when the 1912 Disestablishment Bill was being discussed, and the provision about cathedrals was eventually removed.)[32] However, Gladstone assured a Welsh Liberal MP that he still accepted the justice of the broad principal of disestablishment for Wales. There seems no reason to doubt this. Gladstone, after all, had come to recognise that Welsh nationality existed – but also that the Welsh national movement differed fundamentally from that in Ireland. The land question in Wales was more amenable to a compromise settlement. The pressure for separatism was much less intense. Cultural nationalism did not necessarily lead to a demand for political separation or Home Rule. Welsh rural society was not scarred by the endemic violence of tenant–landlord relations in Ireland. The religious denominations were less antagonistic because there was no Welsh Ulster. Wales was, above all, stimulated by a desire for national equality within the United Kingdom as a whole. It was a part of the wider democratisation of British society as a whole.

By the time of Gladstone's retirement, the influence of the Welsh within the Liberal Party, and on the British political scene, was much enhanced. It was to remain powerful until after the First World War, with Lloyd George becoming premier himself in 1916 and passing the eventual disestablishment and disendowment of the Welsh Church (with general all-party endorsement by this time) in 1919. But several major questions, however, remain to be asked about the process we have outlined.

First of all, was the role of the Welsh a symbol of a wider, disastrous movement towards sectionalism, parochialism and eventual disintegration for British Liberalism? This seems a very doubtful view. After all, the Liberal Party had always been a coalition of divergent interests, a kind of popular front, ever since it came into existence in the latter period of Palmerston's reign in the early 1860s. As early as the 1870s, the stresses between the old Whigs, middle-class mercantile Liberals and scattered groups of working-class and other radicals and between all of them and their parliamentary leadership were evident. Dr. T.A. Jenkins's study has shown how the defection of the Whigs was under way from 1874 onwards,[33] and that a range of popular clubs and local Liberal associations was emergent, not least in London. In these circumstances, Liberals had to work out their ideological positions pragmatically as they went along – indeed, this is what they always had done. Attempts to impose a single great, overarching theme on the party had always been misguided, let alone efforts to 'wipe the slate clean' as the Liberal Imperialists tried vainly to do after 1900.

The Welsh, indeed, were a vigorous element in the many-faceted radicalism and pluralism of the *fin de siècle* Liberal Party. Further, the causes of Wales were wide-ranging in their implications. They were not promoted by single-issue pressure-groups, like the Liberation Society or the United Kingdom Alliance, which cared only for their own sole, obsessive concern. The Welsh embraced religious, agrarian, educational, temperance and labour reform, without any necessary feeling of incompatibility or a battle for primacy existing between them. Thus Welsh disestablishment after 1880 merged into a wider nationwide campaign for democratic reform, instead of being the dogmatic narrow theme as propagated by the Liberationists. Gladstone's positive response to the Welsh is a tribute to this outward-looking quality.

Secondly, it may well be questioned whether Gladstone's positive reaction to the pressures of the Welsh Liberals was the product simply of 'political blackmail'.[34] Of course, political pressure by the Welsh played its part, as it always does in politics. Liberal votes among the Welsh, the Scots and religious nonconformists generally were an important consideration, especially after 1886 when Liberalism appeared to have lost its majority in England with the defection of the Chamberlainites and the Whigs simultaneously. There was the proclaimed policy, too, of 'filling up the cup' so that the challenge to the House of Lords from a Liberal government would be as comprehensive as possible.

But there was more to it than that. There was also the force of nationalism – an elemental, almost sacred force for Gladstone in continental Europe and in the United Kingdom as well since his famous protest against Neapolitan tyranny in 1851. Thus it was that his perception of the triumph of nationalism in Italy or the Balkan countries, along with his first-hand observation of communal endeavour in the small nation of Norway which he witnessed in 1885, played its part in Gladstone's mounting understanding of the needs of Wales. He was also aware of the wider social forces released in his party from the 1870s onwards, and only inadequately reflected in the Newcastle Programme. These forces needed sustained, moral leadership.

On balance, he saw Welsh radicalism as a source of strength for his principles and for his party – 'it is not the Irish case all over again'.[35] Welsh radicalism was not self-contained or exclusive. The rural areas made common cause with the mining valleys of the south. The Welsh could build bridges between the Old Liberalism of democracy, civic and religious equality, and the New Liberalism of social reform, with its links with organised labour. It could straddle Tom Ellis in the agrarian uplands of Merioneth, and 'Mabon' in the coal-mining strongholds of the Rhondda. Lloyd George's own career down to 1914 – perhaps later – showed vividly how a Welsh outsider, from a distinct and possibly more classless society, could fuse the Old Liberalism and the New in political action. There was, indeed, a basic strength about British Liberalism in the 1890s, masked by policy divisions – first over Ireland and then over southern Africa, and by tensions over the leadership when Gladstone retired – just as the condition of the Labour Party was more robust in the 1951–64 period than its schisms over foreign policy and the leadership struggle after Attlee departed might suggest at that time. The Welsh fitted naturally into this pattern of growth in the 1890s and Gladstone recognised it.

Finally, what light do the activities of the Welsh shed upon 'faddism', that nebulous concept on which important books by Professors Shannon and Hamer have focussed? In practice, I would argue, 'faddism' brought important new elements of vitality into the Liberal coalition. It helped to extend the Liberal appeal to agricultural voters and to industrial workers alike after 1885, as well as to the long dormant and semi-colonised 'Celtic Fringe'. The analogy Gladstone frequently drew was with the United States, a land which much influenced him, and where he had close contacts such as with the radical Republican Charles Sumner and the tycoon Andrew Carnegie. In such writings as 'Kin Beyond the Sea', Gladstone lavished praise on the United States as a buoyant democracy and the land of future.[36] He told John Morley in 1891 that the 'history and working of freedom in America' was 'the first object and study for every young man'.[37] He was much struck by how the American constitutional and social system could recover from the disruption of civil war after 1865 and adapt to a dynamic democracy.

Despite his own early declaration of support for the secessionist South in 1862 – which later much embarrassed him and which he eventually and somewhat reluctantly recanted – he admired the United States as a pluralist, popular society with diverse cultural traditions, vibrant religious communities (all disestablished) and varied ethnic constituents. It was moving in the right direction – 'the stream of tendency' was satisfactory and healthy. The late Victorian Liberal Party to Gladstone was, in many ways, the United States writ small. It, too, embodied the collective will of 'capable citizens', of 'the masses' rather than 'the classes'. Wales, no less than Midlothian, played a vital part in his understanding here. It was a crucial target for his moral rhetoric and popular oratory. It helped make him a democrat, 'the People's William' indeed.

Time was to show that by 1914 the Liberals, revived by the 1906 election and driven by a powerful programme of major social legislation thereafter, had absorbed many of their sectional strains – with the omnipresent exception of Ireland, which was a problem apart. By 1914 there was some renewed confidence in Liberal ranks, pace Dangerfield's 'Strange Death' thesis. The troubles surrounding labour, insurance and the suffragettes seemed to recede even if Ireland remained insoluble. Ministers commented that 'time is on our side' and that they were 'nearly out of the wood'. Gladstone's legacy was the forging of a new Progressive Alliance, of which the Labour Party, so close in its outlook to late Victorian Liberalism especially in its economics and links with the chapels, was an outgrowth. Had not Keir Hardie himself – 'Labour's Grand Old Man' – paid tribute to it?

The strength of Liberalism down to 1914, like that of the Labour Party after 1931, lay in the fact that it was not monolithic.[38] It was a sectional party with diverse traditions. The relationship of the lively, obstreperous Welsh with their leader, Gladstone, was thus a symptom of a wider renewal, an infusion of new life. Out of apparently arid, outdated arguments about such arcane matters as the origin of tithe, the purpose of educational charities, the title to Welsh land or the lineal components of the concept of Welsh nationhood can be seen emerging a pattern of politics recognisably modern.

Chapter 3

Lloyd George, Keir Hardie and the Importance of the 'Pro-Boers'

The South African War has long been recognised as a great watershed in British history. Its very length and cost raised fundamental questions about public expenditure and taxation, direct and indirect, culminating in the great debate about free trade and tariff reform. It focussed national concern on public health, especially on recruits for the British army, and thus added to the pressures for the social reform that provided the core of Edwardian New Liberalism. The record of British military incompetence during the war, and the marked absence of support from other powers, also raised new questions about British defence policy and the urgency of escaping from the diplomacy of isolation. All of these generated major debates in the immediate aftermath of the peace of Vereeniging, with Joseph Chamberlain. The South African War has long been recognised as a great watershed in British history. It's the major participant and shortly the major victim. All this is very well known. But the focus has usually been on British government policy and the travails over the Empire that beset the Unionist Party from 1900–6, a period latterly compared by historians with the turmoil in the Tory Party in the 1990s over Europe. There is an obvious parallel between the two electoral disasters of 1906 and 1997, both of them without precedent in their day.

I prefer, however, to focus not on governments, but on anti-government dissenters. There is still much to be said, in my view, about the so-called Pro-Boers, opponents of the war if not necessarily sympathisers with the Boer people. The literature on them is still astonishingly thin: the most useful book devoted to them is a volume mainly of documents produced by Stephen Koss a quarter of a century ago.[1] Indeed, it is Americans like Koss and Ernest May who have provided some of what discussion there is on the Pro-Boers.[2] They raise interesting parallels with America's own imperialist adventure – the Spanish–American War in 1898, followed by a singularly inglorious campaign to subdue a Filipino guerrilla uprising under Aguinaldo that evokes comparison with Britain's travails at the hands of Botha, De Wet and De la Rey at roughly the same time. In each case, the moral impetus of imperialism and territorial annexation was lost. In both the United States and Britain, the outcome was a turning inward to progressive measures of domestic social and political reform.

Apart from this possible comparison, the Pro-Boers are well worth examination in their right. They stand in the grand tradition of Alan Taylor's 'trouble-makers', dissenters against British foreign policy whom he described (admittedly in the somewhat bizarre context of the Munich agreement) as 'a triumph for all that was best in British life'.[3] I propose, therefore, to consider them anew, initially through the perspective of David Lloyd George and Keir Hardie, two leading Pro-Boers for whom the war was pivotal in their careers, to try to investigate the causes and consequences of the forces released in Britain between 1899 and 1902. For, in however muddled a form, the Pro-Boers provided an essential launch pad for the radical revival that led to the Liberal landslide of 1906, the triumph of the Lib–Lab Progressive Alliance in the years down to 1914, and to a profound transformation in the mood, rhetoric and sensibilities of the British people in the early twentieth century. To that degree, therefore, South Africa can be termed Britain's Vietnam with the significant difference that in Edward VII's Britain, unlike Nixon's America, it was the protesters who won the day and captured power. Unlike the debacle of the McGovern campaign in the 1972 US presidential election, in Britain the dissenters achieved in 1906 a record landslide election victory, unequalled until Tony Blair and New Labour's still greater triumph of 1997.

*   *   *

David Lloyd George has always, and rightly, occupied a central and honoured place amongst British critics of the South African War. Almost from the very start, certainly well before the British military disasters of 'Black Week' in December 1899, he was a vocal and courageous critic. His escape, dressed in an ill-fitting policeman's uniform, from a Chamberlainite mob in Birmingham town hall has gone down in folk legend. It was generally acknowledged, by the time that peace came, that his stature had been transformed from a marginal Welsh backbencher to a politician of national stature. Yet, as always with Lloyd George in every aspect of his kaleidoscopic career, things were not as straightforward as they seemed. One need not lapse into Keynes's crude view that Lloyd George was 'rooted in nothing' to see some obscurities in his views on South Africa – after all, a country of which he knew nothing whatsoever at first hand. As the war drew near in September 1899, in the tense period that followed Milner's ultimatum to the two Boer republics, Lloyd George was in Canada, desperately trying to acquire firm information on the looming crisis in South Africa. His first instinctive response when war broke out was to feel that, because the Boers had invaded British imperial territory in Natal, it was right for the British army to repel them to within their own borders, before resuming negotiations for a political settlement. He added, though, 'The way these poor hunted burghers have been driven to self-defence to forestall us, aggravates our crime. There is something diabolical in its malignity.'[4] But that was as long as his uncertainty lasted. By the time the war had been under way for a fortnight he was fiercely critical of British policy towards the Boer republics, Milner's provocative diplomacy and the refusal to accept the Transvaal government's reasonable proposals for an interim period for immigrants to win the franchise. He contrasted ironically the Unionist government's tenderness towards the Uitlander's franchise rights with their refusal to extend franchise reform in Britain itself and their giving a central constitutional role to the hereditary House of Lords which no one had elected at all.[5] Thereafter he emerged as the most powerful of the anti-war critics, in parliament, in the press and on the platform. He urged immediate peace negotiations, perhaps mediated by the United States. As is well known, he made a particular point of focussing his attacks on the giant figure of Joseph Chamberlain, the colonial secretary and his own boyhood hero, 'this electro-plated Rome and its tin Caesar'.

Nor did the advent of the 'Khaki' general election of October 1900 persuade him to tone down his criticisms. Despite the fact that he represented a most marginal constituency in Caernarfon Boroughs with a majority of less than 200 votes at the 1895 general election, despite the fact that his constituency included the relatively Anglican-Tory cathedral city of Bangor where his own life was endangered by a violent imperialist mob,[6] he held to his anti-war line throughout the campaign. He retained his seat by the still narrow margin of 296 votes (53.3 per cent), just 102 more than five years earlier. But, along with the successes of his fellow Pro-Boers, John Bryn Roberts in neighbouring Eifion, Herbert Lewis in Flintshire and Arthur Humphreys-Owen in Montgomeryshire, he proclaimed it as proof of the political sanity of Wales. While England and Scotland were 'drunk with blood', Wales proceeded with a clear head along the path of progress and liberty.[7] In fact, the Pro-Boers were as much of a minority in Wales as anywhere else as I shall mention later, but it was the image that was to influence (and mislead) later eminent historians from Elie Halévy to Heny Pelling.[8] In the last two years of war, as for many other Liberals, the dismal methods by which the war was being fought, the atrocities of the farm burnings and the near-genocide of the concentration camps, provided him with much of his ammunition as for other Liberal and Labour Pro-Boers. But he remained unflinching in his opposition to the war in principle as well as attacking its methods. By the time the war ended, he was focussing his energies on the nonconformist-Liberal opposition to Balfour's Education Bill, which would 'put Rome on the rates' in

the popular phrase. But it was South Africa which had made him. There
were a great variety of Pro-Boer dissenters, some surprising like the former
Unionist Cabinet Minister Sir Edward Clarke, or the Cardiff Tory MP John
Maclean, owner of the *Western Mail*. Some of them fell by the wayside like
Leonard Courtney in Cornwall. Other protesters like Sir Wilfrid Lawson,
Philip Stanhope, or Henry Labouchere remained relatively marginal, with
limited nationwide impact. David Lloyd George, a Welsh Baptist outsider
not yet 40, was the most effective and articulate of them all.

But it is important to be clear about Lloyd George's criticisms of the
war. He was never, of course, a pacifist, never another John Bright. Personally he was a pugnacious man, whose private letters and speeches
contain violent imagery – such as the prevalence of the verb 'to smash'. It
is not in the least surprising that the vehement Pro-Boer of 1900 should
be the war premier intent on 'unconditional surrender' and 'a fight to a
finish' in 1916.

Nor was he opposed to the idea of Empire. He had demanded a
vigorous British response to France during the Fashoda incident, and
talked of war. He had real regard for one of the leading imperialist Liberals, Lord Rosebery, and indeed referred warmly to his Chesterfield
speech in December 1901 at the height of the war.[9] He spoke at times
of the Boers as the initial aggressors, and even of the justification for
Britain annexing the Boer republics. But his point here was invariably
that annexation should be pursued not as imperialist conquest but as
the essential preliminary to a longer-term settlement that should provide
stability not just for Transvaal and the Orange Free State, but for the
Cape and Natal as well. By July 1900 he had decided that 'we went into
the war for equal rights but we are prosecuting it for annexation. A war
of annexation against a proud people must be a war of extermination.'[10]
Like most Welsh Liberals, he was sympathetic to a vision of Empire. The
Irish nationalists were not. They sought exclusion from the Empire and
cheered the news of the Boer victories at Spion Kop and Colenso. Welsh
nationalist-Liberals wanted, by contrast, equality within the Empire as
within Britain itself; along with the English and the Scots, they sought
their place in the sun. So it was broadly with Lloyd George. He actually
applauded the deeds of the Royal Welsh Fusiliers in the war. On the
other hand, his vision of Empire, as it emerged in a series of rhetorical
statements in the House and the country was not Chamberlain or Milner's vision. It was an Empire of partnership and of devolution. While
he denied in the House on 4 July 1901 that he favoured absolute independence for the Boer republics, he argued that a settlement in South
Africa should follow Canadian or Australian lines'.[11] As in the United
Kingdom, so in the white dominions, the dominant principle should

be toleration and local autonomy, a 'union of hearts' with home rule all round.

One of his most powerful attacks on Chamberlain and Milner lay in the claim that liberal elements in the Transvaal had favoured a compromise, including eventual rights of citizenship for the Uitlanders. Liberal views had been expressed by Joubert, Burgher and Meyer, and by younger men like Botha and De Wet; as a result of Chamberlain's policies, they were all fighting the British Army, the first three as Boer generals. President Steyn of the Orange Free State had offered mediation which Milner brushed aside. Throughout the war, Boer leaders were seeking a compromise: at the talks at Middelburg in early 1901, they called for an elected legislature for the Republics with limited powers. Even Kitchener, Lloyd George correctly claimed, was sympathetic, as indeed was Milner, but Chamberlain's obsession with war and conquest prevailed.[12] In the end, the war was prolonged for more than another year; the outcome was that the Boers obtained somewhat more favourable terms than they had been offered at Middelburg. Tens of thousands of military casualties, not to mention Boer mothers and little children dying of disease in concentration camps, had been lost in vain.

Lloyd George's rhetoric invariably depicted the British government as aggressive and unreasonable. It was also totally incompetent (as the sequence of military disasters revealed), ill-trained and poorly led. Brodrick, the secretary for war, was an open target. A paradigm for the British military leadership was bone-headed gentry like White and Buller (even though, ironically, some Tories attacked the latter, a Liberal, as Pro-Boer). A huge imperial force of a quarter of a million had been repeatedly humiliated by '30,000 peasants'. At one stage Lloyd George was led to complain that the immense military commitment in South Africa was weakening British security elsewhere in the world; thus in China, British missionaries had to be defended during the Boxer Uprising by a Buddhist power![13] And of course there was a pervasive taint of corruption which Lloyd George exploited with massive effect. His ferocious attacks on the Chamberlain family for war profiteering through their connection with armaments firms such as Hoskins and Sons, Elliott's Metal Company, Tubes Ltd. and especially Kynocks, the cordite contractors, were never conclusively proved at the time, and were later used with ironic effect against Lloyd George himself during the Marconi scandal in 1912. But it cast a shadow over the public reputation of the mighty Chamberlain. He had narrowly escaped censure after the Jameson Raid; he was now vulnerable as never before. It all further undermined the myths of the integrity of British public life.

Lloyd George could dismiss the term 'Pro-Boer' as a calumny. He defended himself as a patriot. Nevertheless, there is plenty of evidence of a sentimental if uninformed enthusiasm for Boer life on his part. The image of sturdy independence by a small people of self-reliant Protestant farmers appealed to the late Victorians who had long admired rural people such as the Swiss from William Tell downwards. It had particular resonance for Liberals in Wales, whose folk-myth of *y werin* corresponded closely with the kind of physical and moral qualities that the Boers appeared to embody. Lloyd George's copious correspondence with his wife, Margaret, his brother William, and even his children, gives ample evidence of his delight in Boer victories and his joy that Britain was given 'a black eye'.[14] David was giving Goliath a hammering, time after time. He showered praise on Cronje and lamented his having to surrender to superior forces at Paardeberg. Botha was 'a great defensive general'.[15] For De Wet and his guerrillas his admiration knew no bounds. De Wet himself is treated in Lloyd George's letters as if he were some brilliant Welsh wing-three-quarter running rings round the stolid English, a popular hero for Lloyd George's young son, Gwilym, at school. The Caernarfon MP told his son of how the British cavalry 'scampered away with the Boers chasing them like deerhounds'.[16] Like many others in the Pro-Boer camp, from J.A. Hobson to G.K. Chesterton and Hilaire Belloc, Lloyd George could compare the honesty and manly vigour of the Boer peoples with the degenerate greed of the Anglo-Jews who poured into the gold and diamond fields anxious for quick profits.

There is no doubt that, especially in the guerrilla campaigns in the last two years of the war, the Boer farmers attracted widespread admiration and support amongst British liberal opinion. The writings of Olive Schreiner on African farm life had given them some popular appeal. There is equally little doubt that the nature of their society was not well understood, particular in relation to the treatment of the black majority. Lloyd George himself did not ignore the plight of native Africans as is sometimes claimed. He certainly drew attention to the low wages and poor working conditions of black workers on the Rand; he denounced capitalists like Hays Hammond for giving black miners a false prospectus. British troops were 'dying to restore slavery to the British flag'.[17] But in general, he had little to say about the position of black Africans, either in terms of civil or economic rights, or of their own subjection to 'methods of barbarism' in concentration camps. The blacks were in the main a dialectical tool, used with much effect to ridicule claims that Milner and the Uitlanders were fighting to uphold the African majority, rather than an issue that stirred him in their own right. Amidst a culture of Darwinian stereotypes, Lloyd George was no more enlightened than most of his contemporaries.

What really governed Lloyd George's opposition to the war, in my view, was neither his belief in an imperialism of partnership nor his sympathy for and understanding of Boer society, of which of course he knew very little. Even his genuine moral outrage at the farm burnings on the veldt and the deaths in the concentration camps, which he compared to Spanish rule in Cuba and on which he was briefed by Emily Hobhouse herself, were not fundamental to his outlook.

The anger that the South African War aroused in him was based above all on what it revealed about the state of Britain itself. The hysteria of wartime jingoism, the 'brutes' in the street celebrating the relief of Mafeking,[18] were redolent of a sick society. Britain at the *fin de siècle* he saw as class-ridden and deeply unequal. The boom city of gold-rich Johannesburg, with its tramps and millionaires, was its paradigm. In the later 1890s, the traditional British class system had reasserted itself, with massive hand-outs to the Church in the 1897 Education Act, doles to the squires through the 1896 Agricultural Rating Act and the eternal power of the drink interest: a British government that claimed to be regulating the liquor trade on the Rand had 'floated to power on beer'. Now this privileged world was building up links with the new plutocracy spawned by finance capitalism, company promotion and the profits of imperialism.[19] Lloyd George's assaults on the contracting practices and profiteering of the Chamberlains, following a fierce muckraking press campaign in the *Morning Leader*,[20] underlined the connections popularly made between the old wealth and the new, and did so at a politically sensitive moment of transition. Imperialism, far from being a noble crusade taking up the white man's burden, was a squalid conspiracy to promote underhand corruption. Even a minister as apparently unworldly as Balfour was linked with 'the world of cosmopolitan finance'. It was a popular cry in radical and Labour circles long before J.A. Hobson gave it powerful intellectual backing in his *Imperialism: A Study,* a classic inspiration for the international left from Lloyd George to Lenin, shorn of the crude anti-semitism of his earlier writings on South Africa. Meanwhile, vivid war reporters such as Edgar Wallace and Erskine Childers drew the distinction between the energy, fortitude and integrity of the Boers contrasted with the idle Randlords, the goldbugs and itinerant profiteers of uncertain race (frequent hints of anti-semitism here). Even officials in the British War Office voiced dismay at a decaying British army, recruited from 'the scum of the cities' fighting far away on behalf of rootless *nouveaux-riches* while the nation at home languished.[21]

For Lloyd George, along with other Pro-Boers in the Stop the War Committee or the League of Liberals against Aggression and Militarism, the consequences of this domestic corruption were far-reaching. Profits for the few meant deprivation for the many. Social reform was indefinitely postponed. Lloyd George himself told the people of Carmarthen that every lyddite shell on the veldt carried away an old age pension.[22] The physical condition of the British army was itself a powerful argument for improved health and housing, and chimed in with cross-party demands for 'national efficiency'. Political allies of Lloyd George like C.F.G. Masterman or C.P. Scott in the *Manchester Guardian* urged that welfare reform, not overseas glory, should be the main priority; only with the rapid end of the war and total change of British policy in southern Africa would this be achieved. Lloyd George also feared the impact on the national psychology which he linked, characteristically, with the power of the press to which he was always acutely sensitive. Hence his immensely important initiative at the end of 1901 to persuade George Cadbury, the Quaker, to purchase the *Daily News* and turn it into a Pro-Boer journal, with A.G. Gardiner soon to become its editor.[23] It was an astute and influential piece of secret diplomacy. By the time of Vereeniging, the Liberal press was turning sharply against its earlier pro-war sympathies: the *Manchester Guardian*, Stead's *Review of Reviews* and the *Morning Leader* were to be joined by the *Daily Chronicle* and J.A. Spender's *Westminster Gazette* as the horrors of the concentration camps became widely known. Mass-produced pamphlets based on press articles by Emily Hobhouse and others took the campaign further afield.

Lloyd George, however, wanted not merely to regenerate the press but to reform his party. Even in his most intransigent moments, he saw that a party divided between Lib Imps and Pro-Boers, with Campbell-Bannerman, the party leader, hovering unhappily in the middle, was in no state to win power. The three-way split in the party on Sir Wilfrid Lawson's motion on 25 July 1900 and the eventual 'agreement to differ' reached at the Reform Club in 1901, was a road to oblivion. In fact, the Pro-Boers held their ground surprisingly well at the polls, and the party henceforth regrouped under the leadership of Campbell-Bannerman, who coined the immortal phrase 'methods of barbarism', one he had earlier rehearsed at a meeting with Emily Hobhouse.[24] Lloyd George was central to this process. He kept his leads open to Campbell-Bannerman; he was able to work with Imperialists like Grey over domestic issues like education; he claimed to see hope in Lord Rosebery's Chesterfield's speech that would keep him in the Liberal tabernacle.[25] He tried to frame a peace settlement to which all Liberals could agree. Lloyd George, in short, approached the latter stages of the war in South Africa both as a humane moralist and a deft party tactician. He would never be one of those impractical virgins, poor but honest, derided later by his fellow countryman Nye Bevan, who preferred to cherish their purity in the wilderness rather than sully themselves with the compromises of power. The Anglo-Boer War thus offered him a stage to relaunch Gladstonian Liberalism, redesigned as the New

Liberalism of social reform. The war in South Africa led Lloyd George to reframe his priorities, seek a wider horizon, ideologically as well as geographically. He helped make the fragmented, 'faddist' Old Liberalism the instrument of long-term progressive change and of the cult of the new. There was something else, too. The imperial crisis of 1899–1902 built up a lifelong connection between Lloyd George and some of the Boer leaders. At the peace conference in Paris in 1919, when Lloyd George was by now prime minister, his delegation included from his Cabinet General Smuts, whose intellectual gifts he much admired. Another participant at Paris was Louis Botha, since 1910 the South African premier, a child of nature for whom Lloyd George's regard was even higher – the 'embodiment of wisdom in speech and action – truly a great man'.[26] The British delegates also included Lord Milner as well as Joseph Chamberlain's elder son, sitting alongside Smuts, so the wheel had come full circle in a fascinating manner.

* * *

Keir Hardie, the main founder of the Labour Representation Committee (LRC) in February 1900, elected junior member for Merthyr Tydfil in industrial South Wales at the Khaki Election, seems much less complicated than Lloyd George in his response to the war. He knew nothing of South Africa at first hand (though he was to visit the country briefly in 1907), and did not need to. It was simply a straight, evil war of aggression, waged by capitalist imperialists anxious for quick profits on the Rand against a free, independent small people. It was, he repeatedly urged in the pages of his *Labour Leader* and on the platform, an unjust and corrupt imperialist war, the work of the 'war gang' headed by Cecil Rhodes. The incompetence with which it was run was wholly predictable because British generals were accustomed, not to skilful opponents like the Boers, but 'to shooting naked savages or unarmed Dervishes'.[27] He was almost unqualified in his condemnation of it – I say almost, because even Hardie weakened briefly to congratulate Baden-Powell on the relief of Mafeking – 'never was tribute more genuinely earned'.[28] Similarly, during his opposition to the First World War in 1914 he seemed to imply that it could be justified as a war of national self-defence.[29] More than most of the Liberal Pro-Boers he was lavish in his praise of Boer society. On the imperial side, there were British investors, merchants and speculators imposing bondage on native contract labour. But, as he wrote in the *Labour Leader*,

> as Socialists our sympathies are bound to be with the Boers. Their Republican form of government bespeaks freedom, and is thus hateful

to tyrants, whilst their methods of production for use are much nearer our ideal than any form of exploitation for profit.

And again, 'Try to imagine what the free Yeomen of England were like two hundred years ago and you have some idea of Boer life.'[30] He compared them with another small people, the Welsh he had seen singing their hymns during the six-months stoppage in the Welsh coalfield in 1898:

> What more wonderful than that the language of the little nation who thrice repelled the hosts of Rome two thousand years ago, who endured conquest after conquest, and even had their language penalised, should be heard at all in this distant day.[31]

So was it with the Dutch-speaking Boer farmers. After visiting a miners' *eisteddfod* in south Wales, he added flamboyantly:

> Owain Glyndwr, William Tell, William Wallace – are not these among the world's most priceless possessions? And now the De Wets, the Bothas and the heroes serving under them are adding their names to the list. The oppressors of Wales, Switzerland and Scotland were the Imperialists of their day. Now they are remembered chiefly for their follies and their ignoble crimes. So will it be in days to come.[32]

For Hardie there were simply no arguments to deploy on behalf of the war at all. He brushed aside claims that the war was at least good for trade and employment. On the contrary, the cost of maintaining troops in South Africa, the diverting of British mercantile marine, the disruption of overseas trade and the crippling burdens on taxation, direct and indirect, would lead to financial disaster. He pointed to a drop in exports in the first six months of 1901 according to Board of Trade returns. Further, the erosion of civil liberties, the new militarism shown in the use of troops in industrial disputes such as the Penrhyn quarry strike, the corrupting effects of racism and jingoism all threatened the very existence of democracy itself.[33]

After his return to parliament for Merthyr Tydfil, he used the war as a way of launching further attacks on some of his other *bêtes noires* such as the monarchy and the established Church. He deplored the use made of Queen Victoria's funeral for militaristic purposes by the 'war party' and their clerical allies.[34] He launched a particularly violent attack on the new King Edward VII for receiving Milner formally at court:

> It is no secret that His Majesty has been all along a party to the policy of the war gang in South Africa. What his personal holding may be in Rand shares I have no means of knowing, but his son-in-law the Duke of Fife was a director of Rhodesia [sic] at the time of the Raid.

The King, then Prince of Wales, had used his influence to help Cecil Rhodes escape interrogation by the Commons select committee after the Jameson Raid.[35] Elsewhere he called for a re-opening of the Jameson inquiry to establish Chamberlain's complicity.[36] Thereafter, the news of the brutalities of Kitchener's concentration camps pushed him to new heights of fury. So was it to the end of the war. As John Bright had memorably proclaimed of the Crimean War, the South African War was simply 'a crime'.

But there is more to be said of Hardie's outlook than this. He was not only a fount of emotional protest. He was also a shrewd tactician, keenly concerned with maximising popular radicalism both within and without the Labour movement. And, amidst all his emotionalism, he raised two issues of fundamental long-term significance which Lloyd George and the Liberals never quite managed to do.

As regards party tactics, his main priority at this time was not the war in South Africa but creating a Labour Party at home. He had been in the years since 1895 the main architect of the movement to build up an alliance of the socialist societies, notably his own ILP and the Fabians, with the mass working-class membership of the trade unions. Along with ILP comrades like Ramsay MacDonald and Bruce Glasier, he had successfully resisted moves to merge the ILP with the Marxists of Hyndman's Social Democratic Federation (SDF) under the doctrinaire banner of 'socialist unity'.[37] In February 1900 he achieved his great objective, when the delegates of the Trades Union Congress (TUC) met with socialist representatives such as himself at the Memorial Hall, Farringdon Street, in London, to create the LRC. But Hardie's Labour Alliance came into being only through its flexibility. Its programme called simply for collaboration on behalf of the needs of labour, not for socialism or any other ideology. The object of the new party was simply the creation of 'a distinct Labour group in parliament', for what precise purpose was left unclear. Among other things, this meant trying to accommodate both the pro-war sympathies of some, though not all Fabians, including the Webbs, and Bernard Shaw, and Robert Blatchford's distinctly jingo *Clarion,* and the anti-war passions of the ILP and most trade union leaders. Attitudes to the war were thus left an open question. Further, when Hardie himself was a candidate simultaneously for Preston in Lancashire and Merthyr in South Wales (a very odd situation for him), in each he tried to play down his anti-imperialism somewhat in favour of themes such as housing or temperance that might appeal to Liberals. In Preston, where his Irish nationalism went down badly with Tory Orange voters without winning him much sympathy amongst Catholics either, he ran badly.[38] In Merthyr Tydfil, where the coal trade was booming in wartime conditions, he tried to divert attention to domestic themes, notably labour and Welsh issues. His tactical opportunity came because there were two sitting Liberals, the coalowner D.A. Thomas, centrist on the war issue, and the flamboyantly pro-war Pritchard Morgan. Hardie's strategy was to draw away sufficient Liberal support from Morgan to be returned as the junior member behind D.A. Thomas: he well knew that socialists in Merthyr and Aberdare were a small minority, many of them unenfranchised.[39] The policy worked. Hardie later claimed that he had been elected as an opponent of the war in a constituency with a long anti-war tradition going back to the pacifist Henry Richard returned back in 1868. 'To the Celt' he declared, 'Socialism has no terrors.'[40] But it seems clear that it was as a radical not a socialist that he was returned.

Just as Hardie was preoccupied with political strategy within the Labour tabernacle, so he was equally busy outside. He was convinced that the impact of the war was to produce a massive political dissolution in which the old party system would disintegrate. There was now an opportunity to create a new Progressive popular front. Old enemies were forgiven. John Burns, now passionately anti-war, was welcomed back as a comrade. Lloyd George and James Bryce, previously attacked by the ILP for their inadequacy on social issues, were now hailed as popular tribunes. Links were forged with Michael Davitt and other Irish Nationalist critics of the war, previously regarded as social conservatives who were misguided on issues like education and welfare. Most emphatic of all, John Morley, whose dogmatic resistance to the eight-hour bill had led Hardie to travel to Newcastle in 1895 to urge the electors to vote Tory as a punishment, was now briefly seen as a popular tribune. An anti-war speech he made at Oxford in June 1900 was greeted by Hardie in ecstatic terms. Hardie now claimed that socialists like himself were really 'altruistic individualists'. The principles of freedom laid down by Bentham and Mill would 'lead logically to Socialism'. Would Morley now 'cross the Rubicon' to combine the working class with the new radicalism?[41] In fact, Morley, known as the 'Grand Old Maid' of the Liberal Party, made no attempt to do so, although Hardie kept up his hopes for months to come. By the end of the war, Hardie had concluded that Official Liberalism was really 'disguised Toryism'. Even Lloyd George had let him down by his sympathy for Rosebery and his declared support for annexation of the Boer republics. However, Hardie concluded, 'the consolation is that we have still the Boers to call back upon'.[42] It seemed that the fledgling LRC stood in a position of total neutrality between both the established parties. However, when the war was over, the strategic lead for Labour was taken by Ramsay MacDonald who devised, with Hardie's somewhat reluctant agreement, the secret 'entente' with the Liberal whip, Herbert Gladstone, was concluded which was to guarantee Labour about 30 seats in the next general election. Labour thus cast its lot with the Liberals, in any case the natural choice for most nonconformist working men.

Hardie's views on South Africa, therefore, were simplistic and emotional, within a context of party fluidity and manoeuvre. But they also included two major aspects which largely eluded the Liberal Pro-Boers. First, Hardie pointed out the threat from the war to the rights of labour. So did all the nine Lib–Lab members returned in 1900 and nearly all trade union leaders. Boer employers, they claimed, had protected workers' wage levels. But the exploitation of workers on the rand by *arriviste* employers was as one with the exploitation of workers at home. The use of the courts against the unions, most notably in the Taff Vale case of 1901–2, which seemed to undermine the right to strike, the attacks on union tactics such as the boycott, the use of 'free labour' by employers like the shipowners to destroy the unions in major industries, the ultimate sanction of the use of the military by the police authorities in major disputes – in all these ways, South Africa provided a warning and a goad to action. Hardie was amongst the first to draw a parallel between the causes of war in South Africa and the new aggression shown by industrial Milners and Chamberlains in Britain itself.[43] Soon after the war ended, this became a major theme with the use of so-called Chinese Slavery on the Rand as a threat to organised labour. Labour leaders thundered against the new menace to free trade unionism in Britain, on industrial, humanitarian and perhaps also on racial grounds: one miners' leader evoked the threat of Chinese workers being propelled into the slate quarries of Ffestiniog in North Wales. In 1904–5, the most effective use of the war made by former opponents of it was via the issue of indentured labour. Graham Wallas noted the use of villainous-looking Chinamen on hoardings which aroused 'an immediate hatred of the Mongolian racial type'.[44] The high and the low road were trodden simultaneously. It was another instance of the new LRC and its trade union allies showing a concern for the civil rights of labour and the corporate status of trade unions which somehow eluded Lloyd George and the champions of the New Liberalism.

An even more profound issue that Hardie raised was that of the ethnic majority in South Africa. Almost all Liberals treated it as a white man's war; the loss of life amongst blacks as combatants, as residents of concentration camps or as victims of the siege of Mafeking and Ladysmith was virtually ignored. Not so in the case of the fledgling socialist movement. Ramsay MacDonald's *What I Saw in South Africa* in 1902 strongly emphasised both the working conditions and the civil rights of the Africans.[45] So did left-wing journalists like H.W. Nevinson and H.N. Brailsford. It was a constant theme of Hardie's from the wartime period onwards. His correspondents in the South African socialist movement kept him primed on key issues affecting 'Kaffir' workers. He spoke strongly in the House in 1906 on the suppression of the black uprising in Natal and the need for blacks to retain their own farming land under the new Transvaal and Orange Free State constitutions.[46] His earlier idealisation of the Boers was set aside as he spelt out their unwillingness to grant elementary rights to the black majority. Some of his South African socialist correspondents were frankly racialist. They emphasised the fundamental cultural and biological differences in their society: 'they were created different races and must remain so'. Another complained how the goldfield had created a new race, 'half Kaffir, half Chinese'.[47] When Hardie finally visited South Africa in October 1907 and specifically raised the 'native question', he had a violent reception. He was attacked at Durban for suggesting that blacks might enter the trade unions. His hotel was stoned at Ladysmith. At Johannesburg he tried to raise the question of 'Kaffir' squatter farmers when his meeting was broken up by a mob: a Union Jack from the meeting was kept as a proud memento at his flat in Nevills Court thereafter. In the parliamentary debates on the Union of South Africa Bill in 1909–10 he was almost alone in the House in pointing out the way in the rights of the black majority were totally swept aside. The vestigial franchise and other rights the Africans still retained in Cape Colony and Natal would be reduced to the total colour discrimination of Transvaal and the Orange Free State. After all, the wholly racialist Transvaal constitution had been underwritten in the peace Treaty of Vereeniging.[48] In 1913 he was condemning his old heroes, Botha and Smuts, for suppressing black workers on strike in the Rand and for proclaiming martial law. Substantial British forces were being maintained around Johannesburg to 'protect the mineowners and millionaires of the Rand in their struggles with the workers'.[49] Hardie was not as well briefed on these issues as he was, say, on India. Nevertheless South Africa was but one of many international issues where he proved to be a liberator. With all his limitations, he was well ahead of his time. He detected, as few contemporaries were to do, the origins of that oppressive Afrikanerdom that in time were to lead directly to the horrors of Sharpeville and Soweto.

*   *   *

Lloyd George and Keir Hardie, then, illuminate varied aspects of the outlook, strengths and limitations of the Pro-Boers between 1899 and 1902. But, of course, they were but part of a wider transformation of British public life in the period, for which the war was a catalyst. In one area after another, the South African War had massive long-term effects. Perhaps its least effect was the one which attracted most contemporary attention, namely the impact on organised religion. After years in which the antagonism between Church and chapel, from the Church rates in 1868 to tithe, seemed to be receding (in England if not in Wales), the war generated a massive crisis of conscience, especially amongst the nonconformist bodies. Apart from a few critics such as the Liberal Bishop of Hereford and the Anglo-Catholic Canon Charles Gore of Westminster, Anglicans took the establishment line in giving their blessing to the imperialist war. Nonconformists, by contrast, were much divided. The Wesleyan Methodists, underlining their quest for public respectability, were almost uniformly pro-war, witness the Rev. Hugh Price Hughes or 'Imperial' Perks.[50] Others, however, saw it as a classic challenge to conscience. One of their number, the former Methodist minister and novelist, Silas Hocking, summed up, 'The Quakers were with us. In the main Unitarian ministers were on our side. A considerable number of Baptist ministers gave us their support, and a few Congregationalists. The Methodists on the whole ignored us.'[51] In Wales, Lloyd George's own base, while many nonconformist ministers especially in South Wales, were pro-war ('the Salem chapel jingo'), many others, especially in Welsh-speaking rural Wales were emphatically anti-war, sometimes on pacifist grounds as with the Rev. Evan Jones, Caernarfon (Calvinist Methodist) and Rev. Josiah Towyn Jones (Independent). In general the Welsh-language press was far more Pro-Boer than its English-language counterpart: this applied not only to the weekly newspapers like *Baner ac Amserau Cymru* but also to newspapers such as the Calvinist Methodist *Goleuad,* the Independent *Tyst,* and the Unitarian *Ymofynydd* (to which might be added the ILP's organ *Llais Llafur,* the voice of Labour).[52] As time went on, the dire news from the concentration camps led to a marked swing of opinion against the war in denominational assemblies and the religious press. Only in a limited way, perhaps, the war helped rekindle the sense of moral protest amongst some nonconformists: as with Dr. Clifford, it foreshadowed the Luther-style 'here I stand' passive resistance against the 1902 Education Act, an outlook also fostered by a young Indian lawyer, Mohandas Gandhi, amongst his own community in South Africa. It hastened progress towards the 1906 general election which saw almost 200 nonconformists elected to parliament, the greatest dissenting victory since the days of Cromwell.

Another area where the war had its impact was in the ethnic/national pluralism of *fin de siècle* Britain. The 1890s had seen major debates on the diversity of the so-called United Kingdom: issues like Welsh and Scottish disestablishment and land reform, quite apart from the endless debates over Irish home rule, raised themes not to re-emerge until the debates over devolution a hundred years later. The war certainly had its profound

impact on Ireland, both Nationalists and Unionists. The Irish Nationalist Party found a new unifying cause, since all of them, Parnellites or
anti-Parnellites, wanted the Boers to win and cheered news of British
defeats. After a series of Nationalist votes condemnatory of the war had
been raised in the House, the two wings of the party reunited in early
1900 under the chairmanship of a former Parnellite, John Redmond. In
South Africa, Irish Uitlanders fought with the Boers, among them John
MacBride, the father of a future Irish foreign minister.[53] The war certainly made the Irish the more aware of their separate aspirations and
their non-Britishness. It had almost the reverse effect in Scotland, where
Unionism was powerful and links with the Empire, from the shipyards
of the Clyde to the missionaries of the Presbyterian Church, were overwhelmingly strong. At the Khaki Election, although an ardent Pro-Boer
like Dr. G.B. Clark was defeated by a pro-war Liberal in Caithness, the
'peace party' just about held its own. Even so, the result saw a narrow
majority of Unionists returned in Scotland, 36 to 34 Liberals, and a small
swing to Unionism there (0.8 per cent) compared with 1895.

Wales is a more complicated story.[54] On the face of it, its response was
not so different from that of England, which is strongly pro-war down to
the Khaki Election, gradually moving in a radical direction from the start
of 1901. Lloyd George was a dissenter in his own land. The majority of
Welsh Liberal MPs were pro-war, with only four, including Lloyd George,
voting for Pro-Boer motions in the House. The same seems to have
applied to Welsh constituency workers: in several seats in South Wales,
Cardiff, Swansea Town and Gower, for instance, Pro-Boers were rejected
as candidates by local associations in favour of Liberals sympathetic to
the war. This appears to have been broadly true of Welsh opinion as a
whole, including in the Khaki Election in October 1900. The Liberals
won back four seats lost to the Liberals in 1895 but lost one, Monmouth
Boroughs, to Dr. Rutherfoord Harris, Rhodes's agent who gave evidence
on the Jameson Raid. In the event, the Liberals captured 27 Welsh seats
to the Unionists six, along with Keir Hardie winning Merthyr for Labour.
There was a swing to the Liberals almost everywhere, but in an election
fought by them overwhelming on the old domestic issues, church disestablishment, land reform, temperance and the like. It cannot be said
that the Liberal strength in Wales was based on Pro-Boer sentiment. On
the other hand, such sentiment seems to have been much less of a hand-
icap to Liberal candidates than in Scotland, and in the latter stages Welsh
protests against the methods of barbarism along with calls for an immediate peace were as numerous and powerful as anywhere in the Kingdom.
The Welsh were accustomed to seeing other small, often rural, peoples
as role models – the Swiss, the Norwegians and the Austrian Tyrol. The

Boers were another with more immediate impact at home. On balance, the long-term effect of the war seems to have given a new infusion of life into Welsh Liberal ranks, to be shortly reinforced by the 'revolt' against the Education Act, the campaign against 'Chinese slavery' and the galvanising of Welsh nonconformity by the religious revival of 1904–5. The Anglo-Boer War seems to have been one element, if no more than that, in reinforcing the Welsh sense of political identity, perhaps even an urge for the same kind of distinctiveness shortly to be granted to the South African colonies.

The war may also have given a stimulus to gender issues. It was, of course, a man's war, fought by men in uniform, and belonging to the male preserve of overseas affairs. On the other hand, women, especially Liberal women, were markedly involved in the debate surrounding it. Women were active in the South African Conciliation Committee, which had its own women's branch with Emily Hobhouse, the hitherto obscure daughter of a west-country clergyman, as its secretary. So, too, was the National Union of Women Workers. All women's organisations were stirred by the mass death amongst Boer wives and children in the concentration camps. In 1901 the Women's Liberal Federation passed by an overwhelming majority a motion deprecating the conduct of the war and calling for an end of the policy of unconditional surrender. Meanwhile, first-hand witness of the horrors on the Veldt came from Samuel Cronwright-Schreiner, the farmer husband of Olive Schreiner, who toured Britain lecturing on the war. Olive Schreiner's own Pro-Boer sentiments were widely circulated. The greatest stir, without doubt, came from the formidable crusade of Emily Hobhouse.[55] Already well known as an anti-war speaker, 'that bloody woman' was somewhat surprisingly given permission by those frosty bachelors, Milner and Kitchener, to investigate conditions in the concentration camps and she spent four months there, starting with the camp at Bloemfontein. The account she gave on her return was one of unrelieved horror: in the end, so she reported to the South African Women and Children's Distress Fund back in Britain, there were 4,067 deaths recorded early on amongst Boers in the camps, of whom 1,545 were children, victims of disease, malnutrition and elementary lack of hygiene.[56] Eventually, she recorded in *The Brunt of the War,* published after the peace settlement, that there were 10,344 deaths in the Transvaal camps and 9,178 in those of the Orange River Colony [Free State]. She also recorded the deaths of 13,315 Africans. These figures are undoubtedly an under-estimate. The official archivist of the Transvaal government gave the total of Boer deaths as 27,927, of whom over 26,000 were women and children, a quarter of the population of women and children in the entire Boer republics.[57]

Hobhouse proceeded with a nation-wide lecture tour before radical audiences in Britain detailing the horrors on the Veldt, along with strategic meetings with politicians such as Campbell-Bannerman and Lloyd George, and newspaper editors such as Gardiner and Spender. When she was prevented from embarking on a second visit from a ship moored at Cape Town and deported, it made her a radical heroine. Hobhouse's findings were expressed in moral rather than gender terms. The mass loss of life amongst women and children was described in traditional stereotypes as occurring amongst defenceless non-combatants, in no sense part of the war. However, events took a different turn when the government responded with a six-woman investigating committee chaired by Millicent Fawcett. She and Hobhouse were much opposed, not only on the war but on the women's suffrage question where Fawcett was a non-militant, Liberal Unionist, adult suffragist, while Hobhouse was a left-wing supporter of the Pankhursts. Fawcett began with derisive dismissal of Hobhouse's inquiry into the camps; 'they make one rather despair of the new womanhood'.[58] But in the end, her own report produced findings that were scarcely less condemnatory. Eventually, it led to long-deferred medical and relief measures that brought the death toll to an end, but the damage both to Kitchener's reputation and that of his country was incalculable.

The interest of this episode is in part because it was a public debate between women, between Hobhouse and Fawcett, who had very different visions of political and civic life, including the role of women. Hobhouse herself, not obviously raising gender issues in her reports, focussed attention on a public scandal in a highly personalised way, including her later visit to South Africa to try to encourage home industries such as lace-making amongst Boer wives on the veldt. In time she was to use a suffragette argument that contradicted her earlier views. What the war showed, she claimed, was that Boer women were indeed combatants during the guerrilla war, and on that ground alone could claim full rights of citizenship.[59] 'The woman's day dawns' she observed in her Vrouwen-Dag speech at Bloemfontein. She also worked closely in South Africa with young South African champions of women's rights, such as Petronella van Heerden whom she persuaded to read Mill's *Subjection of Women*[60] The feminist Olive Schreiner became a close friend: Hobhouse protested vigorously when Schreiner was kept away from the unveiling of the Boer Memorial at Bloemfontein in 1913. She was buried alongside the Women's Memorial there in 1926, with General Smuts providing the main tribute. The South African war did not produce a massive acceleration in the movement towards gender equality in Britain. But, above all through the remarkable career of Emily Hobhouse (who was not included in the pre-2004 *Dictionary of National Biography,* oddly enough) it did at least mark the end of the beginning.

Social welfare was another area where the Anglo-Boer War and those who opposed it provided an impetus. Its very incompetence, military and administrative, publicly reinforced the claims of those who called for 'national efficiency'. For critics, like the Liberal Imperialists or cross-party Coefficients, let alone anti-war figures like Lloyd George or Hardie, the quality of British government appeared to be a shambles. It had also been the most colossal waste of public resources at a time when journalists, novelists and publicists of all kinds were crying out for new policies to deal with poverty, malnutrition, ill-health and the penury of old age. As is well known, the most dramatic of these issues was the physical well-being of working-class recruits to the army. The Committee on Physical Deterioration in 1904 painted an alarming picture of a general absence of hygiene, ignorance of the rearing of children and widespread environmental squalor. Thus of 12,000 men examined in 1899, only 1,200 were found to be physically fit in all respects.[61] This picture had already been well documented in the sociological studies of Charles Booth and Seebohm Rowntree, and anticipated in a wartime work like Arnold White's *Efficiency and Empire* in 1901. But the stark evidence of physical feebleness in the army itself provided an immense shock to public awareness; after all, national efficiency was, first of all, physical efficiency. The Balfour government's response to the outcry was remarkably half-hearted: keeping down the rates appeared to be the major priority. But the war opened up major national campaigns, for the feeding and medical inspection of school children, for assistance for nursing mothers and for the whole debate that led up in erratic fashion, to Lloyd George's National Health Insurance Act of 1911, the cornerstone of British welfare policy for almost the rest of the century.

But the impact on the social conscience went beyond public policy, enlightened public servants like Llewellyn Smith and Morant, or reforming politicians like Lloyd George and Churchill. It permeated the culture as a whole. By the middle Edwardian years, H.G. Wells could see the war, much reported as it was, as having been a massive literary divide.[62] Before it, lay the relatively uncritical national self-assurance of late Victorian fiction. Thereafter came the social criticism and anxious soul-searching of writers and dramatists ranging from Belloc and Chesterton to Wells, Somerset Maugham, Galsworthy, Compton Mackenzie's *Sinister Street,* and many others. A work celebrating the older virtues like Ferdinand Peacock's *When the War Is Over* (1912), written by one who served as a major in South Africa, seemed frankly bizarre. As in the United States, where authors like Frank Norris, Upton Sinclair or Theodore Dreiser voiced the new social progressivism, British literary sensibility about a wretched war nurtured public concern for 'how the other half lived'. Writers and artists now approached imperial grandeur with something close to disgust. Edwin Lutyens sought to break free from architectural triumphalism to return to his private passion for 'arts and crafts' domesticity. Alas! There was always Herbert Baker, littering South Africa with monumental solemnity, and his rival/colleague in the building of New Delhi during the war, to rein him back, to Lutyens's unhappiness. Similarly, in music Edward Elgar, an aggressive imperialist during the South African War, was in later years to abandon the ostentation of Pomp and Circumstance in favour of the reflective autumnal melancholy of the cello concerto.

As a final point, the Anglo-Boer War served to remove the Empire from its pinnacle as a supreme public ideal and aspiration. Even before the war, there were signs that this was happening: witness the unprecedented booing of Cecil Rhodes by liberal-minded undergraduates at Oxford when he received an honorary degree in the summer of 1899 (almost as remarkable in its way as the rebuff of Mrs. Thatcher that I witnessed in Oxford's Congregation in 1985). After the war, of course, no-one expected the Empire to be dismantled. Nor was it to be after 1919; on the contrary, the mandate system after Versailles made the Empire greater in extent than ever before. Not until 1947 did its disintegration begin. On the other hand, it was at once recognised that a new settlement in South Africa was an inevitable consequence of the Boers' successful resistance; the Union of South Africa in 1910 was accepted with general all-party acclaim (not least, of course, because the black population was totally ignored). What the war seemed to show was that the cause of an ever expanding Empire was no longer acceptable. It should rather be a showcase for calm, orderly government, not a playground for free-booting capitalists or 'prancing proconsuls'. The moral imperative had changed. The young men, mainly Unionists like Kerr, Amery, Robinson, Curtis, John Buchan and others, who worked constructively in Milner's Kindergarten in South Africa after the war and later the Round Table group, were testament to a more serious, socially aware and creative version of imperialism, working if possible with the grain of local society.[63] Chamberlain's tariff reform campaign, of course, showed the clear limits to the imperial gospel, especially when it challenged the shibboleth of free trade. It brought all the Lib Imps (other than Rosebery) back to the heart of their party. An ardent young imperialist like Winston Churchill broke fundamentally with the cause on this issue. The attitude of colonial prime ministers, notably Laurier in Canada, showed that Chamberlain's vision of an integrating Empire was already an illusion.

The war, and the tensions over the Empire, also underlined that growing malaise within Unionist ranks of which Ewen Green has powerfully written.[64] A fundamental ambiguity about the social classes to whom Unionism appealed (the old privileged order or the new suburban plutocracy), about its attitude to social reform, to the constitution and the Union, about its very concept of the state, tormented the party throughout the Edwardian years. It led it to three successive election defeats; and who is to say that another might not have followed in 1915 since the Progressive Lib–Lab Alliance still held and Irish Nationalist support was there for the asking? In short, it was the dissenting minority, the Pro-Boers, Lloyd George, Keir Hardie and their comrades in arms, who triumphed. It was their spokesmen and at least some of their causes that dominated the years down to 1914. The South African war broke out because of local disputes between an aggressive proconsular British government and two introverted rural republics. But they led to major creative redefinitions of British culture and society, and a revolution in our political history. At the outset of the struggle in October 1899 an imperialising people celebrated a land of hope and glory. They won, and yet they lost. By its conclusion, they had precious little left of either.

Chapter 4

The Boer War and the Media, 1899–1902

The South African War that broke out in October 1899 was both very old and very new. It was a traditional war, the last of the old-fashioned British imperial wars, with cavalry playing a significant part. But it was also a very modern war, for instance in the British Army's use of railways to subdue the Boers in the early months of 1900, or the use of trench warfare by the Boers along the Modder River. It was disturbingly new in the way that it changed in the autumn of 1900 from a war between armies to a guerrilla war against a civilian population, most distastefully so in the British concentration camps set up to house Boer women and children. Above all, it was a distinctly contemporary war in its impact on the media, especially the newspapers, and in the interaction between the media and those participating in the fighting. It was a significant war, far bigger than originally expected, and was therefore big news. The British Army, ill-prepared for the original Boer invasion of Natal, at first numbered 75,000 troops. In the end, the British and imperial forces totalled 450,000 with contingents from Canada, Australia, New Zealand and India. The British lost 22,000 men, 13,000 of them from disease. The Boers lost about 7,000 in the field, while another 27,000 (many of them very young children) are estimated to have died in the concentration camps. There were also about 20,000 black and 'coloured' Africans who died in concentration camps, though this was little reported at the time. So it was a major episode in British military history. The impact on British opinion of the relief of Ladysmith and especially of Mafeking in 1900 was quite overwhelming. In a frenzy of 'jingo' celebration, the verb 'mafficking' entered the language. In these circumstances, the consequences of the Boer War on the media and its representation of war were inevitably massive.

The war in South Africa owed its impact in part because it was the first major British war since the advent of mass literacy after the 1870 Forster Education Act. There was a mass readership anxious to read the popular press, while technical advances in telegraphy and news gathering had transformed the methods and scope of the British newspaper industry. The most famous example of this was Alfred Harmsworth's *Daily Mail*, first produced in 1896 at a cost of just one halfpenny. Instead of the traditional, relatively restrained reporting of such newspapers as *The Times* or the *Daily News,* there was now a vibrant press catering to the masses, and one far less elitist and deferential. Thus it was that in the first 12 months of the war, to September 1900 when it seemed the war was over and the British had won an easy military victory, the press coverage of events in South Africa was immense, far more so than in any previous war. In the summer of 1900 there were 58 newspaper reporters in South Africa, up to 20 from *The Times* alone.[1] The *Daily Mail* sent out a range of correspondents, of whom the most famous was the novelist Edgar Wallace, later to be the author of *The Four Just Men* (1906) and *Sanders of the River* (1911). They also used the first woman war reporter, Lady Sarah Wilson, who sent dispatches from Ladysmith during its long siege, and who was briefly captured by the Boers after being used by Baden-Powell to convey secret messages. In early 1900 the daily circulation of the *Mail* reached over a million, a record for any newspaper anywhere in the world at that time.

The Times devoted a particular effort to reporting on the war in South Africa. It had enjoyed a special reputation for war reportage since the dispatches of W.H. Russell during the Crimean War in 1852–5. It believed itself to have a particular authority and was anxious not to be outdone by the Reuters news agency, even though *The Times* reporters also tried to make use of local press agents for their work.[2] *The Times* employed a wide range of reporters, covering a variety of themes, not only military ones; among the more distinguished were Perceval Landon and the youthful Leopold Amery. At first, its writers were intensely one-sided in their writing. They focussed on the gallantry of the British troops on the veldt, and presented coverage of the sieges of Ladysmith, Kimberley, and (especially) Mafeking in idealised, almost romantic terms. In Kimberley, where Cecil Rhodes himself took part, *The Times* simply published pro-Rhodes propaganda, much of it drawn from the hero-worshipping diary of the Hon. Mrs. Rochfort Maguire. The main *Times* reporter in Mafeking, Angus Hamilton, a man of liberal instincts, was repeatedly censored, and once briefly dismissed, when he ventured on a more balanced treatment of the Boers.[3] In the last eighteen months of the war, up to the peace concluded at Vereeniging in May 1902, *The Times* largely dismissed reports on the high rate of deaths of mothers and children in the concentration camps. So far as the deaths there were acknowledged at all, the emphasis was placed not on the British commanders but on the inadequacies of the Boers as mothers in terms of their knowledge of hygiene and nutrition. Emily Hobhouse, whose graphic reports drew the attention of the world to the atrocities in the concentration camps was largely ridiculed as a meddlesome spinster, or, in the bachelor Kitchener's memorable phrase, 'that bloody woman'.[4]

Eventually, even the imperialist *Times* came to adopt a somewhat more balanced view. There was, after all, the need to compete with other newspapers in the accuracy of its reporting, and the British military disasters of November 1899 to January 1900 could hardly be concealed. Increasingly, the military astuteness and patriotic fervour of the Boer soldiers was conceded: indeed the very first military encounter at Tulana hill in the first few days of the war had thrown an ominous light on the Boers' tactical ability. But in general *The Times* made little effort to be objective. Its editor, George Buckle, after all, was an uncritical devotee of Cecil Rhodes and a passionate defender of the Uitlanders, whose demand for the franchise in Johannesburg had originally led to the war. Other newspapers offered different and fairer perspectives. *The Times'* official *History of the War*, published after hostilities had ended under the distinguished editorship of its chief war correspondent, Leopold Amery, was a far more worthy production.

The general impression of the reporters or commentators on the war is that they were a remarkably distinguished group of writers. They comprised a fair range of the literary elite of *fin de siècle* Britain. Rudyard Kipling, already celebrated as poet and storyteller, operated variously in Cape Town and Bloemfontein. He was given special briefings by Roberts, Milner, and Baden-Powell, amongst others. One legacy was his famous poem, 'Boots': 'We're foot-slog-slog-slog-sloggin' over Africa'. As with the Jameson Raid in 1895, he was compelled to observe that the early months of the war proved to be 'no end of a lesson' for the British Empire and its vaunted reputation. In addition to Kipling, as noted, there was the famous novelist, Edgar Wallace, working for the *Daily Mail*, while Sir Arthur Conan Doyle, of Sherlock Holmes fame, contributed two contemporary books of observation of the campaign on the basis of his work in the field hospitals of the veldt. His history of the war went through several editions down to 1903 and took account of Boer publications. Another contemporary account was by Erskine Childers, later famous as author of the spy story, *Riddle of the Sands*, who served in the City Imperial Volunteers in early 1900.[5] On the Liberal side, the *Manchester Guardian* employed J.A. Hobson, whose *War in South Africa* formed the basis for his famous study of imperialism (1902), which was to exercise so powerful an influence on Lenin amongst others, while the *Daily Chronicle* had the prominent radical journalist, Henry Nevinson who operated in Ladysmith during the siege. A lesser but interesting figure was E.W. Smith who covered the events in Ladysmith for the *Morning Leader*, whose work brought him a special medal from the Queen.[6] Ultimately the most celebrated journalist of them all was the 26-year-old Winston Churchill, whose reports for the Unionist *Morning Post* first captured nationwide attention for him, and who used his ambiguous status, part soldier, part reporter, with subtle, self-publicising skill. His book *London to Ladysmith via Pretoria* made an impact, as did his celebrated, if controversial, escape from Boer hands.

What could and did they report? Certainly these journalists were much handicapped by the work of the British censors, especially those based in Cape Town. Here, military censorship of letters and telegrams home was supplemented by civilian vetting by the local Postmaster-General's department. However, things did loosen up a good deal when Roberts took over as commander-in-chief at the start of 1900.[7] Newspapers continued to complain, however, that Reuters was given privileged treatment and access to news. By March 1900, for all the work of the censors, there was fierce criticism of Buller, White and other British generals, whose incompetence had led to so many disastrous defeats down to that at Spion Kop. Leopold Amery in *The Times,* like other journalists, directed fierce attacks on General Buller, though an element in this may have been that pro-Roberts journalists would inevitably have criticised Buller, a supporter of Roberts's great rival in the high military command, Sir Garnet Wolseley who was also a Liberal in political sympathies. On balance, the savagery of the fighting did eventually get across to readers. The heavy British casualties in the disaster at Spion Kop, for instance, were certainly given the fullest coverage.

As in all cases, the newspapers showed a distinct difference between their editorials and their factual reporting. The editorials at first, on the Liberal side no less than on the pro-government side, tended to deal in stereotypes. After all, the overwhelming majority of British newspapers were imperialist and pro-war to the very end. Until 1901 there was no 'Pro-Boer' newspaper in London; a leading radical critic like H.J. Massingham was removed from his post as editor of the *Daily Chronicle* early on during the war. London journalists invariably presented the Boers as primitive and backward, isolated, rural people. They were often described in animal terms as 'herds' or 'flocks', whose defeat by the superior civilisation of the British was an inevitable result of social Darwinism and the influence of the scientific principle of natural selection.

But the reporting of events on the front soon became more balanced. There arose growing admiration for the social and moral qualities of the Boer peoples of the republics of the Transvaal and the Orange Free State. After all, British readers were familiar with the emotionally powerful account of African farm life written up in the famous work of the South African feminist, Olive Schreiner. 'Pro-Boers' who opposed the war tended to project the Boers romantically as models of energetic, Protestant, freedom-loving and family-loving people, somewhat in the way that the Protestant Swiss, William Tell, apple and all, was depicted in British Liberal writing and mythology. It was almost their necessary myth, to be used in their critique of the political and social inadequacies of the British at home. The Boers were sympathetically written up by authors like Childers and Amery, and (if allowed) by Angus Hamilton in *The Times*. Childers was unable to fathom the bitterness towards the Boers felt by a South African recruit to the British Army. There had never been evidence of the Boers mistreating their British prisoners of war. He formed 'a friendly impression of the enemy we were fighting'. The famous critic of Empire, J.A. Hobson, normally unsympathetic to Boer backwoodsmen and their culture, nevertheless praised the 'simple mannered, plain living Boer farmers' as historically necessary victims of cosmopolitan/Jewish capitalism.[8]

Most remarkably, these views were shared by many British Army officers in the field. They found the Boers to be doughty enemies whose qualities, physical and moral, they respected.[9] The Boer enemy, a vigorous and manly type, was often compared very favourably with the cosmopolitan and shifting population in the goldfields of the Rand whom the British were supposedly defending (anti-semitism played its ugly part here as when depicting Johannesburg as 'Jewburg'). Certainly the Boer fighting men compared well with the often physically feeble recruits to the British Army, whose poor quality in terms of health was later to be condemned by the Committee on Physical Deterioration in 1904 and its call for a healthier, more 'efficient' population. The treatment of the Boers in some of the writing and reporting during the war anticipated the political settlement eventually agreed with them when the Union of South Africa came into being in 1910. The Boers, unlike Kipling's 'lesser breeds without the law' were fit to exercise freedom. There was an obvious racial aspect to this. The Boers were, after all, white men, and hence by definition more civilised than black adversaries such as the Zulus, or indeed the black and coloured population in Cape Colony and Natal, which supported the imperial cause. Blacks, even though they patriotically embraced the British point of view, were seen as akin to savages. Certainly they were not supposed to be armed (even though armed Baralong played, for example, an important role at Mafeking close to where they lived). For one thing, the black tradition, it was believed, was to be ungentlemanly in war and to take no prisoners.

A striking feature of the role of the press during the Boer War was the unusual degree of interaction between the newspapers and the main participants. This was especially true of Lord Roberts, a most accessible commander-in-chief. He was a media-friendly man, as he had been since he had won fame in marching from Kabul to Kandahar during the

Afghan Wars in 1880, which made him an imperial hero. One of his close friends was the right-wing Welsh journalist, H.A. Gwynne, then working for Reuters in South Africa. Roberts frequently held relaxed press conferences with reporters and allowed them to travel freely behind the British lines. He believed that all publicity must be good publicity. On the other hand, happy journalists who sent their reports back to Britain often found that Roberts's own doctored reports had got there first! As a result he built up his own image substantially. Writers like Childers made much of his popularity among the rank and file soldiers, and of his courage when his son was killed in action. Roberts's media consciousness was never seen to better effect than in the heavy press coverage of his own triumphant march into Pretoria, the captured capital of the Transvaal, on 5 June 1900. It was even rumoured that Buller's parallel advance in Natal had been deliberately slowed up by Roberts so that the glory of his own running up the flag in Pretoria should not be in any way overshadowed. It all made bad news for his implacable enemy – not the Boers on the veldt but Sir Garnet Wolseley back in London.

This media consciousness applied even more strongly to the hero of Mafeking, Colonel Robert Baden-Powell. Reporters shied away from awkward questions such as why he was in Mafeking anyway, and glossed over the fact that most of the time the siege of Mafeking was almost totally uneventful. Instead they focussed on Baden-Powell's personal qualities, as they perceived them. He himself ensured that hostile reports of his command at Mafeking were suppressed, while he used his own local journal, the *Mafeking Daily Mail,* to promote his own qualities and prestige. He was romanticised by Kipling, Conan Doyle and by besotted journalists for his humanity, his calm and resourcefulness, his 'impish' good humour (he himself took part in humorous music-hall sketches in entertainments for the Mafeking population on Sunday nights). Also emphasised was his typically English love of sport. For instance, he promoted cricket and football matches amongst the British troops, while his reports from Mafeking often featured cricketing metaphors, such as '200 Not Out'. He was depicted as the classic strong, silent type, a child of nature who blended imperceptibly into the veldt, and enjoyed the dark of the night. He was described as 'Impeesa', alleged to be the African name for 'the wolf who never sleeps' (the Zulu word 'iMpisi' actually meant the far less complimentary 'hyena'). His style and appearance were highly distinctive and geared to self-publicity, notably the bush hat he wore on his head, later adopted by the Boy Scouts. Even Queen Victoria was moved to object to his self-publicity when some emergency postage stamps issued at Mafeking included the head of Baden-Powell rather than that of the Queen. In the new cinema photography, Baden-Powell achieved iconic status. By contrast, his many negative qualities on which later historians have focussed – his probable pederasty and undoubted racism in his brutality towards the black population at Mafeking (many blacks were thrown out from Mafeking, often to die on the open veldt, to preserve food rations for the white population; others were executed for stealing food) were never mentioned.

After the siege of Mafeking came to an end, the army itself tried to give Baden-Powell a lower profile, by sidelining him to other field appointments (though he did have the important task of creating a new British South Africa Police in the Transvaal). But his romantic legendary status was assured after the delirious excitement of the siege and relief of Mafeking. After the war, his heroic role was carried on into the woodcraft culture of the Boy Scouts in 1907. His book *Scouting for Boys* became almost a sacred text. Its origins lay in a short work, 'Aids to Scouting for NCOs and Men', that he had written during the siege of Mafeking. *Scouting for Boys* became a cult book, widely publicised by Baden-Powell's close friend, Rudyard Kipling. It was a romanticisation of the outdoor life, militarism with right-wing 'patriotic' overtones linked with the need for national military service. In the interwar years, the massed scout jamborees at Gilwell Park were to become the more benign British version of *Jeune Nation* or the Hitler Youth. Kipling also proclaimed it as a form of social control, imbuing the sons of the working classes with the right patriotic ideas. In return, Baden-Powell's post-war invention, the Wolf Cubs, drew heavily on the mystique of Kipling's *Jungle Book*.

Of the other British commanders in the field, even Kitchener, who took over the command of the British armies after Roberts departed in August 1900, had tried in the past to make some use of the press after his triumph over the Mahdi at the battle of Omdurman in the Sudan in 1898. But his great journalist friend, G.E. Steevens, to whom he may well have had a homosexual attraction, was to die of typhus during the siege of Ladysmith.[10] Kitchener later became furiously angry with the *Daily Mail* – with good reason, one may add – when it appeared to impede his efforts to conclude an early peace settlement with the Boers in 1901. A repressed, introspective, inarticulate man, he never enjoyed a good rapport with the media. On one notorious occasion in the Sudan, he swept aside the assembled corps of pressmen with the words, 'Get out of my way, you drunken swabs!'

This was even more true of the red-faced, stolid General Sir Redvers Buller, whose military reputation became perhaps even more dismal than he deserved as a result. On the other hand, even Buller showed some limited awareness of the press. Thus, in stage-managing his entry into Ladysmith at the end of the siege, his ceremonial handshake with General White, the defender of Ladysmith, and his 'order of the day' on

3 March 1900 on how this was a 'glorious page' in the annals of the British Empire, Buller too had the media in mind.

In general the Boer War was a seminal and crucial period in the evolution of the British press. It launched a new phase in Britain's self-definition and self-image. Thus, the young David Lloyd George's great coup in January 1901, when he persuaded the Quaker cocoa magnate George Cadbury to buy up the *Daily News* and to convert it overnight from a Liberal Imperialist to a 'Pro-Boer' newspaper, was an important event in the rise of the new radical progressivism of the Edwardian age. The distinguished editor of the *News,* Sir Edward Cook, was cast into outer darkness. The impact of the press was most evident in the early part of the war, down to what was seen as the inevitable British victory with the capture of Pretoria. Conan Doyle's book, which was concluded in September 1900, described 'the end of the war' as having taken place with the formal surrender of the Boer forces.[11] By now, the number of reporters in South Africa was being thinned out as signs of boredom set in and public attention focussed instead on new excitements such as the Boxer Rising in China. On the other hand, the press also launched the mounting reaction against the war in 1901–2, as will be seen shortly. The war in general created a new kind of reciprocal relationship between pressmen, proprietors, editors and journalists, and the political world, which helped to generate that curious admixture of racialism, patriotism, anti-corruption and anti-semitism that characterised the era of Lloyd George's dominance in British politics between 1906 and 1922 and of which he himself was part patron, part victim.

Apart from the extreme importance of the newspaper press during the Boer War, another distinctive feature of the war was its importance for photography. Cameras were now far more widely used than in any previous war. The invention of the Eastman Kodak in the late 1890s was a revolution in itself; cameras could now be carried and used easily by anyone. The Folding Pocket Camera, with its cartridge film, was the first to be mass-produced.[12] The cheap 'Brownie' camera was invented in 1900 with its simple machinery and roll-film; 150,000 such Brownies were sold in the course of that first year. This meant that light hand-held cameras could be carried by soldiers and journalists alike: E.W. Smith of the *Morning Leader* carried a small camera with him in his knapsack as he wrote his reports.[13] There had been photography of wars for many years, of course, during the Crimean War in the 1850s and very much in the course of the American Civil War in 1861–5. But the visual reporting was largely then by specialist professionals or agencies. By contrast, many of the major photographic records of the Boer War were by amateurs, notably in the case of the photography of the thousands of little victims in the Boer concentration camps.

The visual images of the Boer War were of the first importance. In a quite new way, it was a war you could see and not just read about. The trauma of the British military catastrophe of Spion Kop was brought home directly by the grim photographic evidence of stretcher bearers carrying away hundreds of British corpses, Scottish Highlanders above all. Illustrated magazines like *Pearson's War Pictures* achieved large sales in 1900; the *Illustrated London News* capped its photographic reporting by sending an artist to Ladysmith to provide a visual coverage of events during the siege.[14] The use of visual record extended into the early cinemas and newsreels. Moving pictures of men like Roberts, Kitchener, and especially Baden-Powell were shown in the music halls to build up patriotic fervour and elevate the reputations of the commanders. Baden-Powell in particular benefited from this treatment. When his picture appeared on a film screen in a music hall, the cheering might last for fully half an hour, holding up the playing of 'God Save the Queen' to official embarrassment.

This media treatment was part of a broad projection of the pro-war imperial ethos in popular culture. The music halls resounded to patriotic songs like 'Goodbye Dolly Gray'. Young children in distant North Wales like me later learned little jingles like:

> *Lord Roberts and Kitchener,*
> *General Buller and White*
> *Went out to South Africa*
> *to teach the Boers how to fight.*[15]

Sport was enlisted for the cause, especially football and cricket matches, although it should be noted that cricket was overwhelmingly a game of the white South Africans of British stock, not of the Dutch-speaking Afrikaaners. One distinguished South African batsman, R.H. Poore, served in the British Army and became provost marshal in the South African Field Force. Other notable players like J.H. Sinclair, also fought against the Boers. In 1901, while the war was still going on, James Logan actually arranged a tour of England by a South African representative side. The whole episode was used to provide imperialist propaganda, vigorously followed up after the war by Sir Abe Bailey, who deliberately linked cricket and Empire in a bid to win over Afrikaaner opinion. How wide an impact this imperial propaganda had on the British population has been much debated amongst historians. Richard Price is prominent amongst those who believe that it was largely middle-class people who rallied to the 'patriotic' propaganda. It was young men like white-collar 'clerks' who were prominent in the celebrations of the relief of Mafeking.[16] But, for all the reservations about the war in the working-class world, until the middle of 1901 public opinion would appear to have been strongly pro-war in most of England and even more so in Scotland, where engineers, doctors, missionaries and others had linked the Scots with imperial greatness. This was true to a lesser degree in Wales, however, where Lloyd George became a powerful voice of anti-war dissent and where the Welsh-language newspapers increasingly showed fellow feeling with the Boer republics almost as fellow victims of English colonialism.[17] The Labour movement was divided. Ethical socialists like Keir Hardie and the ILP strongly attacked a capitalist, imperialist war, less volubly did the Marxist SDF, whose leader H.M. Hyndman always had a jingoist streak. However, the Webbs, Shaw, and other leading Fabians endorsed the war as a facet of 'national efficiency' while Robert Blatchford's socialist newspaper, the *Clarion,* was aggressively 'patriotic'.

On the other hand, the media coverage did have an important effect in helping to stimulate anti-war sentiment in the later stages of the war. Emily Hobhouse's graphic description of the mass deaths in the concentration camps in 1901 was fully reported in the *Manchester Guardian,* the *Speaker* and other Liberal journals and had a powerful impact on opinion.[18] They followed earlier accounts of the mass burning of Boer farmhouses to cut off domestic support and supplies for the Boer commandos. Hobhouse's reports described a catastrophe of near genocidal proportions conducted by the British Army under Kitchener. They showed that the British, incapable of protecting the health of their own troops, thousands of whom died of disease, were totally at a loss in dealing with problems of malnutrition and mass disease that spread like wildfire in the cramped and unsanitary conditions of the concentration camps. With horrific news (and pictures) of the mass burial of thousands of tiny children and their mothers, imperialism lost the moral high ground. Campbell-Bannerman, the Liberal leader, in a devastating phrase, spoke of 'methods of barbarism' being used by the imperial forces in South Africa. Hobhouse was relatively innocent of the ways of the media, but she spoke to others far more adept, notably Lloyd George with his important links with key Liberal journalists like A.G. Gardiner. Her devastating findings soon had an immense impact on the public consciousness.

One important readership group that was much influenced as a result was that of women.[19] The Boer War, indeed, with its massive cruelty inflicted on Boer mothers, was a key episode in the politics of gender in Britain. Women, after all, were prominent on such bodies as the South Africa Conciliation Committee, along with the more forceful Stop the

War Committee led by the newspaper man, W.T. Stead. The great debate over the camps between Emily Hobhouse and Millicent Fawcett, opponents in the woman's suffrage debates as well in their judgement on the concentration camps in South Africa, was above all a debate between women. At first Hobhouse denounced the camps for attacking women who were essentially innocent non-combatant bystanders. Later on, notably in her famous Vrouwen-Dag (Women's Day) speech at Bloemfontein in 1913, she was to argue that, on the contrary, the camps showed that the women had indeed been combatants, that they had fought and suffered alongside their men folk during the war, and therefore that they should now in justice receive the full privileges of citizenship, including the vote (not necessarily in itself a popular view amongst Boer men). She devoted much of her time after the war to trying to build up the skills and self-esteem of Boer mothers, for instance by encouraging cottage industries such as lace-making. Her own close friendship with the pioneer socialist feminist, Olive Schreiner, was another powerful influence in changing opinion.[20]

As soon as the war was over, the British media were pivotal in voicing disgust with the concentration camps and the colossal loss of life that resulted: one-quarter of the entire population of Boer women and children in the two Boer republics lost their lives in the space of around 15 months. Henceforth imperialists like Joseph Chamberlain were swimming against the tide of opinion and the public conscience. In the general election of January 1906, another press issue arose to depress the imperialist cause still further. This was the issue of 'Chinese slavery', indentured Chinese labourers in the mines of the Rand in South Africa.[21] Trade unionists and others denounced the use of cheap non-union labour in this way and alleged that Chinese workers might in time be introduced into British factories and mines also. Cartoonists in 1906 made much use of alarming depiction of Chinese labourers with their narrow eyes and pigtails, with the fullest use of racialist stereotypes. It all reinforced the part that the media played in leading the way in promoting an increasingly negative, guilt-ridden view of the once-glorious war in South Africa.

It is difficult to say much about the Boer newspapers: they were published in Dutch, of course, and were mostly suppressed after the capture of Pretoria in July 1900, to resume publication only at the very end of the war. One specific category of South African newspapers, however, was that catering for black or coloured people largely in Cape Colony. Papers like the *South African Spectator* of Cape Town promoted a strongly pro-British attitude in the mistaken view that the Empire would adopt a more liberal policy towards their social and economic status after the war. They urged the need for black combatants to fight in the British Army along-side white troops and turned Abraham Esau, a pro-British black leader murdered by local Boer republicans in January 1901, into a legendary folk hero. The British, inevitably, viewed this ambiguous source of black support with great reserve, for all their public professions of sympathy for the African majority. For instance, press and other accounts by the British authorities, from Baden-Powell downwards, deliberately played down the major role played in defending Mafeking by black contingents such as the 500 armed Baralong people and the Cape Boys' Regiment, let alone black scouts or runners who supplied key military intelligence. It was felt important to preserve the public myth that this was solely a white man's war.[22]

Whereas the British newspapers focussed on home readers, the Boer propaganda effort by contrast, through their newspapers and inter-national agents, was directed internationally in the hope of foreign sup-port and perhaps even military intervention. Men like the ubiquitous W.J. Leyds, Kruger's chief diplomat in Europe and envoy in Brussels, operated with some sophistication. They had particular impact in France, though here reactions may have been influenced partly by sore feelings after the French had been humiliated by Kitchener in the so-called Fashoda inci-dent in 1898. Even so, French republican sympathy was strongly enlisted in solidarity with the Boers, and accounts of British brutality made a powerful impact.[23] There was at least one very prominent French vol-unteer, Colonel Georges Comte de Villebois-Mareuil, who fought with the Boers, was promoted to General, and then was killed in a rash 'last stand' in April 1900. The British press became very angry at French joy on hearing of British disasters during the 'black week' in December 1899 and some suggested sending virile young Englishmen across the Chan-nel to teach the French a lesson – perhaps a precursor of that cherished symbol of the modern English scene, the football hooligan! There was a spate of anti-French books with some postulating a future war. France conducted via a putative Channel tunnel. When President Kruger went into exile he was ceremonially received by the president of the French republic, Émile Loubet.

Elsewhere the Boer propaganda won many friends, in Germany where Kaiser William II wired his support, in The Netherlands (of course), and in Russia. In the United Kingdom, the Irish Nationalists were almost totally hostile, whereas Protestant Ulster was strongly imperial and sup-plied leading Generals such as Kitchener and French. When the news of 'black week' was announced in the House of Commons, the Irish Nation-alist MPs stood up and cheered: after all, they wanted the Boers to win. The war led the Parnellite and Anti-Parnellite factions, divided since the

O'Shea divorce case ten years earlier, to reunite at Westminster in 1900 under the leadership of John Redmond. In Ireland itself, a broad swathe of intellectual and cultural leaders, Maud Gonne, G.E. Moore, Lady Gregory, and W.B. Yeats amongst them, identified strongly with the Boer cause, though not all for the same reasons. The United States, an especial target for Boer propaganda, was more complex in its response. Whereas Irish-Americans and other ethnic minorities were passionately Pro-Boer, the US Republican government tended to favour Britain both on grounds of the naval security provided by the British Navy in the Atlantic, and on grounds of 'Anglo-Saxon' kinship. Theodore Roosevelt, who became President in 1901 on the assassination of William McKinley, was a warm supporter of Liberal Imperialism and of Cecil Rhodes in particular.

The involvement of the media in the Boer War went on long after the war ended in May 1902. After the war, the British media attempted to project the chivalrous, almost light-hearted nature of the war. The appalling bloodshed of Magersfontein, Colenso and Spion Kop, the atrocities of the concentration camps, were forgotten. It had almost been fun, especially when the Boer commandos took centre stage in 1901–2. They were depicted (not least in Wales) rather like enterprising rugby three-quarters, running rings around their stolid English opponents. The journalist E.W. Smith was to note that the Boer War totally lacked the sustained horror of the Great War of 1914–18. Major-General Fuller was to write in *The Last of the Gentleman's Wars* in 1937 that 'by fighting in a sporting way we endowed the war with a chivalrous atmosphere'. The Afrikaaner Denys Reitz's famous book *Commando* commended English officers and men for their general humanity on the field of battle.[24] Meanwhile, in Australia, imposing war memorials in various cities, especially the one beside Government House in strongly anglophile Adelaide, became testimony to the new Commonwealth's sense of being a fully participating member of the great British Empire, fostering the myth of the 'Independent Australian Briton'.[25]

The enduring symbol of a 'good war' was Colonel Baden-Powell, the symbol and leader of the cult of 'Boy Scouts' and the outdoor ethos of the 'illimitable veldt'. The Boy Scouts became internationally renowned as a global youth movement spreading the gospel of wholesome God-fearing patriotism. It became powerful in Africa, black and white: Baden-Powell was to be buried in Kenya, a particular stronghold of the scout movement. Conversely, the Boers projected the war, along with the Great Trek and the Battle of Blood River in 1838, as central to their folk myth as a people: witness the Afrikaaner war memorial at Bloemfontein, which features both a giant sculpture of a Boer woman and child, and a casket of the ashes of Emily Hobhouse. Indeed, Hobhouse, as a humane upper-class Englishwoman, was appropriated by the Boers as a particular symbol of international support. She had become the close friend of General Smuts, as well as of Olive Schreiner. In the fullness of time, her name was given to a new settlement in the Orange Free State, while the Nationalist government in the 1980s actually attached her name to a submarine, which would surely have horrified this radical pacifist.

The media in both Britain and South Africa used the military prestige of the commandos, especially of Botha and Smuts, to further this image. Smuts in particular came to be seen in Britain as a personal symbol of the Commonwealth partnership, a kind of philosopher king, a gallant adversary in 1900, a political leader with Botha after the Union of South Africa came into being, finally a member of the Imperial War Cabinet under Lloyd George (an old Pro-Boer) in 1917–18 who took his place in the peace conference at Paris and the Treaty of Versailles.[26] He was a major influence behind the founding of the League of Nations partly because he saw it as giving strength and coherence to the British Empire. The defeat of Smuts by the Nationalists in his old age in the 1948 South African elections, a year after he had hosted a visit by the British royal family to his country, was seen as the end of an era. On the other hand, Afrikaaners drew very different conclusions about the war. To many of them, men like Smuts appeared rather as traitors to the good old cause. A symbolic point of reference came in autumn 1914, just after war broke out, when a government led by Botha and Smuts imprisoned old Boer leaders like De Wet for treason and also saw Fourie executed and de la Rey shot (the last probably an unfortunate accident). The clashing interpretations of the war resulted in a supreme struggle for the soul of the Afrikaaner people, with the Smuts legend giving way in time to the victory of the Nationalists and the apartheid regime in 1948.

For 97 years, from 1902 to 1999, the media representation of the Boer War took the form of trying to create a sanitised impression of a 'gentleman's war', a war that led to reconciliation and in which, morally, there were no losers. The fact that the outcome was the permanent riveting of white supremacy upon the black population, in Cape Colony and Natal as well as the Boer republics of Transvaal and the Free State, was swept aside. Even in the era of apartheid, a relatively benevolent view of the Boer War was sustained, difficult though that was after events at Sharpeville and Soweto.

But, at the time of the centenary of the war in the very different era of Nelson Mandela and a free 'rainbow nation', the war had become a huge embarrassment. The Boer War and its legacy, its very centrality in the Boer myth, was strongly contested. For most South Africans, it now seemed merely a local war between two of the white tribes of Africa. One problem was what the war should be called. Names such as the South African or even the Anglo–South African War were now more politically correct than the older designation of the 'Boer War'.

The commemoration of the war's centenary in 1999 thus created a huge dilemma for all South Africans as they emerged from the apartheid era. More and more emphasis now was placed on the long-neglected role of black Africans during the war, the impact of war in terms of loss of life and the disruption of their social and economic existence, and their betrayal by the British government when negotiating the Union in 1910 as, indeed, socialists like Keir Hardie had spelt out at the time. By 1999 it was no longer clear what the centenary of the war was trying to remember or honour. A major historical conference at Pretoria in August 1998 (at which the present writer took part) focussed on social, gender, ethnic, and medical aspects, rather than the actual fighting. When the Queen visited South Africa in 1995, she was asked (in vain) to apologise for the concentration camps during the war, just as she had been asked to apologise to the Maoris of New Zealand and the aborigines of Australia. Media reporting of the war in South Africa 100 years earlier had turned from a reporting of events into a jumble of fiction and fact, legend, symbolism and stereotype. It had acquired an embarrassing half-life of its own. One hundred years after the event, the media representation of the Boer War of 1899–1902 had to begin all over again.

Chapter 5

'Blissful Dawn'?
The Liberal Government of 1906

On 7 February 1906, the crofters and fishermen of Orkney and Shetland made their way through the darkness to cast their votes in the general election. The constituency had not elected a Conservative since the general election of 1835 so it was no surprise when 79 per cent of the voters cast their vote for the Liberal, J.C. Wason. What was totally astonishing was that he was (according to my calculations!) the 401st Liberal MP who had been returned. Spread out over four weeks, the excitement began on 11 January with two Liberals elected for Ipswich ('Ipswich leads the way' read the placards). A sequence of Unionist (i.e., Conservative) disasters followed thereafter. The 'Portillo moment', the Southgate of 1906, came very early with the defeat on 13 January in North Manchester of Arthur Balfour, only five weeks previously the prime minister: he had to find sanctuary in that citadel of unregenerate Conservatism – the City of London! In fact, the Liberals captured all eight seats in Manchester, including Winston Churchill, a recent convert, in North West Manchester. Only three members of the former Unionist Cabinet survived: Akers-Douglas, Arnold-Forster and Austen Chamberlain. To the Liberals 401 should be added the 29 members of the newly formed Labour Party and 83 Irish Nationalists, so the effective normal government majority was over 350. The Tories lost 245 seats and ended up with only 157. It is impossible to assess the swing with any precision – there were 114 uncontested seats, and there had been 245 in the previous election, the Khaki Election held during the South African War in October 1900. Where there is a comparable result, the swing seems to have been around 12 per cent, greater than those of 1945 or 1997. Peter Snow, thou shouldst be living at that hour!

Contemporaries noted that something really dramatic was happening. Many of them focussed, as would have been natural in 1906, on religion. The 1906 election, with over 200 nonconformists returned to parliament, was the greatest triumph of the chapels over the Church of England since the time of Cromwell. Great chapels like Whitefield's Tabernacle on the Tottenham Court Road became in effect Liberal Committee Rooms, with charismatic organisers like Whitefield's Congregationalist minister Silvester Horne (father of a famous radio comedian).

For the chapels, it was not so much an election as an epiphany. There was much talk of Children of Israel and the Promised Land, with particular reference to Church schools and 'Rome on the rates'. Religion had a particular impact in nonconformist Wales, where the much publicised 'revolt' of the county councils, led by Lloyd George, against the 1902 Education Act, was reinforced by the huge religious revival of 1904–5, *y diwygiad mawr* in Welsh, a media-conscious event of messianic intensity. In Wales, the Unionists, like a famous British entry in the Eurovision song contest, scored null points.

But the nonconformists were to be disappointed clients of the Liberal victory. In the longer term, much the more significant aspect was that the general election marked the first great direct impact of the working class in British politics. Balfour saw the Liberal Prime Minister Sir Henry Campbell-Bannerman as 'a mere cork dancing on a torrent which he cannot control...It is an echo of the same movement which has produced massacres in St. Petersburg and riots in Vienna...' A few days later, on 12 February 1906, there followed what was clearly the most important outcome of the general election. The parliamentary Labour Party was formed. Its 29 MPs consisted very largely of trade unionists, many of Lib–Lab views, but also included important socialists like Ramsay MacDonald, Philip Snowden, Fred Jowett and Keir Hardie, the member for Merthyr Boroughs who had brought the Labour Alliance into being six years earlier. Hardie was elected chairman by 15 votes to 14. In January 1909, after a vote amongst the Miners' Federation, the 29 were joined by a further 14 miners' MPs, elected in 1906 as 'Lib–Labs'. It has been rightly pointed out that the advent of Labour was hugely assisted by the secret election pact or 'Entente' with the Liberals in 1903 under which Labour had a free run against the Unionists in around 30 seats. It was a pact much helped by the existence of two-member seats where Labour could run in double harness with a Liberal, as MacDonald did in Leicester, Snowden in Blackburn and Hardie in Merthyr Tydfil. But too much has been made, in my view, of excessive Liberal generosity. With the growing strength of Labour in 1903, with Arthur Henderson winning Barnard Castle against a Liberal, the Liberal whips had not much choice but to make a deal. The outcome benefited both sides, financially and politically, and created the pre-war Progressive Alliance.

The background to the election was one of deep national anxiety. The dismal war in South Africa (1899–1902) proved to be, as Kipling famously wrote, 'no end of a lesson'. It demonstrated diplomatic isolation overseas, growing poverty, class division and inequality in the cities at home. The gospel of Empire was irretrievably tarnished by the deaths of at least 28,000 Boer women and children in British concentration camps on the Rand. The memorial plaques of hundreds of children, perishing under the age of five, on the walls of a former concentration camp near Pretoria, which I saw in 2000, are a permanent stain on the name of Britain. Henry Campbell-Bannerman described these camps as 'methods of barbarism'; three words that changed the politics of a generation. There is an interesting parallel with the Progressive reform movement in the United States at this time. There, too, after an imperialist war with Spain in Cuba in 1898 and the cruel suppression of 'insurgency' in the revolt in the Philippines, Americans turned inwards from the vainglorious imperialism of a 'splendid little war' to political corruption and social injustice at home. The great American 'muck-raking' journalists and writers, like Lincoln Steffens, Ida Tarbell, Ray Stannard Baker or Upton Sinclair, paralleled the British journalism of exposure at the same period.

The brash façade of Edwardian baroque barely concealed this anxiety. It was a time of explosive cultural and intellectual energy, which went far beyond the nationalist confines of Elgar's pomp and circumstance. Edwardian literature was galvanised by social protest, especially with problems of the city and the status of women. H.G. Wells is an outstanding example here in novels such as *Tono Bungay, The New Machiavelli* and *Ann Veronica*. Shaw, Galsworthy and many others also illustrate the social concerns of the Edwardians. It was also a heyday of the 'higher journalism' in the great weekly and fortnightly reviews and the national press. The 'two Hobs', Hobson and Hobhouse, are the great exhibit here. J.A, Hobson, later to join the Labour Party but at the time a leading New Liberal ideologue much admired by Lenin, helped to detach the idea of collectivism and an empowering state from the tarnished creed of Empire L.T. Hobhouse, for many years a leader-writer on C.P. Scott's *Manchester Guardian*, was a pioneer of modern sociology. It was high noon for the political public intellectual and man of letters. Literary giants like John Morley, James Bryce and Augustine Birrell were actually in the Liberal Cabinet. The 401 Liberals MPs included eminent authors such as Hilaire Belloc and A.E.W. Mason of *Four Feathers* fame, and the distinguished historian, G.P. Gooch, member for Bath.

At the same time, we should not overdo the high-minded elitism of the Liberal victory. There was also much low-level populism in the Liberal campaign, long before Lloyd George sailed into the House of Lords as 'five hundred ordinary men chosen at random from amongst the unemployed'. There were highly personalised attacks on Joseph Chamberlain and 'sleaze' linked to the arms deals of the South African War, 'While the Empire expands, the Chamberlains contract'. There were rhetorical attacks on 'Randlords' and 'Landlords', and on the 'small loaf' that would result from Tariff Reform. It was claimed that the Tories would drive us back to the Hungry Forties. Most discreditable of all was racialism: the Liberals' campaign against 'Chinese Slavery' (indentured non-union Chinese workers on the rand) made much use of Oriental stereotypes. It chimed in with trade union fears of capitalist bosses bringing in non-unionised 'free' blackleg labour at home, the role of free-booting employers like the appalling Lord Penrhyn in his slate quarries in Caernarfonshire.

So the election campaign was not a model of moral rectitude. But it was also a great and momentous event to which the historian should respond. It embodied what Karl Marx called the sense of historic necessity. It is right that we should celebrate it today. Perhaps we shall celebrate it again shortly when the statue of Lloyd George is placed next to that of Winston Churchill in Parliament Square. Just as Churchill's statue was once targeted by anti-capitalist demonstrators, it is nice to think that Lloyd George's may be some time by the pheasant-shooting branches of the Countryside Alliance.

Are there similarities between the election victories of 1906 and of 1997? (I set 1945 aside because it was conducted under the special circumstances of wartime.) Of course, there are clear differences. In 1997 Tony Blair emphasised personal leadership and the cult of the 'new'. His first major speech as party leader in 1994 used the word 'new' 37 times. In 1906, by contrast, the Liberals campaigned as a team, and took up distinctly Old Liberal themes: free trade, little Englandism, the rights of nonconformity, the 'unholy trinity' of the 'bishop, the brewer and the squire'.

Again in 1997 the 44-year-old Tony Blair emphasised that he and his country were 'young' (a theme later picked up in 2005 by the 39-year-old David Cameron). In 1906 the prime minister, Campbell-Bannerman, was 69 and spent several weeks, if not months, of the year taking the waters in the agreeable German spa of Marienbad. In fact, 'C.B.' was at first a forceful and decisive leader. He led his Cabinet from the left of centre and with much confidence: 'if the tail is wagging the dog, the party is the dog and I am the tail'. He crushed Balfour at the outset in debate in 1906 with his memorable rebuke, 'Enough of this foolery'. He pushed for early self-government in South Africa (in fact, a highly disadvantageous move as far as the blacks of Cape Colony and Natal were concerned as Hardie and the Labour Party pointed out). He endorsed the Labour Party's view on trade union reform, rather than the opinion of his own Attorney-General. The result was the 1906 Trade Disputes Act, the Magna Carta of Labour so-called, guaranteeing them financial immunity from damages in industrial action that, after being reinforced by Michael Foot at the Employment department in 1974–5, survived largely intact until the regime of Mrs. Thatcher.

But there were also clear similarities between 1906 and 1997. First, in each election there was a background of Conservative division and decline. In the 1990s it was all about Europe. In 1906 it was about Empire. The moral impetus of Empire was severely diminished, as Kipling himself pointed out. 'Methods of Barbarism', a phrase suggested to Campbell-Bannerman by that wonderful woman, Emily Hobhouse, who documented the evils of the concentration camps in South Africa, created a new mood of revulsion. It was the methods of the war rather than its ostensible purposes that generated most criticism, unlike Iraq in 2003. In addition, Joseph Chamberlain in 1903 destabilised his party with his crusade for protective tariffs and imperial preference. In response, Free Trade, the gospel of Cobden and Bright and Gladstone, embraced the whole range of Liberal (and Labour) values: cheap food and raw materials for consumers, full employment for workers, a vision of world prosperity and peace.

Secondly, in both 1906 and 1997 there was a uniform swing all over the country. There was a big swing to the Liberals in Lancashire, which had been since the 1870s a stronghold of Protestant Toryism. Even in Chamberlainite Birmingham, where all the seats were just about held by the Unionists, there was a 12 per cent swing. Fifteen of the 22 Unionist-held seats in London were captured. Rural seats in England, hardly ever, or never, Liberal before, were won. Celtic pluralism was much exploited. There were big Unionist losses in Scotland, the one area to swing to the government in the Khaki Election of 1900. In Wales, there was a clean sweep with the Conservatives losing every seat as in 1997 and 2001. The Liberal cause here, as we have noted was boosted by the great religious revival and also perhaps by the ever famous rugby victory over the New Zealand All Blacks at the Arms Park on 16 December 2005, which evoked fanciful comparison with the Welsh bowmen at Agincourt.

Thirdly, both the Liberals and New Labour won three elections, the Liberals also winning both elections in 1910, though far more narrowly. They stayed in office as a single-party government for nearly ten years, until the first wartime coalition emerged in May 1915. Both the Liberals in 1906 and Labour in 1997 established not just a government but a hegemony.

And finally, both governments were dominated by two men. In 1997 it was Tony Blair and Gordon Brown. Then it was Herbert Asquith and David Lloyd George. There were other big figures in the 1906 government, of course, Sir Edward Grey, the foreign secretary, R.B. Haldane, secretary for war, John Morley, secretary for India. There were also one or two makeweights like 'Lulu' Harcourt and John Burns. But Asquith and Lloyd George were the giants. They were certainly not socially or educationally on the same wavelength. It was a contrast between a wealthy product of City of London School and Balliol College, Oxford, and a relatively poor product of the shoemaker's home in Llanystdumwy who never went to university and left school at 14. This contrast is reflected in Roy Jenkins's suitably patrician biography of Asquith, the work of another Balliol man of course. Asquith did not greatly like either Lloyd George himself or the Welsh in general, 'I would sooner go to hell than to Wales' he once observed. L.G. would sometimes make derisive comments on Asquith's addiction to brandy and women, though he also spoke often with affection of his old leader. As someone once said to me about another powerful partnership, Jim Callaghan and Michael Foot, 'they were not best buddies' personally. Asquith was a convert to Anglicanism, Lloyd George was a Campbellite Baptist, an outsider in religion as in politics. There was also a much greater political gulf between them than between Blair and Brown today, with Asquith the Liberal Imperialist in 1900 and Lloyd George the 'Pro-Boer'.

But what a tremendous partnership they were, and over so long a period! It is a great error to read back the split between them in 1916–18 to the pre-war years. Lloyd George and Asquith were not Bevan and Gaitskell, still less Cain and Abel. Their great qualities were complementary: Asquith judicious and clear-headed, Lloyd George charismatic and visionary. Asquith foreshadowed his government's reform programme while chancellor with his budget of 1907 and its new taxation of unearned incomes, and he also introduced Old Age Pensions, which Lloyd George carried on to the statute book. His famous words, 'Wait and See' implied a threat to his opponents, not a symbol of indolence. In April 1908, when Campbell-Bannerman left office to die, and Asquith became prime minister and Lloyd George his chancellor, the pace and tone of public life changed dramatically. Asquith went along with all Lloyd George's radical reforms. They worked together in brilliant combination over the 1909 People's Budget and the 1911 Parliament Act which permanently clipped the powers of the Lords. There was no serious political gulf between them until the coming of military conscription in the winter of 1915–16. The key moment came with the Marconi scandal in 1912 when Lloyd George (along with Rufus Isaacs, shortly to become Lord Chief Justice) was seen to have bought shares from a wireless telegraphy company in contract with the British government. Lloyd George, who actually lost money on the Marconi shares transaction, could well have gone with ignominy. But Asquith backed him up to the hilt. He fought Marconi hard on totally partisan lines. Asquith wanted to remain prime minister, he despised the Tories, he recognised Lloyd George as his greatest asset, and he played to win. The Liberals, with their Labour and Irish allies, took a tough partisan approach throughout (none more so than Lloyd George's close ally, Winston Churchill) and Lloyd George survived, eventually to supplant Asquith himself. Nor were Lloyd George's sexual peccadillos a political problem: in any case Asquith, with his remarkably frank disclosures to Lady Venetia Stanley, was hardly less vulnerable on that ground himself. Tabloid revelations belonged to a later age.

There was one great difference between the two governments of 1906 and 1997. Tony Blair has said, 'We are at our best when we are boldest'. In fact, on most issues, the government of 1906 was much the bolder, almost recklessly so. Setting Iraq on one side, the Blair government has clearly been the bolder on overall constitutional policy, with Lord Irvine's influence of central importance. Both governments had to grapple with the problem of the House of Lords. Asquith in 1911 limited the powers of the Lords over delaying or blocking government measures, but ignored its composition. (Lloyd George actually feared a remodelled House of Lords dominated by the reactionary 'glorified grocers' of Liberalism.) Tony Blair's government has done the reverse. Overall, Labour since 1997 has had a far more sweeping programme of reform, especially over Scottish and Welsh devolution. In 1906 devolution was not significantly on the agenda, though a Scottish home rule bill did make sluggish progress: the main emphasis was on working through an expanded Scottish Office. In Wales, the main theme was disestablishment of the Church of England, but (unlike Ireland 1869) disestablishment was an alternative to home rule, not a precursor to it. Welsh and Scottish national sentiment focussed on greater equality within the Empire, not exclusion from it as was the case in Ireland.

But in all other domestic areas, the 1906 Liberals pressed on with the greater radicalism. They had said very little about social reform in the general election. But under Asquith's regime from 1908 there was far more momentum. Indeed, Asquith's third term, from December 1910, was actually the most radical and effective since it saw, among other things, the passage of both the Parliament Act and the National Insurance Act in 1911. This radical impetus was almost wholly due to David Lloyd George. He had little to say on social matters in 1906 and the *Labour Leader* reasonably observed that he had 'no settled opinions' on them at the time. He told the Welsh National Liberal Federation then that the workers were quite as much interested in Church disestablishment and temperance and land reform as they were in social reform. But by the summer of 1908 there was a mighty change, and he transformed the public agenda. He had until the end of 1910 a tremendous ally in Winston Churchill, almost his disciple and a humane and reforming home secretary with a keen interest in such unfashionable topics as prison reform and the treatment of juveniles. But most of Asquith's government – McKenna, Runciman, Simon, Harcourt, various peers – were pretty much of a dead loss on social welfare. Lloyd George stood alone as a unique link between the Old Liberalism of civic equality and the New Liberalism of social reform. He alone recognised the need for more radical momentum and the ways in which this might be achieved.

The turning point was his visit to Germany in August 1908 to look at Bismarckian welfare programmes (a great episode to be contrasted with his catastrophic later visit to Germany in 1936 to see Hitler at Berchtesgaden). In the autumn and winter of 1908–9 he discussed a planned strategy with Churchill and C.F.G. Masterman, author of *The Condition of England*. There was an immediate need to deal with a financial shortfall – a crisis in local government finance, funding old age pensions and the expensive construction of Dreadnought battleships. But he also sought a new platform for social welfare in the long term.

He aimed boldly to seize the initiative from the tariff reformers. On welfare, the Tories said that 'the foreigner will pay', through tariffs being levied, an idea which Churchill effectively ridiculed. Lloyd George, and his radical journalist friends, replied that 'the rich will pay', echoing the egalitarian argument of Leo Chiozza Money's *Riches and Poverty* (1905). There was, therefore, a commitment to redistribution through the taxation system; unusual, almost unique, in our history. Its new direct taxes, not the land taxes, were the most important feature of his 1909 People's Budget. He and Churchill, with other colleagues, pressed on with labour exchanges for the labour market, trade boards for 'sweated' trades, a minimum wage for miners and others, and policies for children in relation to health and nutrition.

Above all there was his epoch-making National Insurance Act of 1911, a comprehensive system of health insurance and a preparatory system of unemployment insurance. It aroused controversy. Labour members like Hardie and Lansbury did not endorse its contributory method and called it a poll tax. But it offered a new vision of social policy, indeed of social citizenship, and it was the launch pad of Attlee's welfare state 40 years later. This was a distinguished, if angry and often confused, phase of policy-making. Of course, spin-doctors and media figures were in Downing Street in 1911 as they were in 1997 – Lloyd George, with his close links with editors and journalists in Fleet Street, was the most media-conscious figure of his time. But there were also great intellectuals and planners like Seebohm Rowntree, the Webbs, and William Beveridge, a key man in the agenda for social policy in 1908 as he was to be so memorably in 1945.

There was something else underlying Edwardian Progressivism and Lloyd George's policies: fear of Labour. After all, the Liberals were capitalists, for all their humanity. They were backed by coalowners, shipowners and textile magnates. They feared the long violent strikes of 1910–12 with the use of military and the loss of life in places like Tonypandy and Llanelli. There was an underlying fear of the growth of trade union power anyway, violent or not. This was a great worry for the Labour Party too. Keir Hardie himself, always on the left, urged that they should use the state, not destroy it. Even so, accommodating Labour, through protecting the unions' political levy, the payment of MPs, a miners' minimum wage, and other measures, was a continuing priority for the Liberal government. Lloyd George declared that if they did not continue to promote an advanced social programme, they would play into the hands of the socialists of the ILP.

At any rate, there was plenty of energy within the government down to the late spring of 1914. Lloyd George's 1914 budget, with its rating of site values and higher direct taxes, was the most radical and redistributive of the lot. It ran into severe procedural difficulties in the Commons, which dented his reputation as a minister, but it still emerged as a bold, redistributive measure that focussed on the unearned income and the residual estates of the rich, idle and otherwise. He continued to work with radicals like Masterman, C.R. Buxton and C.P. Scott, editor of the *Manchester Guardian*. Seebohm Rowntree was his great intellectual policy adviser. An important political ally was Dr. Christopher Addison, a famous university medical professor in earlier life, along with Addison's fellow East End MP, William Wedgwood Benn, father of Tony Benn of course. Both later joined the Labour Party. If one considers Isaac Foot alongside Wedgwood Benn, it may indeed be seen how the modern Labour left was literally the child of Edwardian Progressivism. With Addison, Lloyd George worked on areas left out in earlier social reform measures – education including technical education, housing reform, the rural poor, and extending health centres in a way that might have anticipated Nye Bevan's National Health Service (NHS). He told Addison they should dream dreams, though base them on existing realities. The government's ninth year in power was one of its most creative.

George Dangerfield's famous book *The Strange Death of Liberal England* has seen this government fundamentally doomed. Certainly it was brought to a shuddering halt by the advent of war. Dangerfield, however, highlights domestic issues – the campaign of the suffragettes for votes for women, the great labour 'unrest', the crisis over Ireland. His book is brilliantly written and highly entertaining. But very few historians pay much heed to its argument now. The suffragettes were surely declining in political impact in 1914 through their own divisions, even if things would change fundamentally later on. The industrial relations troubles seemed even more a problem for the Labour Party, committed as it was to constitutionalism, and were anyhow petering out in 1914. Irish home rule was undoubtedly intractable, perhaps insoluble, an abiding commitment for Lloyd George thereafter, until he achieved the longest-lasting settlement there in the Irish Free State treaty worked out with Sinn Fein in December 1921.

In the long-term, in my view, Edwardian Liberalism was likely to decline. The electorate was going to expand, bringing many more poor voters on to the register along with all women, and this might well have disadvantaged the Liberals fatally. They were already struggling politically. Their tally of seats had fallen from 401 to 272 by the end of 1910 and by elections had reduced it further since then. No one much suggested PR then – usually the demand of losing parties. There were serious losses to the Conservatives or Ratepayers in local government such as the serious loss of the London County Council to the Progressives in 1907. Arguments for traditional free trade would be harder to sustain as the economy changed and relied less on exporting staple industries like coal, textiles and shipbuilding. The political left increasingly linked free trade not with cheap food or consumer citizenship, but with an ever more cartelized capitalism. Nonconformity, even to a degree in Wales, was now something of a fading force, with chapel membership beginning to decline. More generally, Liberals, champions of the free market, could not ultimately accommodate the politics of class.

But these things hadn't happened yet. The Tories under Bonar Law might have been favourites to win a 1915 general election, but they still had their troubles over food taxes and Irish home rule. The Liberals' electoral pact with Labour was still in being and there were even suggestions that Ramsay MacDonald might enter a Liberal government. There was still a mood of prosperity and peace. The economy looked robust with 1913 a particularly strong year for coal and record exports from Cardiff and Newcastle. There had been no war. The 1906 Liberal government had not invaded other countries. Lloyd George was still their greatest asset, still dominating political life. At the Mansion House on 17 July 1914, two and a half weeks after the assassination at Sarajevo, he spoke of the world scene with guarded optimism, 'the sky has never seemed more relatively blue'. Eighteen days later, Britain engaged in a world war, following the invasion of Belgium. Progressive Liberal England suddenly collapsed for ever. The Liberals were to be a supreme casualty of total war. No longer would they be a party of power. It would never be glad, confident morning again.

Chapter 6

Lloyd George and Germany

David Lloyd George has long been recognised as the most puzzling and paradoxical of modern British politicians. He has been typecast forever in Maynard Keynes's sardonic 'Essay in biography: 'Who shall paint the chameleon, who can tether a broomstick?'.[1] Whatever the many limitations of Keynes's diagnosis, the contradictions of Lloyd George's career in domestic British politics, during which the radical partisan of one period became the architect of coalitions with the Conservative enemy of another, are abundantly clear.

But this volatility is no less marked in Lloyd George's perceptions and policies in foreign affairs, for instance in how the 'little England' opponent of the Boer War became the all-powerful leader in an imperial war. Throughout his career, his concern with Germany was clearly a dominant and abiding interest, from the first decade of the twentieth century to the coming of the Second World War. Here, again, apparently wild variations are to be seen. The tough-talking nationalist of the Mansion House speech in 1911 is also the champion of Anglo-German rapprochement shortly afterwards. The belligerent wartime premier who advocated a 'knock-out blow' and 'a fight to the finish' in 1916–18 was later to advocate the appeasement of Hitler. Yet there is also some consistency in Lloyd George's views of Germany, one underscored by his two crucially significant visits to Germany in 1908 and then in 1936, which provide in some ways the parameters of his career. They are vital both to our understanding of Anglo-German relations in the present century, and to our appreciation of Lloyd George as a political animal, and I propose to examine them here.

In his early years as a politician, from his entry into parliament as member for Caernarfon Boroughs in April 1890 to the South African War of 1899–1902, Lloyd George was largely concerned with domestic issues – with land, church schools and temperance, the rights of nonconformists, and the national claims of Wales. So far as he expressed any particular views on foreign affairs down to 1900, they were in general sympathy with France, the cradle of popular revolution in 1789. Lloyd George's early radical sympathies were stirred by readings of Hugo's *Les Misérables*. He appeared to adopt a moderate stance towards France during the Anglo-French crisis over Fashoda in 1898, and he warmly upheld the 'Entente Cordiale' of 1904.

Yet in many ways, it was with Germany rather than with France that his sympathies lay. His view of Germany was in general a positive one, of a modernising, enterprising and above all protestant Germany. For the young Lloyd George, Germany was revered as the home of Martin Luther who had fought for spiritual freedom during the Reformation. To Welsh chapel-goers, Luther was almost an honorary Celt; '*ein feste burg*' was an alternative national anthem. The oratorios or other choral works of Bach, Handel, Beethoven, or Mendelssohn were grist to the mill of Welsh singing festivals, the *cymanfa ganu,* or the cultural *eisteddfodau* in which Victorian Wales delighted. It is worth noting that British Liberal intellectuals, including historians like E.A. Freeman, saw Germany as embodying not Prussian centralism, but a diffuse, pluralist structure which preserved local autonomy and legal initiative. Lloyd George's parliamentary and other speeches tended to be sprinkled with favourable references to German society. This particularly applied to the German education system, unsectarian, comprehensive, geared to the inculcation of technical and practical skills. No less than other Liberals, Lloyd George admired the omnipresent talents of the 'Prussian schoolmaster' and regarded them as the basis of German development in the later nineteenth century, in peace and in war.

In his pronouncements on foreign affairs, the young Lloyd George at various times championed an Anglo-German rapprochement, for instance in the later 1890s as advocated by Joseph Chamberlain, his youthful political hero. This also created something of a bond between the anti-imperialist Lloyd George and Lord Rosebery, the aristocratic advocate of 'national efficiency', to a degree historians have sometimes neglected. For all his professed Celtic outlook, his enthusiasm for the mercurial style and vivacious temperament of French men (not to mention French women), Lloyd George was really a northern European by instinct, an adopted Anglo-Saxon almost, for whom Germany as it emerged from its unification in 1871 was a kind of role model.

In this as in many other respects, the decisive phase for Lloyd George was his time as president of the board of trade, from December 1905 to April 1908, his first cabinet office. He developed at this period new links with commerce and business, and also a special relationship with the trade unions. He became deeply impressed by the abundant evidence of German industrial training and efficiency, combined nevertheless with a comprehensive system of social reform on the Bismarckian pattern. One important source of information for him during this period was the authoritative and prolific author on German welfare, industrial legislation and local government, William Harbutt Dawson, a senior board of trade staff officer.[2] It is worth noting also that, as president of the board of trade, Lloyd George was a good deal less antagonistic to German trade protectionism than were other Liberals. Indeed, his Merchant Shipping and Patents Acts startled orthodox free traders for the ground they appeared to give to tariff reform, the hated creed of the Unionist enemy.

An immense impact was made upon Lloyd George by his first significant visit to Germany in August 1908, shortly after he succeeded Asquith (now prime minister) as chancellor of the exchequer. It is a visit for which remarkably little direct evidence survives, though there is an informative account in the autobiographical volume, *The Fire of Life* by the Liberal journalist Harold Spender of the famous newspaper family.[3] Lloyd George travelled to Germany in the company both of Spender and the Liberal MP Sir Charles Henry (who loaned his car and possibly wife, Julia, who may have been the chancellor's mistress). The use of the newish invention of the motor car made their journey throughout Germany more comprehensive. As chancellor, Lloyd George was already working on schemes to make the treasury the agent of a new far-reaching programme of social welfare. In Germany, he sought to crystallise his views with first-hand investigation of Bismarckian schemes for social insurance, especially invalidity pensions, broadening into health education and taking in en route German labour exchanges created to cope with the problem of unemployment. He began in Bavaria at Nuremburg, went briefly into Austria, and took the spa waters at Carlsbad, travelled up through the southwest via Stuttgart, Carlsruhe and Frankfurt, ending up in Hamburg, Bremen and the North Sea Coast. In Hamburg, the chancellor was much impressed by the seafaring connections with Britain treasured by the mercantile community there, dating from the days of the Hanseatic League.

To Lloyd George, modern Germany embodied the virtues of industrial efficiency and social cohesion. He agreed with Liberal Imperialists such as Rosebery, Grey and (especially) that Hegelian enthusiast Haldane ('old Schopenhauer') in seeing it as the epitome of the ideals of National Efficiency. He noted how universal compulsion in the system of contributory health insurance did not undermine voluntary initiative through private firms and individuals.[4] This point was reinforced by W.J. Braithwaite, an official sent by Lloyd George to investigate further German insurance policies in 1911. It is notable that Germany aroused similar enthusiasm in Theodore Roosevelt (president of the United States, 1901–9) whose Bismarckian programme of economic corporatism, regulation and social welfare in the New Nationalism of 1912 Lloyd George found almost irresistibly attractive.[5] Indeed, it was the kind of policy that Lloyd George himself championed in his proposal for a national coalition in the autumn of 1910, based on social reform and strong national defences. Theodore

Roosevelt was always very much one of Lloyd George's heroes, a kind of democratic Bismarck; Roosevelt's death during the Paris peace conference in 1919 (including the marked failure of Woodrow Wilson to show any grief at the passing of his old adversary) made a marked impression on Lloyd George.[6]

In time, his National Insurance Bill of 1911 was to demonstrate the impact of German welfare schemes upon Lloyd George's thinking. In introducing this measure, the chancellor of the exchequer praised such aspects as the public lectures provided in Germany to instruct the public on health and welfare. Conversely, he was also to use references to the German system when introducing his bill to show that British 'ninepence for fourpence' was a better and more generous option than its Teutonic equivalent.[7]

This notable visit to Germany in August 1908 also brought Lloyd George into the serious consideration of foreign policy for the first time in his career. He had had discussions with Metternich, the German ambassador, in July 1908, prior to his departure for Germany, during which Lloyd George proclaimed the dangers of Anglo-German naval rivalry and the need for better relations.[8] During his visit to Germany subsequently, he gave a number of major press interviews, notably one given at Carlsbad to *Neue Freie Presse* of Vienna, in which he called for Anglo-German concord and naval disarmament. He hoped to meet the German chancellor, von Bulow, but had to settle for a vice-chancellor, Bethmann Hollweg, who he met in Berlin. Here, however, he encountered the other face of imperial Germany – the aggressive, intransigent outlook of the Prussian junkers and the military caste. Bethmann Hollweg's command of English and his son being a Rhodes Scholar at Oxford counted for little. The obstacles confronting Anglo-German accord were starkly demonstrated.[9] The dualism between this autocratic bent, and the 'real Germany' of business enterprise and freedom was to preoccupy Lloyd George from this time on.

In his somewhat fraught talks with Bethmann Hollweg, Lloyd George took a firm line in defence of British national security. Indeed, he was to build on this subsequently as a member of the Committee of Imperial Defence. He was well aware of British naval preparations and the military accord with the French, though he was to criticise the secrecy that surrounded it in his memoirs. He was often prepared to talk toughly towards the Germans in defending British national interests in areas such as Morocco and the Near East, for instance his apparently belligerent speech at the Mansion House in July 1911 during the Agadir crisis. A.J.P. Taylor's quixotic attempt to argue that this anti-German speech was really designed to threaten the French instead does not find much favour from historians.[10]

At the same time, Lloyd George continued his efforts to promote better relations with Germany and to end the naval arms race. He clashed with two First Lords, Reginald McKenna and then his old ally, Winston Churchill, over expanded naval estimates in first 1909 and then January 1914. He tried in vain to slow down the Dreadnought construction programme. He sought to get beyond the abrasive junker mentality to reach the Germany of enterprise, municipal reform and efficiency, Britain's natural trading partner. Even in the early summer of 1914 he was pursuing the dream of Anglo-German accord, the assassination at Sarajevo notwithstanding. In his Mansion House speech as late as 17 July 1914, he declared, with reference to Anglo-German relations, that 'the sky has never seemed more relatively blue'.[11] This was less than three weeks before the First World War broke out. Certainly in his exploration of the central issues in domestic and world affairs down to 1914, Anglo-German relations were a dominant theme.

Lloyd George's view of Germany and the Germans during the First World War appears to be relatively straightforward. After a period of initial uncertainty following the invasion of Belgium, he launched a fierce onslaught on the Germans in a major speech to London Welshmen at the Queen's Hall on 19 September 1914. He was highly aggressive in his references to the German spirit of militarism. Germany was 'the road hog of Europe' he proclaimed. The German invasion of Belgium had made it a war for liberal values, to defend small nations ('the little five-foot-five nations') such as Belgium, Serbia, Montenegro, and by inference Wales. Hitherto pacific Welsh intellectuals like Owen M. Edwards and John Morris-Jones were to follow his lead.[12] Subsequently as minister for munitions, then as secretary for war in succession to Kitchener, finally after December 1916 as prime minister, Lloyd George was the unremitting champion of a 'knock-out blow' and 'a fight to a finish'.[13] He had advocated military conscription as early as August 1915. He replaced Asquith at 10 Downing Street as the uncompromising voice of total war. Right down to the very end of the war, he maintained this belligerent stance, for instance in brushing aside the peace cry embodied in Lord Lansdowne's famous letter of 1917 or the quasi-pacifist calls from Liberal and Labour members. In the 'coupon election' of December 1918, he made several aggressive declarations towards Germany. He called for Germany to pay for the 'uttermost cost of the war' and for the Kaiser to be tried as a war criminal.

But Lloyd George's position was more complicated than that. Some crucial wartime speeches drew an important distinction between the German people and their military and political leaders. Lloyd George did not go in for the kind of unthinking, blanket anti-Germanism manifested by ministers like Hugh Dalton or Foreign Office officials like Vansittart during the Second World War. Lloyd George's important speech at Bangor in February 1915, in which he used the proposed nationalisation of the drink trade as the launch-pad for a wider programme for the mobilisation of national resources, contained some instructive passages. He drew a distinction between 'the best Germany, the Germany of sweet songs and inspiring, noble thought, the Germany of a virile philosophy that helped to break the shackles of superstition in Europe', the humane land of Kant, Schiller and Goethe, and 'a Germany that talked through the raucous voice of Krupps's artillery, a Germany that harnessed science to the chariot of destruction and death'. Against the latter, he proposed to wage 'a holy war'.[14] But the former humane, liberal Germany was never forgotten either.

In the later stages of the war, especially after the publication of Woodrow Wilson's *Fourteen Points*, Lloyd George also began to talk in terms of the kind of long-term settlement appropriate for Germany after the war. He spoke to journalists and the leaders of the trades union congress of the need to confirm Germany's status as a great power, and to ensure that it harboured no enduring sense of national grievance. In fact, Keynes's account, in *The Economic Consequences of the Peace,* of Lloyd George's stance during the 1918 general election is fundamentally distorted.[15] In general, Lloyd George did not spend much time in the campaign advocating a punitive, Carthaginian peace. He spoke largely on themes of domestic reconstruction, including references to a 'land fit for heroes' that were to haunt him during the economic recession and social cutbacks of 1920–2. There was one, highly damaging speech at the Colston Hall, Bristol, on 11 December 1918 when Lloyd George departed from a carefully written script and played to the gallery with a virulent attack on Germany and the need to ensure that it paid the cost of the war 'to the limit of its capacity'. Apart from this discreditable episode, Lloyd George in general dwelt in his speeches on the need for a peace of reconstruction that would promote international territorial security and above all the restoration of commercial and industrial relations between the major enterprising nations of the world.

During the peace conference in Paris in 1919, Lloyd George fought, consistently in the main, for moderation and magnanimity towards the defeated Germans. In time, even Keynes, always emotionally pro-German as is shown by his affectionate references to the German delegate, Dr. Carl Melchior, in his conference memoirs'[16] came to see this essential feature of Lloyd George's position. Indeed, Keynes's later book, *A Revision of the Treaty* (1922), is distinctly more balanced in its view of Lloyd George than in *The Economic Consequences,* written in white heat after Keynes's angry resignation from the peace conference delegation in the summer of 1919. The peace conferences were all, of course, immense media events, buffeted by conflicting political pressures and nationalistic hysteria. Lloyd George himself responded to them and was guilty of many reversals of policy. But a moderate approach towards Germany was a generally consistent theme. His view was reinforced by other leading members of the government, notably the humane minister of education, the historian, H.A.L. Fisher, a significant influence on foreign policy at this time;[17] General Jan Smuts, the South African pivot of the imperial delegation and men like Philip Kerr and Lionel Curtis in the prime minister's secretariat, the so-called Garden Suburb.

One consequence was the famous memorandum drawn up in the meetings in the forest of Fontainebleau between 21 and 25 March 1919. It followed private sessions involving Lloyd George and some close advisers, unhappy at the turn the peace negotiations were taking under the pressure of French demands for revenge: Smuts was prominent amongst these colleagues. In the memorandum, the main themes of reconstruction and of later appeasement (in the best and most constructive sense) were spelt out. First, following Fisher's view, it was urged that it was important that German-speaking peoples in Memel, Danzig, the Polish corridor, the Sudetenland, Upper Silesia and the Saarland were pot permanently placed under alien rule. There should be no 'German Alsace-Lorraines'. Secondly, it was vital to ensure that any reparations imposed upon Germany, whether in money or materials, were rational and limited, and not calculated to undermine Germany as a manufacturing and trading nation. The sums currently specified were far more than Germany was capable of paying. In the hothouse atmosphere of the conference, Lloyd George appeared to go along with the fashionable figure of £6 billion in reparations (Keynes urged that £2 billion was 'a safe maximum figure' for Germany's capacity to pay – itself a vast figure in all conscience).[18] However, the British prime minister also pursued the tactic of pushing the precise assessment of the reparation claim on to a technical Reparations Commission. It would enjoy real authority in quantifying German assets and liabilities, by contrast with the electioneering committee headed by the banker, Lord Cunliffe, in 1918–19. The effect of its prolonged deliberations, Lloyd George hoped and believed, would be that the bulk of the money would never be paid.

Certainly, Lloyd George was prepared to follow Wilson and Clemenceau in indulging in symbols of national retribution in the Versailles treaty. Thus, he insisted on the treaty's retention of the war guilt clause. But he combined it with practical moderation. He remained the champion of the ethos of the Fontainebleau memorandum, though there is substance in French complaints that Lloyd George was the advocate of moderation only when the national security needs of France were concerned. In areas involving British national security (such as the freedom of the seas issue or German colonies), Lloyd George's zeal was much less apparent. The outcome was, however, that there were frequent conflicts at Paris between the pragmatism of Lloyd George and the intransigence of Clemenceau (the moralism of Woodrow Wilson often being enlisted on the side of the latter).

Eventually, Lloyd George was able to register several major successes. He was able to deflect discussions of reparations (article 232 of the Treaty) to the long drawn-out calculations of the commission. He gained significant compromises on Danzig and the future of the Saar. The plebiscite in Upper Silesia in November 1921 was very much Lloyd George's achievement. It was to result in that territory voting strongly for absorption in Germany rather than Poland; in August 1922 the League partitioned it, very much in Germany's favour. He warned, with less effect, on the dangers inherent in the creation of the new unstable hybrid state of Czechoslovakia, which not only placed three million Sudetendeutsch under Czech rule but also yoked together the mutually hostile populations of the mittel-Europa Czechs and the essentially eastern Slovaks (a prescient view to be confirmed eventually by their agreed political separation in 1992). As always, Lloyd George strove to get beyond the rigid posturing of German delegates such as Brockdorff-Rantzau at Versailles to reach the 'real' Germany emerging from the overthrow of the Hohenzollern dynasty and the militaristic legacy of Prussianism.

By 1921–2, Lloyd George, the sole peace-maker of the 'big three' still in power, seemed much nearer to attaining objectives of the Fontainebleau memorandum. Russia was now on the way to returning to the comity of nations. Allied troops were withdrawn and an Anglo-Soviet trade treaty was actually negotiated in 1921. Naval disarmament had been achieved with remarkable effect at the Washington naval conference. Germany reparations were scaled down at San Remo (April 1920) from the fantastic levels of the £24 billion proposed by the Cunliffe committee in 1919, a 'wild and fantastic chimera' as Lloyd George was to write in his memoirs.[19] At Boulogne in May 1921, Lloyd George and Millerand, the new French premier, seemed to have agreed instead on a new level of £4,500 million spread over 35 years. French troops were persuaded to withdraw from some Ruhr towns they had occupied, while at Spa in July modified inter-allied percentages on German post-war indemnities were apparently agreed, despite fierce clashes with the new German chancellor, Hugo Stinnes.[20] To achieve a balanced policy, at his meeting with the French premier, Aristide Briand, at Cannes in January 1922 Lloyd George appeared also to make the historic proposal of a British continental guarantee of France's eastern frontiers against a future putative German threat. Even though a disastrous game of golf on the Cannes links led to a parliamentary crisis in the French National Assembly in Paris which saw Briand fall from power, Lloyd George had reasonable hopes still of a diplomatic settlement at the international conference called for Genoa in April 1922, which would deal with Germany's grievances over reparations and frontier settlements. It would also enable Lloyd George himself to go before the British electorate later in 1922, not as a domestic failure but as the great international peace-maker who had brought stability to a ravaged post-war world.

In the end, Lloyd George's dreams evaporated. On the eve of the Genoa conference, Walter Rathenau, the business-orientated German-Jewish chancellor whom Lloyd George personally admired as a man of action, quite unexpectedly concluded the private international agreement at Rapallo with the Soviet Union. This doomed Genoa from the start. Raymond Poincaré, the right-wing Lorrainer who now headed the French government, was obdurately anti-German; Walter Rathenau was shortly to be assassinated. Genoa led nowhere. Lloyd George himself fell from power in October after his backing of the Greeks against the Turks in the Chanak crisis almost led to war in Asia Minor. But in fact, the common view of Lloyd George at the time of his downfall that he was an aggressive figure in international affairs was largely false. In particular, towards Germany he had pursued since 1918 a four-year policy of sustained, though not uncritical, appeasement.

Throughout the 1920s, Lloyd George continued to urge the modification of the peace terms. On this, as on domestic economic policy, he and Keynes now made common cause. Lloyd George strongly condemned the French invasion of the Ruhr in 1923. He was sympathetic to the moderate policies pursued at the time of Locarno and afterwards by Gustav Stresemann. Some of Lloyd George's leading associates were even more notably pro-German. This was especially true of a survivor of the Garden Suburb years like Philip Kerr, an intense admirer of Germany and of 'Anglo-Saxon' accord, and also of Lionel Curtis. The Cabinet's deputy-secretary, Thomas Jones, a Welsh *habitué* of Lloyd George, was another influence along these lines, and a future pivot of the alleged 'Cliveden' set hovering around Lord and Lady Astor. Lloyd George's book, *The Truth about Reparations and War Debts* (1932), repeated earlier appeals for leniency. The effect was that he took a more charitable view of German foreign policy postures than Churchill did, even after Hitler came to power in January 1933. Lloyd George uttered only mild criticism of the German occupation of the Rhineland in March

1936. Rather than condemn an open breach of the Treaty of Versailles, he claimed it was the result rather of years of failure by successive British governments to promote disarmament and to make the League of Nations effective.[21]

More generally, he repeatedly condemned the failure to revise the peace treaties of 1919–23. Much of the impact of this theme on popular consciousness at this time came through his widely publicised memoirs. His *War Memoirs* naturally depict the strong, though never vindictive, national leader, the man who won the war. In some ways, however, his other, lesser-regarded, two-volume work is more relevant here. *The Truth about the Peace Treaties* (1938) examines, in a somewhat rambling fashion, longer-term aspects of economic reconstruction and lost political opportunities. One notable passage is a fierce personal attack on Eduard Benes, the president of Czechoslovakia who had engaged in wilful misrepresentation, in Lloyd George's view, during discussions about the future status (and, indeed, the numbers) of the Germans in the Sudetenland.[22] As noted above, Benes was felt to be no less untrustworthy over Czech intentions towards the Slovaks: as a Welshman, Lloyd George was particularly sensitive towards issues of linguistic and cultural diversity. Here again, the effect was to produce an argument for understanding and accommodation towards Germany, in many ways presented as the victim of the peace of which Lloyd George was a major architect.

The climax of Lloyd George's German odyssey came with his historic visit to Hitler at Berchtesgaden in September 1936. His companions were his son, Gwilym, his daughter, Megan (a reluctant visitor of Hitler's), the ever-present Thomas Jones, Lord Dawson of Penn, and two younger Welshmen, Ben Bowen Thomas (warden of Coleg Harlech, an adult education college), and Emrys Pride (a junior civil servant). It was, therefore, a highly selective and national grouping. The visit was arranged through the mediation of the somewhat mysterious figure of Thomas P. Conwell-Evans, an ardently Germanophile Welsh academic who had lectured in German universities and who acted as Lloyd George's translator. The background to the visit was the disappointment of Lloyd George at the failure of MacDonald and Baldwin's National Government to adopt his programmes for economic recovery through Keynesian-style government intervention and a public works programme, together with the virtual eclipse of Lloyd George's Liberals at the 1935 general election. At the same time, Lloyd George's dismay at his inability to influence domestic British politics under their current mediocre leadership was reinforced by longer-term alarm at the failure to reach an adjustment of Germany's legitimate national grievances. In many ways, then, the visits to Germany in 1908 and in 1936 followed similar premises.

In 1908, he had failed to meet Chancellor Bulow. This time, Lloyd George successfully aimed at the top. He visited Hitler in his 'Eagle's Nest' at Berchtesgaden and had lengthy and highly cordial conversations with him and with Ribbentrop on 4–5 September. A dictator's wish for international legitimacy chimed in with an old man's desire for influence or perhaps simple vanity. Lloyd George also investigated aspects of the German economic scene, mainly in Bavaria: public works and road building, agricultural improvements, and hospital services. He even met some German Baptists whom the diligent Conwell-Evans had assembled. He returned to Britain in a mood of virtual euphoria. Hitler, he proclaimed to the world was a remarkable leader, a very great man. Lloyd George's old weakness for dominant individuals throughout history, Caesar, Cromwell, Napoleon above all, now vented itself in a near hero-worship of Hitler. An ecstatic interview with A.J. Cummings in the *News Chronicle* was followed by an extraordinary effusion in Beaverbrook's Daily *Express*.[23] Lloyd George wrote here of the new spirit of 'gaiety and cheerfulness' manifest among the people of Germany. He played down both Germany's aggressive intent and its propaganda against the Jewish community. Oddly enough, he said virtually nothing about Schacht's economic and fiscal policies, or the public works programme in Bavaria. For Hitler himself as a leader, Lloyd George's admiration knew no bounds. He was truly, Lloyd George wrote in a phrase destined to haunt him in later years, 'the George Washington of Germany'. It was an astonishing declaration, surpassing even the effusions of right-wing fellow-travellers such as Lord Rothermere. It marked perhaps the rhetorical climax of inter-war appeasement.

At this time, Germany had rearmed and was making evident threats towards territories on its eastern and southern boundaries. But Lloyd George was far more disturbed by Mussolini's attack on 'gallant little Abyssinia' and the League's impotence in dealing with it, and by the assault on republican, democratic Spain by Franco's right-wing, clerical forces. In March 1937 Lloyd George was again calling for a definite lead from Britain to achieve an Anglo-German entente and a security treaty of guarantee. By this time, even Germanophiles like Kerr and Conwell-Evans were warning all about the menacing attitude of Hitler's regime towards the British Empire. When the Sudeten crisis became critical in the summer of 1938, Lloyd George's line was rather to emphasise the feebleness and untrustworthiness of Czechoslovakia (not forgetting the sins of 'that little swine Benes') rather than German aggression.[24] He kept away from the Commons debate when Chamberlain returned from Munich. Only after that did he finally turn against Germany whom he saw as newly aggressive with the demolition of the Munich agreement by its invasion and dismemberment of Czechoslovakia.

Lloyd George now called for an alliance with Russia. He held discussions with the Soviet ambassador, Ivan Maisky, on the need for a guarantee to Poland by Britain and France, in the event of German attack. He derided Chamberlainite diplomacy as consisting of a feeble surrender towards Hitler, and was constrained to admit that Germany was now the main threat to peace. Yet, even after the outbreak of war in September, he would talk in private about the need for peace with Germany and he continued to do so during the 'phoney war' period. His interview with Sumner Welles, the American under-secretary of state, in March 1940, vigorously focussed on the failures of the allies in handling Germany over the past twenty years, and their refusal to revise the peace treaties to remove legitimate German grievances. 'If the German people were thus granted the recognition of their racial unity and of their economic security, such problems as disarmament, a possible European regional federation and colonies would automatically settle themselves.' What was the key to the problem was the need to convince the German people that they had an equality of opportunity with the other great nations, that justice had been done to them and that they could look forward 'with confident hope' to the future. The policy of Great Britain and of France during the past years had achieved exactly the reverse.[25] He totally ignored Hitler's persecution of the Jews.

His general view was that it was unnatural that Britain should be at war with a great nation under a formidable leader, which had overthrown its junker, Hohenzollern past. 'Do not believe them when they tell you that the British people want this war. I know them and I know they do not'. Lloyd George subsequently took a key part in the Commons debate on 7–8 May 1940, which saw the overthrow of Neville Chamberlain. But he remained in a disgruntled critical mood, and turned down Churchill's offer of serving as ambassador to Washington, in succession to Lord Lothian, his old ally, This was probably to the relief of President Roosevelt who had feared that Lloyd George 'might play into the hands of the appeasers'.[26] Philip Kerr. Along with associates like the military writer, Liddell Hart, and Sir Edward Grigg, his former private secretary, he continued to explore the prospects for a negotiated peace, while pursuing the war vigorously at sea and in the air in the short term. It was not surprising that, after a particularly defeatist speech in the House by the 78-year-old former premier in 1941, Churchill should compare his performance with those of papa Pétain in the Reynaud Cabinet in France a year earlier. Lloyd George kept in touch with such disaffected groups of critics as the Peace Aims Group headed by men like Richard Stokes. One of his last political pronouncements in 1944 was to condemn the policy of 'unconditional surrender' which he had himself championed in 1917.

In general Lloyd George's views on foreign affairs, while always creative and dialectically powerful, were erratic. Over the role and effectiveness of the League of Nations he was ambivalent. His attitude towards France showed many permutations from the Fashoda crisis in 1898 to the downfall of the Third Republic in June 1940. His views of the United States, a country which he visited only in 1923 when he was no longer in office, were also fluctuating. He gave little credence to the sentimental notion of a 'special relationship': admiration for both Roosevelts was countered by painful recollections of the academic moralism of Woodrow Wilson. His views also showed considerable shifts and turns on imperial questions. The champion of Boer self-determination in 1900, the critic of Amritsar in 1919, became the almost diehard critic of the Government of India bill in 1934.[27] He was no obvious enthusiast for colonial nationalism: like his contemporaries, he used freely the term 'niggers'. Similarly, in celebrating Abraham Lincoln's urge for a conciliatory peace after the American Civil War, he showed no sympathy for the radical Republicans anxious for racial equality for the former slaves, and displayed a kind of moral equivalence towards North and South on the racial issue.

In relation to Germany, by contrast, his views were generally more consistent. He was a long-term advocate of detente and harmony, even in wartime. He saw it as a natural ally for the United Kingdom, sharing a broad affinity with it as a trading industrial nation with a world outlook. Its corporate planning in government and in industry embodied powerful aspects of 'national efficiency'. Its territorial ambitions were finite and negotiable. But his analysis collided with the realities of power, and in the end he failed.

Elsewhere in his career, Lloyd George had a dazzling record of achievement. Far more than Churchill, an imperialist wedded to the class system and to outmoded notions of national greatness, he modernised and revitalised his country. He extended political democracy for working men and all women, he pioneered progressive concepts of social reform, he successfully patronised both business and organised labour, he brought a meed of political equality to Wales and almost fifty years of peace to Ireland. Many believed he was 'the man who won the war', perhaps more as minister of munitions in 1915–16 than as prime minister. He was an executive leader of genius. But for Lloyd George, as for the rest of his countrymen, a settled relationship with Germany remained an aspiration unfulfilled. Memories of his (and their) failure continued to plague British views of their national and European destiny, fifty years on.

Chapter 7

The Goat and the Tiger:
Lloyd George and Clemenceau

David Lloyd George and Georges Clemenceau, leaders of their countries in the First World War, are the supreme symbols of the Entente Cordiale in its most momentous phase. Both were imperishably portrayed in Keynes's hostile vignettes during the Paris peace conference in 1919. Both were highly image-conscious. Lloyd George was silkily loquacious (though also an excellent listener), instantly recognisable with his long mane of hair, his Inverness cloak and his almost feminine pride in his feet. Clemenceau, at least in Keynes's version, was brusque, usually almost silent, insensitive to his colleagues and his surroundings, equally identifiable with his cape, his cane, his black leather boots with a buckle at the front, and always wore grey suede gloves to hide his eczema.

Their styles as politicians were utterly different. Lloyd George, in personal conversation, was subtle and beguiling, for men and women alike, a man who 'could charm a bird off a bough'. Keynes's 'Essay in biography' saw him as 'a femme fatale'. Clemenceau was aggressive and confrontational, in parliamentary debate and the world outside, famous for his skill in duels with pistol and sword. This took a dramatic form in a sabre duel with the otherwise obscure Paul Deschanel, who, understandably, kept up a permanent retreat until Clemenceau gave up, observing contemptuously *J'avance, il recule*. No magnanimity in victory here. Keynes condemned both prime ministers with equal vigour. Lloyd George had become at Paris the tool of the chauvinists who won the 1918 'coupon election', the 'hard-faced men who looked as if they had done very well out of the war', in Baldwin's famous phrase. In Keynes's famous description, he was a man 'rooted in nothing', 'a vampire and a medium in one'. Clemenceau, the most intellectually eminent of the Council of Four (including Woodrow Wilson and Orlando, the Italian premier, as well), was in Keynes's view rooted in ancient enmities and hatreds, permanently fighting Europe's ancient civil wars.

Arguably, Keynes seriously misjudged both. His view of Lloyd George as devoid of principle or consistency was a travesty; his account of Clemenceau's wilful and negative nationalism was exaggerated. At any rate, throughout the two climactic years 1918 and 1919, the relationships between these two men (Clemenceau being born in 1841, 22 years before his Welsh colleague) were crucial to the world. Each was hailed, for a brief period as, 'the man who won the war'; the world that emerged after Versailles was really their world. Indeed, in their emphasis on ethnic nationality, it is, in Europe at least, even more their world today.

They had met only once before 1914, through the agency of the Irish Nationalist MP, T.P. O'Connor, at the German spa town of Carlsbad in 1910, when Clemenceau was an ex-premier and Lloyd George at the Treasury. They offered very different recollections of it. Clemenceau believed that their conversation was very brief, and was notable only for showing Lloyd George's immense ignorance of international affairs. Lloyd George thought it had lasted much longer, and that Clemenceau rebutted at some length his own views which favoured an Anglo-German rapprochement, especially on naval matters. He had in 1908 made a notable visit to Germany to investigate its social welfare programmes, and had spoken to the press in favour of closer Anglo-German relations. Both agreed at least that the meeting was not a success.

Both were maverick politicians, both natural outsiders. Lloyd George, Welshman, Baptist, man of the people, at least operated within the broad limits of Liberal Party politics until 1916; then his earlier penchant for coalitions, variously demonstrated in Wales in 1904 and in British politics generally in 1910 at the height of the Lords crisis, saw him become head of an all-party coalition, his own Liberals fatally divided. Clemenceau, who had actually been prime minister for three years in 1906–9, remained determinedly out of office during the First World War, until persuaded into the premiership in November 1917. In 1918, it could be said that the leaders of both Britain and France were prime ministers without a party.

Each had much regard for the other's country, free from those traditional animosities dating back to the reign of Louis XIV. Lloyd George grew up as an admirer of the French Revolution and of Napoleon also, an enthusiast for Victor Hugo's *Les Misérables*, an admirer of the French Riviera and especially of Nice, where the Promenade des Anglais offered ample opportunity for female companionship. He had spoken in favour of good relations with republican France even at the time of the Fashoda crisis in the Sudan in 1898, and warmly applauded the conclusion of the Entente in 1904. There was an interesting dualism in his complementary enthusiasm for Germany. The German Empire, industrially thriving, Protestant and the land of Bismarckian social reform, appealed to Lloyd George the New Liberal, the apostle of social welfare. His National Insurance Act of 1911 was heavily shaped by what he had seen in Germany in 1908, and his wider social and economic outlook was influenced by that obsessive Germanophile, W.H. Dawson, who worked for him at the Board of Trade. Germany pushed Lloyd George in the direction of the creed of 'national efficiency'.

France, by contrast, appealed to Lloyd George the Old Liberal-democratic, republican with a unique revolutionary tradition, anti-aristocratic, anti-militarist, anti-clerical. As a child he was excited to hear of the Paris Commune of 1871 (with which Clemenceau had himself been entangled as Mayor of Montmartre). He was particularly stirred by the completion of the disestablishment of the Church in France in late 1905, shortly before a general election in Britain in which Welsh Liberals would campaign for a similar disestablishment of the Church of England in Wales. As time went on, however, especially after his visit to Germany in 1908, this sympathy for France was challenged by his enthusiasm for Bismarckian social reform (a passion he shared with another social radical with whom he enjoyed a mutual admiration, Theodore Roosevelt, the prophet of the progressive New Nationalism in the United States). Germany, not France, was his main overseas inspiration thereafter, arguably for the rest of his life, two world wars notwithstanding.

Clemenceau, unlike Lloyd George, was a serious intellectual and lover of the fine arts, whose close friends included Claude Monet of whom he became a notable patron. He rescued the ageing Monet's career at the end of the war with his support for his great project of mural-sized water landscapes, the *Décoration des Nymphéas*, which was eventually placed in the Orangerie. He devoted part of his retirement to writing a work on the Greek orator Demosthenes. Like Léon Blum and François Mitterrand, he was a genuine intellectual in politics. He actually wrote a novel, *Les Plus Forts,* of which Maurice Barrès derisively observed that all Clemenceau needed to be a good novelist was to find something to say.

Unlike Lloyd George also, he had a serious interest in political ideas. He spent much time in England in the 1860s and acquired a good knowledge of the language: at Paris in 1919 he was the only world leader to understand both languages of the conference. His approach to the Anglo-Saxon world came through its liberal theorists, notably John Stuart Mill. He also became an enthusiast for English versions of Social Darwinism and an admirer of the work of Herbert Spencer and his positivist followers. He also spent some time in America during the civil war – he would recall later his personal reactions to the assassination of Abraham Lincoln in 1865, and married an American woman, though not happily. Later in his career his English political and financial connections were used by political opponents to attack him – in the 1893 elections, he was pursued with ironic cries of 'Aoh, yes!' He became a strong supporter of an Anglo-French alliance, and had vain discussions with the pro-German

Joseph Chamberlain to this end. He strongly supported the Entente in 1904, despite his later breach with its main French architect, the Foreign Minister Théophile Delcassé. While prime minister he tried hard to give military substance to the Entente during the aftermath of the Moroccan crisis, and was dismayed when the British prime minister, Campbell-Bannerman, showed great reluctance to admit that Britain had accepted any continental commitment at all.

For all that, Lloyd George and Clemenceau shared in many ways traditions and common values. Like Lloyd George after 1906, Clemenceau too had been a strong advocate of a positivist liberalism that gave a high priority to social reform. He wrote extensively on poverty and social inequality. He urged that the Third Republic should become a social republic and not narrowly political. While he was never a socialist, his ideas had much influence on socialist leaders like Jean Jaurès and the youthful Léon Blum. It was ironic that in 1906 Clemenceau, a man hitherto regarded as being on the further reaches of the left, became known as a fiercely anti-labour prime minister who used the army to put down strikes by syndicalist trades unionists. Lloyd George, by contrast, made his name not only as a social reformer but also as a patron of labour during his time as president of the Board of Trade in 1905–8 (as in his famous settlement of the national rail dispute in October 1907) and at the Treasury (witness his securing agreement on a miners' national wage in 1912). In December 1916 his good relationship with the TUC was a vital component of his capture of power as prime minister. Even in the class-war atmosphere in 1918–21, he retained close ties with union leaders, and created (in the language of the 1960s) a kind of 'beer and sandwiches' access to No.10 which the TUC later regretted losing in the years of Baldwin and MacDonald.

Both Lloyd George and Clemenceau were supremely skilful and ruthless practitioners of politics. Both made ample use of the newspapers as political weapons. Lloyd George spent time on his relationships not only with journalists but also with friendly editors (A.G. Gardiner and Robert Donald for a time), and also with owners like Lord Riddell and later Lord Beaverbrook. He contemplated buying up *The Times* as a progovernment newspaper when Alfred Harmsworth, Lord Northcliffe, retired to die in 1922, and he subsequently became wealthy through the sale of United Newspapers in 1925. Clemenceau, by contrast, owned his own newspapers, notably *La Justice* in the 1890s and *L'Homme Libre* and *L'Homme Enchaîné* during the First World War, as platforms of a highly personal kind. Both leaders also were singly unfussy in the kind of allies they enlisted. Each was casual in money matters. Clemenceau's career almost ended when he was tainted by the Panama bonds and bribes scandal in 1892–3; Lloyd George was close to political obliteration during the Marconi affair in 1912–13. The Lloyd George fund, accumulated in large measure through the venal sale of titles, became highly controversial after 1918. Each of them had one highly useful and highly dubious ally, the arms manufacturer, Sir Basil Zaharoff, a French citizen of Armenian origin, who used his money to finance Clemenceau's newspaper enterprises in the 1890s and acted as an unofficial intermediary for Lloyd George in Eastern Europe and Asia Minor in 1917–20. He was widely claimed to have been responsible for the immensely pro-Turkish thrust of British politics in the lead-up to the Chanak crisis in October 1922. Some murmured that Zaharoff must have had a hold on both leaders. Certainly another similarity that both Lloyd George and Clemenceau could claim was of having complicated relationships with women. Clemenceau had Mme. Baldensperger, the wife of a Sorbonne professor 40 years his junior, as his *amitié amoureuse* in his last years; Lloyd George had Frances Stevenson as well his wife, Dame Margaret, the two of them taking care of his political needs in Westminster and in Wales. Not for nothing was Lloyd George known as 'The Goat'. As for Clemenceau, 'The Tiger', we need only recall James Agate's perhaps apocryphal story of Clemenceau's remark when he spotted a pretty girl on his eightieth birthday, 'Oh, to be seventy again.'

On balance, there was more than enough similarity of outlook, ideology and style, between Clemenceau the intellectual and Lloyd George the intuitive Celt to make for a good working relationship between the two during the war years and later. They were both socially minded, radical Liberals, strongly devoted to the Revolution and champions of Dreyfus in recent times. Both combined a vivid regard for their own national interests with enthusiasm for the Entente as each understood the idea. There is a touching scene recorded during a lull at the Paris peace negotiations when both Lloyd George and Clemenceau (with Woodrow Wilson joining it) recorded their deep devotion to the values and achievement of Abraham Lincoln. In Lloyd George's case (and he was later to deliver a powerful address on Lincoln at Springfield, Illinois, in a lecture tour in 1923) he was, after all, the nearest that Europe could offer as a cottage-bred man who advanced from log cabin to president, or, in the title of an early admiring biographer, trod the primrose path 'from Village Green to Downing Street'.

Lloyd George and Clemenceau, of course, became inextricably associated in the last 12 months of the First World War, after Clemenceau became premier in November 1917. It was a critical time, with the French army still recovering from the prolonged ordeal of Verdun and the dangerous mutinies of 1917, and the British reeling after the massive losses at Passchendaele of August–September 1917. From the start, major differences emerged. Lloyd George was always an easterner, the advocate of a more peripheral strategy, notably in the Balkans and in the war with the Turks. Clemenceau was always the supreme westerner, anxious for the maximum of force to be brought to bear on the western front, along France's eastern frontier, to protect the territorial base. He found the British slow to take the point; Lloyd George countered by emphasising the supreme importance of the naval side of the war for food and raw materials, where Britain's commitment was supreme and where he himself had pushed on with the convoy system to neutralise the threat of the U Boats. This aspect, he felt, Clemenceau underestimated.

Along with this, Clemenceau wanted the British under Haig's command to take over more of the line. Britain, he argued had only 487 fighting units, as against France's 662, a statistic which Lloyd George did not dispute. Lloyd George, by contrast, was inclined to hold back British troops until the Americans could throw in a decisive force, probably not before the later summer of 1918. Lloyd George, later accused in the Maurice debate of 9 May of deliberately holding back British reserves in the aftermath of Passchendaele, complained that he would have to incorporate 'nigger' soldiers in his army. Clemenceau's riposte was that the French army had no problem with 'niggers': they had enlisted Moroccan and other Africans, and would take 'Ethiopians' if necessary. A related issue was Clemenceau's demand that the British played their full part in building up a strategic reserve on the western front. Lloyd George insisted on the prior needs of the Turkish campaign in Palestine, which would probably necessitate the withdrawal of British divisions from France.

Despite these tensions, relations between the two prime ministers appear to have steadily improved, especially in their close collaboration during the major German offensive in the Amiens sector in late March and early April 1918. In any case, Lloyd George and Clemenceau had one fairly constant enemy in their sights at this time – namely the British generals. Clemenceau rejoiced when Lloyd George succeeded in removing General 'Wully' Robertson as Chief of the Imperial General Staff in February 1918, in a tense political crisis that almost cost him the premiership. After a conference at Beauvais in early April, the two prime ministers worked together in implementing the old objective of unity of command. Foch assumed titular authority over the allied forces on the western front, Haig accepting the situation with some grace. According to Lloyd George's hugely exaggerated account, the main stumbling here was not the British commander-in-chief but rather the old free thinker Clemenceau's distaste for Foch's devout Catholicism. Certainly

Clemenceau and Foch had a tense relationship long-term, but the roots were strictly secular. The later stages of the war saw the Anglo-French partnership probably working more effectively than at any other time. The lead-up to a post-war peace conference in the autumn of 1918 was marked by agreement on many key issues, other than the settlement with the Turks. In the end, a brisk realism ensured that the future of the Ottoman Empire was partially resolved on the basis of the French being given Syria and the British the ominous legacy of Mesopotamia, later Iraq. Palestine became a British mandate while France assumed military control of Cilicia.

From Keynes onwards, observers of the Paris peace negotiations have focussed on the *sturm und drang* of conflicts between Clemenceau and Lloyd George on their approach towards the defeated Germans. Certainly there was much to record. Lloyd George, indeed, became deeply concerned at the way in which Clemenceau's national prejudices and insistence of curbs on a post-war Germany were taking over the entire agenda. The outcome of his anxiety was the celebrated Fontainebleau memorandum, prepared with Lloyd George's aides and colleagues in the woods near that town, notably Philip Kerr and General Smuts of South Africa, in mid-March 1919. It was very much the personal statement of the British prime minister.

The Memorandum was the first formal document arguing the case for the appeasement of the defeated Germans. It had two main themes. The major one in the Fontainebleau document was a call for moderation in the frontier arrangements to try to ensure that large swathes of German people were not placed under foreign occupation. Lloyd George particularly mentioned the Saarland, Danzig, Upper Silesia and above all the Polish Corridor that should not be placed under alien rule. There should be 'no more Alsace Lorraines'. Later in the conference negotiations, he showed his alarm at placing the Sudeten Germans under the governance of the newly created hybrid state of Czechoslovakia. The Czechs he never trusted, especially their leading statesman, 'that swine Benes' for whom Lloyd George was to show scant sympathy during the time of Munich in 1938. Here, Lloyd George had only limited success though he did achieve the triumph of forcing through a local plebiscite in Upper Silesia, which in 1921 voted to stay in Germany.

The other main pivot of the Memorandum, though taken up far more prominently later on in the Paris negotiations, was the demand for German post-war reparations to be kept flexible so that Europe's economic recovery would not be held back by Germany's being undermined as a great manufacturing and trading nation. Here, Lloyd George was erratic. He later was to add widows' and orphans' pensions to the possible bill which almost doubled it. But in the end he succeeded in pushing the reparations issue into the long grass. It was handed over to a Reparations Commission for long-term deliberation which ensured that the most of the money would never be paid. The blame fell largely not on the British prime minister but on the British representatives, Lords Cunliffe and Sumner. Keynes could never fathom Lloyd George's strategy here, but then, Keynes was not a politician!

Clemenceau, naturally, was deeply unsympathetic to the Fontainebleau *démarche*. He noted cynically that it dealt only with issues worrying to France. On issues that concerned Britain, such as freedom of the seas, it was silent. He and Lloyd George had inevitably many fierce arguments on the Memorandum's themes, notably the reparations issue. The two prime ministers also diverged sharply on the Middle East, where France tended to be pro-Turk whereas Lloyd George was as an old Gladstonian Liberal, passionately, even fanatically pro-Greek and a supporter of the Greek prime minister, Venizelos. At one time, reportedly, the two premiers seemed likely to come to blows. Even though Clemenceau was by now almost 78, he was still combative and combustible.

And yet the Paris peace conference is far from only being a story of Anglo-French (or Cambro-French) conflict. In particular, Lloyd George, far more clearly than Wilson, recognised the need for long-term protection of French territorial security. He saw the force of Clemenceau's demand for a British 'continental commitment' and actually offered a serious proposal of a British military guarantee against future German aggression. He promised that his country would 'place all her forces at [France's] disposal.' He even threw in the exciting vision of a Channel Tunnel as part of this – the first time this idea ever emerged in an international conference. In the end, Lloyd George backed down, citing, correctly, the failure of the Americans to offer any kind of assistance themselves – indeed by this stage the United States was lurching fast into parochial hemispheric isolationism. But after the build-up, Clemenceau felt justifiably angry and let down.

But Lloyd George was serious about this issue, as no British prime minister had been since the end of the Napoleonic Wars – the Peninsular war against Napoleon had been the last 'continental commitment' to engage a British government. At the conference in Cannes in January 1922 he again proposed a long-term British treaty of guarantee to the current French premier, Aristide Briand, with whom he had struck up a good relationship, better than with Clemenceau. It would be ratified with other major proposals at a forthcoming international conference in Genoa in April. But, after the famous and much-derided game between Lloyd George and Briand on the seaside golf course at Cannes, Briand's government was summarily overthrown, and his successor Raymond Poincaré, a stern man of Lorraine and bitterly anti-German, refused all Lloyd George's overtures. But the coming together of Lloyd George and Briand did show that the Welshman was perhaps the one international leader of the time who seriously tried to balance charity towards the defeated Germans with security for the victorious French.

After the signing of the treaty in the hall of mirrors at Versailles, Clemenceau had a far shorter political shelf-life than did Lloyd George. He was defeated for the presidency by no less than his old duelling adversary, Deschanel. He lived on for another ten years, writing his war memoirs, and also significant books on Monet and on Demosthenes. He visited the House of Commons in June 1921, while receiving an honorary degree from Oxford University. Here he met Lloyd George once again, rather briefly. Direct as ever, Clemenceau told the British premier, 'Dès le lendemain de l'Armistice, je vous ai trouvé l'ennemi de France.' To which Lloyd George cheerfully replied, 'Eh bien, n'est-ce pas notre politique traditionelle?' Their last meeting was not a success any more than their first had been in 1910. Clemenceau wanted a firm adherence to the letter of the peace terms, not a revision of them. He rejoiced at the news of Lloyd George's downfall in October 1922. In his extreme old age, he loved to walk in the woods of his native Vendée. He is supposed to have said that one of their charms was that he would never encounter Lloyd George there – only squirrels.

Lloyd George remained the dominant figure in world politics for almost another three years. He worked hard for international reconciliation through revision of the treaties. Keynes now changed his opinions radically and applauded Lloyd George's endeavours. Lloyd George sought peace with Germany, a deferring and scaling down of reparations payments. He withdrew all British troops from Russia. He still focussed on keeping the Entente with France alive, in partnership with Briand until his fall from power. But in the end, French nationalism as voiced by Poincaré, American hemispheric isolationism, Russian commitment to world revolution, and German unreliability shown by their treaty of Rappallo with the Russians, were all too much for him. The Genoa conference dragged on inconclusively. A provocative British challenge to the Turks in the Middle East then threatened war in the Chanak crisis. Poincaré shouted at Curzon, the British foreign minister, at their meeting in Paris. Curzon retaliated by bursting into tears. The dominant Conservative element in the coalition government turned against Lloyd George. Bonar Law wrote that Britain could not alone act as 'policeman of the world'. Appeasement was growing apace, Baldwin denounced the prime minister as 'a dynamic force', Lloyd George was overthrown on 19 October 1922 by a Tory revolt, and he never returned to office.

In the remainder of his career, down to his death in March 1945, he was constantly critical of France for its intransigence as he saw it. His wish to accommodate Germany through a pact of mutual guarantee reached a disastrous level when he made a friendly visit to Hitler in Berchtesgaden in 1936. Photographs of their meeting were as disastrous as those of Pétain and Hitler at Montoire in 1940. Although Lloyd George assisted mightily in the fall of Neville Chamberlain in 1940, he continued to advocate a possible negotiated peace with Germany during the war. Churchill in 1941 savagely compared him with Pétain, pleading for peace in the last days of the Reynaud government. At the end, Lloyd George was indeed being compared with the French – but the wrong French, the militaristic, neo-fascist French of Vichy, not the heirs of the democrats and Jacobins of the Revolution of 1789. There was a final *démarche* on 1 January 1945. Wales's great commoner ended up an earl.

In the aftermath, it was Clemenceau's reputation which was to prove the stronger. Lloyd George was tarred forever by his post-war coalition government of 1918–22 with the Tories. His Liberal Party was divided and defeated for ever, and never again returned to power. Not until his papers were opened up to historians at the Beaverbrook Library, run by A.J.P. Taylor in 1967, did a revision of his reputation take place, in which the present writer took some part. Clemenceau, by contrast, emerged as the one acknowledged hero of recent French history prior to de Gaulle, the epitome of republican France. Only in late 2005 was money at last found for Lloyd George's statue in Parliament Square in London, and finally on 25 October 2007 his monument was unveiled there, near the House of Commons he dominated for so long, close to that of Churchill, Britain's other great war leader, four other Tory prime ministers, and a right-wing king. The unveiling ceremony was conducted by Charles, Prince of Wales, entertainingly so in view of Lloyd George's numerous caustic observations on the royal family during his career – 'The whole atmosphere reeks of Toryism.' Just as Churchill's statue was targeted by anti-capitalist demonstrators three years ago, it is nice to think that Lloyd George's statue may in future attract the interest of the pheasant-shooting branches of the Countryside Alliance, the voice of the landowners he despised.

By contrast, Clemenceau has for long stood tall on the Champs Elysees as the indisputable 'Père la Victoire', dressed as in 1917 in his cape and high boots and brandishing a cane. Pierre Nora's *Lieux de Mémoire* notes that his statue is the only one in Paris that most Parisians may be expected to know, along with that of Joan of Arc in Place des

Pyramides. That is Clemenceau in French legend and memory. David Lloyd George, for all his extraordinary achievements and his efforts in his war memoirs (brilliant but less effective than Churchill's in self-glorification) is recalled as a man who promised a land fit for heroes and failed to deliver. In Britain's public memory, the Second World War, Churchill's war, is a symbol of the national identity, Britain fighting alone in our finest hour. The first war, Lloyd George's, is remembered for senseless slaughter, 'lions led by donkeys'. The Cenotaph is non-triumphalist, Armistice Day is an ambiguous celebration of unknown heroes, pain, pride and shame intermingled. To adopt the title of Joan Littlewood's 1960s satire, 'Oh! What a lovely war.'

For all that, Lloyd George and Clemenceau enjoyed a great, if temporary, partnership. They had different views of the international interest and their personal relationship was never easy. But they appreciated each other's qualities. Lloyd George's vivid sketch of Clemenceau in his war memoirs praised him as the greatest statesman of his day, courageous and strong. He told his newspaper proprietor friend, George Riddell of *The News of the World*, that Clemenceau was 'a wonderful old man', full of humour. Clemenceau, while finding Lloyd George baffling as an intuitive, mercurial Welshman, saw him nevertheless as capable of rising, as few others could, 'à la hauteur des grands événements'. Theirs was the most important Franco-British partnership, comparable with that of Churchill and Roosevelt in 1941–5, and far better than that between Churchill and de Gaulle in the Second World War. Together, they provided the historic high noon of Britain's most enduring Special Relationship – the Entente Cordiale.

Chapter 8

The Future at Work: Anglo-American Progressivism

'The fact is that our political issues are so different that it is hard for either nation to understand the other.' So wrote Herbert Foxwell, a conservative economist in Cambridge, England, to E.R. Seligman of Columbia University in 1895.[1] Fourteen years later, he congratulated Seligman and himself on the contrasts between the two nations, 'Englishmen more than ever envy you the extraordinarily conservative character of your constitution. Democracy seems to have hardly any hold on American politics.' Britain, on the other hand, was plagued by 'the crudest budget of modern times – worthy of the shallow and rhetorical Henry George, whom our chancellor, his namesake, much resembles'.[2]

Foxwell's insular view has been echoed by almost all historians of the Progressive reform movement that swept through the cities and states of America in the first two decades of the twentieth century. It has invariably been assumed that Progressivism can be understood only in a purely American context, as the product of a period of self-examination and inward-looking analysis after the excitement of imperialism and the war with Spain in 1898. It was a time of self-purgation after what Richard Hofstadter called the 'psychic crisis' of the 1890s.[3] Equally, British historians have viewed the political upheavals of the Liberals in the years up to 1914 as a period of creative introspection after the divisions and disillusionment of the South African War and gradual revulsion against Empire that resulted. The House of Lords, Irish home rule, Welsh disestablishment, women's suffrage, above all, the 'new Liberalism' of social reform are all taken to indicate a preoccupation with the internal social and political structure of Britain itself, a high noon of domestic radical change from which a self-contained, insular nation was abruptly wrenched by the advent of total war in August 1914. In so far as the United States did impinge on the awareness of British radical reformers in the Lloyd George era, it has been taken to have served as a threat and a warning – as the supreme symbol of uncontrolled monopoly capitalism in its most irresponsible guise. The intimate transatlantic radical community of *ante-bellum* days, a world that perished at Appomattox, had disappeared. To the British left, socialist and non-socialist alike, the United States now provided the model (and to some extent the source) of the evils, the trusts and robber barons, from which British radicals sought to save their society. In short, American historians of the reform movements in their respective countries appear to agree that each nation was self-contained, preoccupied with its own internal stresses and conflicts, comparatively unmoved by the contemporary experience of the other.

And yet, the evidence from contemporary sources, particularly the British and American newspaper and periodical press, is overwhelming that the Progressive movement in each country was transatlantic in its emphasis. The New York *Forum* commented in October 1906 on 'the unconscious influence that the trans-Atlantic branch of the great English-speaking race exercises on the cis-Atlantic branch, and vice versa'.[4] Political commentators like Lyman Abbott and Benjamin Flower felt convinced that American Progressivism was part of a world-wide movement closely paralleled on each side of the Atlantic.[5] Time and again, this refrain was taken up by journalists and politicians in the Progressive movement in each country. Indeed, British reformers, anxious to consolidate the Liberal–Labour alliance in the period after the sixth general election, adopted the name 'Progressive' to identify their creed. C.P. Scott in the *Manchester Guardian*, A.G. Gardiner in the *Daily News*, H.J. Massingham in the *Nation*, wrote freely of the 'progressive alliance'. In London, Manchester and other urban areas up and down the land, radicals on local authorities formed themselves into 'progressive parties'. Political commentators observed how Progressivism in the Theodore Roosevelt/Wilson era and Liberalism in the Asquith/Lloyd George period appeared to have common aspirations – the cutting back of political privilege, the substitution of the 'national interest' for that of 'special interest', the replacement of the ethic of competition with that of collective co-operation, the democratisation of the political process, the promotion of social justice and of industrial and labour reforms, in the interests both of national efficiency and of humanity. There were those who claimed that, just as the Jacksonian Democrats had struck a common chord with the radical reformers in Britain in 1830, just as the American Civil War had lent new impetus to the revived parliamentary reform agitation in the 1860s, so once again radical reformers on each side of the Atlantic were comrades in a common cause. Of course, some of this was exaggerated. The closeness of the Anglo-American connection in the years after 1900 can be overdone. Since the intimate association of transatlantic radicals in the early nineteenth century, British and American politics had taken very different paths. Partly as a result of this, partly the consequence of changing patterns of immigration to America, the two nations had drifted apart. Further, America's rise as a world power had led to serious Anglo-American diplomatic conflicts, as recently as 1902–3 over the boundary between Venezuela and British Guiana. Historians who try to discern a 'special relationship' in these years, or later, are often all too prone to sentiment or wish-fulfilment about the 'English-speaking peoples'. Even so, the reality of the interaction between British and American Progressivism is too pervasive to be brushed aside. A study of its character, and perhaps of its limitations, sheds new light on political change in the two countries. In particular, American Progressivism may be seen, not just as an introspective desire for purification and change at a time of relative national prosperity, but as part of a world-wide quest to control urbanisation and industrialisation, a quest which knew no national boundaries or else soared above them.

Without doubt, the impact of American Progressivism upon British politics in the Edwardian era was episodic and often indirect. American analogies were freely used in debates on the issues by Edwardian politicians – but all too often by Conservatives rather than by radicals. Those checks and balances embodied in the American constitution were widely cited by opponents of the Parliament Bill in 1910–11 to justify the preservation of the House of Lords as a bastion against unbridled democracy. The American idea of a referendum was quoted for the same purpose. The *laissez-faire* climate in which American business had flourished since the civil war was emphasised by *The Times* and Conservatives generally to curb the pretensions of British trade unions, and to oppose the 'socialistic' attacks on wealth and property conducted by Lloyd George and his allies.[6] Above all, sympathy with the United States on alleged grounds of race inspired Joseph Chamberlain and other Unionists to hope for an alliance with the Americans, or at least for a friendly understanding, as a main adjunct to British foreign policy. The war with Spain in 1898 evoked warm sympathy for the American cause from nationalists and imperialists of all shades in Britain, from Chamberlain to Robert Blatchford of the ILP. Strategic decisions which led to the United States patrolling Caribbean waters with its own expanded fleet were held to be a valuable support for British naval supremacy in the north and mid-Atlantic.

On the other hand, ministers in the British Liberal government after 1905 viewed the United States with some detachment. The member most closely involved with the United States, James Bryce, the celebrated author of *The American Commonwealth* (1888), went from the Irish Office to Washington as British ambassador from 1907 to 1913. While this enabled him to make his own unique contribution to Anglo-American cultural understanding, of course it removed him entirely from direct contact with the British political scene. The one remaining member of the government consistently anxious to maintain close relations with the United States, though not in the shape of a formal alliance, was Sir Edward

Grey, the foreign secretary. He believed strongly in the ties created by language, cultural heritage and religion between the two 'Anglo-Saxon' powers, and the diplomatic implications of this. He devoted much time to anxious fence-mending with the Americans, notably over the Canadian reciprocity treaty in 1911 – a policy that, incidentally, led directly towards the downfall of Laurier's Liberal government at Ottawa. When Woodrow Wilson became President of the United States, and sagely dispatched Walter Hines Page to the Court of St. James's, Grey emphasised how closely attuned he felt to the new Democratic administration, headed by an austere, university-trained patrician like himself. Over the Panama tolls issue and policy towards Mexico in 1913–14, Grey made it plain to Wilson that he took a far less narrow view of British national interest than did his foreign office advisers.'[7] Conversely, Grey's highly eclectic attitude towards domestic British issues, in which he often formed an unexpected alliance with Lloyd George on labour, land and other questions, owed nothing to developments in the United States. His transatlantic enthusiasms were for export only.

On the other hand, the radical domestic policies of the British government during the years from 1906 to 1914 did find some transatlantic ammunition. In particular, Lloyd George, far from the inward-looking, parochial figure he is often represented to be, took a keen if not always well-informed interest in events in the United States. American journals often featured interviews with him. Characteristically, the American figure who most captured his imagination was Theodore Roosevelt whom he met during the latter's triumphant visit to Britain in 1912.[8] Roosevelt's version of the 'new nationalism', a strong foreign policy being combined with paternalist social reform, chimed in with Lloyd George's own inclinations. Again, Roosevelt's penchant for commissions of experts to examine questions like the trusts and the tariffs in a scientific and detached way followed closely Lloyd George's own proposals. In his memorandum in 1910, in which he advocated an inter-party coalition which would vault above petty partisan politics, Lloyd George had similarly proposed commissions of experts who would look at 'non-controversial' issues like imperial preference, the Ulster question, the Lords veto, and disendowment of the Welsh Church. Above all, Roosevelt appealed to Lloyd George (as did Franklin Roosevelt twenty years afterwards) as a symbol of powerful central leadership and of broad executive power who would transcend the mundane issues with which the party politicians of the day were consumed. In the *Truth about the Peace Treaties* in the 1930s, he cited Theodore Roosevelt, along with Botha of South Africa, as a 'big man' who provided a new concept of leadership.[9] Like T.R., Lloyd George believed in executives rather than in legislatures. His bid for a

British version of the 'new nationalism', based on military preparedness and social reform, failed in 1910; the reality of party was too strong for him. But in 1916, when the political world was revolutionised by the impact of total war, Lloyd George's vision found new significance. Then indeed the New Nationalism – or 'nationalist-socialism' as Lloyd George and his new ally, Lord Milner termed it[10] came into its own. The machinery of central government was overhauled, quasi-presidential power was vested in the man at the centre, new departments of governments were created, businessmen and non-partisan experts were drafted in to run their departments on practical lines. Indeed, an almost uncritical faith in the judgement of down-to-earth, untheological businessmen – a faith applied by him even in trade negotiations with Krassin and the Soviet government in 1920–1 was one indirect legacy of Lloyd George's flirtation with the New Nationalism. At the time, though, Lloyd George was critical of Theodore Roosevelt for rebelling against the Republican regulars and forming the 'Bull Moose' Progressive Party in the 1912 campaign. 'He ought not to have quarrelled with the machine', Lloyd George observed.[11] It was one aspect of the New Nationalism that Lloyd George himself forgot in 1918, with fatal results for his career. In addition, his admiration for Hitler in the 1930s, much on the lines of his earlier enthusiasm for T.R., was ominous. He could select the wrong messiah.

For radicals and socialists outside the Liberal administration also, the United States provided an attractive impulse during these years. William Jennings Bryan, for all his insularity, received generous acclaim from Liberal and Labour backbenchers when he visited Britain in 1906. He was the symbol of democratic power ranged against the wealth and influence of the 'goldbugs', the apostle of international peace who had fought imperialism in America as courageously as the Pro-Boers had done in Britain. Even the Labour Party did not necessarily view the United States solely as the ugly symbol of big business. On the contrary, the growth of a vigorous socialist movement in the Mid-West and other regions of the United States, the rise of the American Federation of Labor under Sam Gompers in the face of judicial and other obstacles, re-awakened some of the old faith of the left in America as 'the last, best hope on earth'. While the Fabians (as in Beatrice Webb's *American Journey* in 1898) thought American politics corrupt and incompetent, the more internationally minded of the ILP found much encouragement in the American scene. Ramsay MacDonald wrote enthusiastically of the success of the American Socialist Party in Milwaukee and other areas of the Mid-West. He kept up a regular correspondence with Oswald Garrison Villard of the New York *Nation*.[12] Keir Hardie visited the United States three times in all (1895, 1908 and 1912), and each time found something to gladden his weary heart. He was alarmed always by the unbridled power of trusts and cartels in America. He noted, too, the wide gulf that prevailed between the American labour unions and the Socialist Party, their failure as yet to forge the kind of flexible labour alliance that he himself had helped form in Britain in 1900. He was far from being overwhelmed by Debs's success in polling almost a million votes in 1912; most industrial workers still ignored the Socialists, and indeed Debs's most substantial vote, proportionally, came from rural Oklahoma. Even so, Hardie did not despair of American labour. He had wide-ranging contacts with many wings of the American working-class movement, and so had his intimate associate, Frank Smith, the ex-Salvationist. Through Sam Gompers, Hardie learnt of the progress of the A.F. of L., and its steady, if reluctant, involvement in politics in pursuit of its Magna Carta. One outcome was the creation of the new Department of Labor by Woodrow Wilson in 1913. Through Debs, and ex-Populists like Henry Demarest Lloyd in Illinois, Hardie learnt of the grass roots strength of American socialism in such disparate areas as the largely German parts of Wisconsin and Illinois, and the remote silver and copper mines of Montana, Wyoming and Idaho. Above all, Hardie was impressed by the success of the American Progressive movement in spreading the ethic of communal and co-operative activity throughout American society, in counteracting and undermining the ugly, brutal creed of free-enterprise capitalism. Just as Hardie saw the rise of the New Liberalism and the flowering of social reform in Britain as vital forces in helping on sympathy and understanding for democratic socialism and the Labour Party, so in the United States, pressure for a socialised, humanised, more moral capitalism would lend momentum to Debs and his followers – always provided that they retained contact with the industrial masses and did not lapse into the sterile dogma of a Hyndman or de Leon. At all events, Hardie, whose international sense was so closely bound up with his perception of the social and political processes in Britain itself from 1905 onwards, was far from viewing the United States with blank despair. Many on the British left, Liberal and Labour, followed his lead.

The impact of the United States on British reformers, however, was intermittent and partial at best. The influence of British Liberalism on American Progressives, by contrast, was coherent and continuous. For decades, American reformers had imbibed much of their political philosophy from Britain. Carlyle, Ruskin and Morris helped them towards a moral critique of laissez-faire. A.R. Wallace's evolutionary doctrines spurred on the progress of 'reform Darwinism'. Later, Graham Wallas's new 'sociology' impelled the young Walter Lippman and others towards a more scientific methodology in quantifying and categorising social phenomena. He also taught them to take account of the irrational in politics.[13] In Boston from the 1890s onwards, W.D.P. Bliss, Robert Woods, Frank Parsons and other quasi-socialist reformers found in British Fabian socialism, in its *fin de siècle* phase, the inspiration for many of their hopes. In the case of Parsons, his social philosophy took its stand on the sociological analysis of Herbert Spencer, even while it rejected his determinist commitment to laissez-faire. Until the turn of the century, however, this kind of influence was largely abstract and philosophical: it does not lend itself to precise measurement by the historian. After all, as Frederick Howe commented, with some exaggeration, in his eulogistic account of British city government, social reform in Britain had long been almost non-existent, because of the control exercised by vested interests, particularly the landed classes, on the British legislature.[14]

In the Edwardian years, however, the inspiration of British reform movements for American Progressives became tangible and all-pervasive. Indeed, in many ways, Britain, like Germany, Denmark, Switzerland and other European countries, became for American Progressives a kind of social laboratory where new techniques of political and social planning were being tested and refined. They served as a model of how radical reform could be practical – and good business as well. From the turn of the century, the Anglo-American 'connexion' assumed a highly specific form. A stream of young university teachers, economists, social workers, journalists and civic reformers made their way to Britain, particularly to British cities, to observe the progress of reform in the Old World and to assess how it could be transplanted or adapted to the New. This marked a more outward-looking phase of American reform, part of the supersession of Populism by Progressivism. Populists, largely drawn from remote rural areas of the south and west, preoccupied with domestic issues like the currency and the railroads, viewed Britain as a detested stereotype, the mercantile stronghold of Jewish finance and of the 'cross of gold' on which the American democracy, with the assistance of the Judases of Wall Street, was being crucified. But the mainly urban Progressives viewed Britain in a more positive light. While the Progressive reformers Jane Addams, John R. Commons, Richard T. Ely, Charles Beard, Frederick Howe and many others like them remained profoundly American in their assumptions, convinced that the ills besetting their society could best be solved within a native context by the application of direct democracy on the traditional American model, they valued the application of social engineering from Europe, too. It served to give their achievements a more enduring quality, long after the class and sectional cleavages of the Populist era had passed into obscurity.

There was much to interest American Liberals in the British political scene after 1906. They viewed with admiration the onslaught waged by the British government on special interest groups – on the brewers (the 1908 Licensing Bill was a great encouragement to American prohibitionists),[15] on the landed classes and above all on the House of Lords. They followed with keen attention the crisis occasioned by Lloyd George's 'people's budget' in 1909. It was noted that the main thrust of the budgetary proposals came from new taxes on land, for which American Progressives such as Tom Johnson, Frederick Howe and Joseph Fels had long called. With new taxes imposed on the unearned increment on urban land, with the reversionary duties and other new imposts, it was believed that the British city and the British parliament would be freed from the remaining shackles of feudalism, that new bonds would be forged between the middle and working classes, and that a constantly renewable source of revenue for social reform would be found. The liberal editor of the *Emporia Gazette* in Kansas William Allen White wrote emotionally later in his autobiography of himself and his wife holding hands, tears in their eyes, when joining in a mass march on behalf of Lloyd George's 1909 budget. 'We felt were part of something great and beautiful. We did not know exactly what, except that we knew the under dog had slipped off his leash and this was his time to howl.'

American Progressives also approved of the decision to hold a new general election in January 1910 so that radical legislation could be given a direct popular mandate.[16] The progress of British democracy in other respects was also applauded: the payment of Members of Parliament, the Franchise Reform Bill of 1912 and, above all, the growing pressure from the suffragettes. However, it was notable that the more militant tactics of the British suffragettes struck few welcoming chords among American women leaders. Alice Stone Blackwell, in the *Woman's Journal*, wrote sympathetically of the campaign being waged by Mrs Pankhurst and her daughters. But 'one thing upon which in America we are all agreed is that it is not needed here and would not do here', Mrs Blackwell commented.[17] American women's leaders claimed their objectives were achieved by peaceful methods of persuasion on the state and city level: Inez Haynes Irwin, originally a warm supporter of the Pankhursts, noted how thirty-seven states of the union ratified women's suffrage measures from 1913 after a largely non-militant campaign.[18] Even so, close contact was maintained between the women's movement on each side of the Atlantic. The active involvement of American women in the social justice movement made the more socially radical amongst the British suffragettes, Sylvia Pankhurst and Margaret Bondfield for instance, highly congenial to American women, most notably Alice Paul.

Two areas, above all, helped to inspire American Progressives in their most active and creative period: social justice and civic reform. In these two fields, the impact of British Liberal and humanitarian reform was of most direct inspiration.

In the field of social justice, it was the evolution of the British city that in large measure provided the key to the liberal diagnoses of American reformers. It was in Britain and other European countries that the urban stresses arising from uncontrolled industrial expansion were most acute. Episodes like the London dock strike of 1889 afforded British middle-class social critics a new insight into the evils arising from poverty, slum housing and casual labour in the working-class areas of British cities. Marx's analysis of the social residuum that contained the casualties of industrial change seemed all too forcefully borne out: many commentators dreaded the growing appeal of socialism that might result amongst the urban poor. Fear as well as compassion helped in the cause of social reform. These developments, especially Charles Booth's famous survey of the London poor in 1889, were widely read by urban reformers in the United States. In particular, there was the major influence of the British settlement houses, Toynbee Hall in London's East End above all, created by Christian socialists to provide a communal focus for the immigrant and other poor of London. Toynbee Hall had a dramatic impact on the social awareness of American reformers. Jane Addams's memoirs, *Twenty Years at Hull House,* provide a revealing and sensitive testimony to it. She had originally been stirred by Edward Caird's lecture on Abraham Lincoln, which showed her how the intellectual sophistication of Oxford could be fused with human sensibility and compassion. During her visit to Toynbee Hall in 1888, she found the institutional means and the moral ideals which provided for her the essential key to social justice in the American cities. Hull House in Chicago, to a considerable degree, mirrored the principles on which Toynbee Hall was founded. Like its London counterpart, it sought to create a small, face-to-face community in which the urban poor could be protected from the size and impersonality of the modern city. Like Toynbee Hall, it was based on the premise that the cultural traditions of the residents should be, if possible, preserved and encouraged; thus immigrants in Hull House were urged to maintain their national customs, dress and culture. And finally, Hull House, perhaps even more than Toynbee Hall, was based on the premise that a wide, perhaps widening, gulf existed between the middle and working classes. Its organisers viewed the working-class world from the outside. In return, they gained the consolation of social service and of the fulfilment of Christian obligation. Settlement houses were, for Jane Addams, 'a subjective necessity'. In a very real sense, the Anglo-American connection in the social justice movement was a Protestant Christian one: Jane Addams's experiment at Hull House was fired by the special sense of mission, even of personal guilt imbibed by a college-trained, middle-class American girl in the later nineteenth century. Many other women reformers – Edith Starr and Vida Scudder, and later Lilian Wald and Florence Kelley – carried on the ideals of Toynbee Hall into other settlements, into the crusade against urban poverty and environmental deprivation, into the campaign for tenement house reform in New York and elsewhere. Several of them went through their formative years in Britain: for instance Vida Scudder, who studied at Oxford from 1884 to 1887 and was deeply influenced by Ruskin's lectures there. Without the impulse provided by the British connection, the American social justice movement would have taken a different course.

As the movement for social reform broadened in America after the turn of the century, the influence of British and other European reform experiments became more and more intense. Eastern Progressive journals, such as the *Outlook, North Atlantic Review,* the *Arena,* the *Forum* and the *World's Work,* transmitted them in minute detail to eager American readers. British commentators on social problems, like Robert Donald (editor of the *Daily Chronicle*), Percy Alden MP and J. Allen Baker MP of the London County Council, became widely read in America, although they were usually careful to spell out the differences that divided the British and American reform movements. After 1908, the social reforms of Lloyd George and Churchill were widely emulated in the states and cities of America. Labour exchanges, old-age pensions, progressive direct taxation, housing and land renovation, and above all, the British National Health Insurance Act of 1911, made a dramatic impact on American reformers.[19] Even in Wisconsin, where La Follette's Mid-Western Progressives felt far removed from the European scene – and in important senses hostile to it – 'the Wisconsin Idea' borrowed from the British experience features in the drafting of their social legislation. The limitation of working hours, minimum wage provisions, tax reform, workers' compensation for accidents, and factory inspection were areas where American Progressives drew heavily on European examples. Certainly, Germany was an even more compelling symbol for American social reformers, with its long legacy of legislation dating from Bismarck's measures of the early 1880s. But the experience of Lloyd George and his colleagues showed that Liberal reform was compatible with active democratic control as well as with centralised paternalism. The state need not be so servile after all. If some of the more democratic aspects of the Liberal social reforms seemed unscientific and inefficient to a New Nationalist like Herbert Croly in his *Promise of American Life,* they made British Liberalism all the more appealing to the main stream of American social justice pioneers.

Scores of American social reformers made the pilgrimage to London's East End and to other British cities at this period. Amongst the most notable was the historian Charles Beard who worked for two years in Ruskin Hall, the working-man's college in Oxford founded by the American, Walter Vrooman, in 1899. Here Beard refined his awareness of the crippling pressures of urban poverty and of the underlying economic factors that caused it. He began, too, his lifelong association with adult education: he was to found the Workers' Education Association of America in 1921. Beard also became intensely involved with the socialist movement. From Keir Hardie he heard at first hand of the way in which socialists and trade unionists had made common cause in the LRC. Beard almost stayed on in Britain to work for socialism. Some other American reformers did so. Dr. Stanton Coit, a pillar of the Ethical Church, became a zealot of the ILP and strove to become a parliamentary candidate. Joseph Fels, the naphtha soap millionaire, who had founded land cultivation societies in Philadelphia and other American cities, turned to similar ventures in Laindon in Essex and Hollesley Bay in Suffolk, as a remedy for rising unemployment in Britain. He was actively involved in sponsoring the social campaigns of George Lansbury in Poplar in London's East End. He also met Keir Hardie and later helped finance Hardie's tour around the world in 1907–8.[20] The American impact on the British labour scene prior to 1914 is too often discussed solely in terms of the impact of de Leonism and the 'Wobblies' in pushing British miners and railwaymen towards direct industrial action in the period from 1910 to 1914. In fact, documents of industrial revolt, like *The Miners' Next Step* published in the South Wales coalfield at Tonypandy in 1912, had an indigenous origin, and owed virtually nothing to American syndicalist doctrines. By contrast, men like Fels brought a direct American experience to the mainstream of the British Labour movement. Fels's influence lingered on, even when his land colonies collapsed, and even when the more confiscatory aspects of Labour's programme alienated him (since he preferred the single tax on land as a panacea). In return, the growth of a democratic Labour Party, the 'progressive alliance' which enabled Labour and the New Liberals to unite in fulfilling the old Liberal objectives as well as pushing on to new social goals, acted as a powerful stimulus to urban reformers in the social justice movement in the United States. Writers like Sydney Brooks gloried in English Labour's 'stride towards democracy'.[21]

An even more pervasive impact of Britain on the American reform movement came through the medium of municipal and civic reform. This chimed in with one of the most central features of American Progressivism – its urge to democratise and humanise the city. Here Britain, like Germany, was an obvious inspiration. Municipal socialist experiments had been widespread in Britain since the 1870s Chamberlain's measures in Birmingham, the L.C.C. in London and the municipal reforms of Glasgow were already widely familiar. Much use had been made of British experiences by urban reformers in Boston in the 1890s. One of the most forceful of them, Frank Parsons, a lecturer in the law school of Boston University, extended the argument to demand not only municipal socialism in American cities but the state ownership of public utilities such as railroads, coal and water supplies throughout the nation. While he rejected the class hatred of the Marxists, he cited the nationalisation carried out in New Zealand as harmonious instances of socialistic public enterprise in practice. His *Story of New Zealand* showed him to be a great enthusiast for that country. The New Zealand social welfare state had set up 'Manhood as King'.[22]

As the public revulsion against the 'robber barons' was fostered by Ida Tarbell and other muck-raking journalists from 1902 onwards, these collectivist proposals acquired a new appeal and respectability. Another important theorist of urban reform, also much impressed by the British experience, was Albert Shaw, whose *Municipal Government in Great Britain* (1895) attracted wide attention.[23] Shaw emphasised the disinterested and honest nature of municipal government in British cities, and the wide range of services offered by them. Their life was civic, not merely urban. To him, British cities, like those of Germany and Switzerland, seemed to have an independence of spirit and a public-minded ethos which American cities, plagued by corruption and the machinations of selfish private interests, conspicuously lacked. Again, the impact of the 'muckrakers', notably Lincoln Steffens's exposures of urban graft in St. Louis and other cities after the turn of the century, provided a new political momentum for Shaw's teachings.

In city after city from the turn of the century, reform movements were widespread: Progressive reformers like Tom Johnson in Cleveland, 'Golden Rule' Jones in Toledo and Hazen Pingree in Detroit carved out a new nation-wide reputation. The borrowings from Britain were often indirect, although there is a clear link between the spread of commission government and of city managers, and the influence of a municipal civil service in Britain. The National Civic Federation made explicit its interest in the British urban experience: in 1906 it despatched a twenty-two man commission to investigate British municipal government and to promote its major features in the United States. Most urban reformers in this period remained incurably optimistic about the British city, and the popularity of municipal reform in Great Britain. As in the United States they had boundless faith in the natural enlightenment and Liberalism of the British free citizenry, quite detached from considerations of class benefit or economic self-interest.

The most instructive and best-informed of these enthusiasts was Frederick C. Howe, a lifelong reformer from his days with Tom Johnson in Cleveland in the 1890s down to the New Deal period 40 years later (when Howe worked with Jerome Frank in the AAA Programme for agriculture). Howe saw in the British city a symbol of faith for the American nation. Britain and Germany showed him that the city could become the hope of democracy, instead of its downfall. He propounded his beliefs in a series of powerful monographs, *The City: The Hope of Democracy* (1905), *The British City: the Beginnings of Democracy* (1907) and *European Cities at Work* (1913). In addition, he was an indefatigable contributor to Progressive journals in the Eastern and Mid-Western states alike. The message was consistent. In Britain, while parliament was relatively inert because of the control of the landed aristocracy, 'the city represented the high water mark of democracy'.[24] Its local authorities were under close democratic control yet their spirit was generally non-partisan. Furthermore, municipal councils enlisted the voluntary services of prominent local businessmen and tradesmen as their members, without any thought of monetary reward. As a result, there was a natural congruence between private and public enterprise. Businessmen councillors showed the same practical, business-like enthusiasm in the running of municipal services as they did in running their own private firms. This was a major consideration for Howe: as Lincoln Steffens, who accompanied him on some of his European tours wryly observed, Howe 'believed in businessmen'.[25] The results, Howe argued, were dramatically revealed in British city life – in experiments in municipal trading in gas and water services, in the growth of municipal tramways, in the development of local electricity plant, in the creation of garden cities through a combination of public and private support, and above all in the wide range of economic, social and cultural services that the British city naturally provided. They were marked by emphatic financial benefits, too. Howe, an economist by training, delighted to point out how municipal trading in Britain provided a far better return on capital than did private management. Municipal gas or tramway services were highly efficient, notably cheap for the consumer, showed a clear profit, and yet provided a high level of wages for municipal employees.

But the ultimate benefits of the British city were above all, Howe claimed, ethical and psychological.[26] The extent of the activities operated by British city government, the range of social classes it brought into its activities, gave a sense of natural identity and involvement between ordinary citizens and the city in which they lived. The contrast between this and the stagnation or apathy which marked American cities, with the layers of corrupt private interests which intruded between the people and their civic government, was emphasised by Howe, time and again. As Bryce had observed long ago, Americans were not interested in their cities since they did so little. Whereas Americans disliked or feared the city, British people viewed it with hope, even in a city with such acute housing and environmental problems as Glasgow or Manchester. Howe remained generally optimistic about the British city. When the Progressives were defeated in the London County Council elections in 1907, he insisted that this did not imply a loss of faith in progressive municipal government in London, but resulted simply from a local argument about the rates.[27] Howe's main criticism of British cities, indeed, diminished during these years. He attacked the system under which British cities were made powerless by the inflated land values and by the economic stranglehold exercised by the landowners, often absentee. This led to a serious loss of potential revenue for the city, to inadequate city planning and to widespread urban squalor. Howe vigorously condemned the ugliness and low architectural standards of British town centres, and compared them very unfavourably with German cities in this respect.[28] However, to his delight, Lloyd George's 1909 budget made the first serious attempt to tax the unearned increment arising from land after development, and to release urban land for new social purposes. The financial control of the landowners over British cities, a legacy from the Middle Ages, was now dramatically under challenge from a radical chancellor. Therefore, while Howe was more enthusiastic about German cities, which he rightly felt enjoyed more civic independence, he retained his optimistic faith in British cities also. After Lloyd George's budget, he felt that they might serve even more emphatically as the model and the inspiration for American urban reformers.

Howe's enthusiasm for the British city, faithfully reproduced in many American journals during these years, was partly based on a series of half understandings. Indeed, Howe himself eventually became a migrant from the city, and returned to the rural society from which he had sprung. He was too inclined to ignore factors other than the control of the landed classes which shackled the independence of the British city. In particular, he failed to see the ways in which parliament and the central government were encroaching on the powers of cities – and were having to bail them out to keep municipal and county services going. One of the main reasons for the form which Lloyd George's budget of 1909 took was a crisis in local government finance, and the urgent need to find new forms of revenue from the central government to pay for social and educational services. Again, Howe made the government of British cities and counties more neat and tidy than it really was, and largely ignored the overlapping mass of separate authorities for public health, the poor law and (until 1902) education. Had he read more critically the minority report on the Poor Law in 1909 his faith in the social services which British cities were capable of providing might have been somewhat dented. Even so, his conclusions were generally sound enough. He saw in the British city an active, organic democratic unit, widely respected, ever extending its sphere of operations. By contrast, American cities were passive, despised and relatively powerless. The British city served as a model for American urban reformers from 'Golden Rule' Jones (himself a native Welshman) in Toledo, Ohio, onwards. It suggested that urban reform was practicable in American terms also. Progressivism, like charity, could begin at home.

From these main themes of British inspiration for the American Progressive – social justice and civic reform – a typology of American Progressivism, a kind of profile of one major facet of American Liberalism in the Roosevelt-Wilson era can be constructed. This took the form of the rational planner, the detached, non-partisan expert, professional in his administrative operations, yet with the enthusiasm of the well-meaning amateur, elitist in outlook, yet close to the people in his political philosophy. In many ways, he followed on from the Genteel Reform tradition handed on by the Liberal Republicans in 1872, and the later 'mugwumps' who advocated civil service reform on the British pattern, and who achieved the passage of the Pendleton Act in 1883. Like these patrician reformers, Charles Francis Adams, Richard Watson Gilder, Carl Schurz, and E.L. Godkin, the Anglo-Irish editor of the *Nation,* American Progressives also admired the prototype of British government: passionless, elitist, based on ideals of public service and social segregation inculcated by a classical education and the public schools. The kind of public school and university-trained civil servant who had fired the enthusiasm of Godkin in the 1860s (and who still provided an ideal for the anti- imperialists of 1898) was still a model widely admired. New private schools in the United States formed in the last decades of the nineteenth century gave it a new currency. The introduction of new forms of urban and municipal government in the Progressive era after the turn of the century was in some ways an attempt to Anglicise the United States, by curbing the excesses of its democracy with social and political controls. Just as American Progressives admired the detached, philosophical outlook on government which fired non-partisan civic reformers at home, so they were ready to applaud similar examples overseas. The enthusiasm of American Progressives for their own imperialist movement in Cuba, Latin America and China has long been noted.[29] What has not been sufficiently stressed by historians of American Progressivism who have noted the central role played by the 'mugwump' patrician in the reform movement after 1900 is that this was in many ways a direct transplantation of the British Liberal, indeed, Liberal Imperialist ideal. Patrician, enlightened administrators of the type of Cromer in Egypt or Milner in South Africa provided the inspiration for many Progressive commentators after 1900. The *Outlook* praised the choice of a man like Lord Minto as Viceroy of India in September 1905 – 'it may be remarked that Great Britain never chooses any but able and diplomatic men for this important post'.[30] This kind of imperialist stereotype was particularly appealing for New England and other Eastern Progressives who favoured the New Nationalism of Theodore Roosevelt and Croly. Often the class or racial assumptions that underlay this essentially Anglo-Saxon ideal were bluntly underlined. 'The British Empire has been, and is, a tremendous force for the advancement of civilization throughout the world.'[31] It is no surprise that many (though by no means all) Progressives called for restriction of the flood of 'new immigrants' from the Latin and Slav countries of Europe.

Time and again, emphasis was laid on the fact that British administrators and social reformers were Oxford- and Cambridge-trained, of public school background, and that other British universities were emulating their elitist example. The *Outlook* was lyrical in its praise of the type of man who composed the Liberal government that took office in Britain in December 1905. There were, it noted, eleven men from Oxford, five of these from Balliol, 'These represent the highest and finest traditions of self-culture'. Furthermore, these men included the president of the National Physical Recreation Society, an expert golfer, boxer, cricketer, oarsman, fisherman, footballer, and 'pedestrian'.[32] (A bird-watcher might also have been added to this galaxy of renaissance men). Britain's zeal for the active outdoor life, redolent of the public school antecedents of its governors, was never more widely canvassed. Conversely, the presence in the Cabinet of an outsider like Lloyd George, a product of a poor Welsh shoemaker's cottage and Llanystumdwy National School, entirely self-made and largely self-educated, aroused less attention. Some years later, Walter Hines Page, then the American ambassador, took up the same theme. He lavished praise on the British ruling class, symbolised by Morley, Grey and Lulu Harcourt in the Liberal government in 1913: 'gently bred, high-minded, physically fit, intellectually cultivated'.[33] It was British universities above all, particularly Oxford, which kindled the Progressives' patrician ideals: 'for generations English university life has been a preparation for participation in English public life'. The *Outlook* praised the detached, critical spirit in which its products viewed current shibboleths. Morley's proposals for India in 1906, for instance, were commended for adapting political democracy to Indian conditions, that is, not basing it on universal suffrage. Morley, it claimed, had freed himself of some of the traditional errors of the American Liberal, notably the standard belief that universal suffrage was an automatic, universal right.[34] With the proper leadership, a similar style of reform was feasible in the United States also. In their different ways, Theodore Roosevelt, sprung from a Dutch patroon family in the Hudson Valley, trained at Groton and Harvard, and Woodrow Wilson, an austere Presbyterian who had taught at Johns Hopkins before moving on to Princeton, represented similar ideals of elitist leadership in the United States. They each symbolised a contrast with the business and manufacturing classes. They could be expected to put Liberal Imperialism into effect at home. Abroad, America already had her own social imperialist models ready to hand, for instance, General Wood whose improvements of the roads and other civic amenities of Havana provided an antiseptic, Anglo-Saxon Utopia for the advancement of lesser, Latin breeds. British Liberal Imperialism meant for many American Progressives an updated version of the Rome of the Antonines – confident, rational, ordered, and above all, clean. The vision of 'spotlesstown', of a sanitised, organised civilisation, in place, of the squalor, racial tensions and overcrowding of American cities, was in many ways the ideal of the American Progressives. S.S. McClure wrote of his admiration for the hygienic, crime-free character of British cities by comparison with the urban ghettos of America.[35] Britain, and its Liberal Imperialist elite, provided much of the framework for this ideal. In these ways, then, Britain provided much of the momentum for the American Progressives in the era between the Spanish–American War in 1898 and the United States' entry into the First World War in 1917.

At the same time, it is clear that this British influence had its limits. Urban reform in America owed its impetus to native sources as well. The pressure for direct democracy – for primaries, the direct election of senators, the initiative, referendum and recall – were in explicit contrast to the indirect democracy that flourished in Britain. Indeed, Germany, another model for the Progressives, was in major respects profoundly anti-democratic in its social and political system. Furthermore, the stereotype of the patrician university-trained Anglo-Saxon elitist had its appeal mainly for Progressives in the north-eastern states of America. Even here, there were Progressive critics of it. For instance, Herbert Croly condemned Britain's inefficient methods of economic and commercial management, and its dependence on free trade, which would, be claimed lead to Britain's ultimate decline as a major power. 'The best English social type was a gentleman, but a gentleman absolutely conditioned, tempered, and supplemented by a flunky.'[36] Marcus Aurelius was degenerating into Bertie Wooster.

In the Mid-West, La Follette and other Progressives of the insurgent wing of Republicanism reacted sharply against the patrician ideal: this was the kind of schism which produced the decisive breach within the Progressive movement between Theodore Roosevelt and La Follette in 1912, and which ultimately led to the latter throwing his support behind Woodrow Wilson. Here in the Mid- and Far-West, as for the Populists who preceded them, Britain seemed to most Progressives less of a social model than a symbol of the class enemy.[37] However forward-looking in its social policies, Britain for the La Follettes and Norrises still represented a hierarchical, monarchical, interest-ridden society, dominated by reactionary landowners as it was in 1776, and further reinforced by the insidious capitalistic concerns of the City of London. When war broke out in Europe in August 1914, La Follette's sympathy for the social reforms of the British Liberal Government or for his French forbears in no way led him to identify with the *entente* powers. Indeed, he believed that British finance imperialism was in large measure responsible for bringing the war about − with the incidental assistance of the arms manufacturers, later to be christened 'merchants of death'.

Other Progressives were also disillusioned by the more undemocratic aspects of the British scene, long before 1914. These were emphasised for many Progressives by British policy towards Ireland which repelled many Liberals beyond the restricted confines of Irish-American circles. Lincoln Steffens was another prepared to borrow reforming techniques from Britain while rejecting the essence of its social structure. He believed that in Britain there lurked some of the graver evils of the American scene, but in a more subtle form. Corruption, openly displayed in America through political graft, was quietly diffused in Britain through its education system − the career of Cecil Rhodes was an illustration of this.[38] Where America had financial interests, Britain had class privilege, in many ways much more entrenched and more dangerous. There was, Steffens felt, need for a British muck-raking press to expose conditions across the Atlantic. Even Frederick Howe fell somewhat short of a total admiration for the British social and political system. Despite all the reforms introduced by the Asquith government since 1908, he noted that privilege and the power of the landed interest was still pervasive in Britain; a more determined effort was needed to uproot it than the government, even Lloyd George, had so far attempted. Howe was dismayed by the crude imperialism rampant amongst the Liberal social reformers he admired: 'even the Labour Party had a confused veneration for Empire'.[39] Howe did not want an empire that was a greater Birmingham, but rather a Birmingham which was a crown colony writ small with a Chamberlain as its viceroy. When European war broke out in 1914, Howe felt as detached from the melee as did La Follette. After all, the two countries whose social experiments he most admired were ranged on opposite sides.

The criticism of Britain voiced by American Progressives took varying forms. To Croly, and in a sense to Steffens, what was wrong with Britain was that, politically, it was too democratic. All manner of social groups and classes were given freedom to operate and organise – for instance, the influence of the religious denominations on the British primary education system was the despair of many American radicals. In Croly's view, this pluralist system meant a suppression of the concentrated forces of the true 'popular energy'.[40] He favoured a powerful, centralised paternalism, with a heavy concentration on the executive: there were those later who accused him (perhaps unfairly) of Fascist implications. Steffens also admired strong government: hence his distaste for the confusions and ultra-democracy of the British Labour Party, and his later enthusiasm for the totalitarian dictatorship in the Soviet Union. The future 'worked' in Moscow as it simply did not in Manchester or Merthyr Tydfil. Steffens (and Ernest Bevin) despised the ILP radical 'whose bleeding 'eart ran away with 'is bloody 'ead'. Conversely other Progressives felt that Britain remained too undemocratic, its social justice movement unduly based on class segregation, its civic reformers too superior and isolated. Howe had praised the British city because only a small number of its officials were popularly elected,[41] but this could easily be inverted into a major criticism. The moral was starkly pointed out by the mysterious and secretive manner in which Britain, directed by Grey, the very exemplar of the Liberal Imperialist patrician admired by American Progressives, went furtively to war in August 1914. Britain was not a social democracy, and a political democracy only with serious qualifications.

There was another, wider aspect of British Liberalism in these years which tended to alarm Progressives of most shades – its unduly close links with organised labour. Despite their concern for the working man, American Progressives viewed his plight from the outside, as they also viewed the farmer, the immigrant and the Negro. Progressives felt far removed from Gompers and the world of American Labour unionism; they deeply feared the violence and class upheaval symbolised by the 'Wobblies'. Progressives wanted civic and humanitarian reform, but in a conservative, capitalist setting. They did not, in general, openly pose fundamental questions about the distribution of wealth or the control of economic power. They preferred a co-operative commonwealth to a socialist state: Denmark was their 'middle way' as Sweden was for Marquis Childs during the New Deal.[42] Ultimately, perhaps, most Progressives hoped to reform men rather than institutions, to change society through moral enlightenment and civic education rather than through structural reform. Upton Sinclair found that his novel, *The Jungle,* an account of the horrific labour conditions in the meat-packing factories in Chicago, appealed to the middle-class consumer not to the working-class producer. It produced the Pure Food and Drug Act, not factory legislation. Meanwhile, labour conditions in Chicago remained as uncivilised as before. Workers went on voting Republican and Democratic, rather than Socialist, just the same. Sinclair, as he wrote in disgust, had aimed at the public's heart and hit its stomach instead.[43] By contrast, British Liberalism released new formidable forces beyond the capacity of the patrician elite to control. Asquith could not play 'finality Jack' to the Labour movement. The industrial unrest in Britain in 1910–14, at a time of alarming manifestations in the United States with violent strikes and the upsurge of the 'Wobblies', emphasised for many American Progressives that their reforming zeal had its firm limits. It could remould capitalism, but it should not destroy it. It was planned for the working men but did not arise spontaneously from their needs. Even the tenement house reformers were often careless of the wishes of the proletariat whose wretched conditions they sought to remedy, as Sylvia Pankhurst told them bluntly enough during her two American lecture tours in 1911–12. Eventually, most British Liberals felt their links with organised labour in a 'progressive alliance' were becoming closer: in March 1914 there was the real prospect of a Liberal–Labour coalition government. Most American Progressives were still happy to keep their distance from the working man, and to view Debs, distastefully, from afar.

For all its limits, the connection between British and American Progressivism in this period was evidently a close one. Despite the fears of Croly and others, developments in Britain still provided a fund of ideas and inspiration for American reformers down to August 1914. The election of Woodrow Wilson as president in 1912, a man deeply steeped in British political tradition and folklore, a worshipper at the shrine of Gladstonian liberalism in its most traditional form, seemed to make the links between British and American liberals still more complete. Yet, it was Wilson in fact who dramatically underlined the differences between them. His New Freedom in 1913 had virtually no social content: labour was just another special interest which could claim no privileged treatment from the federal government. His main priorities were the trusts, tariffs and banking – monopoly and the concentration of large-scale industrial and financial power were the main targets. None of these held much significance for British Liberals, free traders and the products of a more integrated, less sectional society. Their approach to concentrations of economic power was to place them under public control rather than to dismantle them entirely. In any case, tariff reform had largely been suppressed as a major issue in British politics; it was wider industrial problems, together with the unique hazards of Ireland, which preoccupied British Liberals now. The outbreak of war in August 1914 confirmed the gulf that still existed between Britain and the United States in their political systems and priorities. In any event, the massive immigration into the United States since the 1890s was steadily eroding much of the Anglo-American connection. Despite the temporary enthusiasm of the British left for Woodrow Wilson as a transatlantic Messiah in 1917–18, the old links were never restored. The steady decline of British Liberalism, the rise of a Labour Party, the new polarisation between labour and capital as the central fact of British political life after 1918, coincided with a new surge of business ascendancy under Republican rule in the United States. 'Normalcy' largely killed off American Progressivism, and the British associations that had helped to foster it. In the 1930s, save for a maverick like Lloyd George, the New Deal failed to kindle the old fire amongst the British left. Franklin Roosevelt's brisk destruction of the World Economic Conference in July 1933 revealed the essential nationalism, even isolationism, of his administration. Keynes was a rare British enthusiast for this decision of Roosevelt's to prioritise national currency management – 'President Roosevelt is magnificently right.'

Even so, the transatlantic aspects of American Progressivism should not be ignored. They serve to show how American Liberalism had emerged from its inward-looking cocoon of the Populist years. They showed, too, how the frankly elitist ideals of the civil service reformers and Genteel Reform patricians had merged with wider democratic currents after 1890. American Progressives did not enlist British and other European ideas because they were the apprehensive victims of a status revolution, as Hofstadter argued in his *Age of Reform*. In the main they represented (as did their businessmen antagonists) social groups which had survived, indeed flourished, throughout the Gilded Age and the so-called Robber Baron era. To the university teachers, lawyers, journalists and social workers who provided the ethic and the passion for so much of American Progressivism, especially in the cities, the British experience gave them a confident, optimistic, crusading aspect, not a defensive, alarmist one.

Radical reform was again possible, desirable, even profitable, in the United States. It was rooted in basic American ideals dating from the founding fathers and beyond. But, above all, it flourished 'over there', in Britain in the here and now. In the Old World, Frederick Howe and his friends beheld a vision of the future – and it worked.

Labour

Chapter 9

Seven Ages of Socialism: Keir Hardie to Gordon Brown

Just over twenty-five years ago, for the only time in my life, I met the Queen. The occasion was the celebration of the seventy-fifth anniversary of the Historical Association back in 1906, and a number of us had given lectures around the country on aspects of Edwardian Britain. The Queen politely asked me what my topic had been. With a sinking heart, I replied, 'socialism, Ma'am'. A period of silence ensued. Then the Queen produced the rather striking remark, 'They must have been highly motivated.' I then lapsed into silence before stammering something about the strong Christian beliefs of the founding fathers. It was a brief, difficult conversation. It showed me that the notion of socialism still had the power to stun, perhaps to shock. Yet in fact, from Keir Hardie onwards, the guiding star of the Labour Party has been socialism. The party's election manifesto in 1945, written by Michael Young, declared that:

> The Labour Party is a Socialist Party and proud of it. Its ultimate purpose at home is the establishment of the Socialist Commonwealth of Great Britain – free, democratic, efficient, progressive, public spirited.

In the centenary year of its foundation, 2006, during the Blair government, this socialist heritage was often, understandably, underplayed. The programme of the original LRC in February 1900 was not committed to any particular doctrine. It rejected a motion to endorse socialism and 'recognition of the class war'. Down to 1918, in fact, the Labour Party had no distinctive ideology; it merely stood for the defence of 'labour', loosely defined. When Clause Four appeared in the new constitution of 1918, it was exceptionally vague, little more than a compendium of almost every kind of socialist doctrine known, from public ownership to workers' control, Guild socialism and the Co-op.

Yet without its socialism, Labour would have been nothing. The idea was central to the operations of the Attlee government after 1945. This was acknowledged by perhaps an unlikely source, Roy Jenkins. Writing in a volume of speeches, *What Matters Now,* published in 1974, Jenkins observed that, 'a working-class party without a Socialist philosophy would be a front for vested interests.'

When I asked Jim Callaghan (also thought of as being on the party right), after I had finished writing his official biography, whether he had always been a socialist, he replied simply, 'Of course, Ken, of course'. He was clearly surprised I had felt it necessary to ask him. The foundation meeting of the LRC in 1900 at the Memorial Hall, Farringdon Street, was largely orchestrated by the minority of socialists, some of them Marxists in the SDF. The National Executive that was created reflected this, with five places reserved for socialists out of twelve, for the ILP, the SDF and the Fabians. There were also socialists in key posts in a number of major trade unions like George Barnes in the Engineers, a skilled trade, Ben Tillett in the unskilled Dockers. The South Wales Miners' Federation, the largest and most rapidly growing part of the Miners' Federation of Great Britain, was soon to be dominated by officials and miners' agents who were socialists, often very much on the left, like Noah Ablett. Nor was Clause Four a meaningless document in the 1918 party constitution – Hugh Gaitskell much under-estimated its potency in 1959 when he tried to get rid of it. For decades it provided a compass for the parliamentary variant of socialism. It inspired Labour leaders from Keir Hardie to John Smith (indeed, they included Gaitskell himself). Not until 1994 was Labour led by someone who was manifestly non-socialist, Tony Blair. It was natural, therefore, that with his new authority he should be successful in getting rid of Clause Four forever.

But what was this socialism? Herbert Morrison's famous description during the Attlee period was that it was what a Labour government did. Harold Wilson in 1964 was equally vague – it was 'applying a sense of purpose to our national life'. He added to the sense of bafflement when in his conference speech he declared that socialism was 'about science'. It always seemed an alien, continental word. It had to be translated for Welsh socialists into the comforting *cymdeithasiaeth*. The original invention 'sosialaeth' sounded totally alien. Often socialism conveyed only a broad sense of forward movement, 'on and on and on, up and up and up' in Ramsay MacDonald's legendary formulation. Alan Taylor used to describe sharing a room on a visit to Russia in the late 1920s with an old Scottish socialist, who would wake up in the middle of the night and shout out, 'It's coming in a fortnight'. Anthony Crosland's classic text *The Future of Socialism* in 1956 identified at least 12 varieties, all with some contemporary relevance. The whole notion, so often linked in continental countries with formal statements like the Gotha Programme of the German Social Democrats, has seemed here very British, a melange of political, economic and moral objectives.

The purpose here is to look at seven ages of socialism that flourished during the history of the parliamentary party. They are not comprehensive, and they overlap. Some disappear only to re-emerge in a different form. But each had its place in the sun. Labour's socialism constantly contradicted itself, but like Walt Whitman it contained multitudes.

1. Socialism as Fraternity

At the end of the Victorian era, British pioneer socialists were clear that socialism was more than simply liberty (which could be viewed as pure laissez-faire, after all). Socialism added a different dimension to the socially reformist, neo-Hegelian New Liberalism of philosophers like T.H. Green or L.T. Hobhouse It was also more than simply equality since it sought to transform the economic framework within which social relationships were formed. Labour's mass membership came from the unions, including increasingly skilled unions like the Engineers imbued with the status aspirations of the respectable Victorian Labour aristocracy and much affected by the ethos of nonconformity. Increasingly, socialism focussed on fraternity and fellowship, on an essentially ethical creed of comradeship. This creed was associated most strongly with the ILP, and especially with evangelists like Keir Hardie. It appealed strongly in areas like the West Riding, the North East and South Wales where populist nonconformity had been powerful. In Wales, the religious revival of 1904–5 gave it an improbable boost, inspiring young socialists destined perhaps for the ministry like Noah Ablett, S.O. Davies and Arthur Horner. In the West Riding, it inspired missionaries like Philip Snowden, and even Victor Grayson, the erratic left-wing radical elected for Colne Valley in 1907, and another reclaimed from the ranks of the religious.

Keir Hardie, the ILP's first chairman, viewed socialism as essentially a gospel. It was important that socialism was more than a narrow materialist 'economism'. Socialism, Hardie wrote in *From Serfdom to Socialism* (1907), was 'not a system of economics' and had relatively little concern with the machinery of government. Its inspiring message could bring in middle-class people like the young Clem Attlee and Hugh Dalton, even eccentric aristocrats like the Countess of Warwick. It 'blended the classes' into one human family. Ramsay MacDonald, the ILP's chief political philosopher in its early years, also endorsed this view of fraternity. Further, as one who had some training as a scientist, he gave it important scientific backing. Socialism was biologically inevitable, a product of progressive social evolution. MacDonald's many books on this theme, either side of the First World War, had a high reputation in socialist circles, whatever his subsequent reputation as a rhetorical windbag. Comrades described him as Labour's 'greatest intellectual asset'. The effect of his writings, it was felt, was to give scientific backing to British socialism's essentially moral imperative. Hardie himself was sometimes criticised for lack of focus, but not in his logic but rather in his proclaimed themes. He was attacked at times for giving primacy to other issues, especially the 'woman question' or international peace in preference to the social-ist struggle at home. But of the primacy of his fraternal appeal there was broad agreement.

The ILP's ethical socialism was challenged in the early years by the idea of efficiency. The Fabians championed this doctrine, advocating rational structures of ordered collectivism within a functional state. The Minority Report on the Poor Law in 1909, advocated by Beatrice and Sidney Webb, was a supreme statement of this kind of approach. But its appeal for the early Labour Party was limited. After all, the Fabians before 1914 saw themselves as a pressure group permeating civil society as a whole. Intellectuals like the Webbs tended to be contemptuous of woolly minded working-class leaders like Keir Hardie. From within, they were sharply attacked by H.G. Wells for bourgeois elitism. Until the outbreak of war they were marginal to the political ideas of the Labour movement. Only during the war did they become central to its agenda.

Fraternalism of the ILP type was a gospel for survival in a hostile capitalist world. It was a dominant creed amongst the 29 LRC members elected at the general election of 1906. But in itself it was insufficient. The confrontational world of industrial conflict, major strikes and an employ-ers' counter-attack, the era of Taff Vale and Tonypandy, was increasingly to see the idea of fraternalism linked with the idea of class. The First World War and its aftermath down to the General Strike made it seem like an antique survival from revivalist nonconformity and the Lib–Lab mentality before 1914. What survived, and powerfully so, was a moral message: the Labour election manifesto of 1950 pronounced that 'social-ism does not mean bread alone'. There was also an enduring human legacy, the memory of a once inspirational leader, embodied in party con-ference down to the 1980s, 'If Keir Hardie were alive today'.

2. Socialism as Workers' Power

The 'great unrest' of the years up to 1914, and even more the experi-ence of the war years promoted a far sharper, more confrontational idea of socialism. They saw the growth of huge new combines in industry such as coal mining and steel manufacturing, an immense expansion of trade unions amongst unskilled workers, and a greater diversity of the workforce, including the significant impact of Irish workers amongst the dockers and others. Capitalism, socialists argued, should be resisted by the collective force of workers' power. This was the view, for instance, of the young Ernest Bevin, as he made his way as a youthful organiser of the Transport Workers. Bevin had little time for parliamentary pressure or the imperatives of fraternalism. He shared to the full the outlook of the legendary Yorkshire miners' leader, Herbert Smith: 'On t'field, that's t'place.' In his way, he was a class warrior.

But what form would workers' power as an expression of socialism actually take? There were great debates, notably amongst the miners of South Wales, which left the Westminster parliamentarians and gradualist politicians like MacDonald and Henderson somewhat sidelined. The Miners Federation of Great Britain and other major unions such as the National Union of Railwaymen increasingly endorsed the national ownership of the means of production and distribution. Central government alone could mobilise the miners, docks or railways to promote the public control of resources, and also give a proper return to the workers. Non-militant, non-Marxist union leaders like Vernon Hartshorn of the Welsh miners took this view. They found something of a model in the forms of central control imposed on the economy by Lloyd George's government during the First World War, and these strongly influenced the approach of Clause Four (Clause 3 (d) at that time) in Labour's constitution of 1918. Interestingly, it was a model to which even clearly anti-socialist government ministers like Winston Churchill and Eric Geddes could also subscribe. Not a great deal followed in providing detailed blueprints on how nationalisation might be put into practice before the Second World War. The famous story is that when Manny Shinwell looked in the files of Transport House to find guidance on how coal nationalisation might be achieved, all he could find was a pamphlet by James Griffiths in Welsh. It might be apocryphal but it embodies a wider truth.

A quite different scenario came from small groups like the Plebs League and the Unofficial Reform Committee in South Wales. They cherished a vision of direct industrial power proclaimed by Tom Mann and the Marxist tutors of the Central Labour College, with some indirect influence from the French syndicalism of Sorel. An ideologue like Noah Ablett argued not for central control but for industrial devolution, not 'mines for the people' but 'mines for the miners'. He attacked the bureaucratic approach of state nationalisation. 'State workers', declared Ablett, were always in a condition of servility. Alienated workers, in enclosed communities remote from industrial power, saw this vision of localism as the key not simply to economic but to spiritual freedom. In the biblical words of the *Miners' Next Step,* they would have the means 'really to live as men and not as the beasts that perish'. A historic debate at Trealaw in South Wales in 1912 saw these two visions of national and localised vividly debated before a fascinated mass audience. At stake was not merely the direction of the economy but also the structure of the trade union movement, with nationwide unions and pay bargaining fundamentally challenged. The devolutionists felt that they had won.

The Labour Party was both threatened and stimulated by these ideas. The Russian Revolution, including the later notion of 'soviets' excited many of Labour's leaders, even, for a time, Arthur Henderson himself. They reached their peak of influence in the harsh years of industrial conflict and economic downturn between 1919 and 1926. The TUC General Council soon came to see their limitations. When Bob Smillie of the Miners met the prime minister, Lloyd George in 1921 to discuss a possible national strike by the Triple Alliance, the latter was direct and disarming, 'Gentlemen, we are helpless before you'. But he also asked penetratingly whether the unions were now ready to take over the running of the country. 'At that moment', recalled Smillie, 'I knew that we were beaten'. Pressure for workers' power remained strong down to the calling of the General Strike in 1926. Even Ernest Bevin responded to its heady appeal. 'Governments may come and go' observed Bevin; the facts of industrial conflict would be eternal. But the collapse of the General Strike soon changed his mind. Two years later, he was engaged with employers' leaders in promoting the corporatism of the Mond-Turner talks.

Thereafter, the mirage of workers' power faded away during the depression of the 1930s which promoted solidarity not separatism. Yet in one powerful mind the dialectic continued to rage. The young Aneurin Bevan grew up during the First World War much influenced by Noah Ablett's quasi-syndicalism as expounded in *The Miners' Next Step*. In the thirties he was genuinely ambivalent about the right strategy. Even as a centralising ministers, he lamented that workers within nationalised industries, centrally directed and largely undemocratic, were powerful. But he too was retreating from the vision of socialism as a doctrine of decision-making at the workplace and the point of production. The variegated essays of *In Place of Fear* showed on balance how he had become a political, parliamentary socialist. This meant capturing the mechanisms of the central state. Socialism was about the mobilisation of power, however elusive its location.

3. Socialism as Planning

As noted above, the idea of socialism as efficiency had been promoted by the Fabians before 1914. It was a powerful doctrine of social organisation and orderly political administration, based on a positive science of society. The war socialism of 1914–18 gave socialists like the Webbs a new prominence, and bodies like the Emergency Workers' Committee encouraged the idea of the planning of resources nationwide. But even in the twenties many of Labour's domestic ideas were reproductions of older

Liberalism. Philip Snowden's free trade budgets when at the Treasury in Labour's first two governments of 1924 and 1929 showed him up as the last Cobdenite. Socialism had no distinct economic dimension, no programme for the here and now. Thus ideas of socialism as planning took off anew after the political and financial crisis of 1931. A variety of think-tanks now pressed the case for it – the New Fabian Research Group, the XYZ group and others of that kind – pressed the case for planning. They now had useful models overseas, the Soviet Union, Roosevelt's economic programmes in the United States during the New Deal, and above all Sweden, always hailed as a kind of Fabian utopia, the British planners' very favourite country.

The vision of planning captured the young economists grouped around Hugh Dalton in the thirties – Evan Durbin, Hugh Gaitskell and above all Douglas Jay in *The Socialist Case* (1937). Jay and his friends assumed the endemic decline of capitalism and the elementary need for the rational planning of resources. There was no woolly fraternalism about the lofty Wykehamist fellow of All Souls, Douglas Jay. 'The case for socialism is mainly economic and it rests on fact.' His friend, Evan Durbin, in *The Politics of Democratic Socialism* added other elements – a concern with social psychology which emphasised the human instinct for non-violent co-operation, and an almost mystical sense of patriotism. It was an ethical social democrat's version of Socialism in One Country.

From the mid-thirties, it became clear that the young planners were more than just Keynesians. Indeed the work of men in the XYZ Group and similar bodies preceded the publication of Keynes's *General Theory* in 1936. Dalton, the senior guru amongst Labour economists, was himself a former pupil of Keynes at Cambridge, and saw his old tutor as a philosophic liberal (and no great democrat either) whose philosophy was not essentially congenial to socialists. But they were also able to blend the tenets of economic planning with democratic socialism. Planning was the answer to a democracy that had been betrayed and to a capitalism that was in collapse. It could also take on board a considerable degree of public ownership, about which Labour had done nothing since 1918, as a way of achieving economic rationalisation. The Labour Manifesto of 1937, with many proposals for public ownership on board including nationalisation of the land, is a key document in this shift. The key to British socialism, therefore, was planning, not just centrally but also in local government, where Herbert Morrison's programmes on the London County Council were thought to exemplify the new ethos. Indeed, Morrison's was a prevailing influence because it was his scheme for the centrally administered London Passenger Transport Board in the early thirties that offered just about the only model on how public ownership might actually be carried out.

Planning reached the summit of its influence during the Second World War. The devastation wrought by the Luftwaffe in so many major cities was in itself seen as a major argument for it, in relation to housing, health, town planning and much else. A famous issue of *Picture Post* in 1941 was devoted to this theme, with powerful intellectuals like Julian Huxley, Maxwell Fry and Thomas Balogh writing in it. Younger socialists like Jay, Gaitskell and Harold Wilson were prominent in key agencies of the wartime civil service. Dalton at the Board of Trade launched a new directive approach to end regional disparities in the so-called depressed areas of pre-war. He worked closely with collectively minded civil servants like the famous Richard Clarke, re-christened with the nickname 'Otto' for his sympathy with Prussian styles of central direction, and father of one of Tony Blair's Cabinet ministers. After the 1945 general election, however, planning lost much of its sheen. Neither Dalton nor Herbert Morrison were really planners in, say, Jay's sense. Post-war planning was in any case prejudiced by its being linked with the physical controls retained from the war in the subsequent period of 'austerity'. For political and other reasons, the government was anxious to relax the impact of controls. The 'bonfire' of controls proclaimed by that former wartime technocrat Harold Wilson at the Board of Trade marked a process of retreat. The Tory cry 'set the people free' marked an end of the planning consensus of the wartime years.

Planning also implied serious philosophical difficulties. Was it centralist and directive, as urged by 'Otto' Clarke or merely indicative as advocated by economists like James Meade and Robert Hall? 'Totalitarian' and 'democratic' models of planning contended throughout government; and especially at the Treasury in the era of Stafford Cripps as chancellor of the exchequer (1947–50). Planning as a cohesive policy was in fact difficult to fit in with the rigid, self-contained structures of nationalisation. In practice, the emphasis tended to be placed more on Keynesian-style systems of demand management. Another problem was fitting in British planning into a radically changed international economy after Bretton Woods. In practice, it seemed to resemble a kind of insular protectionism.

Planning did not disappear in the 1950s. On the contrary, Labour spokesmen made much of the rationality of socialist planning compared with Tory muddle-through. The planners were again in the ascendant in the party as the Macmillan government entered its decline after 1960 – hence Aneurin Bevan's earlier complaint of the influence of 'desiccated calculating machines'. Harold Wilson's speeches in 1964 and

Labour's election manifesto had planning almost everywhere – there would be plans for Industry, the Regions, Transport and Prices (significantly not for Wages at this stage). But the Department of Economic Affairs under George Brown, intended to promote a 30 per cent rate of economic growth over the next six years, was relatively ineffective, and his National Plan largely collapsed after the devaluation of the pound in 1967 gave new priority to the value of sterling and the balance of payments. The Treasury retained its iron grip over the key levers of policy. By 1970, planning looked to be another version of socialism that had bit the dust. Neither Labour's right-wing (witness Tony Crosland's *Socialism Now* in 1974) nor its ex-Bevanite left, with its links to the unions, really believed in it. As Ben Pimlott so powerfully stated in his biography of Harold Wilson, 'the death of planning left a void at the heart of Labour's ideology ever after'.

4. Socialism as Equality

In the fifties and sixties, planning was being challenged by a quite different version of socialism, sociological rather than economic. This was the idea of equality. This harked back to the earliest origins of the socialist movement, even back to the radical instincts of the Peasants' Revolt in 1381 when the itinerant preacher, John Ball, asked the immortal question, 'When Adam delved and Eve span, who was then the gentleman'? The essential political equality of the Putney debates amongst the Levellers and their Cromwellian opponents appealed to a writer like Michael Foot (even if his own father was founder of the Cromwell Association). In his famous Halley Stewart lectures of 1929 published in 1931 under the title *Equality*, R.H. Tawney spelt out how inequality of financial resources should lead to redistribution of wealth; how inequality of economic power should mean the public ownership and control of industry; and how inequality of political power should be redressed by decentralisation and a revitalisation of local and regional government. His was a fundamental influence on Labour's thinking about equality from that time on. The Second World War, with its theme of common citizenship and common suffering, made the impact of egalitarian ideas more popular. The wartime writings of Orwell, especially the social patriotism of *The Lion and the Unicorn*, drove home the egalitarian message. Clement Attlee, Labour's leader in 1937, spelt it out in *The Labour Party in Perspective*, 'The aim of the Socialist Commonwealth is equality'.

But the idea only took hold as a dominant principle after the fall of the Attlee government. That famous Labour administration had not in fact given social equality a high priority. The emphasis, if anything, was more on equality of opportunity. The public schools, deeply inegalitarian, remained as they were, while the state secondary schools were divided into three parts like Gaul, with the expectation that secondary moderns would educate the future workers, and the grammar schools cater to the middle-class minority of future professionals. The minister of education, Ellen Wilkinson, was herself a product of Manchester grammar school and had great faith in them as social levellers which would promote a wider mobility. Her successor, George Tomlinson, once a Lancashire textile worker, was so impressed by Eton that he wished he could have gone there himself. Even Aneurin Bevan had to take account of the different aspirations and needs of the various classes in planning post-war housing programmes for the new estates, the professional executives as well as the manual workers. His followers, the future Bevanites, mainly journalists and other middle-class professionals, were largely concerned with foreign and defence policy, and, with the exception of Richard Crossman, were largely empty on domestic policies, such as education and the social services.

A great change came in 1952. Nationalisation, focussing on trivia as Tate and Lyle's monopoly of sugar refining, had now lost its sheen. 'Consolidation' was a polite way of saying that it had reached its appointed end. Post-war planning was linked with restrictions, rationing and control. Then the West Indian economist W. Arthur Lewis famously pronounced that 'socialism was about equality'. Hugh Gaitskell, also an economist, enthusiastically endorsed this conclusion, a natural appeal presenting itself to a former WEA lecturer in the Nottinghamshire coalfield suffused by middle-class guilt. The New Fabian Essays of 1952 also had much to say about equality. Roy Jenkins, remarkably, linked it with financial redistribution in advocating the case for a capital levy on egalitarian grounds. He pointed out that in some ways nationalisation had actually extended financial inequality. The supreme advocate of the idea of equality was Anthony Crosland in his classic text, The Future of Socialism in 1956. He argued here that modern economic circumstances, in effect the success of the capitalist system, had made older versions of socialism such as nationalisation irrelevant and out-of-date. Marxism was not only economically inefficient but also illiberal. The stimulus of American thinking was important for Crosland, in particular the egalitarian, redistributive ideas of John Kenneth Galbraith in such works as The Affluent Society with its mantra of private affluence and public squalor. Crosland, therefore placed the main emphasis on social equality, notably in education through the creation of comprehensive schools, and the redistribution of wealth and not merely income. Crosland's influence was transparent in the 1959 Labour manifesto. It emphasised the 'socialist belief in the equal value of every human being'.

Crosland pushed hard at this policy while he was the secretary of state for education. He did nothing about the public schools (one of which he had himself attended) but dogmatically declared his intention to close 'every fucking grammar school in England'. Yet by 1970, equality too was receding as a priority for socialists. There were fears about the defence of democracy in the attempt to promote equality of outcomes. Within a property-owning democracy, the new middle-class voters that Labour had attracted in 1964 and 1966 were concerned as consumers with freedom of choice including of suppliers. There were also other kinds of equality altogether that now attracted attention, notably gender equality and racial equality in an increasingly multi-racial society. In *Socialism Now* in 1974, Crosland rightly pointed to several achievements in promoting equality after 1964, notably in education, but he also judged the six years of the Wilson government to be a time of relative failure on that front. His whole diagnosis of educational policy now looks distinctly threadbare – he had nothing on the content of education or methods of instruction, for instance, none of the concerns to be raised in Jim Callaghan's Ruskin speech in 1976. On balance, the emphasis on the primacy of equality disappeared after the death of Hugh Gaitskell. In part, it was based on optimism about capitalism that the 1970s undermined. Labour's ideologues now preferred to talk about 'fairness' instead, not the same idea at all.

5. Socialism as Modernisation

By the 1960s, British socialism was stuck in unproductive grooves. There were endless arguments about further nationalisation, and many more about Britain's international role, focussing on the crusades of the Campaign for Nuclear Disarmament, many of whose leaders were neither socialists nor politicians. In his celebrated speech to the Scarborough party conference in October 1963, Harold Wilson brilliantly achieved the trick of getting away from 'theology' by adopting the cause of 'modernisation'. He also added his own social colouring. He drew a vivid contrast between a northern grammar school boy like himself, a product of the new meritocracy, and the grouse-moor image of the fourteenth Earl of Home. This chimed in with contemporary diagnoses by men like Michael Shanks, Anthony Sampson and Michael Young at the time, with their texts on 'what's wrong with Britain?' and attacks on the paralysing grip of 'the establishment' (a term actually invented by a Tory journalist, Henry Fairlie).

Wilson, who was viewed as a man of the left since he had resigned with Aneurin Bevan over health services charges in the 1951 budget, linked the cause of the left with innovation. In part this meant reviving the idea of planning, with new talk of a national plan that would stabilise the economy and prevent the lurches familiar during the 'thirteen wasted years' of Tory rule. A vital component of his doctrine was the key role of science.

> We are restating our socialism in terms of the scientific revolution... This is what socialism means – a unity of direction for all the decisions a government has to take ... That means planning. (*The New Britain*, 1964)

He also talked about the wider modernisation of the civil service, of parliament, and, more daringly of labour relations with a less adversarial approach. This chimed in with current preoccupations with the existence of 'two cultures', the one humane but effete, the other scientific and forward-looking, popularised by C.P. Snow in some famous lectures. It also focussed attention on the need to compete with other countries such as the French and the Germans, already well advanced with economic and governmental modernisation. There were several overseas technocratic models, a famous one being that of Jean-Jacques Servan-Schreiber, a liberal French intellectual, in *Le Défi Américain*. This argued powerfully that European nations could only meet the technological challenge from the United States (whose dynamism he much admired) through themselves undergoing a wholesale modernisation in their technology, science education, management and marketing.

Modernisation as an idea was essentially value-free. Wilson's own background lay in wartime technocracy under Beveridge, flavoured by some enthusiasm for Soviet planning (which apparently attracted the later interest of MI5!). He extended the cult of science in the Ministry of Technology (originally, strangely, occupied by the trades unionist, Frank Cousins, later by Tony Benn), and using scientific advisers like Solly Zuckerman over defence technology, and Professor Patrick Blackett, an intellectual neo-Marxist survivor of the thirties. C.P. Snow also received employment. The Robbins report on higher education was vigorously followed up, purportedly to develop science, pure and applied, but in fact resulting in a massive expansion in the humanities and social sciences instead, especially among women students.

This creed of socialistic modernisation was not without its achievements. There was indeed an emphasis on investment in higher education and the new Colleges of Advanced Technology, plus the remarkable social innovation of the Open University for part-time students. However, the stimulus to science was only partly successful – Professor Blackett resigned, a disappointed, even bitter man. There was also little enough modernisation either of the civil service or of the parliamentary system. Wilson's proposed reform of the House of Lords collapsed amidst charges of patronage, with even the minister responsible for it, James Callaghan the home secretary, openly sceptical. In industrial relations, the trade unions were strongly hostile to state or legal interference, and successfully resisted Barbara Castle's Industrial Relations Bill in 1969, while a senior trade union leader like Jack Jones tended to favour the syndicalism and local bargaining of his youth in Merseyside. In the end, planning and modernisation seemed less important than saving the pound.

The main heir of this modernisation creed was in fact the Conservative leader Edward Heath, who became prime minister partly on this programme in 1970, the Europhile moderniser cohabiting uneasily with the unreconstructed free marketeer that was 'Selsdon Man'. Labour in Wilson's final phase after 1970 turned inwards to pursue its old class premises. Modernisation gave way to corporatism, a philosophy for the protection of vested interests on both sides of industry. In the 1970 general election, Wilson used the word 'socialism' once, and that was once more than most ministers. It was goodbye to all that. The quest for the socialist golden fleece went on.

6. Socialism as Nationalism

In the 1970s, ideological debate was overlain by massive economic pressures, especially after the huge inflation of oil and other prices after the Arab-Israeli war of 1973. Most of the old socialist themes were thus in considerable intellectual difficulty. Jim Callaghan had some residual interest in both ideas of equality and economic planning, but both were impossible to reconcile with other aspects of government policy, notably the Social Contract with the unions. None of them seemed of much help for the declining purchasing power of lower-paid workers. A more fundamentalist or traditionalist attitude now came to the fore – socialism as Nationalism, to which in their different fashions both putative leaders of the left, Tony Benn and Michael Foot, subscribed.

In the turmoil of in the seventies, it was widely felt among socialists that there was an urgent need to resume lost powers, including powers of national sovereignty, in the face of the failed doctrines of both Keynesianism and corporatism. The socialist response to the crisis of capitalism was vividly portrayed in a book such as Stuart Holland's *Socialist Challenge* published in 1975. A fierce attack was launched here against the power of multi-national giants and their 'meso-economic power' which overrode national democracies. An alternative economic strategy thus came to power, linked with the residual power of the trade unions, British socialists' answer to the new global fluidity introduced with the end of the post-war Bretton Woods world.

A British Labour government, it was argued, should reclaim sovereignty, stop the outward flow of investment, impose import controls and conduct a siege economy of planning agreements and directives. There should also be a total rejection of membership of Europe, a capitalist club into which Britain had been enmeshed since 1973, a decision confirmed in a referendum in 1975. This was a version of socialism in one country, and much reinforced by historical patriotism in the case of a literary socialist like Michael Foot. But it ran into trouble within the Labour Party, with the unions aiming to override government or Treasury priorities, and was in time overwhelmingly rejected by the voters. The political aftermath was Thatcherism and 18 years of Tory government. Michael Foot, an old leftist, was buffeted about almost uncontrollably during his years of party leadership (1980–3). He still retained the authority to turn his oratorical fire at the Bennites, accusing them of pursuing not socialism but democratic centralism, more Lenin than Trotsky. It proved almost impossible to reconcile the central control of the levers of economy power with the voluntaryist and separatist instincts of the trade unions, and even more with failed workers' co-operatives at Meriden and elsewhere. The ideological argument between Foot and Benn in the early eighties was a major doctrinal event, a contest for the historical roots, perhaps the soul of British socialism. In the end, they both lost. Labour, fighting the 1983 general election on its most left-wing programme since 1934, suffered its worst defeat since the party had assumed its modern form in 1918.

In the Thatcher years, socialism as nationalism, now popularly though inaccurately defined as 'old Labour', ebbed away. Neil Kinnock was a product of Welsh valleys socialism, but his book *Paying Our Way* (1986) said nothing about it save for the obligatory quote from Nye Bevan. Roy Hattersley in 1987 based his more libertarian view of socialism on the progressive egalitiarian philosophies of John Rawls but still failed to give the old doctrines any fresh credibility. One of the few reviving the socialist idea, or even the word, was Gordon Brown in *Where There Is Greed*, an attack on Thatcherism, published in 1990. 'Socialism', wrote Brown, 'has always been about more than equality'. The phrase was coined 'supply-side socialism', an amalgam of old socialism with new technocracy, an attempt to link old ethical values with modernisation. In the end, in a global economy, together with the ending of the Cold War which dispelled fantasies of the Soviet model for all time, a purely nation-centred version of socialism, incoherent in itself, just could not be sustained. One of its advocates then was the younger Ken Livingstone. But when he was elected mayor of London in 2000, in defiance of the Labour Party machine, he made his city not a fortress of socialist purity but an open, easily permeated centre for global capitalism in its most mobile form. Its ironic legacy emerged during the near-collapse of the British banking system in 2008, within a context of the worst economic recession for 70 years. Perhaps nationalism might have helped after all.

7. Socialism and New Labour?

It would appear *prima facie* that there is simply nothing to say under this heading at all. Tony Blair had an early stab at talking about 'social-ism' but that was about all. Of the previous forms of socialism, workers' power was rebuffed by the unions, themselves much marginalised in any case, planning was dismissed as unworkable in a flexible, unregulated market economy, equality was supplanted by 'fairness', which could mean anything and nothing. Blair's leadership began with the symbolic rejection of Clause Four, replacing it with a patchwork of verbiage of extreme vacuity. The Third Way, a 'melange of generalities' in the attractive phrase of Blair's biographer, John Rentoul, lacked coherence or focus. Ideologically, by the 2005 election, there seemed nothing left. Labour's election manifesto, incredibly, was called 'Forward, not Back'. Nor did the succession of Gordon Brown to the premiership in 2007 show any revival of enthusiasm for socialist ideas. On the contrary, when the Northern Rock bank failed, as a result of serious mismanagement by its directors, in October 2007, it was with the very greatest reluctance and embarrassment that the government decided to nationalise it, all other policies having failed. It was followed by the equally reluctant nationalisation of the £150 million assets of the demutualised Bradford and Bingley building society, and then by the government taking a controlling interest in the newly merged Lloyds-Halifax Bank of Scotland the following March. Old leftists could rejoice that the nationalization of some banks, a feature of the party manifesto back in 1935, had actually taken place. But the emphasis was always on its being temporary and in no way a threat to the privately run banking and credit institutions that formed the props of British free-market capitalism. As signs of some economic recovery returned in mid-2009, government ministers stood benignly by as the old, self-remunerating culture of the banks returned. It was left to Lord Turner of the Financial Services Authority, not members of the Labour government, to write in *Prospect* magazine condemning some of the banks' activities as 'socially useless' and calling for a Tobin tax to be imposed on their profits.

Yet the Blair/Brown governments did pursue some socialist objectives, however reticent they were in proclaiming them. There were redistributive initiatives with individual and family tax credits, the Minimum Wage and attacks on child and other poverty. Fuller employment was promoted in the New Deal. Modernisation was certainly pursued in some areas, most spectacularly in the reform of the constitution. Gordon Brown's Donald Dewar lecture in October 2006 drew on socialist traditions with its celebration of an 'enabling state' and the egalitarian tone of its social programme. There was also awareness of an ethical community, echoing Ruskin or William Morris, not to mention the Christian socialism of the Scottish manse, together with newer themes of ethnic and gender equality that had been ignored by all politicians earlier. The moral thrust was very different now, since the economic basis of Thatcherite policies were adopted almost unchanged, with some embellishments such as the minimum wage from the European social chapter. But commentators wondered whether a Labour government under Brown could revitalise the civil service and the governmental machine, and breathe new life into aspects of the old socialist ethic.

There were under New Labour two important new emphases. Socialism was being wrenched away from centralisation. This was quite absent in writings on socialism since the heyday of Laski in the thirties. Crosland's socialism was totally uniform and homogeneous in its view of the British Isles and society generally. All its inhabitants, it seemed, from Lands End to the Old Man of Hoy, lived in identical 'little boxes' as in the famous ballad of Pete Seeger. But now devolution in Scotland and Wales, and possibly in regional England at some future date, linked socialism with diversity and local options. The other novelty was the idea of socialism being linked with citizenship. The constitutional and legal reforms of the New Labour period, even if stripped of old ideological baggage of any kind, have opened up the possibility of a civil, libertarian social citizenship, with democratic choice and control, of a kind hitherto unknown in our history. The Green Paper on *The Governance of Britain and Constitutional Renewal* introduced at the start of Gordon Brown's premiership in 2007 made much of this theme. But the government's later legislation on the subject proved to be a disappointment. Old Labour, concerned with inequalities of means, and New Progressivism, concerned with inequalities of power, seemed impossible to reconcile. Whether there is any house-room for socialism in the Labour Party now seems doubtful. In the Commons, it is no longer a workers' party in any meaningful sense. If anything, its defining theme is gender rather than class. Relatively more of its surviving proletarian parliamentary members can be found, improbably, largely on the green seats of the House of Lords, along with a greater number of representatives of ethnic minorities and the disabled. When Ken Livingstone, the leftist mayor of London, was defeated by a right-wing Tory in the elections of 2008, it was noticeable that he polled much more strongly than centre-right Labour councillors elsewhere in

Britain, who lost in droves. In the spectacular financial collapse, especially in the retail banks and the credit system, in the autumn of 2008, Gordon Brown and other ministers combined disapproval of 'irresponsible and selfish' behaviour within the financial community, with an insistence that the substance of semi-regulated free-market capitalism would essentially remain unchanged. The response to global disintegration of the capitalist system, starting in the American sub-prime mortgage market, but with severe knock-on consequences in Britain which were a direct result of the decontrol of business since the 'big bang' of 1986, should be more regulation, not more socialism. Unlike the years after 1931, the extraordinary disparity of reward and risk between different social classes under the Thatcher–Blair regime was not thought to make a case for the old ethical values of the founding fathers. Indeed, there has been no significant statement of socialist doctrine in this country – perhaps in any country – since Crosland in the mid-1950s.

But something of its early vision – Keir Hardie's socialism, where the socialist idea is seen as 'a question of ethics' – survives. John Cruddas of 'Compass' gave it expression in September 2009, in recalling Tawney's judgement years back that Labour's gravest weakness was that it 'lacked a creed'. Significantly, Cruddas's call came in a 'Hardie lecture' delivered in the founding father's constituency, Merthyr Tydfil. For what little it is worth, Keir Hardie, championed by the present writer, was enthusiastically voted at the Manchester party conference in September 2008 as 'Labour's greatest hero'. Interestingly, party delegates placed Hardie easily top of the poll, whereas MPs put him close to the bottom. This outcome offers an appropriate view of a post-modern Labour Party with a diminished commitment to older institutional models including parliament itself, not to mention a total detachment from the class divisions of the years of Attlee, even of Wilson. Certainly socialist-inclined bodies survive in vigorous vitality even under New Labour, especially after the capitalist near-collapse following the credit crunch: 'Compass' and think-tanks like IPPR are amongst the most dynamic of them at the present time. It could be an ultimate irony that under New Labour, proclaiming its Newness, its unconcern with history, its pride in its liberation from a dead past, fresh meaning could be given to that immortal phrase, 'If Keir Hardie were alive today'.

Chapter 10

Labour and British Republicanism

Sherlock Holmes famously solved a case by referring to 'the dog that did not bark'. In the past 400 years of British history, ever since the ignominious end of Cromwell's brief Protectorate, republicanism has been another silent canine. This is particularly true of, supposedly, our most radical major political party, the Labour Party. Over the monarchy, as over constitutional matters generally before Tony Blair's government, Labour's instincts have been anything but revolutionary. Even after 1997, when the new Labour government, under the dynamic leadership of Lord Irvine, did indeed embark on major constitutional reforms – devolution for Scotland, Wales and Northern Ireland; an elected mayor of London; the dismissal of nearly all hereditary peers from the House of Lords; incorporation of the European Convention of Human Rights into British law; a Freedom of Information Act; winding up the historic office of Lord Chancellor and creating a Supreme Court – the hereditary monarchy survived unscathed. It remained totally off the parliamentary and public agenda.

All Labour's prime ministers, Ramsay MacDonald (1924, 1929–31), Clement Attlee (1945–51), Harold Wilson (1964–70, 1974–6), James Callaghan (1976–9) and, up to a point, Tony Blair and Gordon Brown have remained deferential towards their King or Queen and their entourage. Elizabeth II had by far her worst relationship with a Conservative prime minister, Margaret Thatcher, who did not share the Queen's enthusiasm for a multiracial Commonwealth. With another Conservative, the bachelor Edward Heath, notoriously frosty towards women in general, relations cannot have been the greatest of fun. But Labour has generated only a handful of incidental protests, such as the 'anti-jubilee' number of the *New Statesman* on 3 June 1977 (in which I took part), described by the *Daily Mail* of the time as showing 'the termites of the left coming out of the woodwork'. In the past 30 years the British monarchy has certainly lost in public esteem. But this owes far more to its self-inflicted wounds, notably during the prolonged saga of bad relations between Charles and Diana, and the investigative and intrusive journalism of the tabloid press than to anything done, or proposed, by the Labour Party.

In the mid-nineteenth century, there had been an active tradition of working-class republicanism. Early trade unions and socialists were naturally republican since they saw themselves as democrats and opposed to heredity and aristocratic influence. There were many Republican Clubs especially in London, in the 1870s, and politicians such as Charles Dilke and Charles Bradlaugh expressed pronounced republican views. The French Commune of 1871 excited widespread sympathy and encouraged republican ideas in Britain, especially with the Queen's withdrawal from public prominence as 'the widow of Windsor' following the death of Prince Albert. Bradlaugh was nominated by the city of Paris as a candidate in the French assembly elections of February 1871 as Tom Paine had been 80 years earlier. The victory of the republican United States in its civil war in 1861–5 provided more encouragement. There was also a popular cult of the Protector, Oliver Cromwell, often projected, however bizarrely, as a kind of working-class hero who cut down aristocratic privilege, a hereditary House of Lords and an established Church, along with the Stuart monarchy. But this republican movement, such as it was, rapidly fell away in the past 20 years of the century, as the Queen emerged from the isolation of widowhood to identify herself with popular sentiments of patriotism, unionism and imperialism. The title Empress of India in 1876, artfully orchestrated by Disraeli, the Golden Jubilees and Diamond Jubilees of 1887 and 1897, all encouraged a broad populist enthusiasm for the Queen. The culture of the music hall, of horse-racing and of popular sport, became strongly royalist in tone, with the Prince of Wales and others of the royal family identified with all of them. In the music hall in particular, crises such as the Eastern Question in 1876–8, the death of General Gordon at Khartoum and the outbreak of the South African War in 1899 all gave further impetus. Working-class audiences in the galleries of the music halls would bellow out stirring patriotic choruses such as 'We're soldiers of the Queen, my boys'. At the turn of the century, musical patriotism gave the monarchy further momentum with Elgar's 'pomp and circumstance' marches, embodying a strident royalist nationalism somewhat removed from the introspective and Germanophile personality of Elgar himself.

The Independent Labour Party (ILP) founded in 1893 as a democratic socialist body, was initially republican in sympathies. Its founder, Keir Hardie, was always so. His speech of April 1894 in the Commons, at the time of the birth of a royal grandchild (the future King Edward VIII), condemning the House for finding time to celebrate a royal baby at the very moment that 251 Welsh miners had been killed in a terrible mining accident at Cilfynydd in the Taff valley, created a sensation. Hardie had written in his weekly newspaper, the *Labour Leader* (30 June 1894), that 'the life of one Welsh miner is of greater commercial and moral value to the British nation than the whole Royal crowd put together, from the Royal Great-Grand-Mama to this pulling Royal Great-Grandchild'. It gave Hardie a reputation for revolutionary extremism which lasted all his life. His republicanism was more damaging for his reputation than his socialism, his feminism or his pacifism. Hardie remained an outspoken republican, a view widely popular in his Welsh constituency of Merthyr Tydfil, which he represented in the Commons from 1900 to his death in 1915. During the South African War, Hardie used the crisis to further attack the monarchy, to claim, for example, that King Edward VII had financial links with Cecil Rhodes's mining enterprises in South Africa: 'it is no secret that his Majesty has been all along a party to the war gang in South Africa'. He went on to allege, more convincingly, that, at the royal funeral in 1901, militarists and their clerical allies had 'used the Queen's dead body as a recruiting sergeant' (*Labour Leader*, 11 July 1901). In 1907 Hardie and other Labour MPs were denounced for condemning Edward VII's visit to meet the hated Czar of Russia by sailing up the Baltic in the royal yacht (the crew, incidentally, including the father of a future Labour prime minister, Jim Callaghan). Hardie claimed that the visit meant that the King virtually condoned the atrocities of the Czarist regime in Russia, including the suppression of the Duma in 1905. He continued to attack the King's privileged and debauched lifestyle, including his many affairs with young women (among them, the Countess of Warwick, later a picturesque recruit for the ILP). For his pains, he was excluded from royal garden parties at the Palace – in fact, it is inconceivable that Hardie would ever have attended anyway!

But the Labour Party generally was most reluctant to follow this lead. After all, virtually all European countries were monarchies or empires prior to 1914. Ramsay MacDonald, leader of the party in 1911–14 and then 1922–31, was most anxious to show his party as a moderate, constitutional party. After the First World War, when so many imperial dynasties disappeared, and Bolshevik revolution triumphed in Russia, MacDonald gave his party's constitutionalism still further emphasis as a way of showing that Labour was fit to govern. In its entire history, Labour had just one formal vote on the future of the monarchy, at the 1923 party conference. There, a republican motion generated just 15 minutes of debate, and was humiliatingly defeated by 3,690,000 to 38,000.

All Labour governments have been highly sympathetic to the monarchy. Jimmy Thomas's formal dress when attending court levees, became a famous symbol of Labour orthodoxy. In his two Labour administrations of 1924 and 1931, MacDonald built up a good formal relationship with George V. Indeed, this helped to shape MacDonald's policy in 21–24 August 1931 in forming a National Government with the Tories and fatally dividing his old party and casting it into the wilderness. In forming his first government in February 1924, MacDonald kept George

Lansbury out of his government after that old socialist had attacked the monarchy in a post-election speech at Shoreditch town hall, and had referred George V to the sad fate of Charles I back in 1649: 'A few centuries ago one King who stood up against the common people of that day lost his head – lost it really (laughter and cheers).'

As it happened, when Lansbury, serving as minister of works in MacDonald's second government in 1929, in his capacity as Chief Warden of the Royal Parks, actually encountered George V, the two got on perfectly well, cheerfully swapping tales of their experiences on the operating table.

MacDonald, like Snowden, J.H. Thomas and other Labour ministers, was always well aware of the renewed popularity of the monarchy after the First World War, the way that George V identified himself with popular festivals such as the football cup final, first played at Wembley in 1923, and also built up a convincing image of the monarchy as a symbol of the family (a great trap for Charles and Diana, amongst other royals, in the 1990s as the royal family of the day proved spectacularly dysfunctional). As we have seen, the Crown was a helpful factor in the formation of the National government under MacDonald's leadership on 24 August 1931. After that event, left-wingers like Harold Laski and Stafford Cripps strongly attacked the role that the Crown supposedly played then, and the secret links between King, government, the establishment and the banking community, as they saw them. Laski vigorously condemned what he called 'the Palace Revolution' of 1931 in his pamphlet *The Crisis and the Constitution* (1932) and other writings. Yet Labour still fought shy of advocating republicanism. Hugh Dalton's otherwise radical *Practical Socialism* (1934) made a particular point of regarding the monarchy, in its present constitutional form, as standing well above party politics and therefore in no way a target of Labour's future programme of reform. In 1936 it was said that Labour MPs of nonconformist, working-class background were important in persuading Stanley Baldwin that he should remove Edward VIII by forcing him to abdicate after his affair with his mistress and future wife, Mrs. Simpson, and replace him with a more orthodox monarch. Labour, after all, stood for traditional principles of respectability and moral probity, the sanctity of the home and the primacy of the family, what Margaret Thatcher, the daughter of a Methodist grocer from Lincolnshire, was to call 'Victorian values'.

After Labour's landslide victory in 1945, Attlee developed a warm personal relationship with George VI. He felt a genuine sympathy for him and the Queen Mother for his patriotism and sense of duty in taking over from the errant Edward VIII (suspected of fascist sympathies) and his service in London during the blitz, and also for his grappling with personal and physical difficulties. Indeed, George VI's speech impediment even created a bond of a kind between him and the most left-wing member of the government, the minister of health, Aneurin Bevan. Attlee and the King had among things a common interest in the future of India, even if 'Ind. Imp.' disappeared from British coinage after the transfer of power in India and Pakistan in 1947. In October 1951, Attlee disastrously hastened the calling of a general election since the King was due to go on a royal tour of the Commonwealth in early 1952. In fact, the King had contracted cancer and never toured the Commonwealth at all. Labour went on to lose the general election.

In 1964, Harold Wilson developed a good relationship with Queen Elizabeth – the *New Statesman* was to refer to him as 'the working-man's Melbourne' (a reference to Victoria's emollient prime minister, Lord Melbourne, in 1837–41). When the Postmaster-General Anthony Wedgwood Benn (later recycled as Tony Benn) proposed issuing pictorial postage stamps without the Queen's head on them, Wilson vetoed the idea. He also persuaded the Queen to have Charles formally invested as Prince of Wales at Caernarfon castle in 1969, a colourful if somewhat bizarre ceremony, which had the effect of helping to stifle the growing nationalist movement in Wales. Thereafter, Prince Charles enjoyed a strong relationship with such senior Welsh Labour figures as George Thomas, Cledwyn Hughes and Lord Elwyn-Jones, although a brief term as a student at Aberystwyth, running the gauntlet of nationalist demonstrators who called him 'Carlo', was not an experience which the Prince wished to recall later on.

After 1976, Wilson's successor, James Callaghan, had a warmer relationship still with the Queen, even managing to compliment her on her dress sense (remarkably!). Over the Commonwealth and the illegality of the unilateral declaration of independence by white-led Southern Rhodesia under Ian Smith, Westminster and Windsor were as one. The Royal Jubilee of 1977 was well stage-managed by Callaghan who much enjoyed the entire event. During a naval ceremonial in the Solent, he was able to share with the Queen memories of his father's service on the royal yacht over 60 years earlier. He resisted proposals from Tony Benn and others to cut back on the Civil List or to end the Queen's immunity to personal taxation. After much debate, the Cabinet had a 'whip-round' to collect money and give the Queen a silver coffee-pot, chosen personally by Mrs. Callaghan. Others had offered different suggestions – Shirley Williams a saddle, Elwyn-Jones a clock carved from Welsh slate, Tony Benn a vase carved out of coal by a Polish miner. The Queen would surely have been happy with her coffee-pot. Even Callaghan's successor as leader in 1980–3, Michael Foot, left-wing socialist, unilateralist and a known republican much admiring of the French revolutionary Jacobins who put paid to Louis XVI, was by no means hostile to the monarch. He struck up a good personal relationship with the Queen with whom he discussed the politics of Queen Anne's reign and Welsh corgis. When the Queen objected to the King of Spain's hostility to the royal yacht's calling in at Gibraltar during Prince Charles's honeymoon – 'after all, it's my son, my yacht and my dockyard' – Michael Foot congratulated her on patriotic sentiments worthy of Elizabeth I at Tilbury. 'She was standing up for her country', he told Roy Hattersley. He also had friendly times with the Queen Mother, who called him 'Michael' and expressed admiration of the famous 'donkey jacket' at the Cenotaph, much abused by so many critics at the time, 'Michael, that's a warm, sensible coat for a cold day like this'. Foot recalled later on that he would much sooner have the support of the Queen Mother than 'that woman Thatcher'.

After 1997 Tony Blair was harder to assess, so pragmatic a politician was he. The Queen now did pay some personal taxation; there was marginally greater transparency in publishing her accounts; the royal yacht and aircraft were axed as an economy move. But Blair's political antennae led him to help choreograph the public mourning of the death of Diana in Paris in August 1997, 'the people's Princess' as Blair called her (a phrase suggested by his press secretary, Alastair Campbell). He supported the Queen's response in that crisis (well brought out by Michael Sheen's performance in the later film *The Queen* with Helen Mirren's portrayal of the monarch there variously making her an Oscar winner and a Dame). Blair handled Diana's funeral superbly and read a lesson there. Later he was also prominent in the celebrations of the Queen's Golden Jubilee in 2002 (the funeral of the Queen Mother, with arguments about precedence, did not go quite so well). At a grand banquet, Blair announced, excruciatingly, that the Queen was 'simply the best of British'. He declared that he was of the Disraeli school in prime ministerial attitudes towards the monarch. The only note of republicanism, remarkably, was struck by Cherie Blair, who refused to curtsey to the Queen on a visit to Balmoral after Diana's funeral. When another spate of criticism flared up in late 2002, with the collapsed trial of the somewhat disreputable former butler of Princess Diana, Paul Burrell, after the Queen had surprisingly intervened herself, Blair was quick to rush in and proclaim that the Queen was totally blameless and the royal prerogative in no way impugned. If Blair combined respect for the Crown with an anti-establishment style, his successor, Gordon Brown, appeared to be wholly orthodox in his approach, and his pleasant wife certainly did her share of curtseying.

Now why precisely has Labour been so sympathetic to the undemocratic, hereditary Crown and the royal family? Why has it never come close to embracing republicanism unlike, say, the Socialist parties of France, Germany or Italy? In part, it must be because the monarchy has been remarkably skilful in identifying itself with a variety of popular movements and aspirations after the First World War. The King was present to see Arsenal beat Huddersfield Town to win the cup in the 1930 Cup Final. After all, George V was acutely aware of the terrible fate of his cousin, the Russian Czar Nicholas II, during the Russian Revolution, especially after he refused to allow his cousin refuge in Britain on grounds of prudence. The monarchy variously identified itself with the transition from an Empire into a Commonwealth in the years after 1945, and with the growth of a multi-ethnic, multi-faith culture in Britain after 1960. Prince Charles's highly effective Trust was a significant factor here as were his efforts to identify with the values of the Muslim community and other religious minorities. The monarchy has also gone along with pressures for devolution in Scotland and Wales, despite their likely effects in helping to disunite the United Kingdom. In a remarkable Jubilee pronouncement before the Scottish parliament at Edinburgh in 2002, the Queen warmly commended devolution for Scotland as strengthening the ties of loyalty and sentiment that bound Scotland to Britain as a whole. This kind of adaptability has enabled the Crown to deflect criticisms that it was out of date and out of touch. Indeed, the Golden Jubilee celebrations in June 2002 were sufficiently relaxed to have the music of the Beatles and other pop groups resounding across the formal lawns and flower-beds of the Palace. A decision one year to stop the Christmas broadcast by the Queen was rapidly reversed after much public complaint. After the Iraq invasion in 2003, some commentators mused that the current sense of alienation from elected politicians amongst the British public could even reinforce the standing of the unelected sovereign by contrast.

A popular perception has been that the Crown has always been there at times of crisis, unchanging, imperturbable. A powerful image was of the King and Queen staying on in London during the blitz when indeed Buckingham Palace itself was fire-bombed. A legendary event was the Queen Mother tip-toeing through the rubble of bombed houses in the East End of London in 1941. When the Palace itself was struck by the Luftwaffe, she famously observed, 'Now we can look the East End in the face again.' This was important not only for the wartime sense of solidarity but also for the ethos of the war, the Battle of Britain especially, as an abiding symbol of British identity. This came out strongly in the cult of Churchill and 'our finest hour', and the monarchy was one important part of it. It has helped in fuelling the suspicion of continental Europe in recent times, and its supposed threat to British sovereignty. One popular objection to Britain's adopting the Euro after 2000 was that the Queen's head would no longer appear on our currency.

On the other hand, it is clear that the public attitude to the monarchy is far less deferential than in the 1940s and 1950s. There has been a marked decline in royal symbolism. There is far less playing of the national anthem: it has long ceased to be played at the end of cinema performances or at sports event or concerts, and in Scotland and Wales has virtually disappeared on such occasions as rugby internationals. The last night of the Proms featuring 'Land of Hope and Glory' is unique in its raucous patriotic symbolism. The Union Jack (or flag as it was renamed) is flown far less often and was commonly identified with neo-fascism and the working class, allegedly racist supporters of West Ham United football club in the east of London. Since the turn of the century, with evidence of a modest English nationalism emerging in the wake of Celtic devolution and resentment over the financial distortions of the Barnett formula, the Union flag has tended to be supplanted in England by the long-neglected flag of St. George. Since the 1970s, indeed ever since Prince Philip memorably complained that he was so hard up that he would hardly be able to play polo, there has been criticism of the style of the Crown – its vast, mainly untaxed, wealth; its lavish and undemocratic lifestyle (though at least presenting 'debs' at Court has long since disappeared); its social exclusiveness such as the educating of royal princes at exclusive private schools like Eton; its antique modes of speech – such as using 'one' instead of 'I' – and a curious pronunciation of vowels. The spectacle of an uneasy Queen dropping in at a pub or having a nervous cup of tea with the tenant of a Glasgow council house provoked widespread derision. Satire directed against the royal family, first evident in the revue *Beyond the Fringe* in the early 1960s, became for a time a major industry with Fergie, Sophie, Edward 'Count of Wessex', the Duke of Edinburgh and other baroque figures tending to become figures of fun. There was scant public sympathy for the death of Princess Margaret, perhaps the most cultured and intelligent of all the royals, yet commonly seen as 'the guest from hell' in her social habits. And yet when my parents were told, on the morning of their wedding day, 21 August 1930, that a little princess had just been born, it was said by their friends and families to be a sign of almost divine blessing!

The monarchy went through a dreadful time in the 1990s from the *annus horribilis* of 1992 with the memorable fire at Windsor, the long-running saga of Charles and Diana, their divorce added to the divorces of Prince Andrew and Princess Anne. It was hard indeed to identify the British monarchy now with the 'family values' cherished by George V or George VI, or indeed the young Elizabeth II. The Jubilee of 2002 seemed to go well until the Paul Burrell case and other financial apparent irregularities led to a further slump in esteem. The inquiry by Sir Michael Peat into the administration of the royal finances, and Prince Charles's in particular, led to some improved transparency. But there was much comment in the press that, since it was conducted by a royal employee, it was far from an independent audit, and would carry only limited authority.

Recent events therefore have shown that the position of the monarchy is potentially fragile, and it is conceivable that some future radical government could take an interest in it. Regard for the Crown is strongly linked to personal respect for the Queen – and even that was shaken by her bland response to the Windsor fire in 1992, her initially cold reaction to Diana's death in 1997 and the intervention in Paul Burrell, the royal butler's, trial in 2002. Prince Charles, should he succeed as King Charles III, could be a more controversial monarch with his strong opinions on such issues as fox-hunting or rural affairs (he claimed that farmers faced worse problems of discrimination than did black Britons), not to mention religion, alternative medicine, Shakespeare, modern architecture and the teaching of Latin, and his inclination to spray them at ministers at every opportunity. As the example of Edward VIII, with his populism and apparent sympathy for Hitler's Germany, indicates, an opinionated, as opposed to a demurely constitutional monarchy could pose a real problem. At least on the personal side, we seem to have moved on from the immediate emotions of Diana's death, and Charles and his long-term mistress, the equally divorced Camilla Parker-Bowles, were married without controversy at a quiet ceremony in Windsor town hall in 2005. But a reaction against the monarch could be sparked off by some more public issue. There were already strong pressures for a republic in Australia, with the new Labour premier, Kevin Rudd, intimating in 2008 a fresh referendum on the question. New Zealand and Canada (with its large French Quebecois population) show much of the same sentiment and it is perfectly possible to see the role of the Crown as head of the Commonwealth slowly becoming redundant. For many years, bodies like Charter 88 have called for a fundamental reform of the monarchy as part of a move towards a written, formal constitution, based not on informal convention or precedent, but on clear principles of accountability and the rights of citizenship – in other ways, to make Britain more like France or the United States, not subjects, but citizens, and to enable the British to declare meaningfully, like the Americans, 'we the people'.

The survival of the monarchy, then, owes much to the capacity of that institution for renewal and redefinition. But it has met with such limited criticism in Labour circles because the party has never seen republicanism as one of its priorities. Certainly it has never appeared as any kind of electoral vote-winner. None of Labour's political ideologues has raised the issue since Harold Laski did so in 1932–3. Democratic socialism, so far as Labour has followed that creed, has been concerned with social and economic change, rather than with institutional reform, with issues of class not of hierarchical authority. Labour has sought power – *la conquête de pouvoir*, in Léon Blum's famous phrase – but strictly within the existing constitutional framework and notions of identity. The brief antimonarchism after 1931 soon passed away. The allegedly radical Army Bureau of Current Affairs during the Second World War conducted for troops in the deserts of Africa or the jungles of Burma, cited the democratic sentiments of the Levellers at Putney in 1647. But it also hailed the idea of 'the King in Parliament'. That was the basis of our liberties. That was what we were fighting for. The war led to an orgy of Unionism and to decades of veneration for our constitution arrangements. There were only isolated critics in parliament like the Labour backbencher (who was otherwise no left-winger) the Scot Willie Hamilton. There was only one dissentient in June 2002 in the Scottish parliament when a loyal address was presented to the Queen – he was the Independent Socialist Tommy Sheridan, whose reputation later collapsed for reasons connected with his private life. The Labour MPs in the early years of the new millennium probably included many dozens of republicans: they were rumoured to include such ministers as Clare Short and John Prescott. At least 20 Labour peers (including myself) were members of a republican group led by Lord (Jack) Dormand. But the issue seemed most unlikely to be raised publicly.

I chaired a Fabian Society Commission on the monarchy in 2002–3: its report, *The Future of the Monarchy*, appeared in July 2003. It was a daring initiative because the Crown is hardly ever publicly discussed in parliament or the Courts. We do not have royal commissions on the monarchy; its precise influence and key aspects of its management and finances are unknown. The Commission looked at the political and legal roles of the Crown, its relationship to the established Church of England, its finances and property, and also its social projection. We tried to disentangle the various strands that were too often confused – the role of the monarchy in the constitution, the role of the Crown in our law, and the social and personal roles of the royal family as individuals. But we were instructed not to consider advocating a republic (a topic on which our members had different views) since it would make the eventual report appear quixotic or irrelevant.

The main conclusions therefore looked elsewhere. First there was a critique of the royal prerogative in government, exercised in effect by the prime minister of course, notably in relation to patronage and the appointment of bishops and other public figures, the conclusion of foreign treaties, and the right to declare war. After all, when the British air force battered civilians in Baghdad and Basra in March 2003, it did so in the name of the unfortunate Queen, however archaic this might seem. This line of criticism did eventually bear fruit, partly as a result of the fierce public controversy over the invasion of Iraq.

Thus the green paper on the *Governance of Britain* issued at the outset of Gordon Brown's premiership in June 2007 proposed the ending of the prerogative powers in key areas, with authority given to parliament instead. Parliament would have the right to scrutinise and approve foreign treaties, while powers to make war would now be vested not in an archaic royal prerogative but in parliament, though whether this would be achieved by legislative procedures or by special or other resolution remained open to debate. A further inquiry into prerogative powers was promised in the document *Constitutional Renewal* in April 2008, which would be followed by major legislation. The formal power to make war or send troops overseas would no longer be a royal concern, but would be dependent on parliamentary resolution (though not on statute as many wanted). The broad legal justification would also be made public, after all the controversy surrounding the legality of the invasion of Iraq. Again, treaties with other countries would similarly fall within the powers of parliament: a new parliamentary Joint Committee on Treaties would sift treaties laid before parliament and give a formal verdict on their appropriateness. Royal patronage over key appointments would be further diminished. The formal role of the monarch, therefore, would be severely reduced still further, with residual powers relating to such matters as the appointment of a prime minister, the dissolution or recall of parliament or the royal assent to legislation also to be dealt with. In the event, the Brown government's Constitutional Renewal and Governance Bill in 2010 included parliamentary approval for foreign treaties, but not for the power to go to war or send troops abroad, a partial advance only. Still, it was likely that the diminution of royal authority in this way would merge into a wider discussion of general themes of centralisation, unaccountability and secrecy within the forms of the British constitution, with a possible bill of rights to follow on, though not immediately, it seemed, a written constitution which would clearly need an immense amount of parliamentary time. On the other hand, the institution of monarchy would be sustained. Since the purpose of the exercise of constitutional renewal, as the Brown government saw matters, was strengthening national cohesion and the sense of a British identity, the historic role of the Crown in this area was felt to be a vital source of strength, along with the more conspicuous flying of the union flag on public buildings, and Britishness force-fed into the very idea of citizenship.

The other area considered by the Fabian Commission was the vaguer one of the Crown as a social institution, detached from the mass of the population in its style of life, but yet seen historically as a powerful social glue, giving Britain an ancient continuity since the later seventeenth century to a degree paralleled by few, if any, other European countries. In late 2002, opinion polls showed that a more democratised, accessible monarchy, even if one more formal than the bicycling style of the monarchies of Scandinavia, was the most popular option. A republic was supported by only 10 to 12 per cent of the population, even amongst the young. Most people felt it was no great priority anyway. At a time of flux and doubt about the future of a United Kingdom and the endurance of any kind of British identity – with the various changes implied by multi-ethnic immigration, a transatlantic imported culture, membership of Europe, Celtic devolution and the wider social destabilisation enforced from late 2008 by untamed, globalised capitalism – a monarchy, even one with virtually no powers of any kind, remained a point of continuity, and perhaps of stability.

In early 2008, republicanism appeared nowhere on Britain's political radar. But you should never say never. David Marquand's *Britain Since 1918*, published in September 2008, made a considerable impact in its championing of an admittedly discontinuous and distinctly shadowy democratic republican tradition, a philosophy the author variously detected in Milton in the 1650s, Tom Paine in the 1790s and John Stuart Mill in the 1850s. Commentators, observing other radical proposals for constitutional reform, especially in the wake of the MPs expenses scandal in the summer of 2009, ventured to write of 'Britain's republican moment'. Certainly, the revived interest in doctrines of citizenship (some of them stimulated by proposals for constitutional change put forward by the prime minister, Gordon Brown, himself) seemed likely to promote new visions of a more open, accountable, participatory political order, perhaps even a truly democratic one. The United Kingdom has undergone extraordinary changes in the decades since 1945, and continues to do so. A phenomenon like the growing nationalism of Scotland (where Elizabeth II is historically viewed as mere Queen Elizabeth I) is only one of many uncertain elements in the

British melting-pot. For all the ingrained constitutional conservatism of the Labour Party, the republican Keir Hardie's once socialist creation, it is conceivable that, some time in the distant future, the established Church, the pound sterling, the Commonwealth and even the monarchy could follow the hereditary peerage, the Empire and the Union into the dustbin of history.

Chapter 11

Imperialists at Bay: Britain's Finest Hour

Roger Louis, a friend and colleague for almost 30 years, is foremost amongst the historians of the British Commonwealth and Empire. He has written, with matchless knowledge of archives from Cape Town to Canberra, on the movers and shakers of the British imperial experience in the present century. He has covered equally champions of Empire, like Churchill and Amery, and the international forces (especially the actions of the United States) that compelled the liquidation of that Empire, especially in two outstanding monographs covering the years from 1941 to 1951. This chapter focuses on two somewhat underestimated aspects of this theme. The emphasis will be on the British Labour Party, shortly to celebrate its centenary, whose approach to Commonwealth and colonial matters has seldom received the attention given to its domestic, social, economic and industrial policies. My own recent official biography of Lord Callaghan was kindly considered by the reviewers but almost entirely in terms of domestic issues such as *In Place of Strife* and the *Winter of Discontent*. Callaghan's important role as a colonial spokesman and his later involvement with the ending of Empire in relation to Rhodesia, the Falklands and many other matters received no attention.

There is also value in focussing not on the great occasion of the transfer of power to the Indian sub-continent in 1947, which stood on its own as a grand liberationist gesture, but on the period after 1951. It was in the 13 years of Conservative rule when the real sustained process of rapid decolonisation took place and when the Labour Party, albeit from the comfort of opposition, was a major player in public debate and policy. This may shed light on several of the themes pursued by Roger Louis over the years, not least how far the ending of Empire was the inexorable consequence of historic political, economic and military weakness in the face of nationalist upsurge in several continents, how far there was a simple failure of national will. The long debate (which casts its shadow even over Britain in the late 1990s in arguments over Europe and devolution) as to whether decolonisation was an abject scuttle, a pragmatic Anglo-American realignment or the product of a vision of a multiracial commonwealth of partners may thereby be illuminated.

(i)

Empire and colonisation, so central a theme in British history over a hundred years from the time of Palmerston to that of Macmillan, had been surprisingly marginal to the history of the Labour Party since its foundation in 1900. Prior to 1914 and for some considerable time thereafter, the party focussed almost entirely on domestic issues and the defence of the unions and the working class. On Empire, Labour was governed by a simple gut instinct that it was against it, just as it was against capitalism and war. This was a compound of Karl Marx and John Morley, an aversion to imperialism as a bastardised version of monopoly late-capitalism, and a moralist little Englandism inherited from the late-Victorian radical past. But Labour specialists on Empire were thin on the ground. Even over India the main critics of the Morley-Minto policies tended to be Liberal MPs like Sir Henry Cotton and radical journalists like H.W. Nevinson. The most famous contemporary tract on Empire was, of course, that by J.A. Hobson in 1901, who linked imperial expansion overseas with poverty and underconsumption at home. But, until the 1920s he remained a free-trade Liberal. There were, broadly, two main strains of thinking on imperial and colonial matters that Labour inherited in its years of power after the Second World War. The first was associated with the ILP some of whose key figures in the early years had taken an incidental interest in imperial questions. Both Keir Hardie and Ramsay MacDonald wrote influential works on India in the Edwardian years.[1] They had their obvious defects, such as an unduly benevolent view of the demands of the early nationalists like B.G. Tilak, but they helped to publicise the main objectives of nationalism prior to Congress. In the interwar years radical journalists like H.N. Brailsford and the younger Fenner Brockway kept colonial nationalism, and especially pressure for Indian self-government, well to the fore: they were encouraged by Congress politicians active in England such as Krishna Menon, a prominent figure in the Socialist League. But by then the ILP was well in decline and its socialist critique absorbed (and diluted) in the mainstream Labour Party.

The ILP's specialism was moral outrage. The other major theme, that of the Fabians, was imperial development. The Webbs and most of the earlier Fabians saw imperialism as a facet of national efficiency. This was a proconsular vision with strong overtones of Social Darwinism. It is not surprising that the Webbs's choice as first director of the London School of Economics was the Tory imperialist, W.A.S. Hewins. The Empire would be a greater London County Council, a model of planned order, run by experts and specialists, moderated by gradualist injections of democracy. Although the Fabians lost early credibility through their sympathy with the South African War, their main diagnosis held sway in Labour circles after 1918, if only because of the absence of any serious alternative. In the second Labour government of 1929–31, Sidney Webb (now Lord Passfield) was an unambitious colonial secretary. Indeed, apart from the Round Table conference on India, Labour offered no innovations in imperial or colonial policy. By the mid-1930s the party's outlook was summed up by its leader, Clement Attlee. The Empire was going to continue into an indefinite future; Labour, free from imperialist nostalgia and committed to the principle of constructive planning, was the party to run it. The new economic planners of the thirties, the young men who gave Labour a revived social and economic policy after the debacle of 1931, were themselves sympathetic to ideas of colonial investment and partnership. Hugh Gaitskell was the son of an Indian civil servant whose brother was a colonial economist who worked on irrigation schemes in the Sudan. Douglas Jay, an enthusiast for Shakespeare and cricket, also came from a Wykehamist background sympathetic to benevolent views of Empire, while Evan Durbin's Baptist minister father had been a missionary in Ceylon. Men like this felt an instinctive urge to develop and plan rather than to cut and run. Other than in India, Labour in the thirties was not a party committed to rapid decolonisation.

The main feature of Labour's policies on colonies and empire in the thirties, however, was not their conservatism but their unimportance. A major work like Hugh Dalton's *Practical Socialism for Britain* (1935) rated colonial matters worth just two pages at the end. 'The Colonial policy of the Labour Party may be summed up in the two words – socialisation and self-government'. Clement Attlee's *Labour Party in Perspective* (1937) did much better with 20 pages, though these were distinctly lacking in precision. H.N. Brailsford wrote two books on India, of which *Rebel India* (1931), the product of a seven-week visit to the sub-continent originally published as articles in the *New Leader* still retains some interest, particularly in his assessment of Nehru whom he interviewed in prison in Allahabad. There were really only a handful of authors on the left with a sustained interest in colonial matters, although they are worth recalling. The most active and interesting was Leonard Barnes, a former Colonial Office man whose well-researched works such as *The Duty of Empire* (1935) and *Empire or Democracy?* (1939) called for a policy of trusteeship and long-term economic reconstruction of the colonies: however, Barnes's Marxism and his wartime sympathy for the Soviet Union helped to marginalise him in post-war debate. His essentially Leninist economic analysis seemed dated. Although he lived on to a considerable age, dying in 1977, he was no longer a major ideological influence. Another Labour publicist on Empire was Professor W.M. Macmillan, a

South African émigré historian from Witwatersrand (which he had to leave following marital infidelity), a specialist on the Caribbean, who favoured a more consensual programme of collaborative development. Others active in this area were a former doctor in East Africa, Norman Leys, and the journalist and cartographer Frank Horabin, who founded the left-wing anti-colonialist journal *Empire*. One of its main themes was race relations and the prevalent 'colour bar' in colonial territories. But, in truth, their collective influence on Labour Party policy-making was slight and none ever came within sight or sound of Transport House. On colonial issues, the party did not need a Leo Amery to urge them to 'speak for England'.

It was in the years of power from 1940 to 1951, the wartime coalition and even more the six-year Attlee government, that Labour developed a sustainable policy for empire and colonies. The main inspiration undoubtedly came from the Fabian Colonial Research Bureau, founded in 1940 by Rita Hinden, a South African Jewish émigré of social democratic outlook, and Arthur Creech Jones of the ILP. For the first time, Labour evolved policies of long-term colonial development, economic, educational and technological. Creech Jones carried them out with much effect as Attlee's colonial secretary down to 1950 when he lost his Shipley seat through redistribution. He had in any case apparently lost Attlee's confidence as a departmental head. In later years, Creech Jones, an uncharismatic figure, became hailed as the pioneer of a multi-racial Commonwealth, and so in some ways he was. But his party's achievement was strictly qualified nevertheless. Labour as a whole remained paternalist. It adhered to a traditional view of the Commonwealth dominated by the white dominions, shaped by the needs of the sterling area during the post-war dollar shortage, and with the sterling balances to provide an open-ended subsidy to the mother country. In any case, while there were important constitutional advances in the Gold Coast and Nigeria, and in the West Indies, the prevailing assumption, even by enlightened civil servants like Andrew Cohen at the Africa division of the Colonial Office, was that Commonwealth and colonies would survive for decades to come. The Victorian legacy cast a long shadow. In 1945–51 no one foresaw the imminent end of Empire: indeed Bevin in 1945–6 even contemplated expanding rather than curtailing the Empire by taking over former Italian territories such as Cyrenaica, Eritrea and Italian Somaliland.[2] There was, of course, the massive decision to withdraw from India. This owed much to the leadership of Attlee himself, with the transfer of power to India and Pakistan followed by independence for Burma and Ceylon (Sri Lanka). The colossal cost of possible military action in any case meant that staying on in India was not an option. But few imagined that this would or could be extended in the near future to other British territories in Africa, Asia or the Caribbean or Oceania. Creech Jones's own reputation as a far-sighted planner was severely dented, not only with Attlee, by the fiascos of ground nuts in East Africa (at a loss of £30 million) and of Gambia eggs.

His successor, James Griffiths, an idealistic Welshman, nevertheless committed Labour at first to the concept of a Central African Federation – this despite massive evidence of African hostility shown at the Victoria Falls conference.[3] Elsewhere, the Labour government fought the good fight against Chinese guerrillas in Malaya (with its invaluable tin, rubber and palm oil), it stood firm on the rock of Gibraltar, it showed no immediate sign of withdrawal from the Suez Canal base even if it refrained from military action in the Abadan crisis with Persia in 1951, it was remarkably illiberal in bowing to South African pressure to remove Seretse Khama from Bechuanaland. The Colonial Office under Labour (as Professor Northcote Parkinson of the University of Malaya and *Parkinson's Law* delighted to point out) grew massively in 1945–51 in its commitments and in personnel, with giant corporate bodies created like the Overseas Food Corporation, headed by the future Labour MP Sir Leslie ('Dick') Plummer, and the Commonwealth Development Corporation. It was the most active phase of British colonial government since the days of Joseph Chamberlain. Labour in power was not, therefore, broadly a decolonising government, certainly not Bevin, nor Morrison who spoke fondly of 'the jolly old Empire'. Some of its initiatives, such as the new constitution in the Gold Coast in 1951, were designed to enable Britain to share a role with Conservative chiefs and a limited range of nationalists after recent riots. Its vision of long-term partnership and trusteeship retained its appeal for Britain within a Commonwealth which the wartime years had shown to be still supremely important. The future direction of colonisation and the rate of change were still remarkably vague when Labour left office in 1951. The advent of that veteran imperialist Churchill as premier hardly seemed to herald any real change of policy.

It was, therefore, really the 1950s when Labour had to produce a comprehensive blueprint for the process of decolonisation. It did so not necessarily through choice but because circumstances made the imperial heritage, especially in Africa, a central issue in British politics for the first time since the late Victorian period. Labour's successive spokesmen on colonial matters, Jim Griffiths (to early 1956), Aneurin Bevan (briefly in 1956 when restored to favour as deputy leader) and above all the younger and relatively unknown James Callaghan, from the end of 1956 to December 1961 had to pronounce on imperial themes with a clarity and force unknown in Labour's previous history. For the first time, Labour evolved a coherent, powerful critique of colonial affairs, one that helped to create a new cross-party consensus and effect the rapid demise of an empire that had lasted for 300 years within less than a decade. It took Labour half a century to devise a credible colonial policy: it did so just as the need for having one at all was passing away.

A variety of influences helped to shape Labour's approach to decolonisation in these years. The most important at first was still the Fabian Colonial Research Bureau, especially after Rita Hinden took over and edited the monthly *Socialist Commentary*. The bureau's publications had gained intellectual weight and substantive detail since 1945, notably through important pamphlets on colonial development by the West Indian economist, W. Arthur Lewis. On the other hand, it may be that the bureau was now something of a diminishing force. Creech Jones himself did not return to parliament until 1954 and was not thereafter the influence he had once been. Rita Hinden concentrated on the domestic Gaitskellite agenda of *Socialist Commentary*. The bureau as a whole was now widely criticised by more radical nationalist leaders in the Commonwealth for being unduly paternalist and cautious, for favouring a continuing British military presence in areas such as Guyana and Malaya, and being insufficiently aware of the massive speeding up of the decolonisation process demanded by African and other nationalists.

(ii)

Other kinds of influences, therefore, began to take the bureau's place. Not the least were a new generation of younger nationalist leaders from Commonwealth countries, such as Julius Nyerere, Kenneth Kaunda, Tom Mboya and Joshua Nkomo from Africa, Michael Manley and Grantley Adams from the West Indies, and the charismatic young Cambridge-trained lawyer Harry Lee (Lee Kuan Yew) from Singapore. They socialised with Labour leaders like Gaitskell, Griffiths and Callaghan at summer schools and party gatherings at Buscot Park, the home of the patrician socialist, Lord Faringdon. A natural affinity was created between a Labour Party still in throes of revisionism and reassessment after its fall from power in 1951 and the spokesmen of the vocal nationalist movements of the third world. The fifties also saw the emergence of a new generation of leftish journalists specialising in colonial themes, such as Colin Legum of the *Observer* and Patrick Keatley in the *Guardian,* and further on the left, Basil Davidson. Another important source was academic life, notably in Oxford. One powerful intellectual force was Dame Margery Perham at Nuffield College, Oxford, whose Reith lectures of 1961, *The Colonial Reckoning,* were highly influential; another was Thomas Hodgkin of Balliol and Oxford's Extra-Mural Delegacy. A wide variety of development economists and specialists on soil science and other areas also worked with Labour's colonial spokesmen: one of the more important was Arthur Gaitskell, brother of the party leader elected in 1955, and himself politically a Liberal. In short, a new colonial discourse, informative but liberationist, galvanised Labour thinking. It made it the better equipped to confront conservative ministers like Lennox-Boyd, Hopkinson, Macleod and Maudling in an area where the political right was traditionally felt to be far more authoritative. Increasingly it was Labour that was calling the tune.

Transport House also responded for the first time to the new pressures from the colonies, conflicts in Guyana and Malaysia, rapid movements for decolonisation in first West, then East Africa. An important development in 1954 was the appointment of John Hatch, a South African with a left-wing ILP background, as colonial officer. He had worked closely with African nationalist leaders like Julius Nyerere of Tanganyika, to produce a stream of well-informed background papers on the constitutional and economic aspects of colonial questions. He helped to make the Commonwealth Sub-Committee of the National Executive a leftish fount of initiatives on colonial matters. There had never been anyone like Hatch before in Labour's history: after 1964, when the main crises of decolonisation other than Rhodesia were over, he retired to the Lords and became something of a forgotten figure. But in the mid- and later 1950s he was a key influence on party policy and especially on Callaghan as colonial spokesman. He certainly deserves to be resurrected as a major force.

There were also significant political elements in the parliamentary party to push colonial affairs to the fore. Some were survivors from Keep Left and the Bevanite group, but by no means all. They ranged from near veterans like Fenner Brockway to much younger figures like Anthony Wedgwood Benn. There was a general thrust towards an early and precise timetable for decolonisation in general, quite apart from advocates of particular causes like allies of Dom Mintoff in Malta and partisans of the Greek Cypriots such as Barbara Castle and Lena Jeger. They all found a voice in the Movement for Colonial Freedom (MCF), founded in 1954 at a time of crisis in East Africa with the Kikuyu uprising in Kenya. This was an articulate pressure group with much depth of support. It belongs to the grand tradition of British dissent along with the Anti-Corn Law League or the Union of Democratic Control in the past. It was backed by 72 out of 294 Labour MPs and also, remarkably, by two not especially left-wing major unions, the Engineers (AEU) and the shop-workers union USDAW. It adopted a broad pluralist structure similar to the anti-apartheid movement at the end of the following decade, and was a major (if dissenting) voice of anti-colonialist opinion in political life, with a rare record of assiduousness in parliament itself. Even if it was becoming sidelined by the end of the 1950s, as its diagnoses were thought too one-sided and polemical, with some Communist infiltration an additional difficulty, it undoubtedly gave a sense of centrality to colonial issues unknown in British history since the First World War.

But the precise influence of any one of these elements in the mix at any given time depended on Labour's front-bench spokesmen. The priority given to colonial matters was shown by the fact that James Griffiths, spokesman until February 1956, went on to be deputy leader under Gaitskell. His successor, Aneurin Bevan, was to succeed Griffiths as deputy leader after the 1959 general election, just before his fatal illness. Both of these, naturally, were important voices on a range of Commonwealth and colonial themes. Griffiths became an effective voice of moral protest as evidence piled up that his own cherished Central African Federation, launched in 1953, faced the most intense and virtually unanimous African opposition, most of all in Northern Rhodesia and Nyasaland. He was also much involved in Nigerian affairs, as late as the Biafran secession in the civil war of the late 1960s. Nye Bevan inevitably made an impact, especially in Middle Eastern matters, through his own charisma and stature: his later visit to India and Pakistan in April 1957, when he was now shadow foreign secretary, was a memorable affirmation of his vision of the Commonwealth. He did not flinch from instructing Indian nationalists to avoid extremism over the dispute with Pakistan in Kashmir. His becoming colonial spokesman at all was interesting: in 1950 Dalton had argued against his moving to the Colonial Office because of Bevan's sympathy for what Dalton, with insouciant, tasteless racism, termed 'pullulating, poverty-stricken, diseased, nigger communities'.[4] On the other hand, Bevan's tenure was a brief one and his time was much occupied with events on a wider stage, notably during the Suez crisis. Here he appeared somewhat more sympathetic to the Eden government's resistance to President Nasser than was his party leader. Bevan, for once, found himself getting a good press from the Beaverbrook newspapers as a true patriot compared with the traitor Gaitskell.

The most important colonial spokesman, however, was James Callaghan who took over at the end of 1956. A relatively young man aged 44, he was constantly on the move, to Africa above all. Lord Home told Welensky he was 'a bouncy young customer'.[5] In 1958 he flew to various Commonwealth countries 14 times. Although apparently a home-centred politician, his background in colonial affairs was stronger than might have appeared. He had served in Asia during wartime service in the navy, and had taken a keen interest in the affairs of Ceylon. He had gone on an important mission to West Africa, notably Sierra Leone (where he struck up a friendship with the liberal-minded governor, Sir Alan Bums) in the winter of 1946–7. As a result he had made a series of influential and cogent pronouncements on African matters at successive Labour Party conferences.[6] Further, with his wide-ranging interest in foreign affairs, defence (he was a former Admiralty minister), finance (he once worked for the Inland Revenue) and to a limited degree race relations (his constituency around the Cardiff docks was distinctly multi-ethnic), he had a positive background for his new portfolio. He shared in the liberal, anti-colonial assumptions of the time and worked reasonably well with radicals like John Hatch. On the other hand, he came from an old-fashioned patriotic-imperial background in the naval town of Portsmouth: his father had served on the royal yacht. This gave his outlook an unusual degree of pragmatism, or perhaps balance. He was fortunate that in the period 1957–62, decolonisation in Africa, especially the Central African Federation, came to the forefront of British politics. By 1962 he was celebrating his move to become shadow chancellor since a shrinking British Commonwealth might well cause the colonial spokesman to shrink also, as was to happen later to Anthony Greenwood.[7]

But in these crucial years, he was the pivot of Labour's response to colonial challenge. The late fifties and early sixties were elsewhere a difficult time for Labour, with a heavy defeat in the 1959 general election and savage infighting between followers of Gaitskell and left-wing radicals in the Campaign for Nuclear Disarmament (CND). The 1960 Scarborough party conference, with the defeated Gaitskell warning his opponents that he would 'fight, fight, and fight again' was a rare moment of internecine warfare that some speculated might divide the party with fatal effects. By contrast, the mood in colonial matters was relatively consensual. Labour presented itself as a forward-looking party, one that reflected, far more genuinely than the Tories could, the aspirations of the rising nationalist movements of the developing world. It became the natural voice of colonial liberation movements everywhere, in a way denied the French Socialists, tainted as they were with Algeria and Suez. In colonial matters, Labour emerged as the party of the future, in its analysis as well as in its idealism. A new prospect of power, after the flagging momentum of the later Attlee period, presented itself. Callaghan himself was not the least cause of this long-term renaissance.

There were several specific features of Labour's new awareness of post-imperial priorities from 1957. First there was the continuing centrality of the Commonwealth in its thinking, but in the form of an updated, multi-racial partnership. Its role in Labour's ideas in 1945–51 had been in large measure a legacy of the war – the importance of the links with the mother country in terms of defence, the sterling area and raw materials. In the later 1950s the Commonwealth was a very different kind of association. The paradigm was the conference of Commonwealth prime ministers in London in April 1946 where the official photograph featured Attlee, Lord Addison, Mackenzie King, Smuts, Herbert Evatt and Peter Fraser. The Commonwealth was reorganised in British defence terms in the later fifties, to take account of the Egyptian take-over of the Suez Canal: Middle East Command moved to Aden. However, it was also a far more inclusive Commonwealth after decolonisation in Africa, with new territories ranging in size from Nigeria to Zanzibar and Mauritius, and the consequent break-out from a club-like gathering of white Dominions.[8] There was also the momentous effect of changes in South Africa, the establishment of a Nationalist regime imposing apartheid from 1948, the treason trials from 1956, and the Sharpeville massacre in 1960. The various 'winds of change' were responded to in much the same way by the Macmillan government as by the Labour Opposition, although perhaps the latter, which after all had staunchly opposed the Suez venture, was viewed by Commonwealth countries as coming to the conference table with cleaner hands. Labour was also viewed with far more enthusiasm in India where the transfer of power gave the Attlee administration a hallowed status.

(iii)

Where Labour did perhaps show some originality was in taking a wider view as seeing the Commonwealth as an international laboratory of experiment for a broad programme of economic advance, technological improvement and educational change to raise the skills of the third world. It gave a far higher priority to overseas aid and to fixed prices for major commodities. Callaghan himself called for a Colombo Plan for Africa to target aid without political strings attached. In practice, this meant that Labour was suggesting that Britain might have to delay the process of decolonisation in some instances to ensure socio-economic changes in which a working democracy could take root. Callaghan described Britain's remaining colonial role in language he reserved for the trade unions' role in the Labour Party. It would be 'a steadying influence'. It might be added also that Labour enhanced its credentials in Commonwealth countries through its endorsement of mass Commonwealth immigration into Britain throughout the 1950s, and its strong opposition, headed by Gaitskell himself, to the restrictions imposed by the Immigration Bill of 1962. When in government in 1968, the Labour Party (and Callaghan himself, now at the Home Office) found it harder to retain its consistency on the immigration issue, and its moral credit suffered.

This same prudence – many in the MCF used far harsher language – governed Labour's approach to areas of actual or potential insecurity. Cyprus was aflame in the mid-1950s: EOKA terrorists waged war against occupying British forces on behalf of 'enosis' with Greece, and the Troodos Mountains turned into a killing field. A total rejection of earlier Conservative approaches towards Cyprus – when a Conservative minister, Henry Hopkinson, had foolishly declared that the island could 'never' achieve self-government in view of its importance as a British base – was commonplace in the Labour movement. Labour also severely criticised the more draconian aspects of the regime of Governor Harding, the exiling of Archbishop Makarios to the distant island of Seychelles, and the failure to pursue a possible political settlement such as talks with the Turkish Cypriot minority over a partition. On the other hand, Labour was careful not to attack operations by British troops or lapse into what Callaghan saw as the sheer partisanship of Barbara Castle and others who urged immediate union of Cyprus with Greece. 'I simply will not be party to condemning the British troops when a much heavier responsibility rests upon Makarios and EOKA as well as on the British government.'[9] The succession of Hugh Foot, Michael Foot's older brother, as governor of Cyprus in place of Harding in 1957 greatly softened Labour's view of British policy there. The eventual settlement of Cyprus in the Zurich accord of February 1959 left Labour without commitments there, although the continuing conflict between the Greek and Turkish Cypriots was to haunt Callaghan when he became foreign secretary in 1974.

A similar pragmatism coloured Labour's approach to Malta, another Mediterranean island recently of much importance to British defence needs. Here the campaign by the Maltese Labour Party under Dom Mintoff to secure possible integration by Malta with Britain aroused the same localised enthusiasm within the British Labour Party as the Greek Cypriots had done: in particular the economist of Hungarian origin, Thomas Balogh, who knew Mintoff personally, bombarded the Labour front bench with excited demands on behalf of his Maltese friend.[10] Callaghan at least found himself somewhat more in sympathy with the Conservative government on the issue. He approved of the package that Lennox-Boyd introduced for the island; apart from other considerations, the Baileys firm which ran ship construction in Malta was based in his own Cardiff constituency. Labour was as careful to keep its distance from Dom Mintoff as from the Greek Cypriot champions of enosis. Negotiating with him, Callaghan told Gaitskell, was 'a fruitless and frustrating pursuit'.[11] Events were to confirm the broad wisdom of this assessment.

Africa, however, would provide the ultimate test of Labour's colonial statesmanship. All over the continent, from Suez to the Cape, there was a ferment of change and frequent violence to which Labour would have to respond. In West Africa, there was not much that needed to be done other than to endorse the successive independence granted to Ghana (1957), Nigeria (1960) Sierra Leone (1961) and Gambia (1963). Callaghan, however, knew these territories at first hand, and was a good deal less ingenuous than many about the prospects for stability there. In particular, the endemic ethnic warfare within Nigeria concerned him, long before the civil war over the Ibos of Biafra in the late 1960s and the endless breaches of human rights that were to follow. Labour was especially effective in pointing that independence was merely a starting-point, and that without a transformation of local agriculture and the production of skilled workers and managers the prospects for these fledgling African states were bleak.

East Africa was far more turbulent. Callaghan was in close touch with Iain Macleod, the new colonial secretary from 1959, in pressing on with rapid self-government in Tanganyika: his own close relationship with Julius Nyerere was a factor in the British government's assessments. In time, a pact between Macleod, and the Tanganyika African National Union (TANU) Party of Julius Nyerere led to independence for the newly named Tanzania in 1961. Uganda was also consensual as it moved towards independence. Labour endorsed the federal compromise with the Kabaka of Buganda which led to Uganda's independence under Dr. Milton Obote in 1962.

Kenya was a different matter. After the ending of the Mau Mau emergency, progress seemed slow towards self-government there: prominent black Africans headed by Jomo Kenyatta were resident in British gaols as Gandhi, Nehru and so many other third-world leaders had been before them. Labour pursued a middle course here that proved effective and influential. On the one hand, the British government was condemned for a dilatory approach towards drafting a new constitution, and the need for land redistribution in the white highlands, and for agricultural and educational development under the Swynnerton Plan. Macmillan and Lennox-Boyd felt that British forces should stay on in East Africa for a decade owing to the importance of the air bases at Nairobi and Entebbe and the sea base at Mombasa for Britain's defence needs. Labour argued that it would be disastrous to poison relations with Black Africa for such an extrinsic reason. On the other hand, Callaghan himself used his close relationship with Tom Mboya, a recent product of Ruskin College, Oxford, well known in Labour Party circles, to push the need for moderation and gradualism amongst the KAU in Kenya, certainly for avoiding ethnic violence. Callaghan offered his good offices to Lennox-Boyd and Sir Evelyn Baring in persuading Mboya to agree to an amended form of state and legislative council.[12] In May 1959 he told the latter there was 'an opportunity for a substantial move forward' in Kenya which, in turn, would exert leverage on the more difficult issue of the Central African Federation. He also urged the importance of avoiding tribal rivalries.[13] Years later in 1969, this warning proved sadly apposite since Mboya, himself from the minority Luo people and now a key minister in the Kenya government under Kenyatta, was to be assassinated by Kikuyu. It was a break with tradition for a Labour spokesman to urge black Africans to heed the rightful demands of white farmers in the highlands, and the MCF did not like it, but it played its constructive part in speeding up the move towards independence.

When news broke of an atrocity at Hola Camp in which 12 Kikuyu had apparently died in mysterious circumstances which were then covered up by the camp commander, Callaghan and others launched a ferocious assault on Lennox-Boyd and demanded a proper inquiry.[14] Lennox-Boyd, a suave right-wing figure who had tried over the years to smother Callaghan with establishment gentility, found himself assailed and reminded of his pre-war record of support for Franco. The cross-party consensus on Africa did not entirely evaporate, but Labour was able to convey the affront to world opinion with this latest addition to the dismal saga of colonial atrocities dating from Amritsar. Lennox-Boyd's apparent evasiveness over Hola Camp tarred his reputation permanently and tended to obliterate memory of the more positive aspects of his policies in British East Africa. In time it was again Macleod, working in close consultation with the Labour Opposition, who used Michael Blundell's multi-racial New Kenya Party to persuade white settler opinion to compromise, and Jomo Kenyatta completed the transition from British political prisoner to president of the new Kenya in 1963.

The main issue of the time, however, and the basic test of whether Labour had something significant to say on Africa, other than moral posturing, was the Central African Federation. By 1957 it was lurching into something close to anarchy. Here Callaghan was largely left on his own to work out his own approach. Central Africa was not an issue in which either Gaitskell or Aneurin Bevan took a close interest, and only James Griffiths of Labour's front bench had much first-hand knowledge. In fact, Callaghan steered over five years, from 1957 to 1961, a remarkably effective course, in a way that raised both his own and his party's standing.

Labour, as has been seen, initially had welcomed the Central African Federation as a project that would raise up the economies of the three territories concerned through the benefits of integration. This would especially assist the poorest areas of Nyasaland and Northern Rhodesia where the economies were least productive and the white settler population relatively tiny (a mere 9,000 in Nyasaland). Some of the more right-wing members of the Labour front bench, notably the former commonwealth secretary, Patrick Gordon Walker, were still heard to use this argument, along with a much more curious view that a Federation might somehow act as a bulwark north of the Zambesi river against a supposedly expansionist Nationalist regime in South Africa. Callaghan himself, at the time of his first visit to Southern Rhodesia in September–October 1957, was to endorse the economic benefits that would flow to the African peoples from Federation. These, he argued, 'could not reasonably be challenged'.[15] He also responded to the physically bracing atmosphere of southern Africa, its spectacular scenery and mood of pioneering enterprise, in terms reminiscent of Henty or Rider Haggard.[16] In time he was also to become personally friendly with the controversial Prime Minister of the Federation Roy Welensky, a former trade union leader and heavy-weight boxing champion.

But the plain reality was that the British Conservatives had imposed the Federation in 1953 totally against the wishes of the huge black African majority. A massive political and guerrilla campaign spearheaded by men like Hastings Banda in Nyasaland and Kenneth Kaunda in Northern Rhodesia, both of them well known in British Labour circles, was launched. A quarter of a million whites were seen as entrenching their ascendancy over black Africans. The effect on Britain's position in Africa as a whole could well prove disastrous: the United Kingdom could be confronted with the kind of chaos that resulted in the former Belgian Congo. The reasoned opposition of the British Labour Party at this time was thus of immense significance for stability in southern Africa and for world geopolitics as a whole. Callaghan and his colleagues repeatedly urged that the Federation was unsustainable in defiance of black African opinion. They emphasised the hostility of Africans to constitutional amendment that would reinforce the position of Southern Rhodesia, with its relatively large white settler population. The minute number of blacks who appeared on the voting rolls spoke for itself. In addition, a controversial visit by a parliamentary delegation to the Federation territories in September–October 1957 gave Callaghan and his Labour colleagues a rare opportunity to dictate the terms of the debate.[17] They spelt out the poor living standards and working conditions in the mines of the Rhodesian copperbelt, the obvious evidence of racial discrimination especially in Salisbury, the lack of educational and professional advancement for blacks, and the deep distrust felt for Welensky himself. In debates in the Commons in 1958–9, Callaghan urged the need for a rapid move towards a black African majority in the territorial legislatures of Nyasaland and Northern Rhodesia and for retaining a residual role for the British government instead of a headlong rush to an integrated Federation with possible dominion status that could lead to a bloodbath. As he noted, the black view was that it should be constitutionally possible for Nyasaland to secede from the Federation entirely.[18]

What is striking about the debates in the Commons is the defensiveness of the conservatives and the normally super-confident Lennox-Boyd. Back in southern Africa, Welensky sensed this failure of will – 'What in God's name has come over the Tories?'[19] In 1959 the Monckton Commission was appointed to consider the future prospects of the Federation: Callaghan and Barbara Castle, who had been mooted as possible members were ruled out by Macmillan on the spurious grounds that neither was a Privy Councillor. Its findings, however, were remarkably similar to those put forward by Labour in debate after debate. Black opposition to the Federation was overwhelming. There should be African majorities in both the legislatures of Nyasaland and Northern Rhodesia, and political prisoners should be released. Some powers should be transferred back from the Federation to the territorial authorities. No move towards dominion status should be attempted. Although the Monckton report still voiced a generalised sympathy for the long-term benefits of Federation, the effect was to make the position of the federal government increasingly unreal and Welensky a beleaguered figure. The fact that Iain Macleod had now succeeded Lennox-Boyd at the Colonial Office and that his own view of the Federation was scarcely more positive than that of Callaghan (with whom he had a good personal relationship) intensified the pressure on Salisbury. Macleod's private objective was to be the last British colonial secretary.

The Central African Federation, however, was not only a matter of constitutional debate or the formalities of racial partnership. It was also a crucial issue of law and order, with growing and alarming racial violence. Here again Labour led public debate by exposing remorselessly the inadequacies of the Conservatives' defence of the Federation and its governors. There were strikes by African workers in both Northern and Southern Rhodesia, and massive disturbances in Nyasaland. Twenty people were killed at Nkata Bay in March 1959. A state of emergency was declared by Governor Sir Robert Armitage. Under pressure from Labour, Lennox-Boyd appointed a commission of inquiry under the distinguished judge Patrick Devlin. He concluded bluntly that Nyasaland was 'a police state', that Hastings Banda was being wrongly detained, and that claims of a black 'murder plot' were absurd. Debates in the Commons on 3 March and 28 July 1959 were dominated by Labour's spokesmen.[20]

Callaghan himself spoke with new authority in both; he was backed up by Aneurin Bevan who spoke of incipient fascism in southern Africa, to the fury of Welensky sitting in the Commons gallery at the time.[21] The apparent failure of the British Colonial Secretary and Attorney-General to accept the Devlin report, eminent though its author was and thorough as his interrogation of over 1,700 witnesses had been, further undermined Conservative credibility in Africa.

The result was an abrupt change of policy after the general election of 1959. It was reinforced by the impact made on Macmillan early in 1960 by the 'wind of change', which he detected in South Africa and indeed throughout the continent. Macleod was seen by right-wing critics like Lord Salisbury to be working to undermine the Federation. Callaghan in turn encouraged fundamental changes in the Federation including an overhaul of the voting rolls, guaranteeing an African majority in the federal assembly, and an agreed right for Nyasaland and Northern Rhodesia to secede. Macmillan no longer had the authority or the will to rebut Labour's reasoned criticisms. The denouement for an increasingly ghostly Central African Federation came with the appointment of R.A. Butler, to take charge of African affairs in July 1962 in the course of Macmillan's 'night of the long knives' which saw the dismissal of a third of his Cabinet. In the stampede of withdrawal that followed, Nyasaland and Northern Rhodesia moved rapidly towards total independence. Hastings Banda and Kenneth Kaunda were released from their traditional lodgement in British gaol as potential prime ministers. In less than two years their countries were independent. On New Year's Day 1964, unloved and unlamented, the Central African Federation ceased to exist.

That left only Southern Rhodesia, a self-governing territory since the 1920s, in an anomalous position on its own. Figures like Edgar Whitehead, almost liberals in Rhodesian terms, were succeeded by the United Front, a whites-only party headed at first by Winston Field and the up-and-coming figure of the former RAF pilot Ian Smith. Their emergence in 1964 foretold problems to come. The unilateral declaration of total independence by Rhodesia in 1965 was to plague a succession of British administrations, including that of Callaghan himself in 1976–9, until the final creation of a new Rhodesian constitution with a black African majority at the Lusaka conference in late 1979. The future of Zimbabwe/Rhodesia was a troubled one, and only resolved finally with the direct assistance of the United States and *sub rosa* pressure from the Nationalist government in Pretoria. By the turn of the century, the authoritarian regime of Zimbabwe under Robert Mugabe was the focus of international scandal. Yet the wisdom of winding up a wholly indefensible Federation in Central Africa was beyond dispute.

Like all the other mooted federations of this period, in the West Indies, East Africa, southern Arabia and the original scheme for Malaya, it was one with Tyre and Nineveh.

There is no doubt that Labour, including Callaghan, played a major part in avoiding catastrophe in southern Africa. They helped to dictate the political and moral agenda. But what lent authority to Labour's position was its pragmatism and balance. The anti-imperialist rhetoric of the MCF was marginalised; Callaghan himself repeatedly rejected its demands, including demonstrations against South Africa at the time of the Commonwealth Games held in Callaghan's own Cardiff base. Labour repeatedly put pressure on black African leaders like Banda and Kaunda to urge their followers to avoid violence, to follow the constitutional path and steer clear of 'narrow ingrowing racialism'.[22] Labour always emphasised that independence for the African territories would be but the start of the real campaign for liberation, given the low level of agricultural development, the lack of skills amongst black farmers and industrial workers, the total absence of black managers, the poor provision for education and technical training, the relationship of economic advance in tropical Africa to wider schemes of third-world development and to the growth of the global economy. The problems of a country like Nyasaland (Malawi) were less ones of brutal imperialist oppression than of economic backwardness, mass illiteracy and ignorance. The implications were rapidly picked up by African leaders like Tom Mboya, a powerful figure in Kenya as minister of economic planning until his assassination following the tribal resentment that his land redistribution programmes aroused in his country. The later history of the various liberated black countries in Africa from Sierra Leone to Zimbabwe was often to be one of crises and disappointments, economic weakness, feeble currency, political instability, tribal factionalism, endemic corruption and mass abuses of human rights for decades to come. Many of them were foreseen in Labour's critique of decolonisation in the 1950s and 1960s. But, without doubt, a continuation of a discredited, half-hearted imperial regime at that period was politically and militarily impossible. It was, of course, Conservative governments which showed wisdom and statesmanship in carrying political independence through. But it was Labour which in large measure supplied the policies and the moral impetus.

The rapid decolonisation of so much of the old Commonwealth in these few years was a powerful boost to the morale of the Labour Party. Elsewhere the years of opposition brought fierce internal conflict on issues ranging from public ownership to nuclear weapons. Not until Wilson became Labour leader in February 1963 with the expressed aim of bypassing 'theology' over party policies, was a new sense of unity imparted.

Colonial policy, by contrast, was a rare focus of harmony and moral uplift; if a radical body like the MCF could feel sidelined by 1964, it could claim that Labour's policies had largely absorbed its message, while prominent MCF figures like Barbara Castle and Anthony Greenwood served in the Cabinet of Harold Wilson, himself a former member of the movement. For Callaghan himself, the years as Colonial spokesman gave him for the first time the mantle of statesmanship. While some of his views were products of their era – in particular, the belief that the newly liberated colonial peoples would look uniquely to Britain as their constitutional model and source of aid and ideas – in other respects he managed a genuine fusion of moral criticism and constructive prescription. His speeches on constitutional change, economic advance and race relations especially in Africa, which he knew best, were genuinely visionary. More directly, the relationships he struck up with men like Kaunda and Nyerere gave him an unusually wide-ranging political base which won the respect of foreign leaders like Carter and Schmidt in years to come. As foreign secretary in 1974–6, the Commonwealth dimension of his role was always central to his thinking, even if events in Cyprus and Rhodesia were not there to remind him. As prime minister, he imposed his personal authority on Rhodesian matters in particular; his civil servants noted how first Crosland and then Owen at the Foreign Office tended to defer to him here.[23] In short, the Commonwealth and Africa in particular turned him from a routine party operator into something approaching an international statesman. He was no longer just a coming man.

(iv)

For the outcome of the imperial legacy on which Roger Louis has so luminously written, Labour's role in these years is perhaps a somewhat underestimated factor in the equation. Britain, after all, withdrew with astonishing swiftness in a massive range of territories especially in Africa, but without leaving the armed conflict or the chaos in French Algeria, the Dutch East Indies, the Belgian Congo, the Spanish Western Sahara (Rio de Oro), or Portuguese Guinea, Angola and Mozambique. It did so without massive party contention of a kind that had coloured earlier debates over Empire from the Boer War to the independence of India, and Labour's contribution was an important one. When Labour took office in 1964, colonial issues were already much less prominent in public debate. Apart from the abiding issue of Rhodesia, the imperial domain survived only in a variety of small territories in the West Indies, the South Atlantic, Indian Ocean and the Pacific, in Hong Kong, Gibraltar and the unimportant Falklands. Some were uninhabited. Labour had few novelties to propose in any of them: Greenwood cut a relatively minor figure as colonial secretary in 1964–5, as did his successors, Lord Longford and Fred Lee. When told by Tony Greenwood in October 1964 that his new post of colonial secretary would retain Cabinet status, Barbara Castle was surprised. 'I thought his job was small beer'[24] In January 1967 the Colonial Office disappeared from history, while the Commonwealth Office was subsequently to be absorbed by the Foreign Office. The Commonwealth dimension, however, remained significant, notably in co-ordinating support, economic and moral, for sanctions in South Africa. Callaghan himself took his Commonwealth responsibilities very seriously while both foreign secretary and prime minister. His handling of the sporting and other boycotts of South Africa at the 1976 Commonwealth conference at Gleneagles enhanced his reputation for world statesmanship, as had his earlier effective ban on the MCC cricket tour to South Africa after the d'Oliveira affair in 1970 when he was home secretary. The whole Commonwealth area remained a source of his – and Labour's – moral strength. As prime minister he was greeted in India in 1978 as an honoured emancipator, a survivor from the esteemed Attlee government which had liberated (though also divided) the sub-continent. Only on South-East Asia, with which he was relatively less familiar, was he felt by Lee Kuan Yew to speak with less authority.[25]

Why the British withdrew from their empire, both formal and informal, so precipitately after 1945 is a large question which Roger Louis and others have often raised. After all, even the remnants of the Portuguese empire, Goa, Guinea-Bissau, Angola and Mozambique, clung on, admittedly amidst prolonged civil war in the last three cases. In 1998 the Portuguese enclave of Macao still remained detached from China even after the British lease had ended 150 years of occupation in Hong Kong. Obviously there was a massive awareness of diminishing economic and military resources: as Roger Louis has written, Bevin's policy in the Middle East after 1945 was governed by 'a reluctance to endorse political or economic settlements that might have required British bayonets'.[26] Beyond that, however, it was clear that the British people had long resolved that imperial withdrawal was inescapable, with the last rites enacted east of Suez in 1971. It was a recognition that can be detected even under the Lloyd George coalition after 1918, with the independence of Egypt, the moves towards self-government in India under the Montagu-Chelmsford proposals, and of course most spectacularly in the total reversal of policy in Ireland which resulted in the Irish Free State coming into being in 1922. Where Arthur Griffith led, Gandhi and Nehru were to follow on.

In the immediate aftermath of victory after 1945, the British response was heavily coloured by simple emotional and physical exhaustion after six years of total war, along with the renewed military burdens of the Cold War era. There was also much indirect American pressure in the Middle East and South-East Asia, with the result that British imperial power often came to be replaced by a kind of Anglo-American condominium, heavily shaped by capitalist pressures from the US oil and other industries. In the fifties, there was something more positive, not so much a failure of national will but a recognition that Britain's world role rested on other premises. Only a handful of partisans on the furthest reaches of the Tory right urged a long-term retention of power: men like Hinchingbrooke and Waterhouse amongst the Suez rebels in 1954, the anachronistic imperial message peddled by the Beaverbrook press, were relatively unimportant. An old camp-follower of Empire, Leo Amery's son, Julian, bowed to the facts of life and even served in the Macmillan and Heath governments.

Rather was it that, perhaps for the one time in twentieth-century history, an informed and settled view of the problems of an ageing Empire, the strategies for economic development, the parameters of new multi-racial political settlements, the relationship of black and other national-ist movements to global shifts of opinion, shaped political dialogue in Britain. The politicians, intellectuals, lobbyists and journalists in, or associated with, the Labour Party were central to this process, including ex-Liberals like Dingle and Hugh Foot and Honor Balfour. The Tories paid the piper but Labour often called the tune. Their spokesmen were used by Conservative ministers like Home or Macleod to stiffen the spines of their own Cabinet colleagues. It was not a failure of will, but rather a sharper perception of what that will was based on, not passive surrender but creative redefinition. For Labour it also meant something else. At a time of ideological uncertainty, with the party still poised between social-ists and the revisionists (as Harold Wilson in his over-subtle ambiguity recognised in 1964), colonial policy enabled Labour to cleave to the old imperatives. For the one time in its history, the party had evolved an intel-lectually coherent approach to Britain's colonial possessions that embod-ied both the ethical idealism of the ILP and the constructive positivism of the Fabians. It was an ideological popular front that spanned the whole range of viewpoints from Rita Hinden to Leonard Barnes. The ending of Empire, even with difficult problems remaining in Cyprus and Rhodesia, was in many ways Old Labour's greatest moral victory. To adapt Alan Taylor's controversial phrase (originally applied to Munich) it was a triumph for all that was best in British life. The civilised acceptance of a post-imperial role was the great enduring triumph of British history since 1945. The inability to reach a similar consensus over continental Europe in the same period has been the supreme failure. Labour has been as hesitant and insular here, from the rejection of the Schuman Plan in 1950 to the opt-out over European Monetary Union (EMU) in 1999, as it has been morally assured over decolonisation. The white man's burden has been emotionally relocated from the Himalayas to the white cliffs of Dover, to no one's advantage. But that is another, less appealing, story.

Chapter 12

Labour and the 'Special Relationship'

The attitude of the Labour Party to the Anglo-American alliance presents us with a great paradox. Traditionally, Labour, as a supposedly socialist party, has been the more anti-American of the two main British political parties. The United States was the citadel of capitalism, of Uncle Sam, of Wall Street. Its malevolent intent towards a socialist government in Britain was demonstrated, so Labour legend had it, in August 1931 when sinister pressures from the New York bankers J.P. Morgan helped to overthrow the second Labour government during the financial crisis of that time. American bankers have been on Labour's 'hate list' ever since.

And yet, in the years since 1945, it has been under Labour governments that the so-called Special Relationship between Britain and the United States has been most flourishing. It was never closer than under the governments of Attlee, Wilson, Callaghan – and, indeed, Tony Blair. Conversely, it was under the supposedly pro-American Conservatives, when Anthony Eden was prime minister, that Anglo-American relations experienced their greatest crisis – the Anglo-French invasion of Suez in 1956. Even under Winston Churchill (1951–5), at a time when his old wartime comrade Eisenhower was president of the United States, Anglo-American relations underwent many difficult periods, particularly in relation to the Cold War and policies towards China. The British prime minister least sympathetic to the United States in the years since the Second World War has been the Conservative, Edward Heath (1970–4). When I interviewed Henry Kissinger for my biography of James Callaghan, he described Heath's attitude towards the United States as 'horrible'.[1] Fences were mended under Mrs. Thatcher, but as recently as the premiership of John Major, relations with America were strained by his aides having worked in the 1992 presidential election not for Bill Clinton but for his Republican opponent, President George Bush.

The post-war Labour government of Clement Attlee (1945–51) had its attitude to the United States dictated by the Cold War. Its beginnings certainly did not show the feelings of the American government towards Great Britain and the British people in a warm or sympathetic light. The United States abruptly ended the Lend-Lease arrangements with their wartime ally on 21 August 1945, just a week after the end of the Second World War and the surrender of the Japanese. Negotiations with the Americans over a long-term loan to assist Britain with its immense post-war economic problems in the autumn of 1945 showed no great degree of friendship[2] The Americans were intent on taking over what was left of Britain's traditional financial supremacy and its hold over world markets. They insisted on a loan, not a gift, to the dismay of the chief British negotiator, the economist Maynard Keynes, who had told the Attlee government at the outset in July 1945 that Britain faced a 'financial Dunkirk'.[3] The eventual US loan, which the British government accepted with much reluctance and which 98 British MPs voted against in the House of Commons (including the future Labour prime minister, James Callaghan, just elected to parliament) was not a benevolent arrangement. While its interest charges of 2 per cent over 50 years on a loan of $3.75 billion were perhaps not as severe as they appeared at the time, the insistence on early trade liberalisation was directly harmful to British commercial and industrial interests at such a time, while the decision to force the convertibility of sterling in the summer of 1947 was a catastrophe which had to be ended after six weeks to avoid Britain's going bankrupt. The US loan terms of 1945 did more damage to British trade and finance than all the bombing raids of the Luftwaffe.

And yet, after this bad start, the Attlee government and the United States came ever closer. This was in large measure because Attlee and his foreign secretary, Ernest Bevin, felt it to be absolutely essential to maintain and extend the wartime alliance, and to keep the United States involved in Europe in place of the world isolationism that had governed American foreign policy after 1918. There were many signs in 1945–6 that the Americans still hankered to withdraw from a world role, including the rapid demobilisation of the armed forces. However, other geopolitical factors kept them rooted in Europe, especially their role as part of the administering powers in post-war Germany. A turning point was the Truman Doctrine announced in March 1947 by Anglo-American agreement when Bevin's statement that Britain no longer had the power to maintain a military presence in Greece and Turkey was immediately followed by President Truman's announcement that the United States would establish its forces there instead.[4]

The next four years were a halcyon period for Anglo-American relations: the legend of the Special Relationship now emerged in full splendour. The Labour government found themselves acting very closely with the Americans on all aspects of post-war international policy, political, economic and especially defence. Britain and the Americans collaborated intimately in building up western defence and security, with Britain taking the lead in Europe in 'western union'. They worked together in the implementation of the Marshall Plan in 1947–8 for European economic recovery, when the European Economic Community (EEC) was born, and from which Britain especially benefited. The social reforms of the Labour government, including the NHS, would not have been possible without American assistance. And it was Anglo-American diplomacy, negotiated by envoys like Sir Nicholas Henderson, which produced the North Atlantic Treaty Organization in April 1949. On all the key crises and confrontations with Stalin and the Soviet Union, the Labour government and Truman's administration stood shoulder to shoulder.

The classic representative of this remarkable era, which totally transformed the historic course of US foreign policy, was Sir Oliver Franks, transferred from his role as Oxford don and provost of my own college, The Queen's College, Oxford. Franks was first to organise the distribution of Marshall Aid, and then to serve as a vitally influential British ambassador in Washington from 1948 to 1952. A good friend of his fellow native of Bristol, the trade-union foreign secretary Ernest Bevin, Franks was a traditional internationalist Liberal, the very paradigm of the transatlantic alliance, the ethos of the Oxford Rhodes Scholarships, and the union of the English-speaking peoples of which Churchill wrote. Franks had unique prestige on both sides of the Atlantic: he had indeed been the college tutor at Queen's, Oxford, of a key figure in the US State Department, George McGhee. His intellectual ascendancy over the Attlee government, during crises over Berlin, the devaluation of the pound and the war in Korea, was immense. He told the Labour government when the Korean War broke out in June 1950 that Britain should send detachments of troops to Korea to fight alongside the Americans to confirm that Britain was 'the first in the European queue'.[5] (Indeed, the distinctively post-war concept of the 'queue', with its echoes of shoppers lining up outside shops for their meagre food rations during the era of austerity figures prominently in Franks's observations to his government). Just as he urged sending British troops to Korea for the sake of Anglo-US relations, he advised Attlee and his colleagues not to send them to protect the Abadan oil refineries in Persia, again primarily to protect the Special Relationship. But, he assured Attlee's team, the likely British reaction to any course of policy was the main factor likely to decide American thoughts in decisions about future action.

Franks's ascendancy was reinforced by the close personal relationship from 1949 between Ernest Bevin and the distinctly Anglophile White Anglo-Saxon Protestant (WASP) US foreign secretary, Dean Acheson. The relationship was far less close with Bevin's unfortunate successor as foreign secretary in March 1951, Herbert Morrison, whom Acheson believed to display a London parochialism. Whenever Morrison spoke on foreign affairs, Acheson wrote, you heard the sound of Bow bells (the traditional symbol of the old London).[6] By 1950 the union of hearts and minds of the Labour government was complete. Even the most left-wing member of the government, Welsh Minister of Health Aneurin Bevan, found himself strongly defending American policy in NATO, in defending Tito's Yugoslavia from possible Soviet attack, and in the airlift to blockaded Berlin in 1948: Bevan urged that the allies should consider relieving Berlin with tanks.[7]

The only long-running point of division between the Americans and the Labour government concerned Palestine. American Jewish interests, strong in the Democratic Party, complained bitterly of Britain's and Ernest Bevin's apparent sympathy for the Arabs, their refusal to accept unlimited Jewish immigration after the Holocaust, and their refusal to endorse a new state of Israel until the Jews successfully defended themselves in war in 1948. But even Palestine did not disturb the overall good relationship. More important for the Americans in the Middle East was that Britain maintained a strong military presence there, notably the continuing military base in the Suez Canal zone, and also in the Far East, East of Suez, in places such as Colombo, Hong Kong and especially the great naval base of Singapore. Britain was also a nuclear power, developing its own atomic weapons programme (and a future hydrogen bomb), confirming its apparently 'great power' status, even if the origins of this had lain in British distrust of America's willingness to share its atomic secrets with British governments, and America's distrust of Communist spies or other alleged subversives in the British scientific establishment or even (in the notorious case of Burgess and Maclean) in the Foreign Office itself.

New strains emerged between Britain and the United States during the Korean War from June 1950 onwards. Britain diverged from the United States in its formal recognition of Communist China in 1949, in its scepticism to the regime of Chiang Kai-Shek in Formosa, and in the opposition shown by the Labour government to the 'bomb China' resolution proposed by the US government in the UN during the Korean War. The famous meeting of Attlee and Truman in Washington in December 1950, with Franks in close attendance, generally taken to be a kind of high point of the Special Relationship in the post-war period, was actually provoked by British fears that the Americans might use the atomic bomb in North Korea. It resulted in Britain, through US pressure, taking on an excessively high burden of £4,700 million over three years. This proved impossible to sustain, it meant a higher per capita expenditure on armaments in beleaguered impoverished post-war Britain than in the overwhelmingly wealthy United States, and it led to a severe split in Attlee's Cabinet. As it meant imposing charges on the free NHS, Aneurin Bevan and Harold Wilson resigned from the government.

There was also tension with the Americans over the Abadan crisis over oil in Persia when even as pro-American a politician as the Labour

Chancellor of the Exchequer Hugh Gaitskell felt that American policy was swayed as much by anxiety to take over Britain's oil interests in the region than fears for the strategic and political future of Iran (perhaps a kind of precursor of British feelings about American policy in Iraq in the autumn of 2002). Nevertheless, on balance, relations between London and Washington remained extremely close in the entire period down to the end of Attlee's government in October 1951. It was this that fuelled French fears of 'les Anglo-Saxons' so memorably articulated by President de Gaulle in the 1960s. The cultural union seemed as close as it had ever been. American pop culture, the 'Coca-colonisation' of Britain, from chewing gum to Danny Kaye and Bob Hope movies to American musicals like *Oklahoma* and *Annie Get Your Gun,* was omnipresent. Meanwhile the presence of American GIs in many British cities, resented by some, was at least hugely popular with British girls, charmed or seduced by these virile young men bearing gum, chocolates or nylon stockings in the post-war austerity. (The presence of so many black troops, however, produced its own kind of tension, not least within the US armed services despite their desegregation by President Truman in 1949.)

After this high-point of the Special Relationship, however, Britain's relations with the United States produced great strains for the Labour Party throughout much of its 13 years in opposition, 1951–64. These were years of internal conflict in the party, conflict mainly over foreign and defence policy and especially over relations with America. The rise of the so-called Bevanites after Aneurin Bevan's resignation in 1951 was largely stimulated by Labour's pro-American stance in foreign policy at a time of crises in China, and much criticism of the foreign policy of John Foster Dulles, Eisenhower's secretary of state, in relation to China and the Far East more generally. The dominant group in the party, however, remained strongly pro-American. Its symbol was Hugh Gaitskell, leader of the Labour right who became leader of the Labour Party after Attlee in November 1955 and who remained leader until his sudden death in January 1963. Gaitskell had not been especially involved with the United States in his early life (he never went there until he became a cabinet minister) but from his work in the creation of the European Payments Union in 1950 he became ever more passionately pro-American. In his diary, he talks of his personal chemistry with intellectual 'New Deal' Ivy League types like Dean Acheson ('sensitive and cultivated mind') and Averell Harriman and Chester Bowles. In the great arguments in the Attlee government in March–April 1951 over the rearmament programme, the economist Gaitskell did not in the main use economic arguments (where his left-wing non-economist critic Aneurin Bevan was clearly in the right in terms of the damage it would do to British exports and the economy generally) but rather political arguments about the vital need to be the closest possible ally of the United States during the Korean War. He carried the Cabinet and most of the party with him. He was, inevitably, passionately pro-US during the Suez crisis – when, indeed, the Labour Party generally praised Eisenhower's government for resisting the illegal Anglo-French attack on the Egyptians in Suez and Port Said. As late as the Cuban crisis in November 1962, Gaitskell alarmed a colleague like Denis Healey with the zeal with which he urged that President Kennedy had as much right to protect his country against Russian missiles in Cuba as Britain would have if Russian missiles were installed in Ireland.

The other side of Gaitskell's view was a negative one – his growing antipathy to Britain's joining any kind of united Europe. His passionate speech in October 1962 at the Labour Party conference, with its talk of 'a thousand years of history' which joining Europe would destroy, confirmed the linkage in Gaitskell's mind of a close alliance with the Americans and sympathy for a multi-racial Commonwealth with detachment from any mystical concept of European union, whether a Common Market or a federal super-state. Most of the coming men in the Labour Party in the 1950s shared this view. Anthony Crosland's *Future of Socialism* was much influenced by the way that post-New Deal America had managed and solved the problems of capitalism, and on how the Americans succeeded in removing class differences in their own society notably in education. The writings of Franklin Roosevelt's old adviser, Adolph Berle, taught him much on how the separation of ownership and management had transformed an increasingly corporate capitalist system. America could show British Labour the way ahead. Roy Jenkins, another emerging politician, was another firm admirer of the United States. His first visit there under the Smith-Mundt programme in 1953 had a huge formative impact upon him, even though in his case he combined it with a fervent Europeanism as well. Denis Healey, a more technocratic figure and an ex-Communist, was another to whom the American alliance was axiomatic: in particular, he became a great authority on the interconnectedness of British and US defence strategies. Healey told his comrades at the 1952 party conference, 'We cannot say "All men are brothers except the Americans."'[8] Conversely, Aneurin Bevan, the standard-bearer of the Left and always instinctively anti-American, was now dead, and his old lieutenant, Harold Wilson, was moving rapidly to a centre-right position, especially on foreign policy.

By the start of the 1960s, the great bulk of the Labour leadership was passionately close to the Americans, especially so when John F. Kennedy, a graduate of the London School of Economics, was elected president in 1960. Some Labour leaders took their enthusiasm for America to the extent of having American wives – Anthony Crosland and Anthony Wedgwood Benn (then a centre-right figure) being examples. A notable ideological influence on Labour thinking was the Canadian-American John Kenneth Galbraith. In particular his analysis of the tensions in American society – 'private affluence and public squalor' in *The Affluent Society* (1959) – had immense impact in persuading Labour people that the wastefulness and inhumanity of capitalism could better be removed, not by nationalisation or state management but by egalitarian social policies to eliminate class division. A classic test of Labour's attitude to the United States came with the massive conflict over the Campaign for Nuclear Disarmament (CND) in 1958–61. The CND campaign, directed against any use of atomic weapons and therefore for Britain's leaving NATO, had many points of origin, including simple pacifism, religious and environmentalist idealism, and dislike of Gaitskell and the Labour right, but hostility to America was a key part of much of it. In the end, the symbolic contest – Gaitskell's defeat by CND at the 1960 party conference, his triumph over CND in 1961 – was to confirm Labour's adherence to the Special Relationship as understood in the post-war years. In the period leading up to the October 1964 general election, when Labour was to be returned to power by a very narrow margin, Labour's sympathy for Kennedy-style Democratic liberalism was almost complete. The main point of complaint – the position of blacks in the US South – also began to disappear from 1964 with new civil rights policies under President Johnson. When I was in the United States with James Callaghan in May 1963, while working at Columbia University in New York, the future Labour chancellor's view was clear that American unfailing support for its closest ally would ensure that the next Labour government would always be rescued from economic difficulties.

This confidence did, indeed, shape the initial attitude of the Labour government under Harold Wilson from October 1964 onwards. It gave reassurance to Wilson in his famous, or notorious, decision on his first day in office not to devalue the pound.[9] Indeed, in its early difficult period, down to the summer of 1966, the repeated financial crises that Wilson and Callaghan encountered, with balance of payments pressures and much speculation that the pound would have to be devalued, led to frequent US assistance, through major long-term loans from the banks or via the International Monetary Fund. As early as November 1964 his friend Al Hayes, president of the Federal Reserve Bank of New York, bailed out Callaghan with a rescue package of $3,000 million, following a tidal wave of the selling of sterling. Harold Wilson, when he visited the White House as the guest of Lyndon Johnson, found himself showered with compliments as the fitting heir to Winston Churchill,

Horatio Nelson, even William Shakespeare. The presence of Dean Rusk
as secretary of state appeared reassuring: he had been an Oxford Rhodes
Scholar and observed at an Oxford alumni dinner in New York that, in
the US administration, while Harvard got all the credit, Oxford did all
the work.

When I spent a year at Columbia in 1962–3 and then again in the
summer of 1965, I was struck by the continuing high prestige of British
intellectual and cultural life in the United States, at least on its eastern
seaboard. *The Times Literary Supplement* or *The Economist* were widely
respected; the idiosyncrasies of British historians like A.J.P. Taylor or
Hugh Trevor-Roper were avidly discussed, while Broadway featured a
variety of British productions from Peter Ustinov plays to the Oxbridge
review *Beyond the Fringe,* along with the inevitable Shakespeare. Even
a Welshman like me could take pride that his fellow countrymen were
recognised. Dylan Thomas, who had died spectacularly in a pub in
New York's Greenwich Village, enjoyed immense prestige, while the
marriage of Richard Burton to Elizabeth Taylor was discussed as supposedly shedding light on the Celtic temperament, over both drink and
sex, via Burton's much discussed 'Welsh moods'. As Harold Macmillan
had once claimed, Britain still appeared to be playing Greece to America's Rome.

But in fact, under this Labour government, the obvious weakness
and sense of decline in Britain since 1951 was undermining much of
the substance of the Special Relationship now. There was nobody like
Oliver Franks now to paper over the cracks: indeed the importance of
the personality of the British ambassador in Washington (even David
Ormsby-Gore, a personal friend of President Kennedy) now seemed
much diminished. Britain's feebleness in defence matters was underlined in 1962 by the US cancellation of its Skybolt missile system,
secretly promised to Macmillan by President Eisenhower. The eventual
substitution of US Polaris submarines for British use under the December 1962 Nassau agreement served to underline British weakness, apart
from annoying President de Gaulle. The so-called British independent
deterrent seemed, therefore, an almost contemptuous donation from
the Americans to help their struggling partners.

The growing war in Vietnam produced much opposition to American policy in British Labour circles from 1965 onwards. There was
widespread belief in Britain that the support expressed for the United
States by Harold Wilson was simply surrendering to US pressures or
bribes – support for the pound. In return for support in Vietnam there
was a widespread belief in US diplomatic circles that this was a reality.
Wilson himself observed in February 1966 that 'US financial support is

not unrelated to the way we behave in the Far East.[10] He had to resist strong pressure to send British troops to Vietnam, as the Australians had done, and as the British themselves had done in Korea in 1950 when the 'Glorious' Gloucestershire regiment had gained much renown. Harold Wilson tried at times to act as a kind of go-between the Russians and the Americans over Vietnam, but his efforts (which included such strange moves as sending an obscure Welsh left-wing minister, Harold Davies, to Vietnam to explore a settlement) were treated with contempt. Walt Rostow, a key foreign affairs aide, observed bluntly, 'We don't give a god-dam about Wilson'.[11] There was no talk *à la* Franks of being 'first in the queue' now. Meanwhile the almost total domination of British policy by Washington was disgracefully shown in the decision by the Wilson government to remove the population in the small Indian Ocean island of Diego Garcia, a British colony, to accommodate an American communications and naval base, in direct contradiction of the UN Convention of Human Rights.

In 1967–8, the Labour government took three momentous decisions. All were linked, all showed the diminishing importance of a weakened Britain for the United States and the declining importance of the American alliance for British policy-makers. First, Britain finally devalued the pound in November 1967, from \$2.80 to \$2.40. The US patience had run out with the British economy, its structural weakness and unending liquid debts. The US Secretary of the Treasury 'Joe' Fowler could no longer offer US loans to prop up its ailing ally. The United States was desperate in fact that Britain should not devalue the pound since it was believed that the dollar would be the next target. But Callaghan (who then resigned as chancellor) had no alternative as funds flooded out, and sterling was duly devalued on 18 November. This offended the Americans as easily Britain's major trading partner: the relationship became that much less 'special' as a result.

Secondly, Britain took the major strategic decision to withdraw from East of Suez, despite the bitter opposition of US Defense Secretary Robert MacNamara. Denis Healey, the pro-American Labour secretary of defence, in time came to accept that a retreat from the Far East was inescapable, despite US criticism, on financial grounds, and also because British forces were being exposed in the face of opposition from Asian nationalist movements locally. The US ambassador in London, David Bruce, an Anglophile intellectual, bluntly observed that the idea of a British–US 'Special Relationship' now was 'little more than sentimental terminology'. By the end of 1971, despite protests from Lee Kuan Yew and the Australians, all the British forces in Singapore and elsewhere in Asia had gone, and memories of Empire with them.

And thirdly, and crucially, Britain moved closer towards Europe. Harold Macmillan's Tories had applied to join the Common Market in 1962–3 but this had been frustrated by de Gaulle's opposition to 'les Anglo-Saxons.' As noted above, Gaitskell had led the Labour Party in opposing entry into Europe at that time. But in the summer of 1967, Wilson and his strongly pro-European foreign secretary, the impulsive figure of George Brown, began strong moves to apply for Common Market membership once again. It was a reflection of Britain's growing sense of economic and diplomatic weakness, and its need to re-define its world role. Key Foreign Office figures like Michael Palliser and Roy Denman were urging a far more pro-European stance for British policy henceforth,[12] and warning against appeasing the Americans over east of Suez. Even though de Gaulle again vetoed the British application, from that time onwards, future British membership of the European community was a bi-partisan priority, permanently on the political agenda. By the time that it lost power, at the General Election of 1970, Labour's pro-Americanism had cooled considerably. The new Republican US president, Richard Nixon, was far more lukewarm towards Europe than the Democrats had been. Indeed, Richard Crossman actually preferred Nixon's relative detachment to the anti-Communist crusading instinct of Democrats like Hubert Humphrey, Walt Rostow or Dean Acheson.[13]

The emphasis seemed very much on Europe when Labour unexpectedly regained office in March 1974, a minority government elected during the industrial crisis of the miners' strike. Heath had taken Britain into the Common Market. Labour had opposed this at the time, but many of its key members in fact supported the decision, including Jenkins. Major figures like Wilson and Callaghan were at worst equivocal. Callaghan, now foreign secretary, began a somewhat cosmetic process of 'renegotiating' the British terms of entry with the backing of his ally and friend, the German Social Democratic Chancellor Helmut Schmidt and a good deal of sympathy from the new French President Giscard d'Estaing. In time it was claimed that better terms had been negotiated on such matters as budget contributions and Commonwealth imports like New Zealand butter and Australian meat. A referendum on European membership in June 1975 confirmed it by a large membership – and without splitting the Labour Party either.

In fact, Callaghan as foreign secretary made it a major priority from March 1974 to repair relations with the United States after the coolness of the Heath years. The former trade union official struck up a surprisingly strong relationship with the US secretary of state, the *realpolitik* former Harvard professor, Henry Kissinger.[14] They got off to a bad start in July 1974 with a row over the island of Cyprus. After a coup in Cyprus overthrew the government there (commonly thought of as the work of the CIA), the Turks invaded the island with much evidence of covert assistance from the Americans who regarded Turkey as a conveniently placed strategic anti-Communist ally. In the end, Callaghan had to submit to this *démarche* though he did negotiate a settlement which lasts to the present time of a partitioned island with the creation of separate Greek and Turkish administrations. There was further dissension between Callaghan and Kissinger in other areas, notably the revolution in Portugal (which Callaghan supported as a social democrat) and problems in Belize in Central America, which America's puppet, Guatemala, wished to annex. But on wider issues of security, détente and Western collaboration, London and Washington rebuilt something of the old warmth. In addition, Callaghan, after he became prime minister in March 1976, developed a warm personal relationship with President Gerald Ford, which indeed was to endure long after both senior statesmen had retired.

With Jimmy Carter, US Democratic president from the start of 1977, Callaghan's relationship was more wary. Even so, they had much in common because both were Baptists by origin, each had been a farmer and each had served in the navy during the Second World War. Carter's presidential visit to Britain in May 1977, the royal jubilee year, was a great personal success. More crucially, Callaghan acted as a key bridge-builder for Carter in many critical issues, especially since Carter respected Callaghan's long acquaintance with international issues and personalities, and was also well aware of his own relative ignorance of the world beyond the United States. In the Middle East in particular, Callaghan acted as a key go-between for Carter using his personal ties with Golda Meir and other Israeli Labour Party politicians, and his acquaintance with President Sadat of Egypt. The Camp David agreement of 1979, for which Carter got much credit, was to a fair degree Callaghan's achievement. On wider issues, Anglo-US relations were again close during the years of Callaghan's premiership down to May 1979. They worked intimately together in the Strategic Arms Limitation Talks (SALT II) talks and negotiations on defence and security at Guadeloupe (January 1979), and in the possible delivery to Britain of the Chevaline missile system to enhance Polaris. It was also agreed that Britain might station American cruise missiles on British soil – which duly happened at Greenham Common later on, to much popular protest.

In a quite different area of the world, Britain and America also found themselves closely tied together, namely Southern Rhodesia, where the unilateral and illegal regime of Ian Smith, representing the white settler minority, remained a source of danger. Henry Kissinger, anxious about possible Russian or Cuban subversion in southern Africa, via the turbulent Portuguese former colonies, Angola and Mozambique, attempted to concoct a settlement on his own in late 1976. But his characteristic style of individual shuttle diplomacy did not meet with success. However, with the encouragement of others in Europe, David Owen and Cyrus Vance, respectively the British foreign secretary and American secretary of state, made considerable progress in clearing the ground towards a Rhodesian settlement. In particular, they persuaded Dr. Vorster, the South African nationalist prime minister, that it was in his interests to put pressure on Ian Smith to work out an agreement, and to emphasise his point by denying arms and ways of circumventing international sanctions.[15] By the time the Labour government fell from power in 1979, there had been significant advances in trying to engage the black African nationalists of Zambia African National Union (ZANU) in talks with the Smith regime; a Rhodesian Executive Council had been formed and events were moving towards early elections in Rhodesia with full black African participation. The eventual settlement in Rhodesia in late 1979 and the emergence of the controversial new state of Zimbabwe owed much to the combined force of Anglo-American diplomacy in the Callaghan years.

But in other respects, relations between Britain and the United States remained distant – even if Callaghan paid the Americans the compliment of making his own son-in-law, Peter Jay, ambassador to Washington in 1977. During the crisis over the IMF's negotiations with the British government in late 1976 over the terms that might be imposed on the Callaghan government in return for a long-term loan, the United States kept its distance. Callaghan hoped in November that his old friend Gerald Ford might encourage some assistance from the US banks and/ or Treasury to avoid the necessity of begging before the IMF, and sent a minister, Harold Lever, to Washington to discuss possibilities. But the US Treasury Secretary William Simon, a Wall Street bond dealer in moral thrall to the market, was frankly hostile, and there was widespread belief in Washington that Britain should at long last get a grip on inflation and excessive domestic expenditure, deal with its sterling balances and make a proper settlement. Crucially, President Ford had been defeated in the presidential election earlier that month and had therefore no authority to broker a settlement at all. More and more in 1977–8 it was Callaghan's closer relationship with Schmidt and, to a degree, Giscard d'Estaing who governed his policy. He was becoming more and more of a European as he grew older: in 1978 he seemed to have flirted with the idea of joining a European monetary union, 12 years before Britain actually did so. British economic weakness and military withdrawals made the United States simply much less interested in its old ally. When Callaghan fell from office, the Anglo-American relationship was again increasingly remote, and it was left to Margaret Thatcher, with her suspicion of Europe and her strong ideological links to President Reagan, to restore a relationship across the Atlantic, on a very different basis.

Back in opposition, the Labour Party moved to the left. The Bennite left down to 1984, committed to nuclear disarmament and more socialism at home, was inevitably distant, indeed hostile, towards the US relationship. These policies were abandoned under Neil Kinnock's leadership in the reappraisal of the later 1980s, when Labour committed itself to multilateralism, more liberal economic programmes and a strong commitment to Europe, Social Chapter and all. By the end of the 1980s, it was Labour which seemed the pro-European party, the previously enthusiastic Conservatives which appeared under a fiercely anti-German Mrs. Thatcher to be Eurosceptic if not actually hostile. But Neil Kinnock himself, a Welshman from the very constituency (Tredegar/Blaenau Gwent) of that famous old anti-American, Aneurin Bevan, was not instinctively warm towards the United States, and the instincts of the party showed relatively little change at this point. John Smith's approach to foreign policy was defined by his pro-Europeanism and he had little that was new to say about the Anglo-American relationship.

However, under Tony Blair since 1997, there was a marked swing back to pro-Americanism. Labour again demonstrated a close attachment to the United States on a range of issues from Northern Ireland to Kosovo. Blair proclaimed at party conference at Brighton that it was standing 'shoulder to shoulder' with the Americans after 11 September 2001. Tony Blair's friendship with Bill Clinton, another centre-left exponent of 'the third way', was followed by an almost equally warm relationship with George W. Bush, a man almost as ignorant of Britain as the ex-Rhodes scholar Clinton had been comfortable there. Yet Blair had also been Labour's most pro-European prime minister, and evidently hoped that Britain would join the Euro monetary system. During the Iraq crisis and eventual invasion during 2002–3, this traditional conflict of view again led to familiar tension, not least with France over the role of the UN and its arms inspectors. Britain was excluded by other European powers from talks about the formation of a European Security and Defence Union. Labour under Blair, as once under Attlee, might again have to choose between America and Europe, and decisively so this time. Labour's response towards the Americans was to 'hug them close' as emerged with painful clarity in evidence during the Chilcot inquiry into the Iraq war later on. The dilemma re-asserted itself under Gordon Brown, active in promoting European recovery programmes to combat economic recession in 2009, yet instinctively close to the Democratic Party and the North American model of free-market deregulation in economic policy. The decision to retain Trident missiles, years after the end of the Cold War, also suggested an enduring commitment to transatlantic viewpoints on international defence policies. The advent of Barack Obama to the US presidency, and his evident sympathy for British Labour's interventionist approach towards the economy during the 'credit crunch', made the pro-Americanism of Britain's Labour government all the more pronounced. By contrast, the possible advent of a Eurosceptic Conservative government headed by David Cameron was viewed with apprehension in Washington in 2009.

For much of the period 1945–90, despite much residual anti-Americanism from the Bevanites in the early 1950s to the Bennite left in the early 1980s, Labour was the main British custodian of the idea of the Special Relationship in legend and in reality. The classic period was that of the time of massive American economic aid to Britain, the Atlantic alliance to defend 'freedom' against a perceived Soviet threat, and the harmonious withdrawal of the British from Empire from the late 1940s. It reached its climax in the time of Bevin and Acheson, and the influence of Ambassador Oliver Franks around 1949–51. By 'America', Labour, like most British people, probably meant East Coast America, the America that the British elite understood (people rather like Franks himself) – the America of Churchill's history books, of the English-speaking alliance and the English-Speaking Union, of the Ivy League and the Oxford Rhodes Scholarships, of the Anglo–US colloquia in the elegance of Gibbs's Palladian mansion, Ditchley Park, in rural Oxfordshire. It was a world which saw, during the Persian oil crisis in the summer of 1951, the American assistant secretary of state, Paul McGhee, negotiating with, perhaps being overawed by his old Oxford tutor Oliver Franks. Gaitskell perpetuated this image of anglophile America. It was in the era of Wilson in the sixties when a significantly weaker Britain began a period of long-term reappraisal.

It was in this period too, when, symbolised by Lyndon Johnson, a rough Westerner from the hill country of the Pedernales Valley in Texas, American concern with Britain became progressively less important. The source of power in American politics moved from the more internationally minded northeast to the south and west, in a great arc of more conservative, inwardly directed states from Texas to California, whose main inward migration was Latin-American not European. Under President George W. Bush, with heavy influence in his Cabinet from the south west, and from the southern oil lobby, this sense of distance from Britain and Europe has spectacularly increased. Cynics said that Bush had a bust of Winston Churchill in the Oval Office because he was the only Englishman the president had ever heard of. To claim, as some do, that the accepted Anglophilia of the unique city of San Francisco somehow disproves this historic shift seems implausible.

The other aspect of this enduring Labour attachment to the US alliance has been a sense of detachment from Europe. The decision of Attlee and Bevin to steer clear of the Schuman plan for an iron, steel and coal community in 1950 inaugurated this process. The ideological passion of Hugh Gaitskell talking of 'a thousand years of history' and quoting Commonwealth links at the battles of Gallipoli or Vimy Ridge, like the coolness towards Europe of Wilson or Callaghan (or Brown in his Treasury period), confirmed this tendency. It was part of a particular phase of British history, ended by the collapse of the threat from the Soviet Union, the end of Empire, the new global economy and the new prominence in our lives of a more integrated Europe. It was also part of a particular phase of American history, not merely the decline of the old WASP Anglo-Saxon ascendancy which brought the United States into being in the first place, but also the sense of interdependence with Britain fostered by the Cold War.

Instead, there emerged, for example through the New American Century group, a new American sense of global omnipotence and a return to something like isolationism. There was a rejection of international obligations such as the ballistic missile treaties, the Biological Weapons convention, the Kyoto protocol on global warming, and the International Criminal Court, on all of which the United States seemed prepared to challenge the opinion and the conscience of the world.[16] The Iraq crisis and the various positions adopted towards Saddam Hussein, notably the failure to obtain UN sanction for armed invasion, threw this new nationalism into sharper relief. The chaos and carnage resulting from the Iraq invasion and the unstable occupation by American and British troops that followed it coloured the debate over transatlantic relationships with a new anger. By the time of the 2008 presidential election it was accepted that the Bush years had placed unprecedented strains on relations between Britain and the United States. The vast majority of Britons were left praying for an Obama victory in the election in the hope of making a totally fresh start. The outcome of the election induced a palpable sense of relief. At the same time, the terrifying impact of the US 'credit crunch' and the way in which British economic survival rested on the Americans trying to clear up the mess in their own internal banking and budgetary system gave an unpleasant reminder of Britain's basic position of dependency. The legend of the Special Relationship, then, was the unlikely by-product of Old Labour. After Blair and Brown's New Labour, things will have to be worked out all over again.

Chapter 13

Hugh Gaitskell and International Affairs

Unlike the previous distinguished speaker, Lord Jenkins, I met Hugh Gaitskell on only two occasions. One was in early 1957 in Oxford when I was a student. The other was in Swansea in early 1961 when he had a distinctly mixed reception from party members many of whom had connections with CND.

I have two strong impressions of those conversations. The first was how exceptionally pleasant Gaitskell was to talk to. He was a very good listener to the immature and incoherent views of the young. I was rather surprised at how friendly our conversation was since as a youthful Welsh socialist I was a strong admirer of Nye Bevan. Hugh Gaitskell was not obviously one of my folk heroes as I grew up, but he proved to be exceptionally approachable and agreeable. The other feature that I recall is that the discussions that we had, such as they were, concerned foreign affairs, and international policy. In 1957 Gaitskell had just delivered the Godkin Lectures at Harvard; in 1961 there was the aftermath of the debates about CND, unilateralism, the role of NATO and so on. So I thought it was perhaps appropriate that on this important occasion we take at least a fleeting look at Gaitskell's views on international affairs.

Hugh Gaitskell is thought of mainly as being associated with domestic, social and economic policy. In fact, however, a very large proportion of his speeches as party leader concerned foreign and Commonwealth matters. Indeed I would say that perhaps the four great crises of Hugh Gaitskell's life were rearmament in 1951, Suez in 1956, the Scarborough conference in 1960 and the debate about Europe in 1962 – all four of them concerned with international and perhaps defence issues. So it is appropriate that we say something about what is perhaps a relatively neglected aspect of Hugh Gaitskell's outlook and activities.

In the earlier part of his career I am sure that he was, and was regarded as, very much a domestic politician. Lord Jenkins, in one of his essays, has described him as 'instinctively insular'. This may seem a surprising view because he grew up as a young man in the 1930s deeply aware of the context of international crisis. He was a man who travelled widely in Europe in the 1930s, with his influential visit to Vienna in 1934. He was very active in lecturing on the League of Nations and other features of international affairs. We know that Gaitskell was particularly stirred by what he saw as the surrender at Munich and in this he followed very much the line of Hugh Dalton. This was in contrast to his close friend Evan Durbin who was, among other things, the son of a Baptist minister and was perhaps more instinctively pacifist at this particular time. Even so, I think it could be argued that at this stage Hugh Gaitskell's concerns with Hitler and with Nazi dictatorship were perceived largely from a domestic perspective, from the point of view of the British response to the international crisis. I am not aware that they did at this time encourage Hugh Gaitskell to develop a wider critique of international affairs or the balance of international power.

His main intellectual interest was economics, and he wrote extensively on matters concerned with demand management, pricing, exchange rate policy and so on. The impression I have of those writings is they were conceived largely in terms of British autonomy, the imperatives of British economic policy. There is very little interest shown at this stage in the comparative economic experience of other countries. Rather surprisingly from the point of view of Hugh Gaitskell's later career, I can find very few, or indeed no, references to Roosevelt and the New Deal in the United States, though he must surely have discussed and been very interested in that development. What he was concerned with, certainly as a model for Britain, was the experience of overseas Social Democratic governments in handling economic policy. In this context, he wrote an informative chapter in a book on *Democratic Sweden* edited by Margaret Cole in 1938, on banking and monetary policy. I gather, however, from what was said in that book that Gaitskell did not make any visits to Sweden at that time and therefore his views are, so to speak, abstract and theoretical.

During the 1939–45 war it is, I believe, symptomatic and significant that Hugh Gaitskell stayed at home. He worked as a very impressive Civil Servant or technocrat, as Lord Jenkins has observed. I suggest that perhaps Gaitskell did not at this particular time have the widening awareness of war service that, for example, enlarged the outlook of Denis Healey who fought in the Italian campaign or Jim Callaghan who served in the Navy in the Far East. When he was elected to parliament in 1945, Gaitskell's speeches initially focussed very much on domestic matters, fuel and power and later on the Treasury, at both of which departments he was a distinguished minister. His first major speech on foreign affairs, and it was a very impressive one, was as late as November 1954 when he had been in parliament for the best part of a decade.

The great change clearly occurred when Gaitskell became a cabinet minister after the general election at the beginning of 1950. There came the impact of the Korean War, with Gaitskell himself going to the Treasury in succession to Cripps in October 1950. It was during this period that what seems to me the most decisive feature of Gaitskell's international outlook impinged upon him, namely his attachment to the United States of America. His first involvement, difficult negotiations with American oil companies while he was the minister of fuel and power in 1949, was not an easy experience. But during the discussions about monetary collaboration leading to the formation of the European Payments Union in the summer of 1950, he became decisively thrown in with key American policymakers in working out a multilateral payments scheme on gold and credit. Henceforth, he is remarkable for being passionately, almost uncritically, pro-American for the rest of his career. He wrote afterwards to Averell Harriman, 'On the really important issues we just naturally find ourselves thinking along the same lines. And since, like you, I believe that just about the most important thing in the world is for the United States and Britain to work along together, this experience has been wonderfully encouraging.' He was to show this approach very much as a member of the Attlee government taking a very strongly pro-American view on, for example, the question of British troops being involved in the Korean War to show what a particularly close ally Britain was. There was the same attitude again over the 'brand China' issue at the UN, with Gaitskell urging repeatedly that the US policy on China should be criticised only moderately by the British government, even though Gaitskell himself agreed with many of those criticisms, for example, over American support of Chiang Kai-Shek.

In the summer of 1951 we see Gaitskell taking a restrained and moderate line during the Abadan oil crisis. There were a number of reasons for this but one of those he articulates in the Cabinet is that possible British military intervention in Abadan would be contrary to the views of the United States (which indeed, it might be observed, had very much its own views on Persian oil). He was, and throughout this period remained, a passionate apostle of what he often referred to as the Special Relationship between Britain and the United States. It was highly appropriate that he would celebrate his appointment as chancellor by dancing some, at least, of the night away in a New York nightclub.

Now this was very much a key to his foreign policy, indeed, *the* key I believe. Support for the Anglo-American alliance and NATO was the common coin in Labour circles at this time. Indeed, you could go on to say that later Labour administrations under Harold Wilson and then James Callaghan were notable for being again particularly sympathetic to the United States, in contrast perhaps with the premiership of, say, Edward Heath or indeed for that matter, Anthony

Eden. Callaghan's close relationships with Kissinger and Ford under-line the point. Now I think that Gaitskell added a particular ingre-dient because it seems to me that he held a narrowly defined view of the United States. Broadly speaking, the Americans with whom he came into contact were WASP, East coast, patrician Americans, some-times of Ivy League background, who linked their background and out-look with a particular view of American policy. They were, as Gaitskell himself observed, 'New Dealer economist types'. So it was people like Averell Harriman, Chester Bowles, Dean Acheson ('a sensitive and cul-tivated mind' Gaitskell calls him in his diary) – these were the kind of Americans to whom Gaitskell felt particularly close. He felt indeed much the same later about Adlai Stevenson and to some degree also the Oxford Rhodes Scholar in the State Department in 1961, Dean Rusk. Whether he would have felt the same about the later Oxford Rhodes Scholar in the White House (Bill Clinton) I am not quite sure.

In a way, then, Gaitskell's view of the United States is not only a facet of international history but a facet of intellectual history. He felt this very close policy and intellectual rapport with New Dealer Democrats of this type, during the latter period of the Truman administration in 1950 and 1951. It is a kind of action replay of the intellectual axis there existed between British liberal politicians and certain kinds of American pro-gressive reformers at the end of the nineteenth century, people like James Bryce and E.L. Godkin, for instance. The difference was, however, that during the 1880s and 1890s it was, on the whole, the Americans who looked to Britain, to Gladstone particularly, for their model, whereas to some degree with Hugh Gaitskell it was the reverse.

Now this emerged in the first great crisis, the clash with Aneurin Bevan in the spring of 1951, a highly controversial episode in Hugh Gaitskell's career. There were many other factors involved here, of course – political rivalry between two ambitious men, Bevan's particular role in the creation of the NHS and so on; but underlying it all, I believe, were attitudes to interna-tional policy and above all the Anglo-American alliance. What I find most fascinating about this particular episode is that it was Bevan, supposedly the left-wing extremist politician, who used, in the main, solid economic arguments. It was Bevan who spoke about the effects of the £4,700 million rearmament expenditure, the government's problems in the shortage of raw materials, the difficulties in obtaining skilled labour, the short-fall in machine tools, the effects on exports, possible inflationary pressures and so on. By contrast, the economist, Gaitskell, who was, after all chancellor of the exchequer (and who in private discussions would no doubt expound on many other factors) used in Cabinet primarily political arguments: that it was important for Britain to show itself to be the number one ally of the

United States, almost whatever the cost. He took up enthusiastically the notion of transatlantic burden-sharing. The NHS charges *per se* were, in a sense, incidental to the main theme. Bevan, Gaitskell believed in any case, was basically anti-American, and that was decisive.

It became clear after the summer and after Bevan's resignation that there had to be significant modifications. It was evident that American stockpiling of raw materials was simply making it almost impossible to fulfil this rearmament programme. Britain was experiencing a major balance of payments crisis by the end of the summer. The Americans, contrary to Hugh Gaitskell's expectations, were not proving helpful, with their military equipment, or the supply of machine tools, for example; the effect was that the rearmament programme was very substantially cut back by the Churchill government in 1952 and led to grave consequences in terms of major divisions within the Labour Party. The origin of these divisions, I am sure, lay in this diametrically different political perception there seemed to be at the time between Gaitskell, Bevan and others about the nature of the Anglo-American alliance and its primacy for Britain's national interest.

In the 1950s in Opposition, Gaitskell remained strongly pro-American even though very critical of key aspects of American foreign policy, particularly the policy towards China. He was, therefore, a strong supporter of German rearmament. There was, however, a spectacular coming together of Gaitskell's sympathy for the United States and his wider perception of the international scene and the role of the UN at the time of Suez in 1956. I am not convinced that Gaitskell's initial approach to Suez was as totally consistent as Phillip Williams has suggested in his biography – after all, he began with an ill-judged comparison of Nasser with Adolf Hitler. But it became more consistent and without doubt played a great part, as Phillip Whitehead has observed, in stirring the moral conscience of Britain and of other countries. There were many reasons for this, without doubt a basic determining factor being that Gaitskell felt that the Anglo-American alliance had been fundamentally imperiled, that Eisenhower had been betrayed by Anthony Eden's duplicity and the collusion with France and the government of Israel. This gave Hugh Gaitskell a particular passion and, indeed, it would seem made him very much more outspoken at the time than Aneurin Bevan who was, rather unusually, earning plaudits in some of the right-wing newspapers for his patriotism and statesman-like behaviour, contrasted with the traitor Gaitskell.

Atlanticism of this kind was, of course, central to the next great crisis in 1960, the head-on collision between the leadership of the Labour Party and CND. Denis Healey's memoirs are correct in stating that what

Gaitskell's 'fight, fight and fight again' speech was about was not Britain's but NATO's possession of nuclear weapons. An independent British deterrent was not the main theme. In other words, again the Anglo-American alliance was at stake and this enabled Gaitskell, very effectively in my opinion, to outline the basic inconsistency of unilateralist critics who were unwilling for Britain herself to be associated with nuclear weapons, but nevertheless prepared to shelter behind those of their NATO allies, in the face of a perceived Soviet threat.

Perhaps, however, a more interesting feature of Gaitskell's views on foreign affairs lies in a quite different area at this particular time. In a way, what he was saying fundamentally on NATO and collective security was rather conventional. His response, however, to the change in the international scene, following the death of Stalin and the emergence of so-called peaceful coexistence as a workable concept, is perhaps a more innovative feature of Gaitskell's outlook. It was indeed a central feature of his warmly received Godkin Lectures in Harvard in January 1957, one of which we are told was written for him by Denis Healey. Gaitskell had now been persuaded of the merits of a policy which he had previously derided, namely the idea of continental disengagement and he showed sympathy, perhaps of a rather surprising degree of intensity, with ideas for a nuclear-free zone in Central Europe, indeed a totally non-militarised zone in Central Europe. He was moved to express words of sympathy for the ideas of the Polish foreign minister, Adam Rapacki, who pushed the scheme of one variant of a nuclear-free zone in central Europe at this particular time. It is sometimes argued, although I believe the view is not correct, that Gaitskell was converted by Bevan on disengagement. Bevan had certainly been talking in these terms some two years earlier. In my view, it is rather that the changing contours of the international scene brought Gaitskell and Bevan closer together. The main intellectual influence on Gaitskell, I believe, was that of Denis Healey, with whom his personal relationship became increasingly strong.

In the Godkin Lectures, Gaitskell links two central themes – the idea of a demilitarised area in Central Europe with the reunification of Germany. This led some commentators at times to allude to 'the Gaitskell plan'. There was a whole plethora of plans at this particular time and the Gaitskell version was one popularly put across. The main components, the actual way in which Gaitskell presented it varied quite a bit. The order in which events would supposedly happen not surprisingly diverges from time to time in his exposition. But the central ideas would be the withdrawal of foreign forces from Germany, Poland, Czechoslovakia; the re-unification of Germany, which Gaitskell had previously opposed as liable to leave a power vacuum in Central Europe; a security pact to guarantee German neutrality including endorsement of the present boundaries of Germany based on the Oder-Neisse line in the East; and the withdrawal of Western Germany from NATO followed by the withdrawal of Poland and Czechoslovakia from the Warsaw Pact. Now the interest of this is that these remarkably non-confrontational policies were being put forward by this man who was so passionately committed to NATO, total Western resistance to the Soviet Union during the Cold War, and West German membership of NATO. He argued the case for disengagement on the grounds not of emotion, but of realism, namely that after the uprising in Hungary and the troubles in Poland there were very good reasons for the post-Stalin Soviet Union to be prepared to accept a disengagement policy of this particular kind to avoid destabilisation. Gaitskell continued to put forward this argument for some years to come, indeed down to the building of the Berlin wall in 1961 and the effective ending of this particular line of argument. But in some ways, this remains a more original and innovative phase of his views on foreign affairs.

The final crisis was, of course, Europe. Gaitskell initially seemed to be sympathetic towards Britain being in Europe, and her membership of the Common Market. I was told by Edmund Dell, although neither Philip Williams's nor Brian Brivati's biography confirms the point, that he had been sympathetic to Britain's endorsing the Schuman plan that the European Coal and Steel Community proposed in 1950. Clearly, though, Gaitskell moved towards a more and more hostile position in 1961–2. This had been anticipated, even forecast, in his Godkin Lectures. He talked there about the role of the Commonwealth, and a special relationship with the United States. He observed in passing, though he was to outline the case much more forcibly later, that the economic case for joining Europe, as he put it, was 'grossly exaggerated'. The recovery and expansion of the British economy were quite independent of any consideration of joining the Common Market. He was very critical of the agricultural policy of the EEC which he regarded as protectionist and, in any case, an anti-Keynesian economic absurdity. He used a great variety of arguments in pushing his line of attack against Britain being a member of the EEC. One which is quite entertaining in a way is that he argued that membership of the Common Market would prevent a British Labour government from nationalising more industry, which was a rather curious contrast for one who was opposed to the extension of nationalisation at home.

Now one can see a convincing synthesis of arguments being developed. But the vehemence of his opposition to joining the Common Market in 1962 surprised many people. The famous observation in Philip

Williams's book is instructive, quoting Lady Gaitskell in saying that 'the wrong people are cheering' – this is how she described the Labour Party's response to Hugh Gaitskell's conference speech on Europe in September 1962. There were emotional references to Vimy Ridge and Gallipoli and the Commonwealth and Empire participation there, with the notorious remark about a 'thousand years of history' being brought to a close if Britain joined, at least on present terms, the European Community.

Much speculation has taken place about why Hugh Gaitskell took this view. No doubt he did not want to divide the party again, so soon after the rift over CND. Much stress has also been laid on the Commonwealth and on Gaitskell's background – he was born in India, and he had a strong connection through his brother, Arthur, and his father with Commonwealth affairs. There is much in this. But I would prefer myself to lay emphasis on two other factors. Firstly, there is a very strong, one might say dogmatic, view throughout of British political and legal sovereignty. Sovereignty undermined by mysticism was particularly abhorrent to an eighteenth-century rationalist and positivist like Gaitskell. He thought that Jean Monnet, in a famous meeting in April 1962 to which Lord Jenkins alludes in his autobiography, had simply been irrational, almost theological, on the idea of Europe. As Lord Jenkins shows, there was no meeting of minds between the two. Gaitskell took refuge in a pernickety empiricism. It followed in Gaitskell's view that anything approximating to a federation, or indeed a closer political union, of the European countries would not be acceptable. He compared the possible future status of Britain to that of Texas or California within the United States. He claimed, in effect, that membership of the EEC as presently argued would mean no independent British foreign policy, and no independent British defence policy. The other feature that I am struck by is that to Hugh Gaitskell, at this time at least, Europe seemed to him a limiting idea, a localised, introspective unit tending towards regionalism and trade protectionism. His Atlanticism rebelled against this. Although the Americans were apparently in favour of Britain's joining the EEC, he thought that they had underestimated the danger that Europe could be seen as a kind of third force. So in a way his opposition to joining the EEC was a kind of consummation of his views on international policy over the previous 12 years.

Whether he would have changed his view later on is, as Lord Jenkins quite correctly says in his autobiography, impossible to say. He was a deeply emotional person and the way in which he built up criticism of the EEC, almost indiscriminately, at this time, emphasises the point.

I do not see Gaitskell as having the same intuitive flair on foreign policy that he had on economic policy. But I also think that his views here are of much importance. In many ways Gaitskell is at his most vulnerable in foreign affairs, and therefore, perhaps, at his most interesting. He is probing, he is hitting or missing. There were four main international crises which affected his career. I shall boldly advance the view here that Hugh Gaitskell was probably right on two issues and wrong on two issues. I think he was quite right over Suez, and in upholding NATO in 1960. I believe he was mistaken in 1951 when his commitment to the American alliance overrode his economic judgement. In Europe in 1962 he took, in my view, too negative a position. When Dean Acheson observed at this very time that Britain had lost an Empire and was seeking a role, it is in a way towards the outlook of Hugh Gaitskell that the criticism is directed.

But it remains a very fascinating story. Gaitskell's attitude towards disengagement shows a man trying to find ways of reconciling his support for the Western alliance with the changes in the Cold War following the death of Stalin. So I think I would also conclude that we did indeed lose a deeply impressive leader, in foreign affairs as well as in domestic affairs. The view that Gaitskell is a kind of English Adlai Stevenson, a lost leader, I suppose is mainly associated with his perceptions of domestic, social, and economic policy. But in foreign affairs also, the combination of realism and idealism, of accurate perception and of occasional error, is again a world which we sadly lost in January 1963.

Chapter 14

Nye Bevan, Pragmatist and Prophet

Nye Bevan is firmly established in the socialist pantheon as a hero of Labour. This is not surprising. Like Keir Hardie, he built up a rare charismatic reputation as evangelist, orator and prophet of workers' power. Not only was he a prophet, he was also a great constructive pioneer. His NHS remains, 60 and more years on, a symbol of social solidarity. What is far more surprising is that Nye should have become in time a hero for New Labour. At a great event in Congress House in November 1997, to mark the centenary of his birth, the memory and legacy of Bevan were hailed not only by old Bevanites like Michael Foot and Barbara Castle, but also by Gordon Brown. New Labour's iron (or at least prudent) chancellor passionately lauded Bevan as the model of the social democratic faith.

More remarkably still, Tony Blair has repeatedly placed Bevan in the great line of Labour succession along with Clem Attlee, Ernie Bevin and all the saints who for their labours rest – alongside old Liberal heroes like Lloyd George, Beveridge and Keynes. Nye, the scourge of the capitalist ruling class, has become posthumously a pivot of the Progressive Alliance. In a foreword to Geoffrey Goodman's centenary celebration of Bevan, *The State of the Nation,* Tony Blair acclaimed not only Bevan's 'ideas and personality and rhetoric' and his managerial skill in creating the NHS, but also his call for 'passion in action' as embodied in Bevan's political testament, *In Place of Fear.* Tredegar's class warrior had become a hero of the Third Way, embraced by the establishment. By contrast, his old enemy, the revisionist Hugh Gaitskell, was out of favour as an elitist and an anti-European. Edmund Dell's fiercely critical posthumous account of the Labour movement, *A Strange Eventful History,* almost contemptuous of Gaitskell and Tony Crosland for the muddle-headedness of their attempt to blend socialism and democracy, found words of favour for the visionary and inspirational qualities of Nye Bevan. Meanwhile, Patricia Hollis's biography of Jennie Lee in 1997 saw this stormy petrel of the ILP far left acclaimed as a great minister who had promoted the arts and established the Open University.

Commentators lost few opportunities to contrast Nye Bevan's 'passionate parliamentarism' and the Bevanite 'legitimate left' in the 1950s, with the anti-parliamentary extremism of the Bennites and 'hard left' in the 1980s. Asked in 1980 what Bevan would have thought of the hard left then, Harold Wilson briskly replied 'Nye wouldn't have been seen dead with that lot'. Aneurin Bevan, it seems, has been reinvented as a mainstream patriot, who defended Britain's manufacture of nuclear weapons, and whose NHS represented social citizenship, everyman's idea of what it meant to be British. His disciple, Neil Kinnock, seems to have reached the same view, as have the tabloid press. The ultimate marginal radical has been transplanted into the centre ground.

Is this justified? Is this reinvention of Nye credible, or is it yet another example of a dissenting radical going legitimate in hindsight? British political history is full of instances of people seen as extremists in their day becoming licensed rebels over time. It happened to Keir Hardie and Michael Foot; Tony Benn seems on the verge of suffering the same fate. Bevan was never an establishment figure. Even the Tories whose company he enjoyed were offbeat mavericks like Beaverbrook, Bracken and Randolph Churchill. He was the most hated, as well as the most idolised, politician of his time. A product of the socialist cauldron of South Wales in the early twentieth century, he was a ferocious critic of the conventional capitalist wisdom. Baldwin, Chamberlain, and even Lloyd George were savaged. He was, along with Cripps, expelled from the parliamentary Labour Party for advocating a Popular Front in 1939, and almost was again in 1944 for uncomradely attacks on Ernest Bevin and the unions. The Bevanites were accused by the party right of treachery and fomenting civil war. In 1955, he was expelled again, and almost terminally, for anti-party and anti-union activities, Attlee's prudence and the whims of individual union members of the Labour National Executive saving him at the last. The later reconciliation with Gaitskell was always a shotgun marriage.

Even his record as architect of the NHS led him into trouble. His enemies denounced him as the 'Minister of Disease', a 'Tito from Tonypandy' (deliberately mispronounced and also inaccurate, since Bevan actually came from the equally alliterative Tredegar). His fateful remark when launching the NHS at Manchester in July 1948 that the Tories were 'lower than vermin' became a defining moment in Britain's equivalent of the class war. He received abuse, packets of excrement addressed to the resident of 'Vermin Villa', a kick in the pants in White's from a deranged landowner, appropriately named Strangeways. The hero of Labour's grassroots became the most hated man of his time. By contrast, Benn or Scargill were the darlings of the halls.

And yet this stormy petrel does seem, from the vantage point of half a century later, a more centrist, or at least less extreme, politician than contemporary journalists and political critics would allow. Bevan's later embrace by New Labour in its fullest Mandelsonian efflorescence may be less surprising. From his emergence as a serious politician in the 1920s, he usually chose the mainstream, even if under protest. Not for Nye, with his restless urge for power (even if 'you always saw its coattails disappearing round the corner'), the parochial ILP impotence of Jimmy Maxton and the Clydesiders. (Indeed, many of the latter, including John Wheatley, minister of health in 1924, and Tom Johnston, wartime secretary of state for Scotland, came to forsake the wilderness as well.)

Bevan grew up in the class turmoil of South Wales in 1910–26, between the Tonypandy riots and the General Strike. Those were the stormy years of the Plebs League and the Central Labour College evangelising in the valleys; of industrial rebels like Noah Ablett and Arthur Cook; of the 'betrayal' by Lloyd George over the Sankey Commission's proposals for nationalisation of the mines in 1919 and the climb-down by fellow unionists of the Triple Alliance on Black Friday (15 April 1921); of the titanic coal strikes of 1921 and 1926, and the poverty and unemployment, wage cuts and mass victimisation by the coal-owners that resulted. This was capitalism raw and in crisis. Born in 1897 and sent to work in the mines in 1911 (when Tredegar itself was briefly ablaze not just with strike militancy but apparently anti-Semitic attacks on local properties). The young Bevan imbibed a rich variety of philosophies. He read the novels of Jack London, the revolutionary ideas of the German Joseph Dietzgen, and the American Daniel de Leon, the Marxist texts of the social science tutorial classes run by the Central Labour Colleges in the valleys. He was excited by the quasi-syndicalism of the Rhondda-based Plebs League and its Marxist missionaries, Will Mainwaring, Will Hay and particularly the charismatic ideologue, Noah Ablett. They produced that passionate pamphlet, *The Miners' Next Step*, published by the Unofficial Reform Committee at Tonypandy. The young Bevan's ideas centred on direct action by the miners themselves. His views crystallised in his years at the Central Labour College in London in 1919–21, a workers' seminary for other young socialists like Jim Griffiths, Morgan Phillips, Ness Edwards and the Communist novelist, Lewis Jones. This was a more formative phase in Bevan's ideological progress than his own later, rather languid, account was to suggest. He appeared the prototype of the young industrial rebel, focussing on direct action at the point of production to win for the workers the surplus value that was rightfully theirs for the fruits of their labour. In 1926 he fought shoulder to shoulder with his comrades in the pit. His work as disputes agent for the miners confirmed for him the deep injustice of the benefit system and the wage cuts that afflicted those miners not thrown out of work.

But it is highly relevant that these years still kept Bevan somewhere within the mainstream. The miners' strike of 1921, even more the general

strike of 1926, confirmed for him the sheer futility of industrial struggle doomed to defeat by well-prepared coal-owners, and the anti-strike
apparatus, civil and military, assembled by their allies in government.
For all his bitter anti-capitalist rhetoric, Bevan foreswore strategies such
as the Minority Movement linking up the Miners' Federation rank-and-
file with Communist allies, which attracted the support of a far-left fellow agent like S.O. Davies. Still more did he reject the path which took
another colleague, Arthur Horner, into the *cul de sac* of the Communist
Party, about to enter its extreme form of Stalinist sterility. While Bevan
never wholly abandoned the mirage of industrial direct action (using it
to goad the official TUC leadership during the war and to contrast the
centralism of nationalisation after 1945 with the more vibrant message
of workers' democracy), by the mid-1920s he was essentially an orthodox parliamentary socialist. He became a member of the Tredegar UDC
as early as 1922; he worked on the Tredegar Medical Aid Society (which
influenced his ideas on the NHS after 1945); in 1928 he became a member of the Labour-controlled Monmouthshire county council as councillor for Ebbw Vale. To complete the process, his friend Archie Lush, a
fellow participant in the local Query Club, began a private campaign to
subvert the local MP, the passive Evan Davies, and a very rare form of
re-selection took place. It turned out to be deselection since the miners
balloted strongly in favour of Bevan and in 1929 he was easily returned
as Member of Parliament for Ebbw Vale. He remained its representative
for the rest of his life. A decade of experiment convinced him that it was
in the parliamentary method, the conquest of power in Westminster, that
the workers' route to democratic socialist freedom ultimately lay.

Bevan began as an angry MP of the left. His remarkably controversial
maiden speech on the coal industry featured a ferocious attack on the
great figure of Lloyd George – 'better dearer coal than cheaper colliers' –
which shook that veteran, perhaps as an uncomfortable echo of his own
youthful onslaughts on Joe Chamberlain during the Boer War. Bevan was
foremost, along with the Clydesiders, in denouncing the second Labour
government under Ramsay MacDonald, and even more in condemning
MacDonald's perceived treachery in forming the National Government
with the Tories and Liberals in August 1931.

More bizarrely, the eloquent young Welshman fell into strange company. He became friendly with the Marxist intellectual, John Strachey.
Through him, he briefly followed the lead of Sir Oswald Mosley with
his call for corporate planning, public works, tariffs and revival of the
home market. More personally, he was taken up with Lord Beaverbrook
and hobnobbed socially with such intimates as Brendan Bracken, who
derided him as 'Bollinger Bolshevik, Ritzy Robespierre and Lounge-lizard

Lenin'. This stylish bohemian seemed far removed from the austerity of his native mining valleys. It was noticeable that in the House Bevan moved less frequently amongst the South Wales Labour MPs, many of them elderly union officials of limited cultural sophistication compared with Bevan himself. Jim Callaghan was later to tell me that Bevan would only lunch at the 'Welsh table' in the Commons dining room when he was in trouble.

Yet, he always remained anchored within the Labour movement, never joining diversionary movements like the Socialist League. This was a constant source of passionate debate with his wife, Jennie Lee, a Marxist who kept to the ILP fringe until 1944. Bevan affectionately chided her as 'his Salvation Army lassie', who preferred the sanctity of a political nunnery, cherishing the 'virginity' of her pure little sect when it disaffiliated from the Labour Party in 1932 rather than the broad church of the British Labour movement. In South Wales, this was a bleak time of mass unemployment and the means test, of the harsh operations of the Unemployment Assistance Boards, of wage cuts and hunger marches and fights with the police, of the stay-down stoppages at Nine Mile Point, Abertillery, inspired by syndicalist direct action in the Asturias. Bevan toyed with a variety of approaches, including a bizarre idea for setting up Workers Freedom Groups as a kind of local defence militia. In 1937 he joined the Unity Campaign associated with Sir Stafford Cripps, and condemned by the Labour Party hierarchy.

But he was generally housed within the social democratic tabernacle, never a permanent sectarian. When the international crisis built up in the later 1930s, Bevan called for a united nationwide response. From the standpoint of the Popular Front, which indeed was to lead to his expulsion from the parliamentary party, along with Cripps and George Strauss in 1939, his fundamental cry was always for a broader unity. In the columns of *Tribune,* on whose editorial board he sat from 1937, becoming editor in 1941, his approach was patriotic as well as socialist. Certainly he was no pacifist. Earlier than many, he called for armed resistance to fascism, starting with the rescue of the Popular Front government in Spain. He condemned Munich, on the distinctive grounds that it represented a crisis for the ruling capitalist class. In *Tribune,* he became, remarkably in the light of later events, an advocate of the view that Winston Churchill should be brought into a restructured government. In March 1938 he passionately backed up a powerful speech by Churchill calling for resistance to the dictators. 'The time has arrived to assert the power of the free democracies against Hitler', Bevan wrote, even though Churchill's sympathies for Franco's uprising were a serious mark against him.

During the war, Bevan appeared most detached from mainstream Labour views. He rejoined the parliamentary party almost immediately, but then embarked upon a prolonged campaign of opposition to many of the policies of the Churchill coalition. In the wartime years, Bevan moved from bit player to enjoy top billing as the 'squalid nuisance' of Churchillian oratory. He was remarkably effective in challenging the coalition's strategic decisions, in calling for a Second Front to assist our Russian allies rather than prop up the Empire in North Africa, in condemning carpet bombing by the RAF as ineffective as well as inhumane, in exposing anti-Communist diversions like involvement in the civil war in Greece. At home, he denounced the coalition, as Laski and others on the left did, for obstructing the advent of socialism. His anonymous tract *Why Not Trust the Tories?* (1944) laid waste the policies of a Tory-run government on social welfare, employment and industrial planning. Equally, he condemned Labour ministers for setting their socialist convictions aside and missing a unique opportunity of revolutionary social change. He refused to criticise wartime strikes and stoppages by some miners and other trade unionists, and attacked the great Bevin and 'jaded, irresponsible, cynical trade union leaders' for imposing penal restrictions on the right to strike and for general attacks on civil liberties. These led to a great crisis in May 1944 when union leaders tried to throw him out of the party altogether. Bevan was certainly amongst those (Orwell in *The Lion and the Unicorn* was another) who saw the war as 'a radical moment', a unique opportunity for social transformation.

But Bevan always sought revolution via the ballot box and the parliamentary approach. He saw the war years as having made free institutions, especially the Commons, even more powerful as an instrument of the popular will. *Why Not Trust the Tories?* was a passionate affirmation of free assembly, ending with his much-loved evocation of Colonel Rainboro' of the Levellers proclaiming his egalitarian message at the 1647 Putney debates amongst Cromwell's army. At the height of his alleged extremism as an enemy of the consensus, he always saw democracy as his essential strategy for change. It was never likely in 1944, with victory in Europe in sight and even Jennie Lee on the verge of rejoining the Labour Party, that Bevan would favour the impotence of exclusion. He would never opt for the gesture politics of the 'beloved rebel' Jimmy Maxton. On the contrary, after penning a grudging apology which kept him in the Labour fold, he stood for the first time for the National Executive constituency section and was elected, coming fifth out of seven. From then on, he had a crucial power base within the party structure. He bent his efforts to striving for a Labour victory and to shoring up Labour's own plans for post-war reconstruction, unlike what he saw as the pallid alternatives of the Coalition, with its Keynesian nostrums for full (or fuller) employment when peace returned. As such, he caught the attention of Attlee as a dynamic force who ought to be accommodated somewhere in a Labour government. Bevan was indeed one of the very few Labour leaders who foresaw the popular uprising that would sweep Churchill ignominiously out of office in July 1945. As he had long prophesied, the overwhelming force of mass democracy could be harnessed to destroy the capitalist order for all time. Bevan, unexpectedly sent to the Health Ministry to put the proposed NHS into effect, would carry that process forward.

As a minister in the Attlee government, at least as long as he remained at Health until January 1951, Bevan was a remarkable success. More than almost any other minister, he could point to a record of great legislative achievement which permanently transformed the face of British society. But he was effective in large measure because he went with the grain of political realities. He was a broadly centrist minister most of the time who caused no great trouble for his colleagues. Compared with later Labour ministers such as George Brown or Tony Benn, Bevan was the model of loyalty. His NHS, marked by years of deadlock with the British Medical Association and particularly its key officials, was a triumph of relativist philosophy. At times, Bevan lost his temper as well he might, in denouncing the BMA representatives as 'a small group of politically poisoned people'. They, and especially the serpentine Charles Hill, erstwhile 'radio doctor', violently replied in kind. Later on there was 'vermin'. But he always left contacts open. In the end, his ability to persuade and beguile, notably the Royal Colleges and Lord Moran of the Physicians, 'corkscrew Charlie' to his intimates, was decisive.

The NHS was only roughly conceived when Bevan became a minister, and the early key decisions were all essentially his. Donald Bruce, his PPS, has written of how his charm and passion won the devotion of his civil service staff from Sir Wilson Jameson downwards. The broad concept of a service financed from general taxation and freely available at the point of delivery had been enshrined in Beveridge during the war. Bevan's most radical innovation was to take the hospitals into national ownership and control. This led to fierce opposition from Herbert Morrison and Chuter Ede, backed by Greenwood, Alexander and Tom Williams, who wanted control to remain in the hands of the local authorities. At the key Cabinet on 20 December 1945, Bevan just managed to get his way with the support of the venerable Lord Addison, himself a former medical man of great authority as well as the first minister of health in 1919, and, most crucial of all, the personal backing of Attlee. Bevan argued that local authorities lacked the resources to take over the voluntary hospitals and only central control could ensure a properly national service effective in all parts of Britain. He just carried the day. But this was also the accepted view of men like Arthur MacNulty, the chief medical officer, who had backed proposals in the *Economist* during the war for regional organisation and ultimate nationalisation. As Charles Webster's account makes clear, Bevan's proposal reflected the most effectively argued solution among the technocrats, which was also open to the least political objection from the personnel within the health service. It was the least speculative approach open to him. Whether indeed it was more appropriate than local control, experiment and accountability has been much contested by specialists in public health from that day to this, although Professor Webster himself evidently supports Bevan's view.[1]

In other key respects, Bevan's health service was steeped in concessions. Of course, he made compromises galore with the doctors, and acknowledged bitterly that he 'stuffed their mouths with gold'. He retained private practice in full, and 'pay beds' in the hospitals. He never looked like conceding a fully salaried medical profession. The final settlement, negotiated via Moran and Webb-Johnson of the Surgeons, made the state element only a small part (£4,300) of doctors' remuneration. Limits were waived on specialists' fees and the appeal procedures for doctors coming before NHS tribunals were reformed to meet the criticisms of general practitioners. The sale of practices was indeed ended, but £160 million was provided to compensate GPs for the change. A process of two-tier health provision, with the basic national system left underfunded and circumvented by privately funded medical schemes run by BUPA and others, was already underway.

The NHS, so widely acclaimed at the time and subsequently a talisman of faith for the once-critical doctors themselves, was a skein of compromises which greatly disappointed some on the left. Radicals like Dr. Stark Murray of the Socialist Medical Association (SMA), a pioneer body which had helped put the idea of a NHS on Labour's programme in the first place in the early 1930s, were left in dark disillusion. His colleague, Dr. Somerville Hastings MP, was more positive, though he too became a critic in time. The SMA felt that the opportunity for creating a truly national remodelled health service had been lost. In particular, their own cherished scheme for neighbourhood health centres had been largely set aside. The SMA ended up as a marginalised and largely ineffective pressure group. It was in marked contrast, for instance, to NALT, the Labour teachers' group, who felt that the government's educational policy gave them a platform from which to promote the cause of multilateral or comprehensive schools. Bevan's creation is commonly attacked from the right for its financial provision. This led to a succession of supplementary estimates from 1949 and rows between Bevan and Cripps over the possibility of imposing charges for medical prescriptions. But it should be emphasised, too, how the historic achievement of this socialist minister was equally assailed at the time as a sell-out to rich specialists and private practitioners, almost a betrayal of the values of real socialism.

In other aspects of his role as a minister, Bevan again found that his socialist aspirations were hemmed in. His policy on housing, successful in building over one million new homes, far more so than was often acknowledged, was relatively traditional. Here, he left the initiative firmly in the hands of the local authorities, and rejected proposals for more challenging policies such as a new Housing Corporation, put forward by Douglas Jay and others. Here, too, socialism would have to be put on the back burner. While Bevan concentrated on the public provision of council housing for rent, and severely restricted housing for sale, he was forced to recognise the desire for home ownership as well. He was also compelled to mirror the pattern of the existing class system, for instance in creating special categories of better housing stock to minister to the needs of middle-class managers. On the other hand, Bevan's insistence that local authority housing should be marked by high standards of construction and minimum levels of comfort for council house tenants sees him at his most imaginative and most generous.

Elsewhere, Bevan was not a troublemaker. He liked neither Ernie Bevin nor a Cold War foreign policy. Bevan especially disliked what he saw as a violently anti-Jewish policy in Palestine. On the other hand, the realities of international tensions between the West and Stalin's Russia stirred Bevan as powerfully as other ministers. For all his residual anti-Americanism, he was not and never had been a fellow traveller. His anti-Communism, if only on libertarian grounds, was beyond doubt. The rape of Czechoslovakia and especially Stalin's attack on the socialist experiment in Tito's Yugoslavia powerfully influenced Bevan's responses. He was a strong champion of NATO coming into being, even while insisting that it was progressive policies and ideas, not armaments, which would defeat Communism in the end. On the Berlin blockade in 1948–9, Bevan was one of the hawks, not least because of the Social Democrat base in West Berlin itself. He called for Allied tanks to drive a route through the Soviet zone to West Berlin so that its population could receive food and essential supplies. Most striking of all, Bevan raised no protest when news came out almost accidentally that Britain was manufacturing nuclear weapons. Indeed, he would have favoured this policy, if only to ensure that the Americans alone did not control a nuclear arsenal directed against the Kremlin. Bevan would never accept the quasi-pacifist evasions of Labour foreign policy that had paralysed the party throughout the 1930s, even beyond the time of Munich. He endorsed Britain's atomic bomb, its worldwide defence network based on military conscription, and all the arms budgets until the fateful new policy of early 1951. Britain's socialist middle way needed to be defended against all corners. No mirage of 'a socialist foreign policy' here.

At home, Bevan was well content with the main thrust of policy-making under Attlee. He supported, of course, the policy of nationalisation, and fought strongly alongside Dalton and (surprisingly perhaps) Bevin for iron and steel to be kept on the list in late 1947. But, as an old syndicalist of Plebs League days, he recognised that industrial democracy, let alone any form of workers' control, were casualties of a stern centralism, and that public ownership should be made to work better, including for consumers, before it was blithely extended. Bevan went along with the remainder of welfare legislation, even if it reflected the centrist liberalism of Beveridge, for instance through compulsory contributions, rather than egalitarian socialism. He backed up Ellen Wilkinson in basing educational change after 1945 on the selective grammar schools. In practice, for all his rhetoric, Bevan, like Herbert Morrison, was in effect from 1948 an advocate of consolidation, making the foundations more secure before pushing on to the next phase of the socialist advance. At the Dorking colloquium in May 1950, Morrison and Bevan virtually voiced the same conclusions at that transitional moment.

Elsewhere, too, Bevan was markedly more circumspect, or perhaps simply more loyal, than, say Benn in the later 1970s. He did not lend support to backbench revolts against the government on domestic or external issues, even when they often included Jennie Lee and close friends like Michael Foot, his successor as editor of *Tribune*. He used with advantage his links with old fellow-miner, fellow Central Labour College student and fellow Welshman, Morgan Phillips, the supreme *apparatchik* in Transport House. For a time *Tribune* came perilously close to being an organ of the party faithful.

Nor did Bevan encourage dissent at party conference. This later champion of the left-wing constituency rank and file slapped down critics at the 1947 conference who wanted him to change policy over tied cottages at the behest of the grass roots. Solidarity was crucial, and so was discipline. No 'emotional spasms' here. Imperiously, he kept clear of the party Liaison Committee as well. In 1949 he endorsed the expulsion of the fellow-travelling far-leftists, Platts-Mills, Hutchinson, Solley and Konni Zilliacus from party membership. They were guilty of disloyalty and anti-party activity. Zilliacus, Bevan told Huw T. Edwards, 'had passed the bound of all reasonable toleration'. Equally he strongly condemned industrial rebels, notably unofficial strikers in the docks and gas industry. Bevan had no difficulty, on the Cabinet Emergencies Committee in 1948–9, in supporting the use of troops to break strikes. He gave his backing to the Attorney-General Hartley Shawcross in exploring legal weapons to be used against stevedores encouraging disaffection in the London docks. Britain's socialist experiment should not be imperilled by the self-indulgence and indiscipline of a minority, a view faithfully mirrored by Barbara Castle 20 years later during the debates on *In Place of Strife*. This was also Bevan's own approach during his ill-starred three months as Minister of Labour in January – April 1951. Never, down to Gaitskell's budget proposals at that time, did Bevan openly oppose his own government's domestic policies. Even the necessary retreats in the period 1948–50 – rationing, a wage freeze, devaluation of the pound (which Bevan vigorously defended on socialist grounds in a memorable speech in the Commons) – were all defensible. In any event, they were the work of the new chancellor, Sir Stafford Cripps, an old ally from Popular Front/*Tribune* days before the war, and a fellow victim of expulsion from the party in 1939.

It is not his record in the Attlee government but rather the way he left it that is largely responsible for Bevan's later reputation as an irreconcilable of the far left. In a historic episode, Bevan clashed furiously with the new chancellor, Hugh Gaitskell, initially about the scale of his proposed £4,700 million rearmament programme for 1951–4, and then fatally over the charges to be imposed on the health service to help pay for it. After announcing, almost casually, in a speech at Bermondsey on 3 April that it was a resigning matter of principle, he left the Attlee Cabinet on 22 April, along with Harold Wilson – not hitherto a dissenter but a critic of the arms programme on economic grounds – and the lesser figure of John Freeman. Bevan's disastrous resignation speech included bitter criticism of Gaitskell (whom Michael Foot in *Tribune* compared to the traitor Philip Snowden back in 1931, the ultimate comparison in terms of Labour mythology). A 'party within a party' (so-called) came into being, with its own manifesto *Keep Left* in July 1951, and the Bevanites were born. Labour lost the 1951 general election, plunged into four years of civil war and gained a long-term reputation for being divided and unelectable that lingered on into the 1990s when the advent of New Labour reversed it for good. Bevan, at first, was the figure held to blame.

Clearly, resignation in such circumstances indelibly stamps a politician as a divisive, perhaps destructive, force. The moderation of most of Bevan's conduct in the years 1945–50 was forgotten. Gaitskell and Dalton freely compared their former colleague to Mosley, even to Hitler. A series of ministers, Attlee, Gaitskell, Dalton, Gordon Walker, Shinwell and others, spread the total untruth that Bevan had previously voiced no concern at the new rearmament programme. Bevan was accused of the same mixture of semi-detachment and psychological instability attributed by Downing Street to Peter Mandelson when he resigned, 50 years later in January 2001. Others claimed that Bevan had no problem of principle at all but was consumed by personal jealousy of Gaitskell, a public school upstart who had only entered the Commons in 1945. 'He's nothing, nothing, nothing', Bevan exclaimed, though Gaitskell was hardly more conciliatory for his part. Indeed, Bevan felt a real sense of grievance towards Attlee, never the best premier in promoting or removing ministers, when Gaitskell was pushed into the Treasury in place of Cripps in October 1950, followed by the promotion of Morrison to the Foreign Office in place of Bevin in March 1951, where he was to make a derisory impression. Bevan, denied promotion to the two key posts by Attlee, was given little in return. He was not moved on to the Colonial Office in February 1950, apparently because of his excessive sympathy for black Africans, while his move to the Ministry of Labour was at best a move sideways to a post held without distinction by the elderly George Isaacs for the past five years. After Bevan's glorious achievements at Health, Attlee had given him a curmudgeonly and grudging reward. He reacted with years of quarrelsome behaviour, which Barbara Castle attributed in part to the male menopause.

But this is not why Bevan resigned, and it would be unfair towards both him and Gaitskell to lay the main emphasis on personal jealousies. Bevan resigned not because he was an extremist, not because he suddenly cast considerations of loyalty to the winds, but because Gaitskell's budget raised grave issues that went beyond previous policies. On those issues it was Bevan, not Gaitskell, who was demonstrably right. Contrary to what appears in some later accounts (Dalton, Gaitskell, Gordon-Walker for example), Bevan had twice declared at length in Cabinet that Gaitskell's proposed rearmament programme was impractical and unaffordable. On 1 August 1950, while supporting the Anglo-American position in resisting the North Korean invasion of the south, Bevan condemned the then £3,600 million programme. On 25 January 1951, just after Attlee's talks with Truman in Washington had led to a massive increase in Britain's rearmament burden to £4,700 million, heavier per capita than in the United States itself, Bevan argued at length and in detail that it was quite impractical. He offered major economic objections – the effect on exports and inflation, the bottlenecks in supplies, the disruption of labour, the crucial shortage of machine tools. Gaitskell did not seriously contest them, but in effect argued that Britain had no option but to back America to the hilt. It was the supposed Celtic firebrand Bevan who offered careful economic arguments, the supposed rational economist

Gaitskell who spoke as a politician, underpinned by emotion. Bevan steered clear of financial controversies in a fine Commons speech of 15 February defending British involvement in Korea. But it was well known that he opposed the arms programme, and that helping to finance it by imposing charges on dental and ophthalmic areas of the health service would be a resigning matter for him.

Other ministers did not help. Possible allies like Griffiths, Tomlinson and even perhaps Dalton drifted away. Attlee was ill at a crucial moment, leaving the Cabinet in the hands of Morrison, Bevan's arch-enemy. Attlee's letter from his sickbed, unhelpfully and unhistorically comparing Bevan's actions with Lord Randolph Churchill's impetuous and politically fatal resignation from the Salisbury government in December 1886, made matters worse. The crisis could have been avoided. The gap between ministers was the pathetically small sum of £13 million (£23 million in a full year). Many tried to bridge the narrow gulf – the aged Lord Addison, the dying Ernest Bevin, lesser ministers like Robens, Stewart and Callaghan. But, almost fatalistically, the majority willed Bevan to leave them, and he did. His resignation did not show him up as a fellow-travelling extremist. What it showed was that the inexperienced and highly strung Gaitskell, for all his statistical expertise, had got his sums fatally wrong. Indeed, his one and only budget in 1951 was financially inadequate as well as politically disastrous. It discouraged investment and failed to address inflation. When Churchill returned to power in late October, he took Bevan's side. The arms programme was proved by Ian Bancroft and other civil servants to be quite impractical; they were scornful of Gaitskell's calculations. Labour's original arms programme was cut by Churchill by over a third and phased over four years, not three. They were all Bevanites now, it seemed. But the outcome was disastrous for Bevan's career and long-term reputation, and perhaps for his party as well.

The years of internecine controversy while in opposition between 1951 and 1955 have also been taken to prove Bevan's radical departure from the middle ground. It was a painful period, which did great harm to Labour's standing, with the venerable Attlee in his last phase unable to turn back the tide. But again a careful assessment of Bevan's record may lead to a revision of the conventional wisdom. His dissent was fierce and consistent – but on foreign and defence policy only. On domestic matters, Bevan and Gaitskell, both of them democratic socialists who favoured nationalisation and greater equality, were never far apart. Although Bevan received a great boost from his strength on the constituency section of the National Executive, where 'Bevanites' filled six out of seven places, the great debate was fought out primarily within the parliamentary party. The constitutional assumptions of Bevan and Gaitskell were basically the same. There was intense personal bitterness, and rhetorical broad-sides from Gaitskellites and Bevanites alike. But they did not necessarily emanate from Bevan. Indeed, it was his followers like Foot and Castle who were the main protagonists. Wilson and later Crossman had moved to more centrist positions long before 1955. Bevan himself, however, seemed to keep his distance from his followers. 'Surtout je ne suis pas Marxiste', Karl Marx is supposed to have said. Bevan, almost a proletar-ian Gaitskellite in excellent disguise, might have observed that, above all else, he was no Bevanite. Michael Foot's two-volume biography of Bevan, while a marvellous and vivid contribution to socialist literature, exagger-ates Bevan's antagonism towards the Labour front bench. Foot himself emerges as more intransigent and unforgiving towards the Gaitskellite right than his hero ever was. The same could perhaps be said of Bevan's wife, Jennie Lee.

The great debates were almost wholly about foreign affairs. These were years when, especially after the death of Stalin in 1953, coexistence and conciliation seemingly gripped the international mind. Churchill himself called for summit diplomacy between the great powers (amongst whom he naturally included Britain) but failed to push his old wartime friend 'Ike' in this direction. There were strong arguments for trying to build a new consensus around peaceful coexistence, for moderating the arms race by going slow on the hydrogen bomb, certainly for not slavishly following the Americans in encouraging Chiang Kai-Shek and taking bel-ligerent postures towards Communist China, which shrewd observers believed had only limited congruence of view with the Soviet Union in any case. There were at least grounds for rational debate, but reason was set aside, not least by an impassioned and ageing Bevan himself. For a third time in 1955, he was almost expelled by the comrades, and this time it would have been three strikes and out.

Yet Bevan in these years was still cleaving to the broad centre-ground of the party. Nothing confirms this more strongly than his volume *In Place of Fear* (1952), taken to be a supreme testament to the Bevanite out-look at this time. It is certainly a fascinating book, if distinctly disjointed, really a series of essays written over a period of many years. But it is also very far from being an extreme book, any more than the original Keep Left tract, *One Way Only,* which in July 1951 had been unusually radical with its pleas about the shortage of raw materials, overseas aid and world poverty. *In Place of Fear* is a civilised, qualified statement of the socialist case for parliamentary democracy. It expressed a view of socialism rooted in its time, with nationalisation central to it, but that was standard prior to Crosland's *Future of Socialism* in 1956. It is open to criticism on many fronts, not least for its unrealistic assumption that world trade patterns in no way 'limit the application of socialist policies to the British economy'.[2] Indeed the economic argument of the book, neither Keynesian nor Marxist, is somewhat rudimentary.

But the main thrust of Bevan's argument concerns applications, and here it is immediately recognisable within the mainstream Labour tradition. Financially, there is a strong commitment to public expenditure, Labour's main mantra down to 1997 and far from lost thereafter. Public spending was the essential tool to remove the injustices of an unequal harsh society; the NHS was financed from general taxation, not by a poll tax. Politically, the essential route to socialism was the parliamentary one, 'government by discussion'. As Jennie Lee later wrote, Bevan wrote as a 'passionate parliamentarian', albeit one who felt empirically in terms of relativities. Parliamentary socialism was the route to power, the essential road to the New Jerusalem. And emotionally and morally, Bevan saw democratic socialism as a vibrant creed with values of its own, libertarian, pluralist, the creed of the Levellers and Tom Paine and Bevan's favourite philosopher, the Uruguayan Jose Enrique Rodo. Socialism would never be drowned in the linguistic obscurities of the later Third Way. It was clearly delineated, it had its own lineage – and it was great fun. Not for Bevan the austere joyless desiccation of the Webb–Cole tradition, which Crosland was shortly to memorably to denounce. Bevan's own honeymoon would be spent in sunny Torremolinos, not like the Webbs investigating trade societies in Dublin. He enjoyed the Café Royal and suits from Saville Row. *In Place of Fear* is the testament of a humane, distinctly unpuritanical libertarian, never a work of dogmatic extremism. It retains all the poignant magic of the socialist classic.

Bevan's location in the mainstream was finally confirmed in his last phase. After Gaitskell's election as party leader, there was a reconciliation. Bevan, with his record of disaffection and exclusion, never had a chance of succeeding Attlee. Attempts to discern a possible victory route via secret electoral deals with his old enemy and rival for the leadership, Herbert Morrison, are unconvincing. Bevan, though, was still inspirational in party and country, with an international reputation through his friendships with such as Nehru, Nenni, Djilas, Ben Gurion and Mendès-France. Gaitskell wisely brought him into the Shadow Cabinet as Colonial spokesman in February 1956. He had little time to make much of an impact there, though one revealing episode came that April when Bevan, along with George Brown, led the way in challenging Nikita Khrushchev over the treatment of Soviet dissidents. Bevan's anti-Communism was fully confirmed. No one would have doubted it had they read Bevan's trenchant attacks on Soviet suppression of east European social democracy in his foreword to young Denis Healey's *The Curtain Falls*, back in

1951. Khrushchev sneered that if these were the Labourites, he was for the Conservatives. At the time of Suez, while Bevan strafed Eden and Selwyn Lloyd with ridicule for their humiliating failure over the invasion, people noted that he seemed more measured than Gaitskell in condemning the government. Maybe this was Bevan the old Zionist, friend of Israel, and secret patriot.

As shadow foreign secretary, he and Gaitskell worked together well enough in trying to probe for alternatives to break the sterility of the Cold War. Both took up the cause of 'disengagement' in Central Europe, notably the Polish Rapacki plan for a nuclear-free zone in Central Europe, including in time perhaps a reunified, if disarmed, Germany and the return of the Oder-Neisse territories in the East. In general, Labour with Bevan as its spokesman maintained its traditional pro-NATO stance, with little sympathy for the emergent European Common Market at this stage. Kenneth Younger speculated that had Bevan become foreign secretary in 1959 or in 1964 he would have been a relatively orthodox, even right-wing anti-Communist practitioner of power, but this seems an exaggeration.

The most dramatic instance of Bevan's orthodoxy, the one that caused most pain to friends and disciples, came at the 1957 party conference. With opposition growing against British nuclear weapons, and the Campaign for Nuclear Disarmament due to come into being at Easter 1958, Bevan emotionally defended the possession of nuclear weapons. Britain should retain them as a bargaining counter. It should not send a Labour foreign secretary 'naked into the conference chamber'. Other countries wanted Britain to retain nuclear weaponry, at least for the immediate future, if only to act as a counter to an unpredictable, capitalist United States. A moralistic gesture by Britain to give up its own nuclear stockpile, whatever other nuclear powers would do, would be futile and pointless. It would have no effect on the thermo-nuclear weapons remaining in the hands of other countries, nor would it slow down the progress of a nuclear arsenal in coming states such as China. Unilateralism would be simply 'an emotional spasm', the negation of the politics of power, of real politics in the living world about which he had lectured Jennie Lee in her 'nunnery' so often in the past. Later on, the arguments of both sides seemed questionable. Both pro- and anti-bomb factions laid heavy emphasis on the illusion of Britain's moral influence in the world. Bevan himself became uneasy when pressed by Frank Cousins on whether Britain would engage in 'first use' of the bomb, or whether having the bomb was compatible with non-testing. In the end, he and Gaitskell came up with the half-formed notion of the 'non-nuclear club' just before the 1959 general election. But from the standpoint of Bevan's wider role in the movement, his rejection of unilateralism was highly symbolic. In a supreme crisis, he threw himself behind the leadership, behind a tradition of British participation in world collective security, which had been Labour's watchword since 1939. His friends and allies in CND could never move him from that, though it was perhaps fortunate for Bevan that his premature death spared him Labour's supreme agony over unilateralism in 1960, a purgatory that endured until the leadership of Michael Foot, a generation later.

Bevan's occupation of the centre, even right-wing ground, in defence policy made him more than most a force for unity. In 1959 he became deputy party leader. His status emerged dramatically in the party conference of October 1959 just after a humbling electoral defeat at the hands of Macmillan's Tories. The conference was preceded by Gaitskell announcing, on no clear evidence, that Labour's defeat was due in part to Clause Four in the party constitution, which committed the party to unending nationalisation. This produced uproar in the ranks. Once again Gaitskell was compared with MacDonald and Snowden, the traitors of 1931. Bevan, now in the early stages of cancer, strode gallantly to the rescue. He had already been important in getting the party to accept *Industry and Society*, a document in 1957 which argued the case for a mixed economy and warned against rigid models of nationalisation. Like others on the British left, he recognised the need for an updated form of socialism, attuned to modern circumstances, with an emphasis on social equality and strategies for economic growth. In the 1959 party conference, he saved Gaitskell's bacon with a brilliantly evasive speech, which aimed to reconcile the views of Gaitskell and Barbara Castle over public ownership. He quoted Lenin on the need to capture 'the commanding heights of the economy'. He cited Euclid as evidence that two things equal to a third thing were equal to each other. Unity was preserved; the Clause Four issue disappeared for another 35 years. It was all due to Nye, the great moderate and compromiser. His far less abrasive Welsh colleague, Jim Griffiths, continually referred to himself as a reconciler, as did a younger Welshman, Cledwyn Hughes. So they both were. But, in the key crisis, Nye was the greatest reconciler of them all. A few months later cancer killed him. It was, wrote Michael Foot, 'like a great tree hacked down, wantonly, in full leaf.' (3)

On his election as leader in February 1963, Harold Wilson took his ex-Bevanite colleagues over to the wall to toast the portrait of Nye, the man who ought to have been leader instead. But Nye Bevan was not Labour's lost leader, and the mantle of Nye was as elusive and ambiguous a garment as Keir Hardie's cloth cap. He could never have led the party, given his record of dissent and expulsion, and his usually bad relations with the TUC. Attlee's avowal in 1952 that Bevan should have 'had the leadership on a plate' may be doubted given Attlee's steadfast refusal to give the younger man any significant promotion. But Bevan still remains a giant in Labour's Valhalla – yet a giant as much of the centre ground as of the left. Throughout his career, he cleaved to the majority view on domestic politics, foreign policy and the nature of democracy.

Does he then deserve his emerging role as an icon for New Labour? His socialism was of his time, conceived within a very different global economy and a polarised class structure. To speculate counter-factually, he would never have accepted the Thatcherite creed of a market-driven, 'flexible', deregulated economy, which Labour retained after 1997. On the other hand, he would have welcomed anti-poverty measures like the minimum wage and child poverty programmes, and Gordon Brown's 2002 budget to revive the NHS. He might conceivably have come around to devolution for all his lifelong opposition to Welsh separatism. In 1959 he reluctantly endorsed a Welsh Office being put in Labour's manifesto, while no one who heard his moving address at the Ebbw Vale *eisteddfod* in 1958 could doubt his passion for the Welsh identity and culture. Other policies, ID cards, detention without trial, control orders, ASBOs and the like, might have puzzled an old member of the National Council of Civil Liberties. One could, though, imagine an updated Nye, like an older Neil Kinnock, coming to accept the social thrust of a European Union with the prospects of working more closely with social democratic comrades in Europe, east as well as west. New Labour still has its socialist ingredient, however well disguised. Within it, Bevan and his Health Service, convey the essence of the idea of community, of a commitment to public service, a measured incremental socialism that 'made one freedom safe by adding another to it'. So Tony Blair's enthusiasm for the 'solidarity, social justice and co-operation' embodied in Nye's philosophy is not so bizarre. Sceptic, pluralist, visionary, Aneurin Bevan was a socialist for all seasons, who belongs to the ages. A Latimer for the oldest, finest values of all, he may take his appointed place in the world of the new.

Chapter 15

Sixties Socialism: From Planning to Permissiveness

One popular view of the sixties in Britain is that they were 'swinging' – the land of Mary Quant and the Beatles, of sex, drugs and rock and roll. But it is also commonly believed that they were 'socialist' and that this was demonstrated by the government of Harold Wilson between 1964 and 1970. Certainly, the sixties had a character all their own. They differed from the democratic socialism of the Attlee government in 1945–51, which drew so heavily on the social patriotism and civic solidarity of the wartime years and the defeat of Hitler. But they differ also from the Blair years from May 1997 where the government and prime minister, apart from occasional vague references to Christian metaphysics, could hardly be said to be socialist at all – certainly far less so than European left-wing leaders such as Lionel Jospin or Oskar Lafontaine. It is true that Labour in 1964 had just emerged from a long ideological civil war, with the conflict between Gaitskellites and Bevanites, and the challenge of the Campaign for Nuclear Disarmament. But it still believed itself to be socialist, albeit in the gradualist, Fabian, very British sense. Quite apart from leftish former followers of Aneurin Bevan like Michael Foot and Barbara Castle, on the party right Anthony Crosland had called his famous book of 1956 *The Future of Socialism*. Another author on the Labour right, Douglas Jay, wrote in 1962, a powerful book, entitled *Socialism in the New Society*. It was time, wrote Jay, to 'get back to socialism' whose criticism of laissez-faire was 'unanswerable'.[1] Roy Jenkins, seen as amongst the most right-wing of all the government ministers, was also to say that Labour could not simply be a labourist workers' movement focussing on wages and jobs; it also needed a living core of doctrine and this meant democratic socialism.[2] Thus it was that the Wilson government of 1964–70 left legacies later regarded as controversial symbols of 'sixties socialism' including comprehensive schools and high-rise tower blocks, later to be centres for vandalism, crime and racial conflict as at Broadwater Farm, Tottenham.

But what precisely did sixties socialism mean? At least at the time of the 1964 general election, it implied three main priorities, planning, modernisation and equality, and it is worth looking at each in turn.

Planning, a notion rooted deep in the Fabian origins of the early Labour Party, emerged now as part of the vogue for economic and social engineering in the early 1960s in Britain. This was the high noon of social science, of institutions such as Nuffield College, Oxford, and the Social Science Research Council. Criminology, a new discipline concerned with the social roots of deviant activity, entered upon its 'golden age'.[3] Much was heard of it in the literature of the time, with praise for the planning strategies not only of the French Commissariat but also of Eastern Europe. Michael Shanks's influential *The Stagnant Society* began with lavish praise of the economic planning in, of all countries, Bulgaria.[4] There were constant attacks on Tory failure to plan, and their erratic economic policies of 'stop-go' (or 'red-green' to use an analogy drawn from road traffic) and the alleged role of the Treasury in pursuing this unsatisfactory policy. The national finances since 1955 had been marked by repeated lurches in the economy, frequent pressure on sterling and always much instability in the balance of payments. Chancellors like Butler, Thorneycroft and Heathcroft-Amory had left the Treasury with their reputations diminished. So the answer was felt to lie in planning – and not just by Labour. One of the major converts to a form of planning was the Conservative Chancellor of the Exchequer Selwyn Lloyd when he created in 1961 'Neddy' and 'Nicky', NEDC to plan economic development much as advocated by the young Harold Macmillan before the war, NIC to chart income growth.

But this did the Conservatives little good – nor indeed Lloyd himself since he was 'booted out' in 1962 only 12 months after 'Neddy' was born. Harold Wilson in his election campaign book of speeches in 1964 repeatedly compared Labour planning with Tory muddle-through.[5] It was sub-titled 'Labour's Plan for Britain' and included chapters on 'Housing and Planning', 'Plan for Full Employment' and 'Plan for Commonwealth Trade'. The main instrument of this planned economic policy would be the new Department of Economic Affairs. Supposedly devised in the back of a taxi leaving a London hotel,[6] it would also deal with the political rivalry of Wilson's main Cabinet lieutenants, George Brown and Jim Callaghan, by giving Brown a key job at the Department of Economic Affairs (DEA) while Callaghan went to the Treasury. The latter's credentials as a financial expert were already questioned in many quarters. But the root idea was that the DEA, handling the 'real economy' of production, investment and distribution, would replace the dead hand of the Treasury and the Bank of England. Stop-go would be replaced by French-style long-term indicative planning and sustained, though controlled, innovation and growth.

The theme of modernisation linked the failure of economic planning with Britain's antique time-worn social structure. The literature of the earlier sixties also emphasised how Britain was dominated by class division and the traditional ascendancy of an old, privileged social class. This was the theme of Anthony Sampson's *Anatomy of Britain* (1962), which argued that the country was run by about 200 'top people', all middle-class white males bonded together in public schools, Oxbridge and the London clubs. This argument chimed in with the 'anti-establishment' ethos of the day (the term 'establishment' itself apparently coined by a somewhat louche right-wing journalist, Henry Fairlie, who wrote in the *Spectator*). It focussed attention on elite categories of people, an idea adopted skilfully by *The Times* newspaper in advertisements that claimed 'Top People read the Times'. The idea encouraged the rise of satirical television programmes such as *That Was the Week That Was*, and magazines such as *Private Eye*, one of whose owners, Peter Cook, launched a famous London night-club, called 'The Establishment'. Cook starred, along with Alan Bennett, Jonathan Miller and Dudley Moore, in a celebrated undergraduate review, full of satire and cynicism towards subjects as varied as the Queen, the Church and the Boy Scouts, called *Beyond the Fringe*. In this sense Labour's call for modernisation was more populist than socialist.

Harold Wilson, as leader of the opposition after Gaitskell's death early in 1963, brilliantly exploited this mood about 'the establishment'. He attacked Macmillan's carefully cultivated 'grouse-moor image' (the Conservative prime minister took pleasure in shooting large number of grouse on Scottish moors) and even more Sir Alec Douglas-Home as 'the fourteenth earl' who as prime minister in 1963–4 rashly commented that he worked out his ideas on economics through the use of match-sticks. Douglas-Home effectively countered by saying that Harold Wilson was no doubt 'the fourteenth Mr. Wilson'. For Wilson, 'modernisation' enabled Labour to by-pass theology – to rise above doctrinal differences over such issues as nationalisation or nuclear weapons. He linked modernisation with reform of the civil service, the law and parliament among other things.

But above all he linked it with science. Wilson brilliantly took on board the concern at the time that Britain was neglecting or under-valuing science – the theme of C.P. Snow's famous Rede lectures on 'The Two Cultures' and, in part, of the 1963 Robbins Report on higher education. The need to promote science, including such leading-edge subjects as computer science and information technology, so Wilson argued, gave new force to the case for socialism in Britain. It was noted ironically by commentators that the Conservative government had a minister for science and that Labour had a shadow minister, Richard Crossman. What both men had in common was that neither was a scientist but former

Oxford dons in classics, precisely the kind of figures currently held up for public contempt as irrelevant. Wilson himself, after his work at the Board of Trade under Attlee and in the civil service during the war, felt comfortable with science and the company of scientists. His famous speech at the Labour Party conference at Scarborough in October 1963 talked of the 'white heat' of a new scientific revolution, of the need for Labour to appeal to the 'white-coated' as well as to the 'blue-collar' workers. Socialism, he declared bafflingly, was 'about science'.[7] He brought into his counsels among others, the eminent zoologist and government scientific adviser, Sir Solly Zuckerman, Dr. Jacob Bronowski, famous as a populariser of pure science on television, and the nuclear physicist and Nobel prize winner, Professor Patrick Blackett, to give his rhetoric substance when Labour finally took office. In addition, C.P. Snow, whose novel, *Corridors of Power*, appeared on the eve of the election, went to the Lords as parliamentary secretary to Frank Cousins in the new Ministry of Technology.

Equality had become Labour's main ideological priority ever since Crosland's book appeared in 1956. He emphasised the need not simply of greater equality of opportunity but of equality as such, especially in education. Crosland argued that the economic problems of capitalism, which had preoccupied socialists in years past, were now virtually solved by Keynesian-style demand management and the need for nationalisation of ownership was now redundant.[8] Hugh Gaitskell had often declared that 'socialism was about equality'. Douglas Jay had argued strongly that socialists should press for more equality as the foundation of social justice. Merely equalising opportunity was not enough since it would merely create a meritocracy and therefore make social division ultimately worse.[9] Much was made of the writings of the Harvard-based economist, John Kenneth Galbraith, who argued in *The Affluent Society* (1958) for government action to redress the social imbalance between 'private affluence and public squalor'. Indeed, the impact of American liberals such as Michael Harrington and Galbraith was generally powerful in promoting this theme. The United States appeared to be a paradigm in experiencing the social and technological impact of a post-industrial society. The transatlantic influence on the British left was never to be so great again, perhaps until Barack Obama's election to the presidency in 2008. The popular culture of the time emphasised the social inequality endemic in sixties Britain. There were the 'new wave' films such as *Saturday Night and Sunday Morning* and *A Taste of Honey* which focussed on class division, and also for the first time perhaps treated working-class people as interesting individuals in their own right, as French and Italian films had long done, and not mere social stereotypes as in the cheery, unthreatening

Ealing Studios comedies after the war. Equality indeed was Labour's driving moral imperative at the time. Roy Jenkins had emphasised the unfair and unequal divisions in wealth, income, regional development and lifestyle.[10] It was an idea especially congenial to working-class figures in Labour's ranks. With men like George Brown and Jim Callaghan, both former trade unionists of working-class background who had known real hardship in their early years, Labour was still in touch with its proletarian roots, still the custodian of a version of Keir Hardie's cloth cap.

There was something else underlying all this – a belief that, despite its economic problems, Britain was still manifestly a great power. The politicians were still ambiguous about Europe, after President de Gaulle's veto in 1963 and the issue played a relatively little part in the 1964 general election. But Britain still expected to play a world role. It had powerful links with the Commonwealth across the world, through ethnic and cultural attachments, especially through the role of sterling and the pound's being a reserve currency, and through Britain's strong defence presence east of Suez. But above all Labour placed great store on its partnership (popularly called 'the special relationship') with its transatlantic and ancient ally in two world wars, the United States. Macmillan, himself half-American, had made much of this (other than in the Suez adventure) and talked grandiloquently of Britain acting as Greece to America's role. But Labour also saw the American link as making Britain different. Sir Oliver Franks, perhaps somewhat unhappily, had spoken in 1950 of Britain being 'first in the queue'.[11] British Labour also had strong affinities ideologically to the Kennedy–Johnson Democrats and the old New Dealers. Men like Arthur Schlesinger Jr. and Galbraith were well known in Oxford and Cambridge common rooms, while legions of Rhodes Scholars and products of the English-Speaking Union abounded in high places in Washington to spread the word. Wilson in October 1964 spoke, Roosevelt-like, of his 'hundred days' at the start of his administration. Britain had powerful transatlantic defence ties in NATO which a Labour government had effectively created back in 1949. Most important of all, Wilson and Callaghan were convinced that America would always give Britain backing if there were economic or financial difficulties. If there was a run on sterling or the gold and dollar reserves, Uncle Sam would unfailingly bail John Bull out. They spent time in the States in 1963–4 with liberal-minded US bankers and businessmen to help confirm this belief.

Harold Wilson, who took office with a miniscule majority in October 1964, was a new kind of non-doctrinaire socialist. A brilliant leader of the opposition since Gaitskell's death, he had been a highly flexible figure in Labour's ranks. For long, he appeared as a man of the socialist left, who had resigned with Aneurin Bevan over the imposition of National

Health Service charges in April 1951, but who had also voted for Gaitskell as leader after Attlee resigned in 1955. Really Wilson was neither of left nor of right, but a technocrat, trained as an applied economist. Unlike serving servicemen like Callaghan, Healey or Heath, he had fought the Second World War, not in uniform in some distant land, but behind a desk in Whitehall as a bureaucrat and statistician under Sir William Beveridge. His previous ministerial incarnation was as a 'planner' as President of the Board of Trade in 1947–51 (where his enthusiasm for Soviet planning first led to the intense interest placed in his activities by MI5 and the astonishing notion that Gaitskell might have been poisoned by the Russians to make way for the fellow-traveller Wilson). Wilson had scant interest in ideology. The current emphasis on planning and modernisation thus chimed in with his technocratic outlook, while the appeal to equality was consistent with his own contrived image of down-to-earth Yorkshire folksiness, complete with a love of Huddersfield Town football club and HP sauce, built up by and through the media.

Wilson's main Cabinet colleagues, George Brown and Jim Callaghan, were fierce rivals for power. But, at least for the first years to the summer of 1966, they were largely dominated by Wilson. Brown strongly backed the 'planning' ethos and at the DEA promoted the so-called 'National Plan' for six-year growth at 5 per cent a year. Callaghan went along happily with the idea of equality. A man from a very poor home in Portsmouth, the son of a widow without a pension, he saw himself as a socially aware chancellor, along the lines of Lloyd George in 1910. The coming men in the government were all from the centre-right – planners like Crosland, Healey and, above all, Roy Jenkins. But Wilson placed reliance on his links with the old left. He used Richard Crossman, and especially Barbara Castle, the last a kind of keeper of Labour's conscience, to keep him true to the old faith. He used Michael Foot to keep him in touch with radical dissent on the back benches and in the Tribune group. He also employed a notably left-wing adviser, the relatively youthful Peter Shore. Above all, he retained a special relationship with his old ally Aneurin Bevan's widow, Jennie Lee. He gave her free rein (and much financial support) in her work as minister for the arts and in starting up the Open University, itself a great social landmark in promoting part-time, life-long education, and a historic British achievement that owes much to Wilson's own support. Through Jennie Lee and others, the prime minister could underline his own historic affiliations with the Old Labour left. He had even told Crossman before the election, however improbably, that he was running a Bolshevik revolution with a Czarist shadow Cabinet.[12]

How far did the government succeed in promoting these objectives? The main successes came with the drive towards equality. Resources were pumped into the social services, and especially into education from primary schools to universities including the innovative Open University. There was between 1964 and 1970 a sense of greater social mobility in British life. The gulf between social classes and the various regions of Britain was narrowed through state action. But from 1967 onwards, cuts in public expenditures meant a loss of momentum: for instance, the raising of the school-leaving age did not go through. More generally, critics complained that the government's policies did not go to the root causes of social inequality. Many of the reforms mainly benefited the middle class. They used the NHS freely at the point of delivery. It was middle-class not working-class students who rushed to join the newly expanding universities on full maintenance grants and with free tuition. Even the Open University in time proved to be an agency for middle-class professionals like teachers or social workers seeking a formal qualification rather than manual workers or housewives. The public schools, a fundamental sign of social division, the training-ground of all the main civil servants at the time, along with Oxford and Cambridge, were left totally untouched, even as Tony Crosland's campaign to abolish 'every fucking grammar school in England' undermined the best of the state system of maintained schools.[13]

Otherwise, planning did not mean that much in practice. The Treasury inevitably retained much residual strength, especially through civil servants such as Sir William Armstrong and Sir Alec Cairncross, while Harold Wilson's own dogmatic commitment to defending the exchange rate of sterling and not devaluing in 1964 proved to be harmful to effective planning. The new Department of Economic Affairs turned out to be a failure, almost a fiasco. There was a total lack of clarity about what it was supposed to be doing, or in defining the line of demarcation between its remit and that of the Treasury. Since the latter retained powers of taxation and the exchange rate, the DEA was hamstrung from the start. There was constant bickering between Brown and Callaghan over the rival claims of their two departments. They were two formidable and aggressive politicians. But even had they been plaster saints, the DEA would have led to trouble. In December 1964, an agreement was drawn up by the Civil Service (the French word Concordat was used by Peter Jay) to draw up lines of demarcation between the Treasury and the DEA. They were a total mess. It was laid down that the Treasury would deal with the short term but that this would not necessarily exclude the long term, while the DEA would deal with the long term but that this would not necessarily exclude the short term.[14] It is difficult to imagine a formula more likely to lead to future argument. George Brown's National Plan, introduced with a fanfare of publicity, lacked credibility and proved to be hopelessly optimistic. The DEA then lost one set of responsibilities after another, though under its last minister, Peter Shore, it did retain important powers over regional policy. Perhaps it would have been better conceived as a minister of regional development. Its ghostly existence came to an end in 1969. None mourned its passing. In 1997, Gordon Brown strongly and rightly resisted anything like it being set up again.

Planning policy was, therefore, a failure. Anthony Crosland noted in *Socialism Now* that Labour achieved a growth rate of only 2.3 per cent in 1964–70, whereas the Tories had managed 3.8 per cent in the troubled years 1958–64.[15] It gave way to the deflationary policies of Roy Jenkins's 'hard slog' in 1968–70. As Ben Pimlott has written, after that the idea of planning lost its central place in Labour thinking forever, and there was nothing to replace it. Its absence left a void at the very heart of Labour policies thereafter. Roy Hattersley's distinctly revisionist *Choose Freedom* (1987) significantly downgraded planning as the centrepiece of Labour's strategy. It contained problems both semantic and philosophical. 'It cannot in itself bring about the more free and more equal society which socialists seek.'[16] This led directly to the undoctrinaire flexible managerialism that formed the essence of New Labour in 1997.

As for modernisation, this was in the main a story of projects that were not fulfilled. The machinery of government and the civil service, the House of Lords, the structure of industrial relations were not really modernised at all, even if Wilson's instincts were correct on all of them. The mobilisation of science brought some achievements, as in the development of Colleges of Advanced Technology, the encouragement of the computer industry, the modernisation of the Post Office by Tony Benn and the controversial project of the Anglo-French Concorde. But in general it was not a great success. Frank Cousins, the Transport Workers' leader sent to the Ministry of Technology, did not really carry credibility and finally resigned over prices and incomes policy in 1966. Professor Patrick Blackett became hugely disillusioned by what he saw as the government's failure to carry science forward, and finally left the government service. By 1970 nothing was heard of claims that 'socialism was about science'. By 1974 Tony Crosland was openly sceptical about the claims of the scientists to have found the key to human happiness. He emphasised rather the need to impose social controls on rampant scientific development, for instance in dealing with damaging problems such as air pollution.[17]

What can be said of the United Kingdom's standing as a great power? In fact, as Sir Michael Palliser and others have shown, the record was not one of success in external policy, in Rhodesia, the Middle East, Europe and elsewhere. It was fatally scarred by support given to the American's unwinnable war in Vietnam, deeply disappointing to much of the Labour rank and file. There were some wise decisions. The Wilson government rightly decided to cut its losses financially and in 1968–70 accepted the realities of the end of Empire by withdrawing its forces from east of Suez, despite the vocal protests of Commonwealth leaders such as Premier Lee Kuan Yew, of Singapore. However, the government's overall external policy was conducted against a background of economic weakness culminating in the devaluation of the pound in November 1967. This time, the United States would bail out the ailing British economy no longer, even if the US Treasury felt that British devaluation might also mean a new threat to the exchange rate of the dollar. Harold Wilson's claims to enjoy a special relationship with Lyndon Johnson, and even more with Richard Nixon from 1969, were based on a largely illusory belief in British influence. When the prime minister visited the White House in 1968 the musical entertainment provided saw the censoring from the programme of *I've Got Plenty of Nuthin* and *The Road to Mandalay*. It was felt that these were inappropriate to serenade a prime minister who had devalued the pound and withdrawn his forces east of Suez. The obvious alternative for Britain, it would seem, was membership of the European Common Market. Harold finally came around to this view in 1966–7 and persuaded most of his Cabinet to agree. But President de Gaulle applied his veto, and the issue remained in the air until the election of June 1970 when it was given little prominence during the campaign. By this time, much of the Labour movement was drifting back into the anti-European prejudice it inherited from the time of Gaitskell, with key ministers such as Callaghan, Healey and Crosland all unenthusiastic.

A variety of policy failures came together in a climactic third week of July 1966. This proved to be what journalists called the defining moment of the Wilson years and the socialist sixties. It came just after the popular rejoicing that attended England's winning of the football World Cup – defeating the West Germans in the final, to huge national glee. 'Two world wars and one world cup' as the football fans chanted on the terraces. A sudden crisis driving sterling down and a massive loss in the gold and foreign currency reserves led, so Wilson declared, to 'Britain being blown off course'. Hysteria followed in Westminster, especially when Wilson was away in Moscow to discuss Vietnam with President Kosygin, and when rumours multiplied of a plot by ministers to overthrow the absent prime minister – hatched, it was claimed, at the elegant home of an elegant woman, Anne Fleming, the wife of the author of the James Bond novels and at various times the mistress of Gaitskell and Roy Jenkins. As an incidental blow, on 14 July Labour lost one of its seats in Wales to a Welsh Nationalist. This grim period in mid-July saw the effective end of the DEA (George Brown soon went off to the Foreign Office to apply his restrained diplomatic talents there) and of the main modernisation programme; it saw cutbacks in the welfare state (relatively minor compared with the Thatcher experience later on, it must be said); the withdrawal from east of Suez and the bid to join Europe, which anticipated Britain's devaluing the pound. Harold Wilson's personal standing never recovered, especially when in November 1967 he was to tell disbelieving television viewers that 'the pound in your pocket has not been devalued'.

There is, however, a very different aspect to this story. Did the government, in spite of everything, manage to renew itself by adopting a different ideological stance? Could and did it try to rescue itself, not by upholding the public interest against the private, or statist collectivism against the free market, but by setting itself up as the guardian of civil and moral liberty? This was the era of so-called permissiveness and personal libertarianism in private behaviour, with the omnipresent miniskirt as its popular symbol, with the ending of capital punishment and of Victorian-style censorship of theatre and cinema, and the personal experimentation in lifestyle variously symbolised by the availability of the pill and the appeal of the drug culture of San Francisco: 'Turn on, tune in, and drop out'. The Lord Chamberlain, the official censor of the theatre, was in full retreat following a play by Edward Bond that depicted Queen Victoria as a lesbian. According to the poet Philip Larkin, 'sexual intercourse began in 1963', between the end of the ban on *Lady Chatterley* and the Beatles's first LP, a view the present writer might confirm.

Roy Jenkins at the Home Office in 1965–7 was hailed as the white knight of this new mood of personal self-expression. It seemed to dispel forever the heritage of Victorian Puritanism which still cast its baleful shadow over much of modern Britain, including that important Victorian legacy, the Labour Party. Harold Wilson himself seemed quite relaxed in his attitude to these changes, for all his nonconformist background in the Congregational church. He sought to identify himself with the new youth culture, for instance, in giving the Beatles the award of MBE (though it should always be remembered that Penny Lane was quite near his once-marginal Liverpool constituency). Perhaps indeed permissiveness, with all its implications for personal and family life, is the most enduring and endearing cultural legacy of the Wilson era.

But there are political factors to be borne in mind as well. First it is by no means clear that permissiveness was helpful to the British left. It was in the main a middle-class enthusiasm, which left most or many working-class voters alienated. Homophobia and misogyny were still rampant, and only a small minority of young girls actually took the pill. Tony Crosland actually saw permissiveness as a kind of bourgeois elitisism, a contempt for materialism, a belief amongst the suburban intelligentsia that the workers should enjoy open-air cafes, an uncensored theatre and a more exciting sex life, rather than cherishing washing-machines, television sets, football and beer and chips on the Costa Brava. He developed his own enthusiasm for following Grimsby Town. Amongst the 'permissive' young, left-wing demonstrators turned against the government – as perhaps they would against any government – especially for its support for the Americans in Vietnam and the breaking of its word over Commonwealth immigrants. The withdrawal of passport rights for Kenyan Asians was widely regarded as a massive breach of faith. Anyway, most of the student young were not rebels. They showed little gratitude for the government's lowering the voting age to 18. In the 1970 general election, most students voted Tory, assuming that they voted at all. Beyond this, the very self-indulgence and intemperateness of some of the movements of the time bred a reaction. There followed a 'taxpayers' revolt' against 'revolting' long-haired students, taking part in undisciplined 'demos' on university campuses while on full student grants and enjoying massive state subsidies, largely benefiting the *lumpenbourgeoisie*. University administrators, deprived of the campus police or quasi-military CRS detachments used by their American or French counterparts, were condemned for their failure to manage. A long-term reaction against universities and their student unions began which was to reach its climax under Mrs. Thatcher. The decision by Oxford University congregation to deny the prime minister an honorary degree in 1985 seemed only to confirm her point. Amongst many core Labour voters, on the other hand, there was much puritan hostility to a sex, drugs and rock and roll culture. In 1969, Jim Callaghan, a working-class boy brought up in the Baptist church in Portsmouth, now home secretary, rejected the call for the legalisation of cannabis. The tide of permissiveness (an ugly word he said) had gone too far. There were cries of 'hear, hear' all over the House of Commons, not least from Labour MPs on the benches behind him.[18] Permissiveness seemed destined only to lose votes for Labour, at least at the time.

Secondly, permissiveness and free expression could not be contained. It was impossible to say that it could flourish freely in one non-political sphere, but be sternly suppressed in another. Two damaging forms of protest made the point. The workers, or at least many of the trade unions, joined in the passion for revolt, and hence the widespread trade union disruptions and unofficial disputes of the late sixties. The shop-floor found new local heroes like 'Red Robbo' in Longbridge and Alan 'the Mole' Thornett in Cowley. This culminated in a cathartic political crisis in 1969. When Barbara Castle's Industrial Relations Bill had to be withdrawn (it was opposed by the working-class James Callaghan and an eventual majority of the Cabinet, by most of the parliamentary Labour Party and almost all the trade unions), it seemed to tell the world that British trade unions were above the law, and uncontrollable. The British government seemed impotent in the face of raw trade union power. A damaging legacy of industrial conflict was left for the 1970s. It was to overthrow the Heath government in February 1974 and, ironically, saw Callaghan himself in 1979 as its ultimate victim.

There emerged another startling new development – the rise of nationalist movements in Scotland and Wales, two of Labour's great strongholds. Without them, Labour could not normally hope to win a majority at general elections. In 1966, it won 48 Scottish seats out of 71, and 32 out of 36 in Wales. Scotland's nationalism was essentially political, that of Wales largely cultural, focussing on the campaigns of the Welsh Language Society, *Cymdeithas yr Iaith Cymraeg*. But both were potentially damaging to Labour and by-election gains (Plaid Cymru in Carmarthen, the Scottish Nationalists in Hamilton) deeply worrying. The party and the unions had been since 1918 resolutely unionist and centralist, deeply committed to the notion of a United Kingdom or union state. Labour believed in British national planning: as a famous socialist Douglas Jay once observed, the 'gentleman from Whitehall knew best'.[19] In time it led to crucial long-term nationalist pressures in Scotland that directly caused the fall of the Callaghan government over the devolution issue, and later still to the Blair government's decision in 1997 to hold referendums for Scotland and Wales, leading to the Scottish parliament and the Welsh assembly being first elected in May 1999.

Sixties socialism, as Crosland admitted in 1974, was basically a failure.[20] It led to disillusion amongst Labour Party workers in the 1970 general election. Prior to the election, things had seemed to be looking up. Roy Jenkins at the Treasury had brought the balance of payments back into surplus; Jim Callaghan at the Home Office had shown the smack of firm government in bringing order back to Northern Ireland, including the use of troops to protect the Catholic minority, a popular decision at the time. Dick Crossman's pension reforms were well received. Opinion polls suggested a Labour win and Wilson went early to the polls. But in fact, on a significantly lower turn-out, Labour's vote went down by nearly a million compared with 1966. There was a 4.7 per cent swing to the Tories, the largest such shift since the war. Labour would have done far less well in terms of seats had not Callaghan deliberately delayed the redistribution of constituencies until after the election for purely party political reasons. A process of long-term decline for Labour was under way; Tony Benn and the SDP attempted their rival, unavailing solution. Perhaps, with the rooted centrality of the trade unions, the party was not an appropriate vehicle for change and reform in the sixties anyway. Wilson, for all his undoubted political skills, was clearly not an appropriate leader for it. Sixties socialism was founded on his personal style: his Yorkshire humour, his pipe and Gannex raincoat. Even though Wilson, unlike Blair, was always clearly leader of a collective team, it all became too personalised and turned sour. Gannex sales collapsed, especially when the maker of that garment went to gaol for fraud. Wilson's leadership methods degenerated into paranoia about plots and 'leaks' and 'moles', and rumours of conspiracies against him by the media or by colleagues. Improbable figures were said to be involved, such as Earl Mountbatten. Wilson had a fairly disastrous array of personal advisers including Marcia Williams as keeper of the gate, and others of his so-called Kitchen Cabinet, and also his personal secret snooper or bloodhound, the sinister George Wigg (ironically himself later prosecuted for kerb-crawling). There was a constant vendetta against journalists on the BBC to no-one's advantage. The BBC had its revenge in 1971 with a partisan documentary by David Dimbleby, *Yesterday's Men*, following which Wilson successfully sued the BBC for libel. In 1974 Wilson returned to office unexpectedly, less healthy and more subdued. He now saw himself as a 'stopper centre-half', rather than the centre forward scoring all the goals, a Stan Cullis not a Tommy Lawton. But Labour's decline was setting in amidst the union troubles of the period. Its internal civil wars, focussing on Tony Benn, who proved to be no Nye Bevan, highlighted the decay of Old Labour. Ultimately, it was the legacy of sixties socialism to make Thatcherism possible.

Under Harold Wilson, a brilliant, personally kindly and popular leader, the high noon of British democratic socialism came and went. At the level of government command strategy, it is difficult to be very positive about its record. Yet there was something else that was important and enduring. In the social turmoil of the permissive, individualistic sixties, with its passions for personal liberation, civil liberty, greater self-management and devolution, and a growing awareness of a multicultural, not-very united, kingdom within a regional Europe, a different vision of a Labour Britain and of a more libertarian socialism began slowly to emerge. Its tone would be social democrat, rather democratic socialist. It would find its roots not only in Keir Hardie's class-based Labour Alliance but in far more ancient traditions of civic democracy and communal republicanism. Roy Hattersley's attempted revisionism in 1987 declared, in effect, that socialism was not fundamentally about equality, planning or modernisation, but about freedom. Earlier, Roy Jenkins had written prophetically that 'one of the main tasks of the democratic left is to widen the area of human choice'. New Labour went part of the way after 1997, with a humanised version of the socio-economic policies of Thatcherism and some redistribution notably through tax credits, alongside constitutional reform, decentralisation of the public services, stress on community and far greater emphasis on social and ethnic diversity within a less united Kingdom. Through such developments as civil partnerships, the personal, gender and sexual liberalisation of the Wilson years has been taken much further, and much social misery and vindictive persecution have thereby disappeared. This survived beyond the crisis of the Iraq invasion to invigorate the early months of Gordon Brown's new government in the summer of 2007. The vision of a statist, centralist, planned New Jerusalem is a world we have lost since the heady days of 1964, probably beyond recall. Bureaucracy like patriotism is not enough. But a democratic, accountable, more sensitive social commonwealth might yet prove to be the unexpected offspring of the troubled epiphany of Harold Wilson.

Chapter 16

The Rise and Fall of Nationalisation in Britain

'Socialised industry in one country' – the key to the rejuvenation of a dying capitalist order in Britain and to the economic advance of the working classes throughout the world. This battle cry in 1933 by the young left-wing publicist and ideologue, A.L. Rowse, encapsulates much of the grandeur and tragedy of modern British socialism.[1] At least as an aspiration, the public ownership of major industries, utilities and natural resources was inseparable from the socialist idea in Britain from the foundation of Keir Hardie's ILP in 1893 down to the Second World War. It reached its heady climax with the Attlee government of 1945–51 when seven major measures of nationalisation went through and 20 per cent of the economy was taken into public hands. Equally, the relative electoral decline and flagging morale of the British left, from the high noon of the late 1940s to the anxious twilight of the early 1980s, were intimately bound up with a diminishing primacy for nationalisation as the coping stone of Labour's programme, and an eroding confidence in either the methods or achievements of public ownership at least as traditionally conceived. No one reacted more violently against these earlier left-wing shibboleths than did A.L. Rowse himself in his later incarnation as academic historian, insatiable author on Shakespeare and the Elizabethan world, and pessimistic patriot who abjured the social enthusiasms of his youth. A brief analysis of the rise and decline of public ownership as a radical panacea, therefore, with a particular emphasis on the subtle subterranean changes that took place in the status and ethic of public ownership in the Attlee years of 1945–51, is central to an understanding of the political and social culture of modern post-imperial Britain that Stephen Koss did so much to illuminate. It takes us close to the heart of the strengths and weaknesses of the British version of socialism in our time.

The dream of nationalisation had been current in left-wing circles since the 1880s.[2] Radicals advocated the public ownership of land, partly in response to the agrarian protests widespread in Ireland (and, to a lesser extent, Wales and Scotland) at the time. The miners became strongly committed to the principle of nationalisation of the coal-mines ('the mines for the miners') after the turn of the century, and it was formally adopted by the Labour Party and the TUC from 1906 onwards. The nationalisation of the railways was also endorsed at Labour annual conferences before the First World War.

But public ownership at this early stage was an aspiration rather than a programme. It was largely the outcome of deteriorating labour relations in major British industries, at a time of serious class conflict and growing economic difficulties, rather than of a carefully worked-out blueprint for social change or technical modernisation. Little interest was taken in the mechanics of nationalisation by trade unionists themselves. The miners of South Wales, for example, were uncertain as to the rival merits of bureaucratic state ownership on the German model or syndicalism or other forms of industrial devolution.[3] A young miner like Aneurin Bevan grew up apparently espousing both these contradictory creeds at the same time. Most of the serious advocates of public ownership before 1914, in fact, were not workers at all. They were mostly middle-class socialists of a theoretical or intellectual bent, ranging from Marxists in the SDF to the more centrist Fabians, such as the Webbs, who pressed the cause of 'municipal socialism' side by side with central state ownership as part of the gospel of gradualism. The First World War, however, gave public ownership a considerable boost. In particular, the unions now came to see it as synonymous with those central controls which had regenerated industrial production in wartime. As a result, the Labour Party constitution of 1918 included the famous clause 3 (d) (later renumbered as Clause Four) which committed the party to the public ownership of the means of production and distribution, with some vague reference to notions of workers' control or joint consultation thrown in as an incidental embellishment.

Despite this apparent priority given to nationalisation, however, its role in Labour's policies in the twenties remained vague in the extreme. Even what it meant was uncertain. R.H. Tawney, one of Labour's sages and moral inspirations, adopted a deliberately eclectic view in *The Acquisitive Society* (1921). While public ownership could mean a central board being set up to manage an industry on national lines (as proposed by Tawney himself for the coal industry in a famous scheme of 1920), he also proclaimed the merits of the co-operative system, the purchase of shares by the state or various forms of 'industrial self-government'.[4] Nationalisation was but one route towards socialism, alongside educational reform, the redistribution of capital, the ethic of equality and much else besides. The objectives of nationalisation were also not clear. Efficiency considerations relating to major industries and services where a high degree of monopoly prevailed; the urge for more harmonious labour relations and greater industrial democracy; demands for higher wages and shorter hours; straight class hatred of private tycoons like coal-owners and railway bosses all played their part. When the Fabians urged nationalisation, they had in mind a functional collectivist model. But when the miners or railwaymen called for the 'the mines for the nation' they implied an industry in some sense owned by themselves and run for their own benefit. 'Nationalisation', avowed Tawney, was 'not an end but a means to an end.'[5] But both the method and the objective were singularly lacking in substance.

If the purpose and method of public ownership were unclear, so, too, were the precise areas of the economy to be taken over. When Labour came to power for the second time in 1929, only coal nationalisation was proposed with any seriousness. Even that was not pursued with much resolution. Earlier plans for the public ownership of the land, power, rail transport or the Bank of England fell by the wayside. Labour's manifesto in 1929 was strong on social reform, the defence of trade unionists, the revival of employment and a generalised compassion that could appeal to idealistic ex-Liberals, or enthusiasts for the League of Nations. But on public ownership, the jewel in the crown for dedicated socialists, Marxist and non-Marxist alike, the party's lack of grasp was painfully clear long before the financial and political debacle of 1931 exposed it for all the world to see. When Labour lost office in 1931, it was still a party committed to social welfare and a generalised defence of the workers' interests rather than to socialism.

The real history – as opposed to the prehistory – of public ownership began in 1931. Between then and 1937, Labour and the TUC for the first time in their history evolved a clear democratic socialist programme, with nationalisation central to it. *Labour's Immediate Programme* (1937) outlined a precise list of industries and services to be taken over by a future Labour government, very much on the lines of that pursued after 1945. The list now included the banks and the land. There were also viable models for nationalisation now in existence. Herbert Morrison's highly influential book, *Socialisation and Transport* (1933), used the precedent of the London Passenger Transport Board to uphold the idea of the autonomous public corporation, free equally from parliamentary interference and internal dictation by the workers.[6] Earlier he had denounced such bodies as 'capitalist soviets'. The TUC in 1932 eventually came to favour much the same kind of approach, although Ernest Bevin for one wanted more emphasis on the principle of having trade union members on the board of directors of the new publicly owned industries.

The main reason, however, why public ownership suddenly became the new conventional wisdom of the British left was that a new school of university-trained democratic socialist economists appropriated public ownership as part of their rationale. Hugh Dalton's *Practical Socialism for Britain* (1935) contained a lengthy treatment of nationalisation, including the Bank of England whose sinister role during the alleged 'bankers' ramp' of 1931 had been widely condemned.[7] On the other hand, a much younger writer like Douglas Jay in *The Socialist Case* placed significantly less emphasis on nationalisation and concentrated largely on Keynesian-style economic management, the planning of investment and the reform of taxation to redistribute wealth. Jay's book contained only four pages referring directly to public ownership, and even they focussed on the relatively narrow issue of the compensation of private stock-holders.[8] The same was broadly true of the various writings of Evan Durbin, another prominent Oxford-trained economist at the time, whose views in part reflected the trade-cycle theories of Hayek at the London School of Economics. He did argue, however, that replacing a private employer with a manager appointed by a democratically elected government would remove the social gulf in industrial relations.

On balance, though, the basis for the new appeal of public ownership in the thirties lay in the fact that it was harnessed to the idea of planning. It became part of the attempt by some gifted young intellectuals to fuse Keynesianism and the mixed economy with the moral imperatives of democratic socialism. Public ownership was for them part – perhaps not the most important part – of an organically conceived machinery of planning to co-ordinate and control production, distribution, investment, pricing policy and (within limits) consumption, and to rectify the inefficiencies, perhaps even more the inhumanities of the market economy. The vogue for planning in the 1930s gave public ownership a new credibility. Even Chamberlain's 'national' government shared in this enthusiasm to some degree, with the state ownership of coal-mining royalties in 1938 and the creation of the British Overseas Airways Corporation in 1939 following on such earlier instances of state enterprise as the Central Electricity Board.

The Second World War, of course, gave the notion of public ownership an enormous boost. The support of the unions became even more committed, especially among miners and railwaymen. The newly launched National Union of Mineworkers in January 1945 included the nationalisation of the mines, on corporatist lines, as their first objective. There was, however, significantly less enthusiasm from steel workers, although they, too, were now formally committed to nationalisation rather to the central planning board for steel they had advocated in the thirties. In addition, a variety of middle-class groups were also strongly pledged to growing state intervention in the economy. The wartime thrust towards centralised planning; the redistribution of industry to restore employment in depressed communities such as Tyneside and South Wales; the wartime control of industries like coal and shipping; the introduction of nationalisation into munitions production with the take-over of Shorts Aircraft by Stafford Cripps in 1943[9] all helped advance the cause of public ownership. Professional, technical, managerial and administrative groups, through such organisational voices as the Town and Country Planning Association and PEP, became strongly dedicated to public rather than private enterprise. They were anxious not to repeat the errors of decontrol and the wanton return to private ownership such as had occurred after the First World War in 1919–21. The wartime surge towards planning and social direction chimed in with Labour's creed of public ownership, while young socialists like Gaitskell, Wilson, Jay and Durbin all served in important posts in the civil service (Jay at the Board of Trade to work on regional development) to push their ideas further. But throughout, as in the writings of the one-time Guild Socialist G.D.H. Cole at this period, the call for nationalisation was advocated primarily in terms of practical objectives of efficiency and modernisation rather the beguiling vision of socialism.

The Labour Party itself reflected this new commitment. There were fears, indeed, that Labour's leading ministers in the Churchill coalition government – Attlee, Morrison, Greenwood and Bevin – were veering towards the watered-down idea of central control rather than state ownership of basic industries. There were angry protests by Labour MPs in the Commons in 1942 when the government's white paper for the mining industry, to which Attlee and Morrison had given their blessing, suggested a form of dual control of the mines during the war years rather than outright public ownership.[10] The wartime emphasis, indeed, appeared to be on compromise schemes for state control rather than uninhibited nationalisation. On the left flank, Harold Laski urged on the 1942 party conference the need to take the banks, land, shipping, transport and civil aviation into public hands, along with sources of energy such as coal, gas and electricity.[11] The main tendency of wartime economic policy, however, was rather to favour a pragmatic extension of the financial controls and physical planning of the wartime emergency, but to leave the capitalist structure intact. The socialist utopia was still far off, while Emanuel Shinwell blandly admitted to the 1943 party conference that major details of Labour's public ownership proposals still had to be worked out. 'We are not yet in a position to submit a final report.'[12]

An important episode took place at the Labour Party's annual conference in December 1944.[13] It was typical of the way in which political activism at the grass roots continued to mount between 1940 and

1945. When the Labour Party national executive, with Noel-Baker and Shinwell as their spokesmen, tried to push a generalised motion on behalf of a more controlled and integrated economic policy, an amendment from the Reading Labour Party, moved by Ian Mikardo, and strongly endorsed by James Callaghan, prospective candidate for Cardiff South, was carried without a vote. This committed Labour unambiguously to public ownership. Indeed, the amendment included iron and steel as well, which the National Executive (NEC) had desperately tried to omit. The Executive had to give way. Afterwards, Morrison put a friendly hand on Mikardo's shoulder, 'That was a good speech you made – but you do realise, don't you, that you've lost us the general election.'[14] In April 1945, despite strong opposition from Herbert Morrison, the NEC drafted a strong, precise policy of nationalisation, including iron and steel, for its forthcoming election manifesto.[15]

Labour, therefore, for the first – and only – time in its history went before the electors in July 1945 with the nationalisation of major industries and utilities as a major objective. On the other hand, it is highly significant what the list did not include. Some of the proposals outlined in *For Socialism and Peace* in 1934 were omitted, notably the land (where Labour, following the wartime Uthwatt and Scott reports, now preferred an emphasis on town and country planning), the joint-stock banks and cotton-spinning. Labour showed though much reluctance in moving into manufacturing industry or in dealing with the private banks or other financial institutions. From the start, it had a precise, but limited and finite programme. It was committed to working out the old agenda of the thirties, rather than looking forward to new fields for state ownership.

Judged from an international perspective, Labour's schemes down to 1945 remained highly distinctive. The programme and the models for nationalisation followed, in the main, domestic ideas such as those of the Fabians or native prototypes such as the public corporation enshrined in the LPTB in 1933 or BOAC in 1939. It was a pragmatic, national approach, heavily influenced by theories of planning derived from the 1930s and reinforced by the experience of a victorious war in which Britain, almost alone amongst the countries of Western Europe, was not occupied by German troops. Nationalisation in a curious way was thus associated with a kind of patriotism, with the social unity newly created by a people's war.

Within this context, European ideas of workers' control had little influence on the British Labour movement which, from Ernest Bevin downwards, was committed to traditional policies of collective bargaining in which the unions maintained their historic role of representing the workers. French-style 'syndicalism' of pre-1914 days, which had found some echoes in the Welsh mining valleys and in Clydeside in Scotland amongst engineering and shipyard workers, faded from the scene in the 1920s. Nor did Italian-style corporatism have an influence in Britain (apart from a few neo-fascist fringes such as in Plaid Cymru). The only continental country that had much impact at all on Labour's planning, indeed, was one more geographically more isolated – Sweden, a potentially socialist state with a Social Democratic government from 1934. A book edited by Margaret Cole and Charles Smith for the New Fabian Research Bureau in 1938 sang the praises of Swedish social democracy. The authors noted that in Sweden, alone in Europe apart from the Soviet Union, the socialised sector was already extensive. It included the Post Office, most railways, most electric power, forests, the central bank, the Riksbank, air transport, radio, tobacco, liquor and even some iron-ore mining. Even so, the main appeal for young socialists, such as Hugh Gaitskell, lay rather in its inter-weaving of exchange rate policy, deficit budgeting and a public works programme as part of its 'middle way'.[16] In any case, apart from the marginal case of Sweden, the idea of nationalisation in Britain was largely conceived in insular terms. Much of its later history can be explained by reference to this fundamental, historic fact.

The political situation in July 1945 determining the history of nationalisation in Britain was a most remarkable one. Labour won the general election with a huge landslide majority, winning 394 seats as against the Conservatives' 210. Nationalisation, therefore, was the product of a massive political revolution in which the Labour government could carry all before it. Apart from the great enthusiasm within the Labour Party and amongst trade unionists such as the miners and transport workers, the programme of public ownership carried out in 1945–7 seemed to win broad agreement across the political spectrum. The Conservatives did not resist nationalisation measures to any great extent until they began to oppose the 1947 Transport Act, mainly over road haulage. After all, in industries like gas, electricity and civil aviation there was already a high degree of public intervention, national or municipal. In addition, coal and the railways were industries with bad records of modernisation and industrial relations during the decades of private ownership. Many government inquiries, such as the McGowan report on electricity or the Heyworth report for gas, called for public control on technical, efficiency grounds. The civil service, notably the planners like James Meade in the Economic Section of the Cabinet, a stronghold of Keynesianism, also showed much initial enthusiasm for nationalisation while the press and public seemed more than prepared to acquiesce. A historic measure like the nationalisation of the coal mines on 1 January 1947 aroused passionate rejoicing in mining communities from Lanarkshire to Kent.

The programme of public ownership in the 1945–7 sessions, as has been seen, went through with relatively little controversy. One feature that is apparent throughout is the comparatively moderate nature of many of the changes adopted. In the case of the Bank of England, only a modest reform was affected. No public control of capital movements or the flow of investment was attempted, and the governor of the Bank continued to behave in much the same fashion as he had prior to nationalisation (Lord Cromer's hostile view towards devaluing sterling added much to the frustration felt by Harold Wilson in 1964 when confronted with a balance of payments crisis at the start of his new government). In some industries there was already a high degree of municipal ownership (in electricity, and in the later case of gas). The same applied, it might be said, to the more centralising aspects of Aneurin Bevan's NHS, which nationalised all the hospitals.[17] There was widespread bipartisan agreement on the principle of public ownership in the cases of civil aviation, cable and wireless and the electricity supply and distribution industry. In addition, there were remarkably generous scales of compensation paid to private stock-holders, especially in the case of the railways, in accordance with pre-war decisions that there would be no overt confiscation of assets.[18]

In every case, too, the Morrisonian pattern of the public board was broadly adopted, within each instance a modicum of workers' or trade union representation amongst the directors. The public board was the sacrosanct model at this time, with old socialist ideologues like Harold Laski and G.D.H. Cole giving it their blessing. Cole's former enthusiasm for 'Guild Socialism' was now a thing of the distant past. This commitment to the public board method was strongly endorsed in each case by the Labour Cabinet's Socialisation of Industry Committee, chaired by Morrison, throughout the 1945–8 period.[19] The public board approach seemed to follow naturally from the wartime experiments in public planning and full employment policy. There was no trade union enthusiasm at all for workers' partnership, let alone workers' control. The giants of the TUC, men like Arthur Deakin of the Transport Workers or Will Lawther of the Miners, felt, like all trade union leaders before them, that their role would be fundamentally compromised if union leaders turned into bosses. If trade unionists became members of boards of nationalised industry, as when Walter Citrine became chairman of the Electricity supply industry, or when Ebby Edwards of the NUM became a director of the National Coal Board, they had to resign their trade union posts, to avoid any possible conflict of interests or confusion of identity. In Britain, unlike western Germany or Austria for instance, a broadly adversarial view of the relation between workers and capitalist employers continued to predominate, a legacy of the pattern of industrial relations as it had evolved since the Victorian era.

However, the other point to be made about nationalisation in Britain in 1945–7 is that the idea of consensus and inter-party agreement can be exaggerated. The post-war schemes for coal and transport went distinctly beyond the wartime proposals for planning and control. In some cases, notably coal, the most radical option available was taken up. But the results were not always happy. In the case of coal, the highly centralised system of management and of industrial relations led to many problems, and to the resignation of Sir Charles Reid as director in May 1948.[20] Emanuel Shinwell, minister of fuel and power in 1945–7, was a frequent, caustic critic of the lack of care and attention paid to the details of nationalisation and of the over-centralisation, lack of industrial democracy and adequate machinery of consultation within the coal industry.[21] He later complained that, when he set about nationalising coal in 1945, all he could find for guidance in the Labour Party's files was a pre-war document by James Griffiths written in Welsh! It might be added, though, that since Shinwell himself had served at the Mines Ministry in 1924 and 1929 and had been chairman of Labour's Reconstruction Committee in the latter stages of the Second World War, he was foremost among the guilty men responsible for this neglect. In the event, the achievement of the great prize of nationalisation in a major industry like coal mining was the product of much last-minute hustling and muddle, rather than of purposive long-term planning. Many of the future problems of the British coal industry, including many of the background factors in the bitter miners' national strike of March 1984–March 1985, can be related to the unsatisfactory nature of the nationalisation structure adopted back in 1947.[22] In many ways, the French approach to nationalisation in 1944–7, more varied in technique and perhaps more flexibly adapted to the needs of particular industries and utilities, survived the test of time and economic hammer-blows rather better.

As has been noted, coal was the greatest emotional triumph for British nationalisation. Vesting Day on 1 January 1947 was hailed by mining villages throughout the land and aroused much enthusiasm amongst workers in France and other continental countries. 'Now the mines belong to the people.' Yet it was also coal that became associated with the first serious doubts about nationalisation as a policy. The advent of nationalisation coincided with a terribly cold winter of prolonged freezing weather, from January to March 1947. This led to immense coal shortages, a huge cutback in energy supplies and industrial production and much temporary unemployment. It was perhaps unfair to blame all these problems on the newly nationalised industry: part of the trouble lay in transport difficulties rather than in coal production. But it did draw attention to manpower shortages and the low level of productivity in the coal industry.[23] From the fuel crisis of early 1947, British nationalisation was partially tainted with the stigma of failure. The planners had simply failed to plan. Shinwell, the minister of Fuel and Power, who had blithely discounted fears about coal shortages in 1946, as late as November of that year, was one of the victims. He was finally removed from the Cabinet altogether in October 1947, to be replaced by his enemy, the bourgeois figure of Hugh Gaitskell.

Apart from the disaster of coal, in Britain, as in France, 1947 saw a growing mood of *anti-étatisme*, as the emotion of wartime unity gradually evaporated. After a glorious period in which nationalisation, the ethic of equality, planning and the commonweal had swept all before them, there was mounting public discontent with controls, bureaucracy and the continuing austerity and restriction on personal liberty in the post-war period. To the general public, coal and railways, two declining industries with long-term structural problems, were symptomatic of a wider decay in the socialist ideal.

Added to this psychological mood, Britain, like other Western countries, was gravely afflicted by the economic crises of 1947. In the case Britain, there was a mounting balance of payments crisis and a huge outflow of funds on the capital as well as the current account, culminating in the disaster of convertibility of sterling in July–August 1947. The American loan of 1945, supposed to help Britain until 1951, would, at the present rate of loss, be completely used up by the end of 1947. Hence Marshall Aid, OEEC and the European recovery programme, as a salvage operation mounted in dire necessity. In itself, Marshall Aid did not directly influence the Labour government's will to nationalise, which was shaped by internal party priorities and assumptions. Paul Hoffman of the US European Recovery Program did voice concern with British steel nationalisation in 1948,[24] but this played no part in determining British policy. Marshall Aid to Britain, which came through in vast quantities down to the end of 1950, went partly to maintaining food supplies, partly to building up the infrastructure of British industry and services, public and private. However, the nature and volume of US assistance helped confirm a reluctance to tamper with the character of British industry at a time of acute financial crisis, as grave as 1931. It encouraged widely expressed doubts about the lack of confidence in socialism in terms of economic achievement and productive effect, as opposed to moral ideals of social equality or human justice.

All these doubts surfaced in full in the great Cabinet debates about the nationalisation of iron and steel in the spring and summer of 1947.

No issue showed more clearly the implicit limits to Labour's commitment to nationalisation as a concept and an ideal. The case of iron and steel was significantly different from that of industries and services previously nationalised. In the first place, steel would take British nationalisation into manufacturing industry, including engineering and aircraft production. This was a radical new departure, and one viewed with a lack of enthusiasm by most members of the government. Secondly, the steel industry was not easy to criticise on grounds of poor productive performance. It had done very well during the war, while the Iron and Steel Control Board, a kind of half-way house for nationalisation set up in 1946, performed very efficiently with rapidly rising steel production in 1946–7 and major new steel works like the Steel Company of Wales plant near Port Talbot in South Wales coming into operation. The chairman of the Control Board, Sir Andrew Duncan of Steel House, was praised by Labour's Chancellor of the Exchequer Hugh Dalton as a 'great executive' who was half a socialist himself.[25] Thirdly, it was well known that steel workers were less zealous for nationalisation than were the miners or railway workers. The history of labour relations in the steel industry in the 1930s had been good, despite bitter memories of the closure of Jarrow and the hunger march of 1936. There was not the legacy of conflict that had plagued coal mining for 40 years past. Lincoln Evans, president of the Iron and Steel Confederation, the main trade union, made it very plain that he personally did not want nationalisation at all.[26]

Finally, and crucially important, key figures in the government, including Attlee and Morrison, did not favour steel nationalisation. Morrison had opposed its being inserted in the party manifesto at all in 1945. It was also highly significant that steel was postponed until almost all the other proposed nationalisation measures had been passed before it was considered ripe for legislative action. Even a figure like Emanuel Shinwell was reluctant about steel nationalisation since the steel industry was the major customer for the coal and coke supplies which concerned him as minister of fuel and power. Ernest Bevin himself, the foreign secretary and the most powerful living trade unionist, was also less than wholly committed by now.

Bitter arguments over iron and steel preoccupied the Labour Cabinet in many private sessions between April and August 1947.[27] The records of these meetings are fully available in the National Archives at Kew, with the opinions of individual ministers clearly attributed. In the end, the steel industry was overshadowed by the terrible financial crisis of the convertibility of sterling in the summer of 1947, which increased still further the doubts about the merits of introducing so controversial a measure at a time of great economic emergency. Morrison was hostile to nationalisation throughout, and he proposed to the Cabinet a compromise semi-control scheme (Cabinet Paper [47] 1212) which fell far short of nationalisation. He was supported by other ministers, both in the Cabinet and outside. Among them was John Wilmot, the minister of Supply who had responsibility for steel nationalisation, and who proved strangely reluctant to challenge the steel barons. When Wilmot was removed from office in October 1947, he was to be succeeded by George Strauss, a man with a strong record as a man of the left (he had been expelled, with Cripps and Bevan, from the parliamentary Labour Party in 1939 for advocating a Popular Front). Yet he, too, was to prove a somewhat timid nationaliser in practice.[28] After much anguished ministerial debate, gas nationalisation was given priority for the 1948 sessions, with iron and steel postponed to the 1948–9 session, to allow for a measure to be introduced to reduce the delaying powers of the House of Lords over legislation passed through the House of Commons from two years to one.[29] All this meant that iron and steel nationalisation might not now pass through parliament before another general election.

The entire ministerial debate showed clear and unmistakable doubts within the Cabinet, to the dismay of the Labour left in parliament and in the country. Morrison obviously did not want steel nationalisation at all, even though, ironically enough, he was urging this very thing, along with Bevin, for the steel industry of the British-occupied zone in western Germany at the same period. Evidently he felt more confidence in the British steel owners than he did in the heirs of Krupp, Stinnes and Thyssen.[30] Attlee also showed much uncertainty, and his general attitude led to an overt challenge to his leadership, led by Cripps, in September 1947, which the prime minister survived with difficulty. One civil servant advised Attlee in August 1947 that seven ministers were against nationalisation, and another eight wanted a postponement, while only three (Bevan, Tomlinson, Strachey) wanted the immediate nationalisation of steel.[31] But there were still some powerful voices on behalf of steel nationalisation, too. Cripps, the president of the Board of Trade, retained his old commitment as a man of the left. So, more forcibly, did Hugh Dalton, the chancellor of the exchequer. Aneurin Bevan, minister of Health, who sat for a steel constituency in Ebbw Vale, was vehement on behalf of steel nationalisation throughout. Yet it was noticeable that much of the argument on behalf of it was ideological rather than empirical. With Bevan, as with the left-wing journals *New Statesman* and *Tribune* (the latter edited jointly by Bevan's wife, Jennie Lee), it was less a case of the technical, economic merits of nationalising the steel industry. Rather, steel had become a touchstone of the government's socialist intentions, a beacon of hope in a hostile capitalist world.[32] It was also tacitly assumed, even by Bevan, that steel would in any case be the last measure of nationalisation, at least for some considerable time. There would be no 'second wave' as there was in France over air and maritime transport in 1947 or in Austria with the electricity proposal of 1947. British nationalisation was in retreat, and it would never have the same glamour again.

From the autumn of 1947 the retreat of nationalisation, from the gates of Moscow as it were, was clearly underway. Gas nationalisation went through in 1948, with Gaitskell in charge, while steel nationalisation eventually was passed through the House of Lords in December 1949. It was noticeable, though, that the form of public ownership adopted meant no remodelling of the structure of the 107 firms to be taken over by the state.[33] This meant that it could very easily be denationalised by a future Conservative government – as was to happen in 1954.

The retreat from nationalisation is in many ways easy to understand, if not, perhaps, to justify. Labour's main theoreticians had long implied that nationalisation would be limited in scope. Now that the original 1945 list had been achieved, there was no cause to advance much further. In his book, *The Politics of Democratic Socialism* (1940), Evan Durbin had emphasised, as did many other Labour authors, the need to limit growth of nationalisation on grounds of personal freedom. He always stressed the priority of a pluralist society and a mixed economy in libertarian terms.[34] Further to the left, G.D.H. Cole, writing on *The Socialisation Programme* in 1948, assumed that the bulk of industry and finance would remain in private hands, though it would be a private enterprise more humane and acting more responsibly – and perhaps purified by antimonopoly policies by the Board of Trade. Cole also suggested trying a variety of techniques in pushing through nationalisation, instead of the uniform public board model – the co-operative method and the purchase of equity shares by the state were other measures that he proposed as alternatives. A similar view was to be taken by Aneurin Bevan in 1952 when he upheld the mixed economy and condemned excessive nationalisation.[35] A much younger Oxford economist like Anthony Crosland was to stress, following the American, James Burnham, in his *Managerial Revolution,* the growing divorce between ownership and management in industry. This in effect diminished the unique case for nationalisation and made it seem increasingly irrelevant.[36]

On the National Executive of the Labour Party, discussions on industrial policy from November 1947 onwards showed a clear halt to the drive towards further public ownership. Herbert Morrison, the chairman of the party Policy Committee and the key link between the Cabinet and the party machine, criticised the policy document *Socialism and Private Enterprise* as too doctrinaire. 'We definitely do not want to nationalise the small man – the shop around the corner', Morrison declared, with the approval of most of his fellow executive members.[37] The public arguments about Labour's plans, in its Transport Bill in 1947, to nationalise smaller private road haulage operators, holding C licences (which covered distances of less than 40 miles), had brought the government into bad odour and made it seem illiberal.[38] As has been seen, Emanuel Shinwell, one of the more left-wing members of the government, had made public his doubts about the nature and pace of nationalisation to date. Even Aneurin Bevan, the most committed socialist in the Cabinet, admitted the need to improve on the productive performance of industries and services already nationalised, and to improve on their public relations side.[39] Bevan also well knew that the record of labour relations in the newly nationalised industries was already a somewhat mixed one. In the coal industry, recent damaging strikes in the pits around Grimethorpe in South Yorkshire and some evidence of 'go-slow' working in his own South Wales collieries showed no dramatic improvement in the industrial climate compared with the days of private ownership.

The retreat from nationalisation was further reinforced by the ascendancy in the government of Sir Stafford Cripps, who became chancellor of the exchequer in November 1947 and remained in that key post until October 1950. This may seem strange, since Cripps enjoyed a long-established status as an ideologue of the left and had been expelled from the parliamentary party for his left-wing views in 1939. But he had moved to a far more centrist position during the war years, while his period at the Board of Trade in 1945–7 (when, for instance, he resisted any attempt to nationalise the cotton-spinning industry in Lancashire) had accentuated this tendency. Cripps was, above all, anxious to boost exports, to make Britain financially self-sufficient, and to avoid any further financial crisis of the kind that had almost brought the government down during the convertibility crisis of August 1947. This meant partnership with private industry, and the use of indicative planning within a mixed economy through Sir Edwin Plowden and the newly formed Economic Planning Board, guided by the Economic Committee and Production Committee of the Cabinet, both recent creations also. Cripps had the crucial support now of American Marshall Aid, reinforced by the Intra-European Payments Agreement through which Britain's position as a creditor nation with other western European nations was financed. The objective of making Britain self-sufficient commercially and industrially – an objective which showed encouraging signs of being realised when Britain's balance of payments moved back into surplus by the end of 1948 – was not compatible with domestic political controversy over nationalisation.

As the general election of 1950 approached, Labour's attitude towards nationalisation was hesitant and piecemeal. While the remaining stages of steel nationalisation were forced through by the end of 1949, Labour otherwise went to the electors with a bizarre mixture – or 'shopping list' – of separate proposals. Cement, water supply, meat wholesaling and sugar refining were all added to the list at random, whereas brick-making and the chemical industry were turned down as candidates for public ownership.[40] It all had a harmful effect on Labour's prospects, especially the curious proposal to nationalise the sugar refining enterprise of Tate and Lyle, an admitted monopoly. This threat brought the cartoon figure of 'Mr. Cube' on to every packet of sugar on the breakfast table, a formidable domestic weapon against nationalisation in every household.

More significant was the debate on the party national executive in 1949 about the nationalisation of industrial assurance, as a complement to the 1946 National Insurance Act, which implemented the schemes of the Beveridge Report for social security. Nationalisation of private insurance companies, with their huge funds, seemed, even to a moderate like James Griffiths, a necessary part of creating the welfare state.[41] He was strongly backed by Aneurin Bevan, the minister of Health. But this plan was opposed by Morrison, many trade unionists and also by Cripps, aware of the crucial role of private insurance in boosting Britain's 'invisible exports' through its operations in the United States and many other countries.[42] The Co-operative Society, which had its own insurance activities on an extensive scale, also was strongly hostile.[43] In the end, a modified form of 'mutualisation', or control by the policy-holders, was placed on the party manifesto for 1950. It did Labour no electoral good at all. It meant that every private insurance agent in the land was a potential anti-Labour propagandist from now on. On balance, the 'shopping list' of nationalisation measures was probably a straight vote-loser. Nationalisation played no significant part in the 1951 session of parliament, after Labour's narrow return to power with its majority reduced to six only. Only the final, weary stages of putting the iron and steel nationalisation into effect survived from former controversies. In the 1951 election campaign, Labour made no positive commitment to nationalisation at all, other than pledging itself vaguely to taking over unnamed industries that might in future be 'failing the nation'. Calls from the left, such as from Ian Mikardo, later a leading 'Bevanite', for the nationalisation of aircraft production, machine tools or parts of the car industry, somewhat on the French model, were ignored.[44] For the aircraft industry, ministers like Morrison argued that technical advance required freedom from state control; instead, Morrison proclaimed the need for something called 'Competitive Public Enterprise' which might revitalise private enterprise through the spirit of competition.[45] On the other side in 1951, the Conservatives and their business allies in the organisation 'Aims of Industry' attacked nationalisation for bureaucracy and controls, for inefficiency and waste. In six years, therefore, Labour's priorities had totally changed. Nationalisation, once a great asset and inspiration for the party, had become something of an electoral liability – or even worse, a plain irrelevance.

The long-term success or failure of the nationalisation measures in Britain from 1945 to 1951 raise far wider issues. Certainly, many of the criticisms of the nationalised industries were unfair. For instance, the financial losses incurred by the coal industry or the railways arose from the policy of keeping down prices and fares as part of an anti-inflation programme. These industries could easily have made a large profit if they had been allowed the same freedom to operate enjoyed by private enterprise, and if nationalised enterprises had not been viewed as social services. For all the difficulties in some aspects of labour relations, it could hardly be denied that, at least down to the early 1970s, the relationship between management and the workforce, in the coal industry for instance, showed a dramatic improvement by comparison with the class confrontations of the past.

In fact, there was very little denationalisation by the subsequent Conservative governments of 1951–64. Only road haulage and steel were denationalised in the early 1950s; the rest of Labour's work was broadly left alone. The publicly owned industries did well in the economic expansion and consumer affluence enjoyed in Britain in the 1950s and 1960s. Not until the mid-1960s did they come under attack as the British economy showed signs of slowing down, and government was forced to act increasingly in determining the pricing and investment policies of state enterprises. The public sector was also accused of fuelling the wage inflation that characterised Britain during the 1960s and early 1970s. When state ownership again emerged as an issue after 1974, after the election of another Labour government, first led by Wilson, then by Callaghan, the old cause was advocated in terms of trying to bail out failing enterprises, such as Rolls Royce, British Leyland, ship building or the various clients of the National Enterprise Board, rather than the bold expansion and forward-looking planning dreamed of in the heady days of 1945. In practice, the policies of the 1970s made the public image of nationalisation, popularly linked with a high incidence of strikes in the public sector, rather worse. Labour's leaders tried to play it down in the 1979 general election. The 'privatisation' policy of the Thatcher government launched after 1983, with overt rejection of the post-1945 consensus and zeal to roll back the frontiers of the state took nationalisation back into the domain of public controversy. It had been a central feature of the programme of the hard left between 1979 and 1983. Tony Benn's *Arguments for Socialism* gave it a key role, albeit one linked with greater industrial democracy, links to the consumer and overall planning and economic integration. He looked forward to its being extended into 'profitable manufacturing industry'.[46] It was the left's ultimate Alamo. The notorious 'longest suicide note', the 1983 Labour election manifesto, killed it off for good. Nationalisation, the great cry of the British left for over half a century, simply faded away.

One major consideration is how the British nationalisation programme relates to the experience in Western Europe generally after the Second World War. On balance, the impact of direct influence from public ownership experiments in France, Austria or elsewhere after 1945 (or after 1936 in France) seems relatively small. British nationalisation, like so much else of British history in the twentieth century, appears now like an exercise in splendid isolationism. There was some direct involvement with nationalisation on the European continent after 1945. For instance, as has been seen, proposals for British coal or steel nationalisation to some degree became caught up in plans to nationalise the coal and steel industries of the Ruhr in the British-occupied zone in western Germany at the same period. But little direct interest was shown by British governments in continental experiences from 1945 onwards; I was told by Sir Robert Hall that even the modified *dirigisme* of the Monnet Plan in France from 1947 excited relatively little interest in either the Cabinet or the economic planning sections of the civil service, at least at this period. The British government showed precious little enthusiasm for the economic policies of post-war French governments, even left-wing ones and refused to accept the Monnet plan as the basis for the European Recovery Program.

When pressure built up in 1948–9 for a more integrated approach towards European economic co-operation, a clear lack of any community outlook showed itself between British socialists, and their French, Belgian and Dutch comrades. The British idea of 'Western union' and the French concept of 'European unity' were fundamentally different.[47] While Britain and Bevin led the way in the functional arrangements of OEEC and later the European Payments Union, the 1950 Schuman plan for an integrated coal and steel industrial system in Western Europe was strongly rebuffed by the Labour Cabinet and the unions, even though Cripps and some right-wing figures like Gaitskell and Kenneth Younger showed some sympathy. As Schuman and the French government no doubt expected in May 1950, Britain's socialist movement continued to emphasise its geographical and ideological detachment from the continent and to proclaim its wider links with the Commonwealth and the United States instead.[48] In a curious way, public ownership, and the idea of socialist planning that it was still felt to embody, was a part of that proud detachment.

British nationalisation under Labour, then, was very British, very insular – perhaps, indeed, very English, since ideas once current in South Wales for forms of syndicalism or theories of workers' control emanating from the shop stewards' movement in Clydeside in Scotland were firmly set aside. The whole debate about nationalisation in 1945–51 (as in 1931–45) was largely conducted in domestic terms. After 1945, British industrial authority and leadership in a war-ravaged Western Europe was taken for granted. The impact of worldwide commercial or monetary pressures upon British industry, whether nationalised or in private hands, was seldom adequately considered by Attlee and his colleagues. Such industries and utilities as were nationalised were largely allowed to function on a basis of managerial autonomy rather than as part of an integrated, planned socialist economy. By 1951, even the essentially shorter-term forms of planning adopted after the war were visibly in retreat, as the public mood rebelled against continuing wartime controls. Despite the massive programme of nationalisation, therefore, the British economy and society changed less profoundly than did those of France, West Germany or other continental countries in the post-war years. Nationalisation was debated and implemented in an atmosphere of domestic conservatism and complacency. For this, Britain in the 1980s continued to pay a heavy cost.

Even in 1985, there were centrist trade union leaders such as Alan Tuffin of the Union of Communication Workers who still called, not only for the renationalisation of British Telecom, Britoil and Enterprise Oil by a future Labour government but for nationalisation to be restored as 'the main vehicle for investment and jobs. Labour's economic programme should be promoted so as to highlight this prominence'. Such voices, however, were relatively rare even on the far left. Labour's new leadership in the Kinnock-Hattersley era from 1983 onwards, visibly gave public ownership an infinitely more humble role in future Labour programmes. Enterprise boards run by metropolitan local authorities were one alternative mooted. Meanwhile, the columns of *Marxism Today* contained suggestions that the far left, or some of it, went along with a view that rejected bureaucratic, paternalistic state ownership, especially as personified in the rigid and unappealing figure of Ian MacGregor of the NCB as any kind of route to socialism.[49] The general drift of Labour's policy pronouncements if only through its silences was only to confirm the diminished confidence in public ownership as a panacea, that had been detectable in Labour's ranks from the time of the pivotal debates over steel in 1947 onwards. Both Kinnock and Hattersley in early 1986 affirmed that there would be no further nationalisation by a future Labour government, and that even renationalising concerns 'privatised' by the Tories would not be a major priority. Hattersley wrote in 1987 that 'state monopolies are not, and in themselves cannot be, the path to socialism'.[50] Party leaders were anxious to reassure small investors in British Telecom shares that they would be amply compensated. Labour's Policy Committee in 1986 endorsed a feeble-sounding 'social ownership', in place of the Morrisonian model after 1945 which was deemed to be 'unresponsive' and 'monolithic'.

The regime of New Labour under Tony Blair from 1997 to 2007 completely turned its back on any idea of nationalisation. Indeed, the very idea was held to be a fundamental symbol of the divide between itself and the Old Labour of the past. The Bank of England, nationalised in 1946, was given independence from outside control, notably in the setting of interest rates. Labour's economic programme was hailed now precisely because of its emphasis on decontrol, deregulation and a flexible labour market. The Labour government battled strongly for these propositions against other countries within the European Union and secured a number of 'opt-outs' intended to protect them. In fact, the years of New Labour, down to the time Gordon Brown became prime minister in June 2007, appeared to be a time of serene and steady growth, in marked contrast to the economic crises that had afflicted every previous Labour government going back to Ramsay MacDonald in 1924. It also saw the domination of financial services and the market over the British economy, while the manufacturing industries, variously nationalised and privatised in the past, went into serious decline. Then in 2007–8, the economic climate changed alarmingly, with the 'credit crunch' resulting from failures in the US sub-prime banking system and a sharp rise in the costs of oil and foodstuffs. In these circumstances, the old panacea of nationalisation, almost totally forgotten since the years of the Callaghan government and the 'social contract' with the trade unions in 1976–7, when shipbuilding and British aerospace were nationalised, suddenly reappeared from the shadows.

The collapse of the ill-managed Northern Rock bank in October–November 2007 caused a huge crisis of confidence and led to its eventually being taken into public ownership with Bank of England guarantees for savers and mortgage-holders. Northern Rock shares duly recovered. However in the late summer of 2008, further turmoil in the American banking system (which led to public take-over there of the private banking giant Lehman Brothers and the insurance colossus AIG) led to further catastrophes in the British retail banking system. A second nationalisation now took place, this time of the £150 billion assets of the demutualised Bradford and Bingley building society, with its savings management handed over to a Spanish bank, Santander. In the first week of October, the Bank of England, by lending £100 billion to banks under a special liquidity scheme, and a further £100 billion because banks would no longer lend to each other, in effect nationalised the money markets, an astonishing change of stance by the Bank's governor, Mervyn King. The following March the government intervened to take a controlling share of the newly merged Lloyds-Halifax Bank of Scotland, whose merger had been forced through under prime ministerial pressure when the credit crunch became desperate the previous autumn. In the United States, President Obama's similar intervention in the banking system seemed almost a response to nationalisation measures the other side of the Atlantic.

However, what was most striking about these and the Northern Rock cases was the hesitation and reluctance with which a Labour government, and a Labour chancellor, Alastair Darling, approached the policy of further nationalisation. Much emphasis was placed on these being temporary, emergency rescue packages until the private banking sector supposedly recovered its confidence. Labour's approach now, in industry, finance and the social services, was to place emphasis on decentralisation, localism and consumer choice. Nationalisation had become the last worst option, even when free-market capitalism had so manifestly collapsed. No longer did it point the way ahead to a New Jerusalem. It seemed improbable that any future Labour manifesto would seek to revive it. There was, however, one poignant echo of the past. In June 2008 a leading government minister, arguing in the Lords for a partial privatisation (up to 49 per cent) of the Post Office, referred almost patronisingly to the programme of the Attlee government. It sounded as though he was recalling some lost world unintelligible now. This was Peter Mandelson, New Labour personified, grandson of Herbert Morrison, but in no other sense his heir. It gave a new twist to Morrison's own aphorism that socialism was what a Labour government did.

Precisely why public ownership should so have lost esteem – in contrast, say, with others of Labour priorities such as the idea of a welfare state – is open to debate. Opponents of the very concept of governmental interference in the management of industry, such as the Unservile State group, could argue that the history of nationalisation since 1945 merely confirmed the inherent evils of monopoly, whether public or private, as inevitably tending to inefficiency and the raising of costs for the consumer. But there were, naturally, very few in the Labour movement who would accept this case. After all, even Crosland's *Future of Socialism* (1956), while focussing on other themes such as the promotion of equality, still gave nationalisation a significant role. Indeed, the total failure of Hugh Gaitskell to secure the elimination of Clause Four from Labour's constitution in 1959 was testimony to the enduring mystique of public ownership as a principle and source of inspiration to party activists.[51] No subsequent Labour leader dared to risk raising the issue until Tony Blair secured an overwhelming majority in favour of abolishing Clause Four in 1995, in the first flush of winning the leadership. Perhaps it is indeed the failure of public ownership to command more support that is most and puzzling, in view of the inability of private enterprise (covering over 80 per cent of the economy) to apply itself at all effectively in coping with Britain's industrial and commercial decline between 1951 and 1985. It is not obviously faith in capitalism and the market economy – especially in its abrasive Thatcherite form – that has eroded the faith of the British centre and left in the traditional nostrum of public ownership.

The explanation may lie in something more deeply rooted in the British psyche in the later twentieth century. Public ownership, we have seen, was conceived in a spirit of insularity, even of national self-confidence. Its model, going back from Gaitskell and Durbin in the 1930s, through the Webbs to Chadwick and Bentham, was that of the detached, unemotional public servant, the man in the grey flannel suit altruistically pursuing the path of duty, running economic and social institutions in a way that would transcend sectionalism and invest them with a kind of Platonic purity. It was a domestic, progressive version of the model of colonial rule offered to the young Attlee at Haileybury and to the Wykehamists who joined his administration after 1945,[52] a form of social imperialism with the common touch, not so much Kiplingesque as Rudyard Hardie. Amongst the thirties generation of socialists, Gaitskell was the son of an Indian civil servant whose brother developed irrigation schemes in the cotton fields of the Sudan; Jay's brother served with distinction on the Yangtse; Durbin was the son of a Baptist minister who had been a missionary in Ceylon. If the Victorian Empire (much admired by Bevin, Morrison and other ministers in 1945–51) had been Joseph Chamberlain's Birmingham writ large, the National Coal Board, British Rail, BOAC and even the BBC were Chamberlain's empire writ small, with their chairmen (often retired industrialists or even generals) cast as the Cromer or Lugard *de nos jours*. After 1945, however, the cocoon of confident insularity within which the debate over nationalisation took place soon dissolved. The underlying structural weakness and imbalance of the British economy, whatever its pattern of ownership, became embarrassingly plain to see. At home and abroad, the state lost much of its moral authority; equally the mystique of the detached public servant, the patrician symbol of the governing elite, deferentially obeyed by native and workers alike, became outdated, even discredited. The decline of public ownership in Britain thus mirrored – and partly grew out of – the downfall of Empire overseas. The attendant economic, financial and commercial disintegration of that Empire reinforced the decay at home. In the end, internal colonialism took the same path to perdition as did its external counterpart. It had become one with Nineveh and Tyre, paradise mislaid rather than lost, and was likely to remain so.

Chapter 17

Was Britain Dying?

The Wilson–Callaghan era of 1974–9 is etched gloomily in the public memory – sleaze under Wilson, strikes under Callaghan. Much was made of this perception by Margaret Thatcher later on, when she drew a powerful contrast between her own liberation of Britain from the shackles of post-war socialist corporatism and the cultural despair of the Winter of Discontent. 'Do you remember the Labour Britain of 1979? It was a Britain in which union leaders held their members and our country to ransom...the sick man of Europe.'[1] It was the natural role of the Conservatives to keep these folk memories warm. Perceptions of the Wilson years of 1974–6 were largely of a failure of style – the paranoid mood of the Kitchen Cabinet, the humiliating finale of the Lloyd George-style final honours list of 1976 on the famous lavender-blue notepaper of which volumes of reminiscence by Joe Haines and Bernard Donoughue as late as 2003 faithfully reminded the public. Perceptions of the Callaghan years are rather of failures of policy – a Labour government swamped by trade union militants on the loose; anti-cancer drugs on the Hull dockside uncollected; trade union leaders like Moss Evans or Alan Fisher oblivious to any dangers from wage inflation; hospital wards and primary schools closed down by public sector stoppages; refuse bins overflowing; the classic image of the Liverpool grave-diggers in David Basnett's union refusing even to bury the dead. On the far right, Douglas Eden has added luridly the spectre of major trade unionists like Jack Jones supposedly acting as covert Soviet agents and undermining British democracy.[2] The political literature of the late 1970s is apocalyptic, written in the language of 'collapse' or 'eclipse', a land 'as governable as Chile' in the words of an American politician, conducting the last rites on Attlee's post-war consensus: Americans indeed were especially prominent in this kind of historical pathology. Isaac Kramnick in 1979 captured the mood vividly in *Is Britain Dying?* An authoritative work by Alec Cairncross and Kathleen Burk on the IMF crisis a few years earlier was entitled *Goodbye Great Britain.*

This gloomy view of the 1974–9 Labour governments continued to flourish in the 1980s and 1990s, not only amongst Thatcherite Conservatives but equally within a reviving Labour Party. Neil Kinnock and John Smith urged the comrades to embark on a fresh start, a new sense of discipline and unity without sacrificing the values of democratic socialism on which the party was (allegedly) founded. By the end of Kinnock's period of leadership, all the old left-wing totems had been dropped from Labour's programme – unilateralism, an exit from Europe, mass nationalisation had all vanished. Under John Smith a serious reform was even undertaken of the trade union block vote at party conference. New Labour under Tony Blair's leadership in 1994 went still further in lamenting the party's past. Its strategists drew a stark comparison between the dark days of Old Labour in the 1970s and the bright promise of New Labour under its dynamic, youthful leader. Philip Gould saw the Wilson–Callaghan era as providing crucial evidence of the 'failure to modernise' in 'the century Labour lost'.[3] Peter Mandelson and Roger Liddle in *The Blair Revolution* (1996) attacked the era of the Social Contract which saw 'every wage claim and every strike as justified. ... In the eyes of the public the Labour government appeared a helpless bystander'.[4] If the formation of the Social Democratic Party in 1981 proved ultimately to be an abortive challenge to the Old Labour past, which imploded in humiliating fashion after seven short years, its ethic lived on, not least in the New Labour leadership of 1994–7 which included key ex-SDP intellectuals like Andrew Adonis and Roger Liddle. Blair's battle to ditch Clause Four was a crusade to rid Labour of this symbolic incubus of out dated socialism. The political commentators and historians tended to follow this line, especially in welcoming the Blairite landslide of 1997.

A rare exception was the Oxford-based Australian historian, Ross McKibbin, in 1991. An article of his article 'Homage to Wilson and Callaghan,' celebrated the commitment of the Labour administrations of the seventies to greater social and racial equality, high public expenditure and commitment to the public services.[5] They had, after all, little or no parliamentary majority (they were defeated 59 times in Commons votes in 1974–6 alone). Yet they rescued the country from the miners' strike, the three-day week and 30 per cent inflation. The contrast with the social divisiveness of Thatcherism was underlined. But a favourable analysis of this kind was rare.

Yet, gradually, perhaps inevitably, interpretations of Labour in the 1970s have begun to moderate. Lengthy biographies of both Harold Wilson and Jim Callaghan, predictably no doubt, spread a more positive view, as to a degree, did Edward Pearce's of Denis Healey (2002) and Healey's brilliant autobiography, *The Time of My Life* (1989). Ben Pimlott's and Philip Ziegler's lives of Wilson (1992 and 1993 respectively) focussed much more on the government of 1964–70 and also paid proper tribute to the premier's political skills especially in negotiating the referendum on membership of the European Common Market in 1975 without splitting the party. My own biography of Callaghan (1997) was kindly received although journalist reviewers focussed with predictable unanimity on the Winter of Discontent and the evidence of prime ministerial anomie in the last months in office in 1979, with Callaghan sadly telling his private secretary, Ken Stowe, 'I let the country down.'[6] My attempt to highlight the far longer period of economic and social recovery from the IMF crisis of December 1976 to the late autumn of 1978 (when many people thought Callaghan would go to the country to cash in on his growing popularity, and win an election) met with far less attention as did chapters on foreign, Commonwealth and defence policy. Other writers have noted the high calibre of the members of the government: administrations boasting Healey, Jenkins, Crosland, Dell, Benn, Lever, Foot, Shore or Shirley Williams in this period, did not lack intellectual fire-power. Callaghan's own array of advisers in the Policy Unit – Bernard Donoughue's team of Oxford dons like Andrew Graham and Richard Smethurst, and the brilliant young economist Gavyn Davies – were indeed amongst 'the best and the brightest' of their generation. The Think Tank contained progressive thinkers like Ken Berrill and Tessa Blackstone; there were Keynesian economic advisers like Douglas Wass, Brian Hopkin and Leo Pliatzky. Even at the height of the Second World War, the country had scarcely more able people at the helm. Meanwhile, with Callaghan's press office under the low-key but trusted direction of Tom McCaffrey, the British government of 1976–9 was comparatively spin-free. There were few PR disasters, other than perhaps Peter Jay, Callaghan's son-in-law, going to the embassy in Washington.

Apart from these matters of personalities, historians such as Jim Tomlinson have pointed to the growing economic success of the later 1970s. Douglas Jay rightly wrote of it as 'one of the few examples of any Western government...reducing both inflationary pressures and unemployment at the same time'.[7] The pound's value went up month by month, yet exports improved; foreign currency reserves accumulated down to November 1978. Gloomy contemporary perceptions in the press were at variance with the economic realities. It is also generally accepted that, following the IMF crisis of November–December 1976, the judgements of the Treasury on public sector borrowing proved to be far too pessimistic. With North Sea oil coming on stream, Britain's economic prospects in the Callaghan years were relatively buoyant. The apocalyptic prophets of doom around 1979–81 seem harder to justify now. Even the strike days were exaggerated. Ninety-eight per cent of manufacturing establishments had no strikes at all. Two groups of workers who could have brought the country to a total halt, the electrical power and water workers, fortunately never went on strike at all.[8] Many Blairites were later to recognise that the stark contrast between moribund Old Labour then and modernising New Labour later on was overdone.

It is, therefore, perfectly possible to argue that a more positive view should be taken of the achievement of the Labour governments of 1974–9. But the two should be distinguished because they were quite different. The last Wilson ministry of 1974–6 was a time of survival and self-doubt under an ailing, paranoid and dispirited prime minister who was surprised (and perhaps even disappointed) to win in February 1974 and gained little momentum from his very narrow victory in October 1974. Long before March 1976 he was becoming undermined by ill-health and perhaps addiction to alcohol. The Callaghan years, on balance, saw trust in government and a sense of collective responsibility revive. They are an episode in their own right, not a mere interlude as accounts such as Hugo Young's otherwise comprehensive story of Britain's post-war relations with Europe seem to imply.[9] The last Wilson administration was a troubled one, with inflation soaring to alarming double-digit levels until Jack Jones's flat-rate pay restraint of June 1975. Even so, they were an improvement on the corporate collapse and mass strikes of the Heath years, forever symbolised by the three-day week. Wilson's skilful confirmation of Britain's membership of Europe – aided by Callaghan's canny diplomacy which was 'negotiating for success' and by the powerful diplomatic backing of the German Chancellor Schmidt – was perhaps his major contribution to British history.

Callaghan, a cautious, personally conservative man four years older than Wilson who had never expected to enter No. 10 at all, proved to be an unexpectedly effective leader for much of the time, praised as such as Denis Healey and Tony Benn alike. Healey, speaking at Callaghan's memorial service in July 2005 in the presence of Thatcher and Blair, called him the best prime minister since Attlee. The economy progressed in the wake of Callaghan's handling of the IMF negotiations, while Michael Foot kept lines of negotiation with the trade unions open. In economics, unreconstructed Keynesianism, as conceived 40 years earlier, came to a gradual end, with monetarism and privatisation both making an appearance. A vigorous regional policy brought new life to Wales and Scotland. Callaghan's Ruskin College speech in October 1976 provided a powerful stimulus to national debate on educational standards in the maintained schools, which foreshadowed Tony Blair's famous mantra 'education, education, education' two decades later. There were major reforms in welfare policy, notably the state earnings-related pensions scheme (SERPS), an achievement rightly identified with Barbara Castle before Callaghan sacked her from the Cabinet, and the establishment of the first effective Race Relations Board. Michael Foot's trade union legislation at the Department of Employment in 1974–6 included such valuable innovations as the Health and Safety Executive and ACAS to conciliate in industrial disputes. Devolution first emerged as a legislative priority. It failed to progress in the Welsh and Scottish referendums of 1 March 1979 (it was the switch of Scottish Nationalist votes, not Tory or Liberal opposition, that brought the government down prematurely in the Commons three weeks later), and Callaghan himself was far from enthusiastic, but it was still a powerful portent of constitutional change. To a degree also, the Labour government re-established itself as the party of the nuclear family and of law and order (both under challenge from the far left), with PC Jim, once spokesman for the Police Federation, depicted in cartoons as a Dixon of Dock Green figure advising us all to 'mind how you go'. Whether the public mood really did indicate a 'sea change' towards Thatcherite Conservatism, as Callaghan famously suggested to Donoughue in a pessimistic moment during the 1979 election campaign, is open to question. It does not seem to be a view borne out by public opinion surveys of the time.

Above all, it was a constructive period in foreign policy, quieter than the warlike Blair years, but with more obvious achievement and certainly no perilous adventure like the invasion of Iraq. Wilson and Callaghan played their full part in negotiating the Helsinki CSCE Treaty on European Security in 1975 which closed this phase of the Cold War. Callaghan was quietly effective in protecting the nascent democratic revolution in Portugal against American pressure, the product of fear of Iberian socialism; in defending the Falklands against Argentine threats in 1977 and without war; in working towards strategic arms limitations with the Russians and even in the international conference at Guadeloupe in January 1979, eternally overshadowed by memories of a sun-tanned prime minister coming home to a frozen, strike-bound Britain and saying something like 'crisis, what crisis'? Steve Richards once wrote that Old Labour was popularly thought of as anti-American and weak on defence.[10] That accusation, at least, could never be brought against Callaghan who revived, for good or ill, the British nuclear deterrent, and who really did act as the honest broker between America and Europe that Blair later sought to be. Callaghan's shrewd and highly personal diplomatic style enabled him to serve as a bridge between two world leaders who heartily disliked each other – his fellow Baptist ex-sailor, President Carter, and German Chancellor Helmut Schmidt an intellectual socialist who admired Callaghan as an authentic leader of working-class social democracy such as he had encountered in the Hamburg of his youth.[11]

For a short period, Callaghan basked amidst some international acclaim both as a world mediator and a pilot who had weathered the IMF storms at home. His reputation perhaps reached its zenith around the time of the Camp David Agreement when his links with both Israeli politicians and President Sadat of Egypt proved valuable to a successful outcome. There was also the bonus of a successful Royal Jubilee in 1977, highly congenial to an old naval patriot from Portsmouth whose father was a sailor who had served on the royal yacht under Edward VII. His Cardiff constituents noted too that, in a notably 'Celtic' administration, Wales kept winning rugby's Triple Crown. Cledwyn Hughes told Tony Benn that he hoped Jim would not become swollen-headed with all this success.[12] Maybe, indeed, that is where and why his leader endured nemesis after hubris in the end. Certainly his bizarre rendition of an old music-hall song at the September 1978 TUC conference, which seemed to mislead union delegates fatally, smacked of over-confidence and triviality at a sensitive moment.

There is, therefore, much to be said for these governments and, to a degree, their leaders. And yet the 'declinist' interpretation of these years has its substance. Its prime minister enjoyed high ratings in the polls, far more so than the opposition leader, Mrs. Thatcher. His Cabinets were often successful and effective. The Labour movement was not. The Party had been in numerical and ideological decline since the 1960s. It was becoming barren in ideas and lapsing into factional warfare, symbolised by the deeply divisive if charismatic figure of Tony Benn as the voice of the left. It was unduly dependent on special-interest clients such as unionised public sector workers and council house tenants. No document of genuine intellectual weight came from Labour in these years. Tony Crosland's *Socialism Now* (1974) was in some measure an elegy on the failure of the ethos of planning and economic growth in the 1960s. The trade unions were undoubtedly provoked by Callaghan's later misjudgements, notably the commitment to a 5 per cent pay norm which 'just popped out' in a radio interview,[13] but they were also out of control. The loss of Jack Jones through retirement was a huge blow. With his possible successor, Harry Urwin, also near retirement, the advent of Moss Evans, a man of minimal political judgement, to head the giant Transport and General Workers Union was a political and industrial disaster. However, there were positive features about the 1974–9 period. The country was mostly competently run, with a greater commitment to social equality or public compassion than was shown either in the Thatcher counter-revolution of the eighties, or the Blairite managerialism after 1997. Even in its last months in office, the Callaghan government never displayed the political and ideological barrenness of the Brown government in 2008–10. It never lapsed into non-doctrinal managerialism. But fundamentally a Labour government needed to retain contact with its political and industrial base. The decay of that base, the fundamental fractures within Keir Hardie's old Labour Alliance at time of global capitalist crisis, left the government bereft. The rot was setting in. As a result, attempts to rehabilitate the Wilson–Callaghan governments, let alone pay them homage, cannot be more than a marginal success.

Chapter 18

Michael Foot – History Man

This chapter has two twin themes: the impact of history on the career and ideas of Michael Foot, and his own impact on British history. It is an interesting area in its own right, and it may also shed some light on the possibilities and pitfalls of turning to history as a guide to contemporary public life. It may even have some echoes for the advent to the premiership of our only prime minister with a higher degree in history, that eminent graduate of the University of Edinburgh and biographer of Jimmy Maxton, Dr. Gordon Brown.

As regards the impact of history upon Michael Foot, he probably read more history throughout his life than any other British frontline politician, with the possible exception of Winston Churchill. Michael's father, Isaac, accumulated a colossal library of books on literature, religion and history in his home of Pencrebar on the Devon-Cornish border: works of history alone ran to many thousands of volumes. The young Michael was steeped in books at an early age, and as a schoolboy would have been familiar with the works of famous Liberal scholars like George Otto Trevelyan and J.L. Hammond. He was an immense enthusiast for Macaulay's *History of England* and his expertise here possibly accounted for his success in winning an Exhibition to Wadham College, Oxford in 1931. Certainly it much impressed one examiner, Lord David Cecil. Foot also was steeped in the works of Gibbon and Carlyle, and, in French history (in translation only) the writings of Michelet. Foot himself wrote one significant work of history, *The Pen and the Sword* (1957), about the political manoeuvres during the reign of Queen Anne which saw the downfall of the mighty Marlborough in 1711. Historical themes and quotations abounded always in Foot's speeches and journalism. While editor and leader-writer of the *Evening Standard* between 1940 and 1944, he offered his readers many a historical discussion of such matters as Carnot's direction of the French revolutionary armies in 1793 or Lenin's rationale for the Treaty of Brest-Litovsk in 1918. Among his closest friends in later life was the most famous British historian of the day, Alan Taylor.

Three historical themes were particularly influential for Michael Foot. First, there was the historical background to his upbringing in Plymouth, especially the history of the navy. The symbolism of Drake's Drum was as powerful for Michael Foot in Plymouth as that of the Pompey Chimes was for his comrade Jim Callaghan in Portsmouth. Foot's patriotic fervour about the vessels that set off from Plymouth Hoe to repel the Spanish Armada in 1588 was replicated in *Guilty Men* in 1940 in his passion to ward off invasion by the Germans, and perhaps by his unexpectedly belligerent response to the invasion of the Falklands by the Argentine junta in 1982. It was a strongly naval, patriotic view of history, and indeed a strongly regional and English one. Although Foot was to champion devolution for Scotland and Wales in the 1970s, and take bills through the Commons and on to the statute book, they were a relatively unfamiliar world to the English patriot Foot (even though two of his heroes, Lloyd George and Nye Bevan, were manifestly not English).

Secondly, and crucially, there was the constitutional crisis of the seventeenth century, and especially the English Civil Wars of 1642–51. Those wars had impinged powerfully upon the citizens of Plymouth, a parliamentary stronghold besieged for a long period and with much suffering by royalist armies, a legendary episode perpetuated in the name Freedom Fields in the centre of Plymouth, complete with a statue of Oliver Cromwell. In the West Country, especially amongst nonconformists like the Methodist Foots, the Civil War was still very much alive, and a point of political confrontation. Foot himself had a strong affinity with the issues of the Civil Wars, and especially with the career of Cromwell: his father was a Cromwell fanatic, and the main founder of the Cromwell Association founded in 1939. Isaac Foot once declared challengingly that the test of a man was on which side he would have fought at the battle of Marston Moor (commemorated now by a statue put up by the Cromwell Association in Isaac Foot's time). John Gross wrote perceptively in *The Rise and Fall of the Man of Letters* (1969) that later generations could hardly grasp the central importance of the seventeenth century for the Edwardian man of letters, say John Morley or Augustine Birrell, both Liberal cabinet ministers. It might have been Isaac Foot, still fighting for the good old cause well into the twentieth century that he had in mind. His son, Michael, 'inveterate peacemonger', lifelong opponent of capital punishment, showed no remorse for the execution of King Charles I in 1649; he rejoiced that his own lawyer, Geoffrey Robertson, published a learned and highly legal/historical work on a leading regicide, John Cooke.

Foot was always a devoted parliamentarian. He felt himself to be the direct heir of Pym, Hampden and their brethren three centuries earlier. It was the threat to parliamentary sovereignty in Britain, as he saw it, that led Foot into ardent opposition to British membership of the European Common Market in the 1970s (an issue on which he later changed his mind). It was parliamentarianism too which led him to uphold a constitutional parliamentarian Labour Party in 1980–3 against what he saw as the anti-parliamentary, rather than extra-parliamentary, challenge from

Militant Tendency and the Bennites. Foot remained a child of the English Civil War throughout his life, a lifelong parliamentarian and Roundhead. On only one aspect was he uncertain: how he could maintain allegiance both to the democratic Levellers at Putney in 1647 and also to Cromwell, their establishment opponent who sent Lilburne and other dissidents to the Tower. Paul Foot pointed to this ambiguity in his challenging posthumous book, *The Vote*. In many ways it was a continuing family argument with Uncle Michael, the parliamentary socialist, Aunt Jill, the supporter of the less socialist or even anti-socialist feminists of the Pankhurst family, and especially grandpa Isaac, Cromwell's chief camp follower three hundred years on.

The third and final area where Foot was hugely influenced by history was the French Revolution. Like Fox, like the Lake poets such as the young Wordsworth, Foot always thought it the greatest event of recent history, which had transformed the world. He hugely admired the radical essays of Hazlitt and the even more radical verse of Byron and Shelley on this theme. He relished Hazlitt's enthusiasm for Napoleon; by all accounts, news of the sad events on the battlefield of Waterloo made Hazlitt seriously ill. Foot himself intended to write a book on that great liberal opponent of the war with France, Charles James Fox. He never did so, but he did attend the unveiling of a statue of Fox in Bloomsbury Square early in 2007, perhaps a belated gesture of apology. He also had a fascinating private discussion at the launch of my biography of him with William Hague, author of a biography of the Younger Pitt, Fox's great historic opponent. Foot's interpretation of the Revolution in France was much influenced by Michelet, and by George Lefebvre, amongst more modern authorities. He was delighted to be invited by his literary/political comrade, President François Mitterrand, in Paris in 1989, during the bicentennial of the French Revolution, partly to combat the distinctly anti-revolutionary views recently offered by the non-historian, Margaret Thatcher. The title of Foot's famous pamphlet, *Guilty Men* in 1940 was drawn directly from the demands of demonstrators petitioning the French Revolutionary Assembly in 1793.

These were the aspects of the past that most obviously captured Foot's imagination, none of them more recent than 1815. He did not pay especial attention to the history of the Labour movement, other than in his memorable two-volume biography of Aneurin Bevan. In fact, he was perhaps less attracted to Labour history than was Jim Callaghan, a man who never went to university but on whom the impress of Harold Laski was powerful. Foot's interest in history was also heavily west European. He had limited interest in American history and did not share his father's enthusiasm for Abraham Lincoln. The American

Michael Foot most revered was Thomas Jefferson, whom he rightly saw as a devotee of the European enlightenment culture of the later eighteenth century.

The other point to be made about Foot's views on history is to note that they were frequently drawn less from historical analysis than from literature. He was excited by the insights of Hazlitt, Byron, Heine and H.G. Wells. He saw their literature and politics – and surely his own – also – as all of a piece. In many ways, Foot's emphasis on the political radicalism of his favoured authors – Byron and Heine for instance – gave him insights denied purely literary scholars and biographers such as Fiona McCarthy. Foot's treatment of the politics of Queen Anne's reign was shaped fundamentally by the writings and ideology of Dean Swift, *Gulliver's Travels* and all. His admiration for Disraeli was heavily based on his admiration for his novels, Sybil and Coningsby, with their sympathetic portrayal of industrial relations and also his awareness of the role of women. More recent writers were also important for Foot's historical understanding – Wells and Arnold Bennett for his analysis of capitalist society, George Orwell for his depiction of the radical impulses of Englishness (though less so of *1984*), Arthur Koestler for the illiberalism of Soviet Communism, Ignazio Silone for a vivid portrayal of the cruelty that underlay Italian fascism. This emphasis on literary evidence added a cultural dimension that added distinction to Foot's career as a politician. But it would also lead to a romantic and sometimes idealised, and hopelessly partisan, view of the past.

What of the converse aspect, Michael Foot's impact on British history? Much of it was ephemeral. Much of the time, he was an outsider, a critic, a rebel with or without a cause. He had an unquenchable penchant for lost causes, the Campaign for Nuclear Disarmament above all, and this came out fatally in the catastrophic election defeat of 1983. Perhaps his major impact on his time came not through his political activities but through his books, two or perhaps two and a half of them.

First there was *Guilty Men*, with its title drawn from Revolutionary France. It was written in four hectic days just after Dunkirk with two other journalists, Frank Owen, former Liberal MP for Hereford and editor of the *Standard*, and the distinctly less radical, Peter Howard, soon to become a huge evangelist for Moral Rearmament. They adopted a joint *nom de plume*, 'Cato', chosen by Foot himself. *Guilty Men* was only a polemical squib but it was the most powerful and sensational political pamphlet since the days of John Wilkes. It had a huge sale of over 230,000 copies, despite being banned for distribution by W.H. Smiths and Wymans. Foot and his colleagues pushed barrow-loads through the streets of central London, including Soho where members of the oldest profession bought it avidly thinking that *Guilty Men* was a tract about the ethics of prostitution.

The book focussed the national mind and the national conscience upon the 1930s forever. The popular view of appeasement and the personal delinquency of Neville Chamberlain was dictated for all time by Foot's highly partisan account. A poll of historians on 21 December 1999 decreed that Chamberlain was the worst of all the British prime ministers of the twentieth century, which he certainly was not. All the famous myths and clichés about appeasement are contained in its 100-odd pages, Chamberlain's umbrella, 'Caligula's horse', Hitler missing the bus, faraway countries of which we knew nothing. Attention is savagely focussed on government ministers. Nothing is said about Labour's inadequacies in facing up to the dictators, the equivocation of Churchill about Franco or Mussolini, Lloyd George's calamitous visit to Hitler in Berchtesgaden in 1936, certainly nothing at all about the staunch support for every kind of appeasement down to September 1939 from Owen and Foot's employer, Lord Beaverbrook. But ever since, British and also American public memory about the very idea of appeasement has been set in stone. There was one bizarre consequence. In the lead-up to the Iraq invasion in 2003, George W. Bush and Tony Blair both repeatedly drew on analogies with the 1930s and emphasised the dangers of weakness before dictators. In fact, the ideas they were citing (totally inaccurately in relation to Iraq) came from no less than the venerable Hampstead sage and his *Guilty Men*. It was ironic indeed that the first Iraq anti-war march on 15 February should end with speeches by Foot amongst others at Hyde Park Corner at its conclusion. Here indeed, in the words of Michael's old historical comrade, Alan Taylor, was one of history's 'curious twists'.

Long before Iraq, there had been a previous grotesque abuse of the notion of 'appeasement'. This was the Suez invasion in 1956, when Eden and the Foreign Office variously compared President Nasser of Egypt to Hitler, Mussolini, Napoleon and even Alexander the Great. As a result Foot wrote another *Guilty Men* denouncing that too. But it lacked the panache of the tract of 1940 and made far less impact.

Foot's other major work was his biography of Aneurin Bevan, perhaps the most influential biography of any Labour politician. It is hugely partisan and very unfair to Hugh Gaitskell, Bevan's great adversary who drove Nye out of the Attlee government, but was himself also a socialist of a highly committed kind and certainly no clone of Ramsay MacDonald. The biography reflects the fact that Foot himself was more hostile towards the party leadership than Bevan himself in the later fifties, after all, Bevan served in the shadow Cabinet as spokesman first for Colonial Policy then Foreign Policy and was at the end Gaitskell's deputy leader. In many ways,

Foot's history of Bevan's career is less a work of historical scholarship than a kind of mythic saga of a Welsh giant, like the medieval *Mabinogion*. Yet it is a hugely powerful and memorable book. Not only does it have excellent accounts of such key issues as wartime radical politics or the foundation of the NHS, but it is also the most effective statement we have of what it meant to be a democratic socialist in the mid-twentieth century. It was Michael Foot's most important contribution to socialist ideas and Labour history, and an inspiration to tens of thousands ever since. No other Labour biography can compare with it.

The 'half-book' was *Debts of Honour*, Foot's book of historical portraits published in 1980 just before he became Labour leader. It is an engaging, highly readable and romanticised attempt to construct a kind of alternative radical genealogy. It was an eccentric list. It included only three socialists – the journalist Noel Brailsford, the novelist Ignazio Silone and the cartoonist 'Vicky', – none of them politicians. It also includes Benjamin Disraeli, Daniel Defoe and even Beaverbrook whom Foot always considered a radical outsider. For some on the left it was an inspirational work in the dark days after the return of Margaret Thatcher in 1979. One eager convert was the young lawyer, Tony Blair, who wrote to Foot in 1982, in a confused yet also strangely moving way, about how the book had inspired him in searching for a democratic, non-Marxist radical creed. Perhaps through Gordon Brown, a regular telephone conversationalist with Foot while Chancellor, and himself the author of a book of portraits of courageous politicians, the ideas and audacity of *Debts of Honour* still had some currency in the corridors of power.

What else is to be said of the importance of Michael Foot for British history? Five points of his career perhaps might be emphasised.

First, Foot was a marvellous communicator. He was not a theorist of any importance. He could never be compared with a Crosland or a Jay. He was certainly no kind of economist and the modern world of information technology left him cold. But, he spoke directly to the masses like no-one else, and thrilled them. He was an incomparable platform orator, who also became a marvellous parliamentary performer with a gift for literary allusion and a beauty of language that attracted the admiration of men such as Harold Macmillan, Enoch Powell and John Biffen. But he mainly operated via the printed word, through newspapers, weeklies, tracts of all kinds. *Tribune,* into which he put much money himself, was in this sense an important journal throughout the Bevanite period, as an organ of left-wing, but democratic socialism. Foot, the historian of Swift, the friend of Koestler and Orwell, had a historic commitment to a free press, and treasured his membership of the National Union of Journalists which honoured him in his last years. He saw himself in the line of succession of the great socialist editors like Robert Blatchford in the *Clarion* and George Lansbury in the early *Daily Herald*. During the debates on the trade union legislation Foot brought forward in 1974–6, he claimed in all sincerity that strengthening the collective rights of journalists as against their capitalist employers was a major contribution to the freedom of the press. Many critics, including his brother Dingle, retorted that it restricted rather than liberated writers in the journals and newspapers by forcing them into a trade-union straitjacket through the closed shop. For Foot, however, it was a fundamental issue of social freedom, and he successfully out-argued a variety of owners, editors, journalists, lawyers and others on the matters involved. Always many of his closest friends were journalists: Frank Owen, 'Vicky', James Cameron, and more recently Geoffrey Goodman and Ian Aitken.

Secondly, Michael Foot was central to the existence of the Labour governments of 1974–9, far more so than Tony Benn, a persistently destructive force. Deputy leader from 1976, Foot kept the government afloat mainly through his close links with trade union leaders, especially Jack Jones. Much of his legislation, commended at the time by judges like Lord Scarman, was destroyed by the Thatcher government, especially by Norman Tebbit at the Department of Employment. But important legacies from Foot's time at Employment survive – ACAS for settling trade disputes, the Health and Safety Executive, pioneering legislation on race relations and on the status of women. Foot was important in another way – the negotiation of the Lib–Lab pact of March 1977 in which he was a key player in partnership with David Steel and other Liberal MPs. It was followed by 18 months of generally stable and successful government, and evidently Foot, the youthful Liberal of the early 1930s, found no philosophical or personal problem in running matters with the Liberals in parliament. The Winter of Discontent, after the Liberals had ended the Lib–Lab pact, was in itself a sign not only of the government's waning authority but of Foot's waning influence personally. Jack Jones had retired, and he was replaced by verbose pigmies like Moss Evans. Foot was now condemned by the Bennites for surrendering to the right of the party. Even so, his crucial role in keeping the last Labour government of the post-Attlee era alive and creative should not be forgotten.

Thirdly, while leader of the House in 1976–9 he took up the cause of Scottish and Welsh devolution. It was not a natural issue for him – his idol, Nye Bevan, had always been an opponent of devolution and so was Foot's young friend, another leading valleys socialist, Neil Kinnock. Foot's interest in the administrative minutiae of devolution had its limits, it seemed, as was shown by a tendency, when devolution bills came up, to keep the television switched on in his office during test matches – admittedly with the sound turned down. Even so, despite defeat in the referendums of March 1979 (shattering in Wales), devolution bills went through, a remarkable triumph for Foot's persistence with Labour now a minority government, and devolution has been firmly on the public agenda since, with a parliament in Scotland and an elected assembly in Wales well established for almost a decade, and manifestly accepted. Foot's role as a pioneer was publicly acknowledged by none other than the president of Plaid Cymru, Gwynfor Evans.

Fourthly, and negatively, there was Foot's dreadful period as party leader in 1980. It was the party's darkest hour: the defection of the Social Democrats made it darker even than 1931. Foot himself was not equipped, temperamentally or psychologically, to be a leader, and in any case came into the position in his late sixties when he was physically and perhaps intellectually a fading force. But this period also showed up the incoherence of the Labour Party, its limited impact socially with the decline of the old industrial working class, and ideologically since the heady days of the Attlee years. An old intellectual hegemony dating from the socialist planners in the 1930s was coming to its appointed end, amidst huge internecine acrimony. Fundamental questions were being raised both about the democracy and the socialism of British-style democratic socialism. Foot at this time appeared a totally traditional figure. Election speeches from him in the 1983 campaign looked back to Munich or the Spanish Civil War, events that took place long before many members of his audiences were born. In a way, Foot's gallant but somewhat pathetic campaign in 1983 was the last hurrah for the Guilty Men (e.g. a verbal assault in Oxford town hall on Lord Hailsham, victor in the Oxford by-election at the time of Munich and still in Mrs. Thatcher's government). It showed that at long last the Second World War had come to an end, just as the death of President McKinley by assassination in 1901 was a sign that the American Civil War was finally over, and the 'bloody shirt' could finally be put away.

The Social Democrat Party was founded in 1981, and some of its leading figures like David Owen would have left, whoever was leading Labour at the time. Yet the derided and ridiculed Michael Foot (famous for his allegedly shabby, though actually brand-new, jacket at the Cenotaph) in fact led a kind of fight-back. He consolidated the centre-left of the Tribunite tendency, people like Neil Kinnock and Stan Orme and they formed part of a vital anti-Bennite alliance on Labour's NEC. And in time, Labour did indeed revive after Neil Kinnock's rousing rescue act. Labour intellectuals like David Marquand, Roger Liddle and Andrew Adonis came back to it from the wilderness of the SDP. It was Michael Foot, in his gentle, wordy way, who had begun the process. One returning defector is worthy of note – the veteran intellectual Michael Young who had actually written Labour's election manifesto, *Let Us Face the Future*, back in 1945 when the young Foot first was returned by the electors of Plymouth, Devonport.

The fifth and final aspect of Michael Foot's historical role is more general, but of much importance. He is a striking, late example of the man of letters in public life. It should be noted that a powerful influence upon him for 50 years was that he was married to a considerable woman of letters, Jill Craigie, who was steeped in the writings of visionaries like Lewis Mumford, and herself a dedicated historian of the suffragettes. Michael was to become an iconic figure, Bohemian in appearance with shabby clothes and long hair, an intellectual based in Hampstead and a habitué of the 'Gay Hussar'. He brought with him, via his father and indeed all the Foots in their way, a unique literary and cultural inheritance. His list of heroes was politically complicated: Cromwell, Disraeli, Lloyd George, Beaverbrook, Enoch Powell, Bevan, Indira Gandhi, along with a roll-call of past radicals from the Levellers to the Chartists. Difficult aspects such as the manifold atrocities committed by Cromwell's troops in Ireland or Beaverbrook's enthusiastic support for appeasement tended to be brushed aside. But Foot was more than a slavish litterateur of protest, as the enthusiasm of this old Leveller and Jacobin for the scarcely Whig Dean Swift and the eclectic Edmund Burke, hammer of the French Revolution, indicates.

Contrary to Denis Healey's famous formulation, Foot's passion for literature was no mere 'hinterland'. It was a launch-pad for action and for protest – he emphasised this connection in a lecture at Cardiff in 1983, 'Byron and the Bomb', seeing the poet almost as a founder-member of CND. His cultural background led him into many a crusade from the appeasement controversy of the thirties to the defence of Croatia against Serb aggression in the nineties. Foot's style and rhetoric would have been instantly recognisable to the Edwardian men of letters who were Father Isaac's heroes and colleagues, and indeed to Gladstone. Like them, Michael Foot was fired by the centrality of culture in our society, by the vital civilising importance of history, and by seeing himself as the natural freeborn heir of radicals past, fighting the same battles as Swift, Fox, Tom Paine, Hazlitt and Wells had done in their day. He was a radical of the book: it was reading the social novels of H.G. Wells and Arnold Bennett on the Merseyside trams in 1935 that got him into the Labour Party in the first place. He was always partisan and wrote in ironic condemnation of 'impartial historians' (perhaps impartial biographers as well). His own history writing, other than his account of Dean Swift in *The Pen and the Sword* (1956) is often really high journalism. His career shows the value and also perhaps the dangers of history being pitch-forked into contemporary political debate. When his long life finally ended in March 2010 at the great age of 96, it received extraordinary coverage in the media, indicative that an icon of our public culture had passed away. His memorial service in Golders Green crematorium was a national event: the prime minister, Gordon Brown, led off the list of speakers. Of the polymath literary socialist Michael Foot it was widely observed that that we shall not see his like again.

Chapter 19

The Attack on Iraq

As a historian, I want to reflect briefly on the observable and wide gulf between the views of the government and the views of the British people. Normally in a war crisis, historically government and people converge as they did in 1914 and in 1939. This time, they have grown further and further apart. At the present time, perhaps three-quarters of the British people do not support a war. At least 30 per cent have said that they will not support a war under any circumstances, even with a second UN resolution.

The government says that the facts need to be explained and the message elucidated and then people will form correct views. Well, the message has been elucidated; the spinners have spun; the plagiarists have plagiarised; and the people are more hostile than ever and public opposition to an attack on Iraq has grown stronger. Why is that? Have our people suddenly turned uniformly into Trotskyists and pacifists? They find the government's case unconvincing; they simply do not believe it.

In the first place, it is evident that people are not persuaded that Saddam Hussein is an obvious threat to the United Kingdom – perhaps not immediately a threat to anywhere. After all, he was successfully contained by international force for 12 years previous to this crisis. It was only after 11 September 2001 – indeed, some time after that – that the United States turned its attention, in a way that future historians will find mysterious and interesting to penetrate, from Al-Qaeda to Iraq, which, after all, had been there all along.

The public recognises that Saddam Hussein is an unpleasant man and that his regime is cruel. They do not regard the case for his having weapons of mass destruction – certainly not nuclear weapons – as currently proven. Saddam Hussein certainly has some unpleasant weapons – of course he has, we gave him some of them; the United States gave him others. The United States was responsible for selling Iraq anthrax, West Nile virus and botulinol toxin in the 1980s, the salesman being Donald Rumsfeld.

In spite of that, the reports by Dr. Blix have so far been temperate. Things are by no means satisfactory, but they are moderately encouraging. He talks of positive progress and it is surely reasonable to ask for inspection to be undertaken properly and to reach its appointed time, rather than to resort to the extreme response of war.

Secondly, as many noble Lords have said, people are not convinced of any link between Iraq and international terrorism. The evidence for that is derisory. The people of this country fear that the threat of terrorism will be greatly increased by an attack on Iraq – as may be tension between the different ethnic communities in this country.

Thirdly, people deeply suspect the motives of the United States. That is not just anti-Americanism; our people are not anti-American. I am not anti-American; I taught American history in universities for 30 years and greatly enjoyed it. But there is great hostility to and distrust of an extreme right-wing administration. People distrust the unilateralism of American foreign and external policy in relation to the environment, armaments, the International Criminal Court and many other issues.

There is mass popular distrust in this country about the American concern with oil and the hypocrisy that is shown in not acting against an aggressive Israeli regime with an extremely right-wing government who consistently defy the UN's edicts and deny fundamental human rights for Palestinians. There is great disbelief in this country that the United States, rather late in the day, has decided that this is a crusade for human rights. What human rights, when the Kurds, for example, are specifically omitted? Why are they omitted? Because it would upset the Turks and a large number of Kurds live in Turkey, which is a valuable base.

It is also recognised that the United States has for decades propped up and continues to prop up some of the most atrocious regimes in the world, which have flouted human rights – at present, Uzbekistan, which provides virtually no human rights, but is a convenient base. That is recognised and regarded with a good deal of suspicion.

The British people also believe in the United Nations. Admirably, our prime minister also believes in the United Nations. People in this country suspect that that the Americans do not – at any rate, to nothing like the same degree. The Commonwealth background of this country makes us attuned to dialogue and international discourse, whereas the history, background and outlook of the United States are different. People see the United States apparently overruling or ignoring UN resolutions and probably not wanting to use the United Nations at all, had it not been admirably pressurised into it by Tony Blair. They see the United States regarding the Blix inspection as an irrelevant interlude, as they have already decided on war. They see the Americans trying to impose their definition of regime change unilaterally and in complete defiance of the edicts and principles of international law. They see a United States committed to following its own interests, whatever the rest of the world thinks. Speaking historically, I fear that that is the other side of America's so-called isolationism; it is an interventionist consequence of isolationism. It frightens people.

Finally, the British people fear war because they think that it will be barbarous and may well lead to the death of hundreds of thousands of innocent people – children, the elderly and others – in Iraq. They think that it will be far worse than the atrocities undoubtedly committed by Saddam Hussein and will result in a humanitarian catastrophe. They feel that war should be the last resort and that we are a long way short of the last resort.

In addition to what I have tried to identify as popular concerns about Iraq, there are some more specialist concerns. Economists are anxious about the long-term damage to the world economy and the prospects for economic recovery, particularly given the high price of oil. As we have heard in the debate, military experts are worried about the absence of clearly defined strategic objectives and ask about the purpose of the projected war and possible occupation of Iraq. Those who are expert in international analysis fear the probability of extreme instability for many decades throughout the Middle East. I noticed a remarkable statement by the former prime minister, John Major, pointing out the difficulties of getting a stable settlement in Iraq, given the deep animosities between Shias and Sunnis, the position of the Kurds and so on. The effect of the war will be to exacerbate the problems, not to cure them.

Others worry about the new gulf emerging between us and our allies and comrades in France and Germany and the effect that it will have on the European ideal. We are being alienated from France and cosying up to the neo-fascist prime minister Berlusconi, with whom this country has little common interest.

As a historian, I worry about the crude use of history, particularly our old friend the 1930s. Time and again we hear that this crisis is the 1930s come again. What nonsense. Saddam is not another Hitler. Where is his *Mein Kampf*? Where is his dream of universal conquest? George Bush is certainly not another Churchill; it would be a calumny on the reputation of that great man to suggest it. It is a facile argument, and it disturbs me that Downing Street produces it, all the more because I taught one or two of them. My efforts were clearly somewhat in vain.

We should anatomise public opinion. The polls show the components of alienated public opinion on the threatened invasion. Every element that brought new Labour to power is hostile. Women are strongly hostile, more so than men. At least 70 per cent of women are hostile to war under almost any circumstances. Young people are deeply alienated, as are the trade unions. In Scotland, only 13 per cent of the people would support a war. God help the Labour Party in the elections in May. It will be a bonus for the Scottish Nationalists (SNP) and perhaps, in my own nation, for Plaid Cymru. All faiths are opposed to the war. Today, we heard the bishops speak out with courage and vision. They do not see it as a just war. There is also the powerful opposition of the Pope. All political parties are united, even many conservatives who reject the gung-ho militarism of Iain Duncan Smith.

That opposition was reflected on 15 February in a great and moving protest comparable with any in our history, comparable with the Chartists or the Suffragettes. The extent of that protest shows how the crisis can destabilise our country. Nearer home, it is certainly destabilising the Labour Party. I have been a member of the Labour Party since 1955. I was a member of the Labour League of Youth before Tony Blair was born. It grieves me to see the haemorrhaging of good members from our party. There are masses of them, and friends of mine are leaving the party.

Tony Blair is a brave man who prides himself on being another Churchill. He must be wary of not being another Ramsay MacDonald. This is said to be a listening government; one that listens to the people. They should listen – not to transatlantic ideologues but to the wisdom, humanity and decency of the British people.

Acknowledgements

Versions of the following chapters first appeared in the following works and they are printed by kind permission of the original publishers thus:

1. Published by The Reform Club, 2001

2. Peter Jagger (ed.), *Gladstone* (Hambledon Press, 1998)

3. Wm. Roger Louis (ed.), *Still More Adventures with Britannia* (I.B.Tauris, 2002)

4. *20th Century British History* (OUP), 13, 1 (2002)

5. *Journal of Liberal History* 51 (Summer 2006)

6. *Historical Journal* 39, 3 (September 1996)

7. Antoine Capet (ed.), *One Century of Entente Cordiale* (Palgrave, 2006)

8. H.C. Allen and R.F. Thompson (eds.), *Contrast and Connection* (Bell, 1976)

11. Robert D. King and Robin W. Wilson (eds.), *The Statecraft of British Imperialism* (Frank Cass, 1999)

12. Antoine Capet (ed.), *The Special Relationship* (University of Rouen, 2003)

13. *Contemporary Record* 7, 2 (Autumn 1993)

14. Kevin Jeffrey (ed.), *Labour Forces* (I.B.Tauris, 2002)

15. Michael Parsons (ed.), *The Wilson Years 1964–70* (University of Pau, 1999)

16. J.M.W. Bean (ed.), *The Political Culture of Modern Britain* (Hamish Hamilton, 1987)

17. Anthony Seldon and Kevin Hickson (eds.), *New Labour, Old Labour* (Routledge, 2004)

I wish to pay tribute to the special help I received from my daughter, Katherine, in conceiving and producing this book.

Notes

(Place of publication London unless otherwise indicated)

1 The Great Reform Act of 1832

Based on a lecture given at the Reform Club, 7 Nov. 2000.

1. G.M. Trevelyan, *Lord Grey of the Reform Bill* (Longmans, 1920); David Cannadine, *G.M. Trevelyan: A Life in History* (Fontana, 1993), p. 104.
2. E.A. Smith, *Lord Grey 1764–1845* (Clarendon Press, Oxford, 1990), p. 278.
3. Leslie Mitchell, 'Foxite Politics and the Great Reform Bill', *English Historical Review*, CVIII (1993), 338. Also see Frank O'Gorman, *Voters, Patrons and Parties: The Unreformed Electoral System of Hanoverian England, 1734–1832* (Clarendon Press, Oxford, 1989).
4. Lord Macaulay, *The History of England*, Vol. 2 (Everyman's Library edition, 1964), pp. 380–81.
5. John Vincent, *The Formation of the Liberal Party, 1857–68* (Constable, 1966), p. 212.
6. David Lloyd George, speech at Queen's Hall, 23 Mar. 1910, quoted in *Better Times* (Hodder and Stoughton, 1910), p. 296.
7. Henry Richard, *Letters on the Social and Political Condition of Wales* (Jackson, Walford and Hodder, 1867), p. 80.
8. Kenneth O. Morgan, *Keir Hardie: Radical and Socialist* (Weidenfeld and Nicolson), pp. 97ff., 242–45.
9. Aneurin Bevan, *In Place of Fear* (McGibbon and Kee, 1961 eds.), pp. 199–203.
10. Linda Colley, *Britons: Forging the Nation* (Yale, 1994), p. 345; Norman Gash, *Politics in the Age of Peel* (Longmans, 1952), pp. 373–92.
11. Jonathan Clark, *English Society 1660–1832* (Cambridge University Press, new edition, 2000), pp. 555–64.
12. Gash, *Politics in the Age of Peel*, p. 410; Peter Mandler, *Aristocratic Government in the Age of Reform: Whigs and Liberals, 1830–1852* (Oxford University Press, 1990), p. 164.
13. Westminster Club Committee Book, 1834–38 (Reform Club archives). On 14 Mar. 1835 Disraeli sent a cheque to the Committee of the renamed Westminster Reform Club, but asked for his name to be erased. (I am much indebted to Simon Blundell, the librarian of the Reform Club, for his archival assistance.).
14. Reform Club Minute Book, 1836– (Reform Club archives). The club opened on 24 May 1836 after the purchase of Lady Dysart's house in

Pall Mall and the failure to purchase Gwydyr House in Whitehall. There is an excellent discussion in Gash, *Politics in the Age of Peel*, pp. 403–11. For Inigo Jones's 'double cube', see John Summerson, *Inigo Jones* (Penguin Books, 1966).

15. I am much indebted to fascinating insights into the legal aspects of this case by Mr. Conrad Dehn QC, communication of 27 Nov. 1999. The case of *Charlton v. Lings* concerned the claim of Mary Abbot to be placed on the Manchester voting register. The judges concluded that there was no record of women ever having voted; Lord Chief Justice Bovill, focussing particularly on section 33, noted that there was no provision in the Act of 1832 which entitle women to the right to vote.

16. George Rude and Eric Hobsbawm, *Captain Swing* (Lawrence and Wishart, 1969); lorwerth Prothero, *Artisans and Politics in Early Nineteenth-Century London: John Gast and His Times* (Dawson, Folkstone, 1979).

17. Macaulay to Thomas Ellis, 30 Mar. 1831, quoted in George Otto Trevelyan, *The Life and Letters of Lord Macaulay,* Vol. I (Oxford University Press, 1932 ed.), pp. 186–88.

18. John Cam Hobhouse, quoted in Michael Brock, *The Great Reform Act* (Hutchinson, 1973), p. 192.

19. Brock, *The Great Reform Act*, p. 291. This story inspired a famous cartoon by 'H.D.' (John Doyle).

20. J.M. Prest, *Lord John Russell* (Macmillan, 1972), pp. 3–8ff.

21. Asa Briggs, 'The Background of the Parliamentary Reform Movement in Three English Cities', *Cambridge Historical Journal* (1950), 293–317.

22. John Belchem, *'Orator' Hunt* (Oxford University Press, 1985), p. 107.

23. E.P. Thompson, *The Making of the English Working Class* (Goilancz, 1963), pp. Iff.

24. Shelley, 'Mask of Anarchy', canto XCI. Mrs. Shelley noted that Leigh Hunt did not print it in the *Examiner* in 1819 because he felt that 'the public at large had not become sufficiently discerning to do justice to the sincerity and kind-heartedness of the spirit that walked in this flaming robe of verse'. Shelley's 'Song to the Men of England (1819) was published by Mrs. Shelley, 1839. More generally, see Paul Foot, *Red Shelley* (Sidgwick and Jackson, 1980) and materials in Keats House, Piazza di Spagna, Rome.

25. Belchem, *Orator Hunt*, pp. 29ff.

26. For the Bristol riots of 28–31 Oct. 1831, see M. Harrison, *Crowds and History: Mass Phenomena and English Towns, 1790–1835* (Cambridge University Press, 1988), 289ff., and Geoffrey Amey, *City Under Fire: The Bristol Riots and the Aftermath* (Lutterworth Press, Leicester, 1979).

27. For Merthyr, see Gwyn A. Williams, *The Merthyr Rising* (Croom Helm, 1978), and D.J.V. Jones, 'The Merthyr Riots of 1831' in *Before Rebecca; Popular Protests in Wales, 1793–1835* (University of Wales Press, Cardiff, 1975), pp. 133–58.

28. Williams, *The Merthyr Rising*, 194.

29. Gash, *Politics in the Age of Peel*, pp. 3ff.

2   Gladstone and the New Radicalism

Based on a Founders' Day lecture at St. Deiniol's library, 27 Jun. 1985.

1. *Ardrossan and Saltcoats Herald*, 27 May 1887 (written by Hardie under the pseudonym 'Trapper').
2. *Labour Leader*, 28 May 1898.
3. See Roy Hattersley, *Choose Freedom* (1987). For some interesting observations, see Eugenio Biagini, 'Prophet for the Left. Gladstone's Legacy 1809–2009', *Journal of Liberal History*, 64 (Autumn 2009), 23–7.
4. *The Times*, 6 Jun. 1887, 14 Sept. 1892.
5. William George, *My Brother and I* (1958), p. 176; A.S.T. Griffith-Boscawen, *Fourteen Years in Parliament* (1907), p. 47.
6. See esp. D.A. Hamer, *Liberal Politics in the Age of Gladstone and Rosebery* (1972) on this theme.
7. Ibid., pp. 173 ff.
8. Henry Richard, *Letters on the Social and Political Condition of Wales* (1867).
9. See C.S. Miall, *Henry Richard MP* (1889), p. 143.
10. *The Times*, 20 Aug. 1873. On these themes, see Kenneth O. Morgan, *Wales in British Politics, 1868–1922* (3rd ed., 1880), esp. Chapters 2 and 3.
11. See Kenneth O. Morgan, 'The Member for Wales: Stuart Rendel, 1834–1913', *Transactions of the Honourable Society of Cymmrodorion* (1984), 149–71.
12. *Parliamentary Debates (hereafter Parl. Deb.)*, 3rd series, 201, 1295.
13. H.C.G. Matthew, ed., *Gladstone Diaries*, Vol. 7, Jan. 1869–Jun. 1871, Introduction, pp. xxxiv–xxxvi; R.T. Shannon, *Gladstone* (1982), I, p. 317. Gladstone added that 'It would be an error to recognize a knowledge of the Welsh tongue as dispensing with any of the still more essential qualifications for Episcopal office.'.
14. Gladstone to the Archbishop of York, 12 Jan. 1870, BL, Gladstone Papers, Add. MS 44424, fol. 90.
15. Gladstone to the Bishop of Durham, 28 Dec. 1892, BL, Gladstone Papers, Add. MS 44478, fols. 271–72.
16. Gladstone to H.A. Bruce, 18 Jan. 1870, BL, Gladstone Papers, Add. MS 44086, fol. 123.
17. Joshua Hughes to Gladstone, 20 Mar. 1870, BL, Gladstone Papers, Add. MS 44425, fol. 29.
18. Lord Aberdare to Gladstone, 31 Dec. 1882, BL, Gladstone papers, Add. MS 44087, fols. 165–70.
19. See Kenneth O. Morgan, 'Gladstone and Wales', *Welsh History Review*, 1 (1960), pp. 72–73.
20. *Parl. Deb.*, 3rd ser., 260, 1772 (4 May 1881).
21. Ibid., 247, 1160 (1 Jul. 1879).
22. Morgan, *Wales in British Politics*, pp. 48–49.
23. Ibid. pp. 52–53. Aberystwyth was at first granted only £2,500, in contrast to £4,000 each for Bangor and Cardiff, but the new Conservative government under Lord Salisbury provided the balance of £1,500 in 1885. This followed a great fire which burned down much of the old college at Aberystwyth.

24. A.C. Humphreys-Owen to Rendel, 20 Jun. 1886, National Library of Wales, Rendel Papers, 14, fol. 293.
25. Belchem, *'Orator' Hunt*, pp. 29ff.
26. *Parl. Deb.*, 3rd ser., 336, 135 (15 May 1889).
27. *Eisteddfod Genedlaethol y Cymry: Cofnodion,* E. Vincent Evans, ed., National Eisteddfod Association (Liverpool, 1889), pp. xxiv–xxx, for the text.
28. See Lord to Lady Aberdare, 3 Jun. 1887, in *Letters of Lord Aberdare* (Oxford, 1902), ii, p. 224.
29. *Parl. Deb.*, 3rd ser., 250, 1264ff. (20 Feb. 1891).
30. *Parl. Deb.*, 3rd ser., 9, 277 (23 Feb. 1893).
31. Gladstone to Asquith, 10 Nov. 1893, BL, Gladstone Papers, Add. MS 44459, fol. 154; draft Welsh Disestablishment bill, 1893 (Bodleian Library, Asquith Papers, box 14).
32. *The Times*, 19 Jun. 1895; Morgan, *Wales in British Politics*, pp. 154, 268–69.
33. T.A. Jenkins, *Gladstone, Whiggery and the Liberal Party, 1874–1886* (Oxford, 1987), esp. pp. 14ff.
34. See Morgan, 'Gladstone and Wales', p. 65.
35. Gladstone to Rendel, 12 Nov. 1892, BL, Gladstone Papers, Add. MS 44549, fol. 39.
36. W.E. Gladstone, 'Kin beyond the Sea', *North American Review*, 127 (Sept.–Oct., 1878).
37. John Morley, *Gladstone* (1903), iii, p. 491. Also the valuable thesis by my former pupil, M.M. Gerlach, 'British Liberal Leaders and the United States 1874–1898' (unpublished D. Phil. Thesis, University of Oxford, 1982), esp. pp. 223–76.
38. Excellent accounts of the popular Liberalism of Gladstone's later period appear in two works by Eugenio Biagini, *Liberty, Retrenchment and Reform: Popular Liberalism in the Age of Gladstone, 1860–1880* (Cambridge, 1992) and *British Democracy and Irish Nationalism 1876–1906* (Cambridge, 2007).

3   Lloyd George, Keir Hardie and the Importance of the 'Pro-Boers'

1. S. Koss, ed., *The Anatomy of an Anti-War Movement: The Pro-Boers* (Chicago, 1973). Mention should also be made of the pioneering work of Arthur Davey: A. Davey, *The Pro-Boers* (Cape Town, 1978).
2. See E. May, *American Imperialism* (New York, 1968), pp. 321ff.
3. A.J.P. Taylor, *The Origins of the Second World War* (1961), p. 235.
4. National Library of Wales, Aberystwyth (hereafter NLW), William George Papers, David Lloyd George to William George, 16 Oct. 1899.
5. *Parl .Deb.*, 4th ser., LXXVII, 782–83 (27 Oct. 1899).
6. NLW, Penucha MSS, David Lloyd George to J. Herbert Lewis, 14 Oct. 1899: 'The mob was seized with a drunken madness and the police were helpless'.
7. *South Wales Daily News*, 8 Oct. 1900.
8. E. Halévy, *Imperialism and the Triumph of Labour: History of the English People, 1895–1905*, (new ed., 1951), p. 96; H. Pelling, *Popular Politics and Society in Late Victorian Britain* (1968), p. 93.

9. M. Fry, *Lloyd George and Foreign Policy*, Vol. 1 (1977), 53–54. Lloyd George would have referred to Rosebery's speech in his meeting at Birmingham town hall (18 Dec. 1901) which was broken up by the mob.

10. *Parl. Deb.*, 4th ser., LXXXVI, 1210 (25 Jul. 1900).

11. *Ibid.*, XCVI, 890ff. (4 Jul. 1901).

12. *Ibid.*

13. *Ibid.*, LXXVIII, 762 (6 Feb. 1900).

14. Lloyd George to Margaret Lloyd George, 27 Sept. 1899, in Kenneth O. Morgan, ed., *Lloyd George: Family Letters, c. 1885–1936* (Oxford and Cardiff, 1973), 122.

15. David Lloyd George to William George, 21 Feb. 1900, 5 Jun. 1900, in W. George, *Lloyd George: Backbencher* (1983), pp. 307, 315.

16. David Lloyd George to Margaret Lloyd George, 12 Mar. 1902, in Morgan, *Family Letters*, p. 129.

17. *Parl. Deb.*, 4th ser., LXXVIII, 762 (6 Feb. 1900).

18. David Lloyd George to William George, 19 May 1900, in George, *Lloyd George: Backbencher*, p. 314.

19. See G.R. Searle, *Corruption in British Politics, 1895–1930* (1987) on this theme.

20. *Morning Leader*, 18 Sept. 1900 and subsequent issues.

21. K. Surridge, 'All You Soldiers Are What We Call Pro-Boer: The Military Critique of the South African War, 1899–1902', *History* 82 (Oct. 1997), 582–600.

22. J. Grigg, 'Lloyd George and the Boer War', in A.J.A. Morris, ed., *Edwardian Radicalism, 1900–1914* (1974), p. 15.

23. S. Koss, *The Rise and Fall of the Political Press in Britain*, Vol. 1 (1981), pp. 396–400.

24. J. Hobhouse Balme, *To Love One's Enemies* (Cobble Hill, BC, Canada, 1994), p. 220.

25. George, *Lloyd George: Backbencher*, pp. 343–46.

26. D. Lloyd George, *The Truth about the Peace Treaties*, Vol. 1 (1938), 257–60.

27. *Labour Leader*, 23 May 1899.

28. *Ibid.*, 26 May 1900.

29. *Merthyr Pioneer*, 28 Nov. 1914.

30. *Labour Leader*, 6 Jan. 1900, 17 Mar. 1900.

31. *Ibid.*, 4 Nov. 1899.

32. *Ibid.*, 24 Nov. 1900.

33. K.O. Morgan, *Keir Hardie, Radical and Socialist* (1975), p. 105.

34. *Labour Leader*, 2 Feb. 1901: 'The Queen's Funeral: A Protest'.

35. *Ibid.*, 11 Jun. 1901.

36. *Ibid.*, 10 Feb. 1900.

37. Morgan, *Keir Hardie*, 87–90.

38. *Ibid.*, 114.

39. See 'The Merthyr of Keir Hardie' in K.O. Morgan, *Modern Wales: Politics, Places and People* (Cardiff, 1995), pp. 268–86.

40. *Labour Leader*, 13 Oct. 1900.
41. *Ibid.*, 16 Jun. 1900, 'On the Banks of the Rubicon: An Open Letter to John Morley'.
42. *Ibid.*, 21 Dec. 1901.
43. *Ibid.*, 3 Feb. 1900.
44. Pelling, *Popular Politics and Society*, 98.
45. D. Marquand, *Ramsay MacDonald* (1977), pp. 76–78.
46. *Parl. Deb.*, 4th ser., CLXVII, 1107–11 (17 Dec. 1906).
47. Morgan, *Keir Hardie*, p. 197.
48. *Parl. Deb.*, 5th ser., IX, 987ff. and 1571ff. (16 Aug. 1909).
49. *Ibid.*, 5th ser., LVI, 814ff. (31 Jul. 1913) and LVIII, 385ff. (2 Feb. 1914).
50. See S. Koss, 'Wesleyanism and Empire', *The Historical Journal*, 18, 1 (1975), 105–18.
51. S.K. Hocking, *My Book of Memory* (1923), 180. His book on his experiences as a Pro-Boer was turned down by publishers at first, but was successfully published in 1914.
52. K.O. Morgan, 'Wales and the Boer War', in Morgan, *Modern Wales*, esp. pp. 52–53.
53. F.S.L. Lyons, *Ireland since the Famine* (1973 ed.), pp. 260–61.
54. See Morgan, 'Wales and the Boer War', pp. 46–58.
55. For Emily Hobhouse, see R. van Reenen, ed., *Emily Hobhouse: Boer War Letters* (Cape Town and Pretoria, 1984); Hobhouse Balme, *To Love One's Enemies*; J. Fisher, *That Miss Hobhouse* (1971); and B. Roberts, *Those Bloody Women: Three Heroines of the Boer War* (1991), esp. pp. 177ff.
56. E. Hobhouse, *Report of a Visit to the Camps of Women and Children in the Cape and Orange River Colonies* (1901) and E. Hobhouse, *The Brunt of the War and Where It Fell* (1902).
57. Hobhouse, *The Brunt of the War*. She records the population of the camps as growing to 105,000 by Aug. 1901. There is a fascinating discussion of the concentration camps (drawing on his skill both as a surgeon and as an historian of war photography) by my much-lamented late friend, Emanoel Lee, in *To the Bitter End: A Photographic History of the Boer War 1899–1902* (1985).
58. Van Reenen, *Emily Hobhouse*, p. 401.
59. *Ibid.*, p. 407.
60. *Ibid.*, p. 506. Van Heerden was the first Afrikaaner woman doctor.
61. *Report of the Committee on Physical Deterioration*, 1904 (Cd. 2210), p. 123.
62. H.G. Wells, quoted in S. Kemp *et al.*, eds, *Edwardian Fiction* (Oxford, 1997), p. 38.
63. See J. Kendle, *The Round Table Movement and Imperial Union* (Toronto, 1975) on the Kindergarten.
64. E.H.H. Green, *The Crisis of Conservatism* (1995).

4 The Boer War and the Media, 1899–1902

1. Tabitha Jackson, *The Boer War* (1999), pp. 80–81.

2. Jacqueline Beaumont, 'The Times at War, 1899–1902', in Donal Lowry, ed., *The South African War: A Reappraisal* (Manchester, 2000), pp. 72–73.
3. Raymond Sibbald, *The War Correspondents: The Boer War* (Stroud, 1993), pp. 130ff.
4. See Brian Roberts, 'Those Bloody Women': *Three Heroines of the Boer War* (1991); J. Hobhouse Balme, *To Love One's Enemies* (Cobble, BC, Canada, 1994); John Hall, *That Bloody Woman: Cornwall's Forgotten Heroine* (Truran Books, 2008).
5. See Andrew Lycett, *Rudyard Kipling* (1999), pp. 434ff.; Margaret Lane, *Edgar Wallace: The Biography of a Phenomenon* (1938); Arthur Conan Doyle, *The Great Boer War* (1900 and subsequent editions); Erskine Childers, *In the Ranks of the C.I.V: A Narrative and Diary of Personal Experiences with the C.I.V. Battery in South Africa* (1900).
6. Papers of E.W. Smith, Harry Ransom Humanities Center Library, Austin, TX.
7. Jacqueline Beaumont, 'The British Press and Censorship during the South African War', *South African Historical Journal* 41, special issue (Nov. 1999), 267–89.
8. Stewart Weaver, 'The Pro-Boers: War, Empire and the Use of Nostalgia in Turn of the Century England', in George K. Behlmer and Fred M. Leventhal, eds., *Singular Continuities: Tradition, Nostalgia and Identity in Modern British Culture* (Cambridge, 2000), p. 523; Childers, *In the Ranks of the C. I. V.*, pp. 252–53.
9. Keith Surridge, '"All you Soldiers are what we call Pro-Boer": The Military Critique of the South African War, 1899–1902', *History* 82 (1997), 582–600.
10. Philip Magnus, *Kitchener. Portrait of an Imperialist* (1958), p.136. Steevens appears in Giles Foden's attractive historical novel, *Ladysmith* (1999). For Kitchener's criticisms of the reporters, see Field Marshal Lord Carver, *The National Army Museum Book of the Boer War* (1999), p. 239.
11. Conan Doyle, *The Great Boer War*, Chapter XXIX.
12. Emanoel Lee, *To the Bitter End. A Photographic History of the Boer War* (Harmondsworth, 1895, republished Pretoria, 2001), pp. 1–11.
13. Papers of E.W. Smith, Harry Ransom Humanities Center Library, Austin, TX.
14 Bill Nasson, *The South African War* (1999), pp. 243ff.
15. I was taught this song by my grandmother (then aged around 65) in Wales during the Second World War. My other grandmother had a large painting in her dining room of Colonel Mahon being greeted by Baden-Powell at the relief of Mafeking.
16. For cricket, see the excellent volume Bruce Murray and Goolam Vahed, *Cricket and Empire* (University of South Africa Press, 2009). Richard Price, *An Imperial War and the British Working Class* (1972), pp. 132ff.
17. Kenneth O. Morgan, 'Wales and the Boer War', in *Modern Wales: Politics, Places and People* (Cardiff, 1995), pp. 52–53.
18. Balme, *To Love One's Enemies*, 220ff.; Rykie van Reenen, ed., *Emily Hobhouse: Boer War Letters* (Cape Town and Pretoria, 1984).

19. Kenneth O. Morgan, 'Lloyd George, Keir Hardie and the Importance of the Pro-Boers', *South African Historical Journal* 41, special issue (Nov. 1999), 307–9.

20. Emily Hobhouse to Mrs. Steyn, 30 Oct. 1913, cited in Reenen, *Emily Hobhouse, p.* 393, notes that Olive Schreiner was not invited to the unveiling of the Boer Women's memorial at Bloemfontein in 1913.

21. Henry Pelling, *Popular Politics and Society in late Victorian Britain* (1968), pp. 96–99.

22. Bill Nasson, *Abraham Esau's War* (Cambridge, 1991); Justin Cartwright, 'Mafeking Revisited', *Guardian,* 21 Jul. 2001. Since this article was written, two immense volumes on the Siege of Mafeking, edited by Iain Smith, have been published by Brenthurst Press, Johannesburg.

23. Donal Lowry, 'The Wider Impact of the South African War', in Lowry, ed., *The South* (Manchester, *2000),* pp. 214–15. Villebois-Mareuil has been said to have provided the model for his cousin, Edmond Rostand's version of the dashing fictional hero, Cyrano de Bergerac, in 1897.

24. E.W. Smith MS autobiographical fragment, in Smith Papers, Austin, TX, Folder 1/11; Eversley Belfield, *The Boer War* (1937), p. xxv.

25. Of 28,777 Dominions troops serving in the war, 16,310 came from Australia.

26. See Lloyd George's comments on Smuts in his *War Memoirs, Vol. I* (1934), pp. 1032–34 ('a fine blend of intellect and human sympathy') and on Botha in his *Truth about the Peace Treaties, Vol. I* (1938), pp. 256–60: 'The great head, the steady, dauntless, understanding eyes full of fire and light, the deep, husky, commanding voice – as I sat opposite him for hours, I found myself drawn to gaze upon him. I thought of him leading his men in a charge and I felt I would rather be by his side than facing him'. For Smuts's role in the founding of the League of Nations, see Mark Mazower, *No Enchanted Palace* (2009), pp. 29ff., 'Jan Smuts and Imperial Internationalism'.

5 'Blissful Dawn'? The Liberal Government of 1906

Based on a lecture at the London Guildhall, 7 Feb. 2006.

6 Lloyd George and Germany

1. J.M. Keynes, *Essays in Biography* (1951 edn), pp. 32–33.

2. His *Who's Who* entry said of Dawson, 'Most of his books have been written for the purpose of interpreting German thought, life and character to English people, and particularly of expounding German practice in the treatment of social and industrial questions…'.

3. Harold Spender, *The Fire of Life* (n.d.), pp. 161–66. At Carlsbad, Lloyd George met Clemenceau for the first time.

4. *Parl. Deb.,* 5th ser., xxv, 615–16 (4 May 1911).

5. Lloyd George was in touch with Theodore Roosevelt during the 1912 presidential campaign. See D. Lloyd George to Mrs Lloyd George, 16 Oct.

1912, in Kenneth O. Morgan, ed., *Lloyd George: Family Letters, c. 1885–1936* (Oxford and Cardiff, 1973), p. 164.

6. D. Lloyd George, *The Truth about the Peace Treaties, I* (1938), pp. 231–2.

7. *Parl. Deb.*, 5th ser., xxv, 615–16, 638 (4 May 1911). See E.P. Hennock, *British Social Reform and German Precedents. The Case of Social Insurance 1880–1914* (Oxford, 1987), pp. 180ff.

8. D. Lloyd George, *War memoirs* (1938), 1, pp. 8–16 (with the Kaiser's annotations included).

9. Ibid. 18–19.

10. A.J.P. Taylor, *The Struggle for Mastery in Europe, 1848–1918* (Oxford, 1954), p. 471.

11. *The Times*, 18 Jul. 1914.

12. See Kenneth O. Morgan, 'Peace Movements in Wales, *1899–1945*', *Welsh History Review x*, 1 (1981), 406–7.

13. Notably in his interview with Roy Howard of the American United Press, published in *The Times*, 29 Nov. 1916.

14. Lloyd George's Bangor speech is printed in a volume of his speeches, *Through Terror to Triumph* (1915), pp. 75–89.

15. J.M. Keynes, *The Economic Consequences of the Peace* (1919), pp. 127–33.

16. Robert Skidelsky, *John Maynard Keynes*, Vol. 1, 1883–1920 (1983), pp. 358–61.

17. Kenneth O. Morgan, 'Lloyd George's Stage Army: The Coalition Liberals, 1918–22' in A.J.P. Taylor, ed., *Lloyd George: Twelve Essays* (1971), pp. 230–1. Also see H.A.L. Fisher to Lloyd George, 17 Mar. 1919 (House of Lords Record Office, Lloyd George Papers, F/16/7/39) in which Fisher warns against either Danzig or Posen being given to Poland.

18. Keynes, *The Economic Consequences of the Peace*, pp. 186–87. He added that Germany would not be able to pay this amount.

19. George, *The Truth about the Peace Treaties*, I, p. 461.

20. An entirely new kind of capitalist, dark and fanatical: Philip Kerr to Lord Curzon, 25 Jun. 1920 (National Archives, FO/800/153), fols. 289–90.

21. See Lloyd George to Kingsley Martin, 28 Mar. 1936 (House of Lords Record Office, Lloyd George Papers, G/14/2/3).

22. George, *The Truth about the Peace Treaties*, I, pp. 930ff.

23. *Daily Express*, 17 Sept. 1936.

24. Colin Cross, ed., *A.J. Sylvester: Life with Lloyd George* (1975), p. 219 (5 Oct. 1938). See also R.A.C. Parker, *Chamberlain and Appeasement* (1993), pp. 315–16.

25. 'Special Mission to Europe of Sumner Welles', *Foreign Relations of the United States*, Diplomatic Papers (Washington, 1940), pp. 85–6.

26. Richard Toye, *Lloyd George and Churchill* (2007), p. 376.

27. A.J.P. Taylor, ed., *Lloyd George, a Diary by Frances Stevenson* (1971,), pp. 256–57 (21 Feb. 1934) 'We should keep a strong hand in India', observed Lloyd George. Also ibid. pp. 272–73 (14 May 1934). He was unsympathetic towards attempts to conciliate Gandhi.

8   The Future at Work: Anglo-American Progressivism

1. Herbert S. Foxwell to E.R. Seligman, 24 Nov. 1895 (Butler Library, Columbia University, Seligman Papers).
2. Foxwell to Seligman, 23 Jun. 1909 (Butler Library, Columbia University, Seligman Papers).
3. Richard Hofstadter, 'Cuba, The Philippines and Manifest Destiny', in *The Paranoid Style in American Politics* (Vintage Books edition, 1967), pp. 148ff.
4. *Forum,* Oct. 1906, pp. 176– 77. These comments were written by A. Maurice Low.
5. See Benjamin O. Flower, *Progressive Men, Women and Movements of the last Twenty-Five Years* (New York, 1914), pp. 134–41.
6. Henry Pelling, *America and the British Left* (1956), pp. 70ff.
7. Keith Robbins, *Sir Edward Grey* (1971), pp. 274–77.
8 David Lloyd George to Mrs. Lloyd George, 16 Oct. 1912 (National Library of Wales, Aberystwyth, Lloyd George Papers, MSS. 207 431 C).
9. David Lloyd George, *The Truth about the Peace Treaties, Vol. I* (1938) pp. 226, 231–32. Lloyd George was also a lifelong admirer of Abraham Lincoln.
10. Lord Riddell, *War Diary* (1933), p. 324.
11. Harold Spender, *The Prime Minister* (1920), p. 359.
12. See the Villard-MacDonald correspondence in the Houghton Library, Harvard University, 6. MS. Am. 1323.
13. See Charles Forcey, *The Crossroads of Liberalism* (Oxford, 1961), pp. 100–1.
14. Frederick Howe, *The British City – The Beginnings of Democracy* (New York, 1907), pp. 9, 273–309.
15. Samuel J. Burrows, 'The Temperance Tidal Wave', *The Outlook,* 4 Jul. 1908, p. 513.
16. *The Autobiography of William Allen White* (New York, 1946), p. 419; The *Outlook,* 20 Nov. 1909, pp. 605–7.
17. *Woman's Journal,* 15 Jun. 1912, pp. 188–89. The views of an English anti-militant women's suffragist, the Anglican preacher, A. Maude Royden, were widely cited.
18. 'The Adventure of Feminism', Inez Haynes Irwin Papers (Radcliffe College Library). Only nine western states had done so by 1912.
19. Gertrude Amy Slichter, 'The European Backgrounds of American Reform' (PhD Thesis, University of Illinois, 1960).
20. Mary Fels, *Joseph Fels: His Life-work* (1920) pp. 58–59; John Shepherd, *George Lansbury* (Oxford, 2002), pp. 60–62, 135–36; Ramsay MacDonald to Bruce Glasier, 29 Aug. 1908 (Independent Labour Party archive); *La Follette's Magazine,* 1 Jan. 1910.
21. *The Outlook,* 7 Apr. 1906, pp. 797–800.
22. See Parsons's articles in *The Arena,* December 1906 ; January, February, March, April, October (1907); Arthur Mann, Arthur Mann, *Yankee Reformers in the Urban Age. Social Reform in Boston 1880–1900* (Cambridge, Mass, 1954), pp. 139–40
23. Slichter, 'European Backgrounds', p. 191.

24. Frederick Howe, *The City: The Hope of Democracy* (New York, 1905), p. 136. There is an excellent discussion of the contemporary context for Howe's ideas in Daniel T. Rodgers's important book, *Atlantic Crossings. Social Politics in a Progressive Age* (Cambridge, MA, 1998), esp. pp. 139–44, 155–59.
25. Lincoln Steffens, *Autobiography, Vol. I* (New York, 1931), p. 648.
26. Howe, *The British City*, p. 123.
27. Ibid., p. 213 n.
28. Ibid., p. 243; Howe, *European Cities at Work* (New York, 1913), p. 323
29. William E. Leuchtenburg, 'Progressivism and Imperialism: The Progressive Movement and American Foreign Policy, 1898–1916', *Mississippi Valley Historical Review XXXIX* (Dec. 1952), 496ff. There are, of course, many exceptions to this generalisation.
30. *The Outlook*, 9 Sept. 1905, p. 52.
31. Ibid., 6 Jan. 1912, pp. 4–5.
32. Ibid., 23 Dec. 1905, pp. 957–99.
33. Page to Herbert S. Houston, 24 Aug. 1913 (cited in Burton J. Hendrick, *Life and Letters of Walter Hines Page, Vol. I* (New York, 1924)), p. 139.
34. *The Outlook*, 25 Aug. 1906, pp. 923–24.
35. S.S. McClure, *Autobiography* (1914), pp. 255–6.
36. Herbert Croly, *The Promise of American Life* (New York, Paperback edition, 1963), p. 238.
37. *See La Follette's Magazine,* 9 Jan. 1909.
38. Steffens, *Autobiography*, pp. 652–63, 704–8.
39. Howe, *Confessions of a Reformer* (Kent, Ohio, 1925), pp. 296–98.
40. Croly, *The Promise of American Life*, p. 238.
41. Howe, *The British City*, pp. 234–35.
42. Howe, 'A Commonwealth Ruled by Farmers', *The Outlook,* 26 Feb. 1910. Marquis Childs wrote enthusiastically of 'Sweden: The Middle Way' during the 1930s.
43. Louis Filler, *Crusaders for American Liberalism* (New York, paperback, 1961), pp. 165–68.

9 Seven Ages of Socialism: Keir Hardie to Gordon Brown

Based on a lecture given to the Labour History Society, South Bank University, 29 Nov. 2006.

11 Imperialists at Bay: Britain's Finest Hour

1. J. Keir Hardie, *India, Impressions and Suggestions* (1909), J. Ramsay MacDonald, *The Awakening of India* (1909).
2. Memorandum by Bevin and George Hall, 'The Future of the Italian Colonies and the Italian Mediterranean Islands', Sept. 1945, FO/371/50792, U 6540/51/G70, National Archives (NA). Bevin proposed absorbing Eritrea, British and Italian Somaliland and Abyssinia in a Greater Somalia in the Horn of Africa, under British trusteeship.

3. Memorandum by Griffiths and Gordon Walker, 'Closer Association in Central Africa', 5 Oct. 1951, DO 121/138, NA.
4. Hugh Dalton diaries, 27 Feb. 1950, British Library of Political and Economic Science Library, Dalton Papers, 1/38.
5. J.R.T. Wood, ed., *The Welensky Papers* (Durban, 1983), p. 572.
6. For example, Callaghan's speech in 1947, *Report of Annual Labour Party Conference,* 1947, 115; also Callaghan to Sir Alan Burns, 14 Oct. 1949, Bodleian Library, Callaghan Papers, Box 4.
7. See Ruth Winstone, ed., *Tony Benn. Years of Hope: Diaries 1940–62* (1994), 330 (10 May 1960); also my entry on 'Anthony Greenwood' for the *New Dictionary of National Biography* (Oxford, 2004).
8. Callaghan's notes on Commonwealth conference, Jan. 1959, Callaghan Papers, Box 4.
9. Callaghan to John Hatch, 7 Oct. 1958, Callaghan Papers, Box 4.
10. Callaghan to Thomas Balogh, 23 Jul. 1958, Callaghan Papers, Box 4.
11. Callaghan to Gaitskell, 23 Jun. 1961, Callaghan Papers, Box 4.
12. Callaghan note of a meeting with Lennox-Boyd and Baring, 11 Dec. 1957; Callaghan to Mboya, 18 Dec. 1957, Callaghan Papers, Box 4.
13. Callaghan to Mboya, 28 May 1959, Callaghan Papers, Box 4.
14. *Parl. Deb.,* 5th series, DCVII, 352–61.
15. For example, Callaghan to T.D.T. Banda, Blantyre, 10 Dec. 1957, Callaghan Papers, Box 4.
16. Report of speech (to a joint meeting of the Royal Africa and Royal Empire Societies) in *African Affairs,* Jan. 1958.
17. Report of Commonwealth Parliamentary Association visit to the Federation of Rhodesia and Nyasaland, Sept. 1957, draft in Welensky Papers, Rhodes House library, Oxford, 194/5; Callaghan's articles in *Reynolds News,* 8, 22, 29 Sept., 6 Oct. 1957.
18. *Parl. Deb.* 5th series, DLXXVIII, 808–20.
19. Welensky to F.S. Joelson, 3 Dec. 1957, Welensky Papers, 628/5, fol. 60.
20. *Parl. Deb.,* 5th series, DCI, 279–87, and DCX, 335–53.
21. Materials in Welensky Papers, 596/5.
22. Callaghan to Hastings Banda, 10 Dec. 1957, Callaghan Papers, Box 4.
23. Interview with Lord Hunt of Tanworth, London, 17 Oct. 1996.
24. Barbara Castle, *The Castle Diaries, 1964–70* (1984), p. x.
25. Interview with H.E. Lee Kuan Yew, Istana Negara, Singapore, 21 Sept. 1993.
26. Wm. Roger Louis, *The British Empire in the Middle East, 1945–1951* (Oxford, 1984), p. 15.

12   Labour and the 'Special Relationship'

1. Author's interview with Dr. Henry Kissinger (26 Oct. 1993).
2. See Robert Skidelsky, *John Maynard Keynes III: Fighting for Britain, 1937–1946* (Macmillan, 2000), pp. 403–59.
3. Memorandum by Keynes, "Our Overseas Financial Prospects" (14 Aug. 1945), National Archives: CP (45), 112, Cabinet Papers, CAB 129 /1.

4. Kenneth O. Morgan, *Labour in Power, 1945–1951* (Oxford, Clarendon, 1984), pp. 252–54; Joseph M. Jones, *The Fifteen Weeks* (New York, Viking Press, 1955).
5. Franks to Attlee (5 Jul. 1950), NA: PREM 8/1405.
6. Dean Acheson, *Present at the Creation: My Years at the State Department* (Hamilton, 1970), p. 505.
7. Kenneth O. Morgan, 'Aneurin Bevan', in *Labour People* (Oxford, Oxford University Press, 1987), p. 212.
8. Roy Jenkins, *Life at the Centre* (Macmillan, 1991), pp. 100–2; see Edward Pearce, *Denis Healey* (Little, Brown, 2001).
9. Meeting of Economic Affairs Committee, MISC 1, 17 Oct. 1964 (NA, CAB 130 / 202); Ben Pimlott, *Harold Wilson* (HarperCollins, 1992), pp. 350 –2.
10. Matthew Jones, "A Decision Delayed: Britain's Withdrawal from South East Asia Reconsidered," *English Historical Review* CXVII, 472 (Jun. 2002), 584.
11. Philip Ziegler, *Wilson: The Authorized Life of Lord Wilson of Rievaulx* (Weidenfeld and Nicolson, 1993), p. 325.
12. Hugo Young, *This Blessed Plot: Britain and Europe from Churchill to Blair* (Macmillan, 1998), 103ff., for Palliser; for Denman, see his recently updated autobiography, *The Mandarin's Tale* (Politico's, 2002).
13. Richard Crossman, *Diaries of a Cabinet Minister*, Vol. III, edited by Janet Morgan (Hamish Hamilton, 1977), pp. 384–85 (25 Feb. 1969).
14. This is based on many interviews with Lord Callaghan and my interview with Dr. Kissinger (26 Oct. 1993). Also see Kenneth O. Morgan, *Callaghan: A Life* (Oxford, Oxford University Press, 1997), pp. 437ff.
15. See David Owen, *Time to Declare* (Penguin Books, 1992), pp. 305–18.
16. See Michael Hirsh, 'Bush and the World,' *Foreign Affairs* (Sept.–Oct. 2002), pp. 13ff., and G. John Ikenberry 'America's Imperial Ambitions,' ibid., pp. 44ff.

13 Hugh Gaitskell and International Affairs
Based on a lecture at the University of Leeds, Jan. 1993.

14 Nye Bevan, Pragmatist and Prophet
1. Charles Webster, 'The Birth of the Dream', in Geoffrey Goodman, ed., *The State of the Nation* (1997), p. 118.
2. Michael Foot, *Aneurin Bevan, 1945–1960* (1973), p. 649.
3. Aneurin Bevan, *In Place of Fear* (1976), p. 51.

15 Sixties Socialism: From Planning to Permissiveness
1. Douglas Jay, *Socialism in the New Society* (Longman, 1962), p. 58.
2. Roy Jenkins, *What Matters Now* (Penguin, 1974), p. 117.
3. Paul Rock, ed., *A History of British Criminology* (Oxford University Press, 1987), pp. 61–62.
4. Michael Shanks, *The Stagnant Society* (Penguin, 1963), pp. 13–17.
5. Harold Wilson, *The New Britain: Labour's Plan as Outlined by Harold Wilson* (Penguin, 1964).
6. George Brown, *In My Way* (Penguin, 1971), p. 89.

7. *The Times,* 2 Oct. 1963.
8. Anthony Crosland, *The Future of Socialism* (Macmillan, 1957), pp. 68–76.
9. Jay, *The Socialist Case*, pp. 178ff.
10. Jenkins, *What Matters Now*, pp. 81ff.
11. Oliver Franks to Attlee, 15 Jul. 1950 (Nat. Archives, PREM 8/1045, pt.1).
12. *The Backbench Diaries of Richard Crossman* (Hamilton and Cape, 1981), p. 973 (entry of 8 Feb. 1963).
13. Susan Crosland, *Tony Crosland* (Cape, 1982), p. 148.
14. Kenneth O. Morgan, *Callaghan: A Life* (Oxford University Press, 1997), pp. 210–11.
15. Anthony Crosland, *Socialism Now* (Cape, 1974), p. 18.
16. Roy Hattersley, *Choose Freedom* (Penguin, 1987), p. 209; see Ben Pimlott, *Harold Wilson* (Harper Collins, 1992), pp. 586–87.
17. Crosland, *Socialism Now*, pp. 151ff.
18. Kenneth O. Morgan, *Callaghan: A Life* (Oxford University Press, 1997), pp. 320–22.
19. Douglas Jay, *The Socialist Case* (2nd ed., 1946), p. 258.
20. Crosland, *Socialism Now*, pp. 23ff.

16   The Rise and Fall of Nationalisation in Britain

1. A.L. Rowse, 'Industry in the Transition to Socialism', in Stafford Cripps et al., ed., *Where Stands Socialism Today?* (1933), p. 126.
2. E. Eldon Barry, *Nationalisation in British Politics* (1965).
3. Kenneth O. Morgan, 'Socialism and Syndicalism: The Welsh Miners' Debate, 1912', *Bulletin of the Society for the Study of Labour History,* xxx (1975), 22–36.
4. R.H. Tawney, *The Acquisitive Society*, pp. 152–57. Also see Rita Hinden, ed., *R.H. Tawney: The Radical Tradition* (1966), pp. 123–43; Ross Terrill, *R.H. Tawney and His Times* (1973), esp. pp. 151–52.
5. Tawney, *Acquisitive Society,* p. 149.
6. Herbert Morrison, *Socialisation and Transport* (1933), pp. 149ff.
7. Hugh Dalton, *Practical Socialism for Britain* (1935), pp. 93–180.
8. Douglas Jay, *The Socialist Case* (2nd ed., 1946), pp. 198–202.
9. D.E.H. Egerton, 'Technical Innovation, Industrial Capacity and Efficiency: Public Ownership and the British Aircraft Industry, 1915–48', *Business History* XXVI (1984), 266–68.
10. *Parl. Deb.,* 5th ser., ccclxxx. 1093ff. and 132ff. (10 and 11 Jun. 1942).
11. *Report of the Forty-First Annual Conference of the Labour Party,* 1942, pp. 110–12.
12. *Report of the Forty-Second Annual Conference of the Labour Party,* 1943, pp. 180.
13. *Report of the Forty-Third Annual Conference of the Labour Party,* 1944, pp. 160ff.; 'Short Term Programme' presented to NEC (Labour Party archives).
14. Kenneth O. Morgan, *Callaghan: A Life* (Oxford, 1997), pp. 52–53; Ian Mikardo, *Backbencher* (1988), p. 77.

15. Hugh Dalton's diary, 11 Apr. 1945 (British Library of Political and Economic Science, Dalton Papers).

16. Hugh Gaitskell, 'The Banking System and Monetary Policy', in Margaret Cole and Charles Smith, eds., *Democratic Sweden* (1938), pp. 96–107. Other contributors included Cole, Postgate and G.R. Mitchison.

17. Cabinet conclusions, 18 Oct., 20 Dec., 1945 (National Archives [NA], CAB 128/1).

18. Nicholas Davenport, *Memoirs of a City Radical* (1974), pp. 180–81.

19. Minutes of Committee on Socialisation of Industry, 1946–48 (NA, CAB 134/687– 8).

20. *New Statesman,* 22 May, 1948.

21. For example, Shinwell's speech to the Co-operative Congress, reported in *The Times,* 3, 6, 13 May 1948. See also Norman Chester, *The Nationalization of British Industry, 1945– 51* (1975).

22. Cabinet conclusions, 7 Jan. 1947 (NA, CAB 128/8); Shinwell's paper on 'The Coal Position', 21 Feb. 1947 (NA, PREM 8/ 8449).

23. Morgan, *Labour in Power,* p. 272 and n.

24. *Ibid.*

25. Dalton, Memorandum on Iron and Steel, May 1946 (NA, T 228/74).

26. Lincoln Evans to Morgan Phillips, 2 Oct. 1950 (Labour Party archives, GS 23/1).

27. Cabinet conclusions, 28 Apr., 24 Jul., 7 Jul. Aug. 1947 (NA, CAB 128/9, 10).

28. Hugh Dalton's diary, 4 Jan. 1951 (Dalton Papers, 1/39); Cabinet conclusions, 2 Dec. 1948 (NA, CAB 128/13).

29. Cabinet conclusions, 7 Aug. 1947 (NA, CAB 129/10).

30. Cabinet conclusions, 7 May 1946 (NA, CAB 128/5).

31. W.S. Murrie to Attlee, 4 Aug. 1947 (NA, CAB 21/2243).

32. Cabinet conclusions, 31 Jul. 1947 (NA, CAB 128/10).

33. Cabinet conclusions, 7, 14 Jun. 1949 (NA, CAB 129/12).

34. See Evan Durbin, 'The Economic Problems Facing the Labour Government', in Donald Munro, ed., *Socialism: The British Way* (1948), pp. 3–29.

35. G.D.H. Cole, 'The Socialisation Programme for Industry', in Donald Munro, ed., *Socialism: The British Way* (1948), pp. 30–56; Aneurin Bevan, *In Place of Fear* (1952), p. 118.

36. Anthony Crosland, *The Future of Socialism* (1956), esp. pp. 462ff.

37. Labour Party Policy Committee minutes, 25 Nov. 1947.

38. Socialisation of Industry Committee, minutes, 8 Mar. 1946 (NA, CAB 134/687); Cabinet conclusions, 7 Jul. 1946 (NA, CAB 128/5).

39. Labour Party Policy Committee minutes, 25 Nov. 1947 (Labour Party archives).

40. *Ibid.,* Feb.–Nov. 1949.

41. *Ibid.,* 30 May, 7 Jul., 24 Oct. 1949.

42. Cripps to Dalton, 16 Mar. 1949 (Dalton Papers, 9/7/9).

43. Meetings of Policy Committee with Co-operative Society representatives, 27 Jul., 24 Oct. 1949 (Labour Party archives).

44. Ian Mikardo, *The Second Five Years: A Labour Programme for 1950* (1948).

45. *Annual Conference of the Labour Party,* 1949, p. 155.

46. Tony Benn, *Arguments for Socialism* (1979), p. 63.
47. Record of International Socialist conference at Selsdon Park, 21–22 Mar. 1948 (Labour Party archives, International department); material in R.W.G. Mackay Papers, section 8, file 3 (British Library of Political and Economic Science).
48. Cabinet conclusions, 2 Jun. 1950 (NA, CAB 128/17); record of meeting of Cripps and Monnet, 15 May 1950 (NA, FO 371/85842, CE 2338/2141/181).
49. Gareth Stedman Jones, 'Paternalism Revisited' *Marxism Today,* Jul. 1985.
50. Roy Hattersley, *Choose Freedom* (1987), p. 189.
51. Philip Williams*, Hugh Gaitskell* (1979), pp. 537ff. Even Gaitskell was prepared to endorse public ownership on a pragmatic basis, for instance in the case of urban building land (ibid., p. 545).
52. See A.F. Thompson, 'Winchester and the Labour Party: Three Gentlemanly Rebels', in Roger Custace, ed., *Winchester College: Sixth Centenary Essays* (Oxford, 1982), pp. 489–503.

17 Was Britain Dying?

1. Speech to 1985 Conservative Party conference at Blackpool.
2. Douglas Eden, 'We Came Close to Losing Our Democracy in 1979', *The Spectator*, 6 Jun. 2009.
3. Philip Gould, *The Unfinished Revolution: How the Modernisers Saved the Labour Party* (Little, Brown, 1999), p. 36.
4. Peter Mandelson and Roger Liddle, *The Blair Revolution: Can New Labour Deliver?* (Faber and Faber, 1996), p. 25.
5. Ross McKibbin, 'Homage to Wilson and Callaghan', *London Review of Books*, 24 Oct. 1991.
6. Kenneth O. Morgan, *Callaghan: A Life* (Oxford University Press, 1997), p. 633.
7. Douglas Jay, *Sterling: A Plea for Moderation* (Sidgwick and Jackson, 1985), p. 162.
8. Andy Beckett, *When the Lights Went Out: Britain in the Seventies* (Faber and Faber, 2009), p. 496, quoting Sir Clive Rose, chairman of the Civil Contingencies Unit.
9. Hugo Young, *This Blessed Plot: Britain and Europe from Churchill to Blair* (Macmillan, 1998) devoted only three thin pages (pp. 299–302) out of 558 to the years of the Callaghan government.
10. *Independent on Sunday*, 1 Jun. 2003.
11. Interview with Helmut Schmidt, 30 Nov. 1994.
12. Cledwyn Hughes diary 2 Mar. 1978 (Cledwyn Papers, National Library of Wales, Aberystwyth).
13. Morgan, *Callaghan*, p. 583.

18 Michael Foot – History Man

Based on the Brian Hodgson lecture given at Charlbury, 18 Oct. 2007.

19 The Attack on Iraq

Speech in the House of Lords, 26 Feb. 2003.

Index